WAR POWERS

WAR POWERS

The Politics of Constitutional Authority

Mariah Zeisberg

PRINCETON UNIVERSITY PRESS

Princeton and Oxford

Published by Princeton University Press, 41 William Street, Princeton, New Jersey 08540
In the United Kingdom: Princeton University Press, 6 Oxford Street, Woodstock, Oxfordshire OX20
    1TW

press.princeton.edu

Jacket illustration: S. E. H. Coyle, *Dynamic Imbalance*, 2010.

Library of Congress Cataloging-in-Publication Data

   Zeisberg, Mariah Ananda, 1977–
War powers : the politics of constitutional authority / Mariah Zeisberg.
      pages cm
   Includes index.
   ISBN 978-0-691-15722-1 (hardcover) 1. War and emergency powers—United States—History.
2. Separation of powers—United States—History.   I. Title.
   JK339.Z45 2013
   352.23'50973—dc23   2012039981

British Library Cataloging-in-Publication Data is available

This book has been composed in Sabon LT Std

Printed on acid-free paper.

Printed in the United States of America

10 9 8 7 6 5 4 3 2 1

For Jeffrey Tulis, Christopher Eisgruber,
and Maryrose Hightower-Coyle

Contents

WAR POWERS

Chapter 1

WHO HAS AUTHORITY TO TAKE THE COUNTRY TO WAR?

In early 2012 President Quaddafi's suppression of popular uprisings in Libya began to arouse concern domestically and abroad. Attention began to focus on what, if any, the US response would be. By late February the UN Security Council adopted a resolution expressing "grave concern" about Libya, and the US Senate unanimously approved a resolution calling for the Security Council to impose a Libyan no-fly zone.[1] By March, the Security Council had authorized member states to use force to protect Libyan civilians, and the House simmered with dispute about the president's constitutional war authority.[2] On March 18 President Obama deployed troops to Libya.

The president's domestic authority to intervene in Libya was conditioned by two authoritative texts: the US Constitution, which grants him the power to command the military, and Congress the power to declare war; and the War Powers Resolution of 1973 (WPR), which creates procedural and reporting requirements for deployments. The WPR declares that presidents may introduce US armed forces into "hostilities" "only pursuant to (1) a declaration of war, (2) specific statutory authorization, or (3) a national emergency created by attack upon the United States."[3] With none of these conditions in place, the president's legal authority

---

1 UN Security Council Resolution 1970 (Feb. 26, 2011); S. Res. 85, *Congressional Record*, 112th Cong., 1st Sess. (March 1, 2011).

2 UN Security Council Resolution 1973 (March 17, 2011); *Congressional Record*, 112th Cong., 1st Sess., 2011 (March 10, 2011); H. Con. Res. 31, 112th Cong., 1st Sess. (March 15, 2011); see also the House's hearings on Libya, *Congressional Record*, 112th Cong., 1st Sess., 2011 (March 31, 2011). This book refers to the president with male gender pronouns for the sake of historic accuracy as of 2013.

3 War Powers Resolution, Section 2(c).

to intervene in Libya under the WPR was suspect from the beginning.[4] Nonetheless, the WPR's procedural requirements created a set of structured expectations about how the branches would respond to one another over the Libyan incursion. On March 21 Obama reported to Congress "consistent with the War Powers Resolution."[5] When US military operations continued past the time horizons of the WPR, still without legislative authorization, members of Congress challenged the president's constitutional and statutory faithfulness.[6]

Instead of either challenging the constitutionality of the WPR, or discontinuing operations, the executive branch argued that the deployments did not amount either to "hostilities" or to "war in the constitutional sense." By early June, a restive House resolved that the Libyan mission had not been legislatively authorized and stated the legislature's prerogative to withdraw funding.[7] Hundreds of senators and representatives expressed constitutional concerns, but this did not translate into a willingness to either authorize or shut down operations.[8]

The legislature's challenge and the president's response constitute a revealing window into characteristic features of a constitutional war powers debate. Consider first that the debate was nowhere judicialized. Members of the House sued the president, but the US District Court threw the case out, noting its "frustration" at being asked to hear the case given

4   Presidents have often claimed constitutional empowerment beyond the terms of the WPR.

5   The White House, "Letter from the President regarding the commencement of operations in Libya" (March 21, 2011). Available at http://www.whitehouse.gov/the -press-office/2011/03/21/letter-president-regarding-commencement-operations-libya (accessed March 7, 2012).

6   See S. Res. 194 (May 23, 2011), supportive of the president, submitted by John McCain and debated on June 14, 2011; S. J. Res. 13, S. J. Res.14 (both on May 23, 2011), emphasizing the importance of legislative war authority and authorizing the war in Libya, submitted by Ron Paul; Amendment SA 381 by Sen. Paul to bill S. 990 (May 25, 2011), stating that the president needed authorization from Congress for the incursion; Kucinich Resolution (H. Con. Res. 51) (June 3, 2011) mandating the president remove troops in 15 days (failed 148–265).

7   Boehner Resolution (H. Res 292) (June 3, 2011) restraining the president from introducing ground troops and stating that "the president has not given Congress a compelling rationale for the operations" (adopted 268–145).

8   268 members of the House voted for the Boehner Resolution; 148 voted for the Kucinich Resolution mandating that the president remove troops in fifteen days. H. J. Res. 68 would have authorized Obama's actions in support of the NATO mission but failed on June 24, 2011 by 295–123. H.R. 2278 would have blocked the president's use of Defense Department funds for the Libyan intervention, but failed by 238–180 on June 24, 2011. Congress did restrict the president's use of defense department funds for Libya in limited ways (Amendments 8 and 13 to H.R. 2219, adopted July 7, 2011).

long-standing precedent.[9] This controversy would be decided through nonjudicial politics. Indeed, the politics of the moment were on vivid display in the reasoning of three prominent executive branch officials— President Obama, Vice President Biden, and Secretary of State Clinton— all of whom argued that this use of the military was constitutional, but all of whom, when they were Democratic senators challenging a Republican president, had emphasized the importance of legislative authorization for war.[10]

The debate pivoted around the meaning of "war"—in the language of the Office of Legal Counsel (OLC), "war for constitutional purposes."[11] Despite air strikes and remote drones, the administration claimed that the Libyan intervention was neither "war" nor "hostilities."[12] President Obama interpreted the meaning of "war" and "hostilities" not through international law, or judicial precedent, or close readings of the Constitution's text. Rather, the administration invoked policy concerns, structural and governance reasons, and historic precedent. State Department legal advisor Harold Koh told Congress that it should interpret the WPR's language in light of the security consequences of their chosen readings, emphasizing that a "mechanical reading of the statute could lead to unintended automatic cutoffs . . . where more flexibility is required."[13] The

9 *Dennis Kucinich et. al v. Barack Obama* (2011), Civil Action No. 11-1096 (RBW), p. 7, fn. 4.

10 On Biden, see Adam Leech, "Biden: Impeachment If Bush Bombs Iran," *Seacoast online.com* (Nov. 29, 2007), available at http://www.seacoastonline.com/apps/pbcs.dll /article?/AID=/20071129/NEWS (accessed January 27, 2012). On Clinton, see Charlie Savage, "Hillary Clinton Q&A," *Boston Globe* (Dec. 20, 2007), available at http://www.boston .com/news/politics/2008/specials/CandidateQA/ClintonQA/?page=full (accessed June 12, 2012). On Obama, see Charlie Savage, "Barack Obama's Q&A," *Boston Globe* (Dec. 20, 2007), available at http://www.boston.com/news/politics/2008/specials/CandidateQA/Obama QA/?page=full (accessed June 12, 2012).

11 Caroline D. Krass, Office of the Legal Counsel, "Authority to Use Military Force in Libya" (April 1, 2011), p. 8 (henceforth *OLC April 1*). Available at http://www.justice .gov/olc/2011/authority-military-use-in-libya.pdf (accessed January 29, 2012).

12 The administration developed this argument in a series of reports and statements. See *OLC April 1*; The White House, "United States Activities in Libya" (June 15, 2011) (henceforth Libya Activities June 15), available at http://www.politifact.com/truth-o-meter /article/2011/jun/22/are-us-actions-libya-subject-war-powers-resolution/ (accessed January 29, 2012); Harold H. Koh, Legal Advisor, US Dept. of State, "Libya and War Powers: Headings before the Senate Committee on Foreign Relations," 112th Cong. (2011) (henceforth *Libya Hearings*), at http://foreign.senate.gov/imo/media/doc/Koh.Testimony.pdf (accessed January 29, 2012); Barack Obama, "Remarks by the President in Address to the Nation on Libya," National Defense University (March 28, 2011) (henceforth *Remarks on Libya*), available at http://www.whitehouse.gov/photos-and-video/video/2011/03/28/president-obama -s-speech-libya#transcript (accessed January 29, 2012).

13 *Libya Hearings*, 5–6.

administration described the importance of US intervention for regional security, for UN and NATO credibility, for humanitarian needs, and for international alliances, especially given the foreign policy imperatives of the Arab Spring. The OLC made these policy reasons one element of a constitutional test, arguing that the president's war authority depended upon whether the intervention served "sufficiently important national interests."[14]

The administration also gave reasons that spoke to the governing capacities of the branches. For example, it cited the president's capacity to respond to "rapidly evolving military and diplomatic circumstances."[15] It emphasized that costs and casualties would be low and that the administration would not ask Congress for appropriations.[16] Apparently concerned about policy intersections between Libya and other legislative security priorities, the administration argued that the intervention would have few policy consequences elsewhere. For example, the intervention would not impact operations in Iraq and Afghanistan, nor was it likely to escalate.[17] The OLC argued that only operations sufficiently extensive in "nature, scope, and duration" required legislative approval.[18] Finally, its citation of OLC reasoning during the Clinton administration amounted to a precedent-based claim.[19]

To argue for the constitutionality of a president's deployment because of its importance for domestic security interests would seem to violate one central effort of constitutional law: to seek answers about procedural authority precisely so as to *avoid* controversy over topics like Libya's security significance. Legal objections either condemned Obama for playing fast and loose with constitutional and statutory language, or challenged the integrity of the OLC's legal process.[20] No constitutional

---

14   *OLC April 1*, 10.

15   *OLC April 1*, 7.

16   *Libya Activities June 15*, 15–16.

17   *Libya Activities June 15*, 21; *Libya Hearings*, 7–10.

18   *OLC April 1*, 10. These arguments were consonant with ones developed during the Clinton administration. See Walter Dellinger for the Office of Legal Counsel, "Deployment of United States Armed Forces into Haiti" (September 27, 1994), 1; Walter Dellinger for the Office of Legal Counsel, "Proposed Deployment of United States Armed Forces into Bosnia" (November 30, 1995); Walter Dellinger, "Did Obama Buck Congress on Libya?" *Politico.com* (March 22, 2011), available at http://www.politico.com/arena/perm/Walter_Dellinger_67654F65-2026-4BE1-A4B9-6D18C15BC77E.html (accessed January 23, 2012).

19   *OLC April 1*, 9. On Clinton administration precedents, see too Jane C. Stromseth, "Understanding Constitutional War Powers Today: Why Methodology Matters," *Yale Law Journal* 106:3 (1996): 845–915, fn. 139.

20   Bruce Ackerman, "Obama's Unconstitutional War," *Foreign Policy* (March 24, 2011); Robert J. Delahunty, "War Powers Irresolution: The Obama Administration and the Libyan Intervention," *Engage* 1 U of St. Thomas Legal Studies Research Paper No. 11–

scholarship found Obama's substantive claims worth investigating: for example, whether the Libyan intervention actually was as significant to regional peace, NATO and UN credibility, and US domestic interests as Obama claimed.[21] Nor did constitutional scholars engage the structural arguments that Obama offered for presidential war governance. Perceiving that the administration was being strategic in its interpretation of constitutional language, some argued that the War Powers Resolution—and perhaps the Constitution itself—were shoddy in their legal draftsmanship, especially in allocating interbranch war authority with reference to a set of slippery terms ("war," "hostilities") that have little definitive content.[22]

It is true that the US Constitution's allocation of the power to initiate hostilities is ambiguous.[23] That the Constitution empowers a federal government to wage war is beyond dispute.[24] But which branch has the power to initiate hostilities? Congress is vested with the power to "declare war," a power whose scope could range from the simple legal

---

17, 12 (September 2011): 122–28; Louis Fisher, "Military Operations in Libya: No War? No Hostilities?," *Presidential Studies Quarterly* 42:1 (2012): 176–89; Trevor W. Morrison, "Libya, 'Hostilities,' The Office of Legal Counsel, and the Process of Executive Branch Legal Interpretation," *Harvard Law Review Forum* 124:62 (2011): 62–74; Michael Isikoff, "On Libya, President Obama Evaded Rules on Legal Disputes" *NBC News* (June 21, 2011), available at http://www.msnbc.msn.com/id/43474045/ns/politics-white_house/t/libya-president -obama-evaded-rules-legal-disputes-scholars-say/#.T7BbYWUbroA (accessed May 13, 2011).

21 For a notable exception see Michael J. Glennon, "The Cost of 'Empty Words': A Comment on the Justice Department's Libya Opinion" *Harvard National Security Journal* (2011), *available at* http://harvardnsj.org/wp-content/uploads/2011/04/Forum_Glennon _Final-Version.pdf (accessed April 4, 2012), pp. 6–7.

22 Louis Henkin, "Foreign Affairs and the Constitution," *Foreign Affairs* 66:2 (1987): 284–310, 300 (lamenting that "above all, the [WPR] suffers gravely from a lack of any definition of 'hostilities'").

23 A technical legal language distinguishes "vagueness," "ambiguity," and "underdeterminacy." An "ambiguous" text has more than one distinct meaning. A "vague" concept has indefinite applications. An "underdeterminate" text constrains, without fully fixing, a legal outcome. Vagueness and ambiguity are two routes toward underdeterminacy. The Constitution's war powers language is both vague and ambiguous. The concept of "war" is vague, and the allocation of the power to "declare war" to Congress is ambiguous as to whether Congress has the power to authorize all military confrontation, or simply the power to name a confrontation as war. See Ralf Poscher, "Ambiguity and Vagueness in Legal Interpretation," *Oxford Handbook on Language and Law*, Lawrence Solum and Peter Tiersma, eds. (Oxford University Press, 2011).

24 Daniel Deudney, *Bounding Power: Republican Security Theory from the Polis to the Global Village* (Princeton: Princeton University Press, 2007); David Hendrickson, *Peace Pact: The Lost World of the American Founding* (Lawrence: University Press of Kansas, 2006); Frederick W. Marks III, *Independence on Trial: Foreign Affairs and the Making of the Constitution* (Wilmington, DE: Rowman & Littlefield, 1986); Michael Oren, *Power, Faith and Fantasy: America in the Middle East, 1776 to the Present* (New York: W. W. Norton & Co., 2007).

power of naming, to an exclusive power to authorize any and all military confrontation. Congress can also pass laws and appropriate funds, regulate the military, and create the structure of the executive bureaucracy, including security-related bureaus. Finally, Congress is vested with the power to "issue letters of marque and reprisal," a common form of limited and undeclared war of the eighteenth century.[25] Yet the president is granted a vague "executive power," and the Constitution designates him "Commander in Chief... when called into the actual Service of the United States." Unlike the legislature and judiciary, the presidency never adjourns, and the structure of the branch is comparatively efficient and unitary. Article II Section 1 also requires the president to swear to "preserve, protect, and defend" the Constitution. These features imply some independent war powers, and the oath implies that those powers are for defensive purposes. The contours of those powers, and the conditions under which they may be used, are never specified. Nor do originalist sources reveal any bright lines.[26] Justice Jackson said that the answer to this question "must be divined from materials almost as enigmatic as the dreams Joseph was called upon to interpret for Pharaoh."[27]

The Constitution also fails to provide for one authoritative institution to settle this controversy. Whereas the South African Constitution designates its Constitutional Court as the "highest court on all constitutional matters," and specifies that the Court "makes the final decision whether a matter is a constitutional matter,"[28] the US Constitution never concretely establishes judicial review. The power of the US Supreme Court to interpret the Constitution is implied, not explicit, and its origins rest in judicial constitutional reasoning that has been sustained and reinforced by other political actors, rather than being mandated, or even explicitly

25   Bernard Bailyn, *The Ideological Origins of the American Revolution* (Cambridge, MA: Harvard University Press, 1967), 27–29; Stromseth, "Understanding," 860.

26   Michael Ramsey's originalist reading of the "declare war" clause in *The Constitution's Text in Foreign Affairs* (Cambridge: Harvard University Press, 2007), chs. 11 and 12, resists the common idea that originalist sources are incomplete. Ramsey admits that his reading was not transparent to all members of the founding generation (pp. 244–45). The Constitutional Convention spent less than a day discussing war powers, and neither the Virginia Plan nor the Paterson Plan contained any procedures governing the power to commence hostilities. Christopher Collier and James Lincoln Collier, *Decision In Philadelphia: The Constitutional Convention of 1787* (Ballentine Books: New York, 1986), 330. Perhaps debates were cursory because delegates were fatigued at the end of the proceedings. Jack N. Rakove, *Original Meanings: Politics and Ideas in the Making of the Constitution* (New York: Vintage Books, 1996), 83–84. See also Stromseth, "Understanding."

27   *Youngstown Sheet & Tube Company, et al v. Charles Sawyer, Secretary of Commerce* 343 U.S. 579 (1952), Jackson concurrence.

28   Republic of South Africa Const, Chap 8, Sec 167, § 3.

contemplated, by the text.[29] In its constructions of constitutional meaning, the judiciary has chosen to limit its scrutiny of "political questions" like the nature of constitutionally authoritative procedures for going to war.[30]

In the domain of war powers, the agents who have advanced and judged claims of war authority are not courts but the elected branches themselves as they formulate and defend their policies to one another and to the electorate. They have often done so in ways that are transparently linked to institutional or partisan policy advantage. Presidents in the twentieth century have made vast claims for independent war-making authority. Truman, Ford, Kennedy, Johnson, Nixon, Reagan, George H. W. Bush, Clinton, and Obama all claimed the power to initiate hostilities without congressional authorization—a claim premised on the executive's authority to decide on his own what constitutes a threat and an appropriate response to threat. Although it was unusual for nineteenth-century presidents to state it explicitly, presidents from Jefferson to Polk to Lincoln to Wilson behaved as if congressional authorization for military hostilities was optional. In fact, while George W. Bush is remembered for bellicosity, his effort to achieve congressional authorization to fight wars in Iraq and Afghanistan was notably sensitive to legislative prerogatives in war. Many presidents have behaved as though whether to engage in military hostilities is not a relevant question for Congress.

Congress, too, has been actively engaged on its own behalf. Early Congresses made assertions of constitutional authority that are breathtaking to modern ears. The debate between Pacificus and Helvidius, one of the first showdowns between the branches, concerned whether or not it is constitutionally appropriate for the president to offer a *point of view* about how a treaty should be interpreted. Partisans of Congress worried that a president's speech about the meaning of a defense treaty would unduly contort the legislature's deliberative space. Many of Congress's esteemed members—Senators Vandenberg, Nye, Taft, Mansfield, Fulbright—were known for their sustained challenges to executive war authority. In 1973 congressional solicitude for its own institutional honor reached a new level of mobilization in the War Powers Resolution. The Iran-Contra hearings and contemporary agitation about executive authority for interventions in Libya show us that even in the age of the "imperial presidency," the legislative branch has its defenders.

---

29   Keith Whittington, *Political Foundations of Judicial Supremacy* (Princeton: Princeton University Press, 2007).

30   See e.g., *Massachusetts v. Laird*, 400 U.S. 886 (1970) and *DaCosta v. Laird*, 405 U.S. 979 (1972) where the Court denies certiorari over the constitutionality of the Vietnam War; *Doe v. Bush*, 323 F.3d 133 (1st Cir. 2003) (rejecting a suit to enjoin the Iraq War on constitutional and statutory grounds).

Both the Constitution's text—which apparently commits the elaboration of the meaning of "war" to a potentially rivalrous interbranch relationship—and the history of war powers debates, where the branches' interpretive claims are transparently driven by partisan, institutional, and policy rivalries, generate one common conclusion: core features of this area of constitutional policy do not intersect well with standard presumptions about the conditions of faithful constitutional interpretation. Conventional beliefs about constitutional reasoning emphasize neutrality, impartial review, and the value of making policy in conformity with the Constitution's procedural requirements as specified either explicitly in the text or through judicial construction. With underdeterminate constitutional language, an interpretive process driven by the politics of motivated and strategic officeholders, and the absence of a final arbiter, the structural conditions of the war powers debate are repugnant to core conditions thought necessary for achieving good practices of constitutional interpretation.[31]

The idea that constitutional fidelity means adhering to the meaning of determinate text, or adhering to the decisions of one authoritative, impartial adjudicator is sustained by reference to an idea about constitutional authority called the *settlement thesis*. The settlement thesis claims that the very point of constitutions is to resolve conflict over basic political questions like the allocation of power between institutions. For the Constitution to be authoritative in disciplining war powers *is* for the Constitution to resolve the basic question of where war authority resides and for all agents to conform their behavior to that settled understanding. Policies may be more or less legitimate, more or less in accord with the "spirit" of the Constitution.[32] But the Constitution as authoritative text is the Constitution whose translation into politics is determinate.

The hope is that constitutions can contain policy controversy within a set of uncontroversial decision procedures. If a constitution offers a set of clear boundaries, then actors can uncontroversially assess the constitutionality of their behavior, and a core function of the constitutional order—to create a stable, procedural, lawful framework—is achieved. The link between settlement theory and judicial supremacy should be transparent: if the primary function of a constitution is to resolve interpretive conflict, then it is important to identify a single institution whose impartial reasoning about vague language can be accepted as authoritative by all others.

Yet establishing stable, legal, procedural frameworks is only one task of a constitutional order. Constitutions also create resources—textual,

31   On "underdeterminacy," see footnote 23.
32   Many thanks to Mitch Berman and Colin Bird for their challenges on this front.

ideological, and institutional—through which actors occupy various roles, or offices, and in turn use those offices to advance their aims in politics. The Constitution creates a politics every bit as much as it creates a legal order. The aims that politicians pursue in this constitutional universe are premised on, and have implications for, the policies and institutions that surround them. The Cold War ferocity of the Republican Party in the 1970s and 1980s was linked to an interpretive claim about presidential war powers; so too, apparently, is the Obama administration's conception of liberal international order. The availability of these textual, ideological, and institutional resources for ordinary politics makes it appropriate to assess constitutional fidelity not only in terms of respect for a legal framework, but also in terms of officials' relationships to a structured politics that is created and sustained through constitutional language and institutions.

Can this politics be assessed in any meaningfully constitutionalist way? Evaluating the behavior and rhetoric of strategic, partisan, and motivated public officials in terms of their adherence to neutral, procedural, nonpartisan standards seems to promise only disappointment. For this reason, some say that we should not assess constitutional fidelity in the area of war powers at all. John McGinnis and Mark Tushnet both argue that the Constitution's failure to advance determinate rules over war powers means that the constitutional text is consistent with, in Tushnet's words, "*whatever* the political process produces."[33]

But it is precisely this constitutional politics that determines the allocation of war authority in practice. And war has been endemic to American statecraft. Since the constitutional founding, the United States has been in an almost continuous state of war, and war has arguably been the single most important engine behind the development of the US state.[34] To refrain from evaluating the interpretive politics behind this tremendous exertion of resources is to remove highly consequential domains of governance from constitutional scrutiny. At the same time, we should be skeptical of accounts of constitutional fidelity that begin with the premise that the ordinary behavior of elected officials is constitutionally deficient.

---

33 Mark Tushnet, "The Political Constitution of Emergency Powers: Some Lessons from *Hamdan*," *Minnesota Law Review* 91:5 (2007): 1451–72, 1468; John O. McGinnis, "The Spontaneous Order of War Powers," *Case Western Reserve Law Review* 47:4 (1996): 1317–29 and "Constitutional Review by the Executive in Foreign Affairs and War Powers: A Consequence of Rational Choice in the Separation of Powers," *Law & Contemporary Problems* 56:4 (1993): 293–325.

34 Mary L. Dudziak, *War Time: An Idea, Its History, Its Consequences* (New York: Oxford University Press, 2012); David R. Mayhew, "War and American Politics," *Perspectives on Politics* 3:03 (2005): 473–93.

Assessing the branches' war powers politics requires an altogether different way of theorizing constitutional fidelity. This book demonstrates that the constitutional politics of war powers can be meaningfully assessed in terms that are congruent, rather than repugnant, to their animating conditions. Constitutional theory need not be disabled in its confrontation with an interpretive politics that is shot through with vagueness, underdeterminacy, structured interbranch conflict, and partisan and policy rivalries. We can generate standards for assessing interpretive fidelity that capture, track, and engage this constitutional politics rather than resist, ignore, and condemn it. Doing so requires new and different theories about constitutional authority. This book is simultaneously about the war power, about the best way to interpret the Constitution's interbranch allocation of war authority; but it also offers a broader way of conceiving constitutional authority, one that is relevant for other dimensions of constitutional policy whose structuring premises, like those of war powers, fit poorly with the terms of settlement theory.

THE PRESIDENT VERSUS CONGRESS: INSULARIST CONCEPTIONS OF WAR AUTHORITY

Constitutional scholarship shares a broad premise that the Constitution should be read to settle basic questions of institutional competence like which institution has the power to start wars. Dispute focuses on what, exactly, it is that the Constitution settles. Since the mid-twentieth century, one set of commentators has elaborated the executive branch's claim that it has the constitutional authority to initiate military hostilities without legislation. Its opponents, dominant since the founding, are partisans of the legislature, arguing that only Congress enjoys the power to authorize hostilities.

Controversy about whether the authority to initiate war rests with Congress, or the presidency, conceals a more basic agreement that structures the war powers literature. Both sides, seeking to shield the constitutional war powers structure from the effects of policy controversy, would locate the sovereign war power in a single branch (perhaps with a few narrow exceptions). If procedures for authorizing war are settled beforehand, then constitutional fidelity involves acting in congruence with those procedures, rather than considering in any fresh way which branch *ought* to be empowered given the context. The branches need not review and justify their interpretations of the war power, so much as act in congruence with settled procedures. Vesting the authority to initiate war in settled, noncontroversial procedures protects the branches from the burden of justifying their constitutional politics to one another. I name these "insular" theories of war authority. An insular account of war authority is one that seeks to shield its favored institution from the burdens of justifying its interpretive position to its rival. In the context of war powers, insular conceptions of war authority run up against obdurate features of constitutional text and politics.

PRO-CONGRESS INSULARISM

For advocates of the legislature, Congress's power to declare war, to pass laws and appropriate funds, to issue letters of marque and reprisal (authorize limited war), and to make rules and regulations for the military all indicate legislative empowerment over war.[35] Louis Henkin writes that the Constitution "gave the decision as to whether to put the country into war to Congress," and doubts that that power can be delegated.[36] Pro-Congress insularists believe that "Congress has the exclusive power to determine whether to introduce forces into war, though in emergencies the President may act."[37]

This last proviso is the wedge that splinters pro-Congress insularism. For no scholar denies that there are contexts in which the president may act on his own authority.[38] This authority is structurally implied: the executive branch is always in session and heads the military. Founding debates reinforce the idea of an implied presidential war power. Congress was empowered to "declare," rather than "make" war, in an effort to grant the executive "the power to repel sudden attacks."[39] The power to "declare" war, which is Congress's, then amounts to something less than a power to authorize all military confrontation. What distinguishes

35   Louis Fisher, *Presidential War Power* (Lawrence: University Press of Kansas, 1995); Michael J. Glennon, *Constitutional Diplomacy* (Princeton: Princeton University Press, 1990); Charles A. Lofgren, "War-Making under the Constitution: The Original Understanding," *Yale Law Journal* 81:4 (1972): 672–702; William Michael Treanor, "Fame, the Founding, and the Power to Declare War," *Cornell Law Review* 82:4 (1997): 695–772.

36   Louis Henkin, *Constitutionalism, Democracy, and Foreign Affairs* (New York: Columbia University Press, 1990), 39.

37   Glennon, *Diplomacy*, 84; Philip Bobbit, "War Powers: An Essay on John Hart Ely's 'War and Responsibility: Constitutional Lessons of Vietnam and Its Aftermath,'" *Michigan Law Review* 92:6 (1994): 1364–400, 1373–74; Stephen Griffin, *Long Wars and the Constitution: Presidents and the Constitutional Order from Truman to Obama* (Cambridge: Harvard University Press, forthcoming 2013), p. 60 in manuscript.

38   See, e.g., Louis Fisher, *Constitutional Abdication on War & Spending* (College Station: Texas A&M University Press, 2000), ch. 2. This book refers to the president using historically accurate male pronouns.

39   See deliberations between Madison, Gerry, and Sharman (August 17, 1787). James Madison, *Notes of Debates in the Federal Convention of 1787 Reported by James Madison* (Athens: Ohio University Press, 1966), 476.

military confrontations where the president is empowered from those where congressional authority is plenary?

This is among the central questions of the war powers debate. From within settlement terms, the answer to the question should be relatively formal so as to avoid interpretive controversy. It will not do to argue that the president is empowered to quickly respond when he *should* do so, or when national security calls for him to do so, or when his office positions him well to respond to the security needs of the moment, because such answers replicate the political controversy that it is a core aim of settlement to curtail. What are the security needs of the moment? Often, the answer is politically contentious. Settlement theorists need criteria that are not subject to political controversy. And yet the Constitution's text provides no clear guidance.

Lacking clear textual answers, pro-Congress insularists may point to a founding-era consensus that the president may repel sudden attacks at territorial borders. But does this mean that a president must wait until the attack has actually occurred to respond? If he is allowed to respond with force as attack is unfolding, how much force? How long can the president fight without legislative authorization? And what does it mean for "attack to be unfolding" when a finely tuned diplomatic and bureaucratic politics holds the key to nuclear war?

Some scholars believe that there are also founding-era consensus answers to these questions that can guide us today. Even if there were, consensus politics, on its own, is a weak place to vest constitutional authority, not least because a modern consensus has emerged in politics that the president is empowered to engage in short-term military hostilities as long as his bellicosity can plausibly be named something other than "war." It is precisely this modern consensus that pro-Congress insularists wish to dislodge. Their reliance on the consensus politics of yesterday hence raises conceptual problems.

There are other good reasons to resist reading consensus politics of the founding into the Constitution's war powers order. Even during the founding, there was a consensus that not all military strikes amounted to "war." President Washington sent federal troops to put down Native American resistance to white settlement of the Pacific Northwest.[40] President Jackson paid militiamen to repel attacks by Native Americans in Missouri, Michigan, and Indiana without specific legislative authorization.[41] In the Second Seminole War in Florida, the War Department

---

40 David J. Barron and Martin S. Lederman, "The Commander in Chief at the Lowest Ebb—A Constitutional History," *Harvard Law Review* 121:4 (2008): 941–1113, 962.

41 See Henry Bartholomew Cox, *War, Foreign Affairs, and Constitutional Power 1829–1901* (Cambridge, MA: Ballinger Publishing Co., 1976), 16.

lent muskets and provisions and dispatched army companies to Florida to fight alongside state militia forces. Federal army units were dispersed throughout the West during the Indian Wars of the mid-nineteenth century. Congress appropriated funds for these and other like ventures, but did not authorize war.[42] Public officials apparently did not conceive of themselves as engaging in war despite the fact that the US government had entered into treaties with Native American tribes, implicitly recognizing some sovereignty. Theodore Roosevelt used these precedents to guide his thinking about legislatively unauthorized bellicosity in Central and South America and the Caribbean. Harry Truman, and later Lyndon Johnson, followed Roosevelt's path when they characterized executive branch belligerency as "police action," not war; today President Obama, with the counsel of war powers scholar Harold Koh, argues that the strikes in Libya amount to a "limited mission," not war.[43] What counts as war is a matter of political judgment, and national consensus has often permitted forms of executive bellicosity that pro-Congress insularists would or should condemn. Looseness in the very concept of war creates textual space for opportunistic presidents to evade the restrictions that pro-Congress insularists demand. Neither the consensus politics of the founding, nor those of today, are reliable resources for pro-Congress insularists.

The concept of "war" corresponds to dividing lines for institutional empowerment, and the Constitution creates branches with the political capacity to challenge one another. The basic tension between Congress's and the executive's authority over military control—a tension not resolved through textually specified consultation procedures—makes textual vagueness consequential for war politics. For these reasons, we should expect enduring struggle over the meaning of that term. Moreover, such challenge is legitimate insofar as some cases of military confrontation truly do not amount to "war." The branches must determine the scope of these exceptions. That Congress's insular power to authorize war is subject to poorly defined exceptions begs the question of how officials and the public are to judge when a state of affairs exists that could justify independent presidential action. Pro-Congress insularism depends on the sensitive judgment of officials, yet offers only limited resources for training that judgment.

42 Cox, *War*, 23, 64–65, 205–206, 211, 302–304; see also Barron and Lederman, "Lowest," 991.

43 Charlie Savage and Mark Landler, "White House Defends Continuing U.S. Role in Libya Operation," *New York Times* (June 15, 2011) available at http://www.nytimes.com /2011/06/16/us/politics/16powers.html?_r=1&pagewanted=all (accessed May 14, 2012).

PRO-PRESIDENCY INSULARISM

Pro-presidency insularism argues that the executive branch has the constitutional authority to engage in defensive military hostilities, and that the president is the only judge of the practical meaning of this category. Truman made the claim prominent when he defended his actions in the Korean War as inherently authorized by the commander-in-chief clause. Since Truman, presidents have used striking language to advance this claim. Although President George H. W. Bush obtained authorization for hostilities in the first Gulf War, he emphasized that "I didn't have to get permission from some old goat in the United States Congress to kick Saddam Hussein out of Kuwait."[44] When Clinton sent troops to Haiti, he argued that "[l]ike my predecessors of both parties, I have not agreed that I was constitutionally mandated" to achieve congressional approval.[45] After the executive branch raised the claim to political prominence, a few scholars took up the work of elaborating and defending what is essentially a political claim deployed in the heat of struggle.

Pro-Executive insularists argue for "exclusive" presidential control over the armed forces.[46] Eugene Rostow tells us that, although the executive's power to call the military into service is a limited power "confined to cases of actual invasion, or of imminent danger of invasion," nevertheless the president himself must be the "sole and exclusive judge" as to when these cases have arisen.[47] Congress's war power is then construed as residual and secondary—perhaps a power to endorse or refrain from endorsing, but never a full power to authorize or bar. Some partisans of the president would interpret the power to "declare war" as a simple power

44 "Remarks of President George Bush before the Texas State Republican Convention," Federal News Service (June 20, 1992) as cited by William Michael Treanor, "Fame, the Founding, and the Power to Declare War," *Cornell Law Review* 82:695 (1996): 703.

45 "Presidential News Conference: Health Care, Haiti and Crime Transcript of President Clinton's News Conference at the White House," *New York Times* (August 4, 1994), A16, as cited by Treanor, "Fame," 704.

46 Bobbit, "War Powers," 1373–74; John Yoo, *The Powers of War and Peace: The Constitution and Foreign Affairs After 9/11* (Chicago: University of Chicago Press, 2005); J. Terry Emerson, "The War Powers Resolution Tested: The President's Independent Defense Power," *Notre Dame Law Review* 51:2 (1975): 187–216; Henry S. Commager, *The Defeat of America* (New York: Simon and Schuster, 1974); Robert F. Turner, "War and the Forgotten Executive Power Clause of the Constitution: A Review Essay of John Hart Ely's War and Responsibility," *Virginia Journal of International Law* 34:4 (1994): 903–79. See also L. Gordon Crovitz and Jeremy A. Rabkin, eds., *The Fettered Presidency: Legal Constraints on the Executive Branch* (American Enterprise Institute for Public Policy Research, 1989).

47 Eugene V. Rostow, "Great Cases Make Bad Law: The War Powers Act," *Texas Law Review* 50:5 (1972): 833–900, 854.

to determine whether a state of hostilities should be called "war" for purposes of international law.[48] This does not insulate the president's use of war powers from review by the electorate. But it does advocate norms of deference to insulate the president's use of powers from repudiation by other institutions. It would shield the president from the political heft of rival institutionalized authority.

Three of the most important arguments for presidential insularism include an argument based on flexibility; an argument that challenge is dangerous; and an argument based on practice. Pro-Presidency insularists often emphasize flexibility.[49] Rostow argued against "put[ting] the Presidency in a straitjacket of a rigid code, and prevent[ing] new categories of action from emerging, in response to the necessities of a tense and unstable world."[50] "[M]odern conditions" require the president to "act quickly, and often alone."[51] Congress, then, should understand its role in terms of cooperating with the president to support his negotiations and diplomacy.

While policy flexibility is important, the relationship between policy flexibility and interbranch behavior is more complex than insularists claim. The president's capacity to independently respond to crisis is structurally guaranteed by a fixed term and by high barriers to impeachment. Given a massive military establishment, he can pursue his policies even if very few people agree with him at all. Congress cannot, except under exceptional circumstances, remove him personally from office. The need for flexibility through independence is guaranteed at the structural level.

There are good reasons not to expand this structurally guaranteed independence into a norm of political insularity. In part, this is because the president's decision space may be restricted by many forces beyond Congress. Presidents who govern unilaterally may discover that their strategy becomes more and more determined by the imperatives of a single force, say the views of a single cabinet. In fact, engaging the conflicting demands of different political realities and institutions can open space for an agent to make flexible decisions in a broader space. A president "freed" from Congress may end up chained by party. In the prelude to World War II, Senator Nye sought restrictive legislation out of a worry that open presidential discretion would leave the president beholden to

---

48 See Rostow, "Great Cases"; Curtis A. Bradley & Jack L. Goldsmith, "Congressional Authorization and the War on Terrorism," *Harvard Law Review* 118:7 (2005): 2047–133, at 2061–65.

49 Bork has written that Congress is "institutionally incapable" of achieving "swift responses with military force." Robert H. Bork, "Erosion of the President's Power in Foreign Affairs," *Washington University Law Quarterly* 68:3 (1990): 693–706, 693, 698.

50 Rostow, "Great Cases," 838; see also Bobbit, "War Powers," 1382.

51 Rostow, "Great Cases," 871.

economic interests against his own will.[52] Roosevelt affirmed this worry, telling certain senators that "[i]f war came in Europe, [he] did not want to be forced to defend American commercial interests blindly—we would prefer to conduct American policy free from emotional and economic pressures."[53] Even imagining a presidency that faces no external pressures at all, groupthink in the cabinet may still restrict the branch's flexibility. Politicians can sometimes achieve policy flexibility in the US constitutional system by working through a crossroads of conflicting imperatives, rather than being freed from any one of them.

Moreover, flexibility is not the only value for achieving a sound security policy. Wisdom, deliberateness, stability, and consistency are also values, and Congress is well-positioned to contribute here. The right response to a threat is often unclear. Diplomacy, embargoes, and even ignoring the incident may sometimes be more skillful than war.[54] Some legislators have more expertise than the president on particular security problems, and they may have creative perspectives borne of long experience in difficult areas.

So too, the inertia associated with decision-making in large groups can be a positive good for achieving policy stability. In certain contexts, like the provision of security guarantees to other nations, long-term policy stability is required for a policy's success. The time and effort it takes to respond to Congress is time and effort spent toward convincing many people that the policy chosen is in the national interest, and toward building and sustaining policy architectures along that path.[55]

A second pro-presidency insularist argument is that the challenging characteristic of interbranch deliberation endangers the well-being of troops in the field by exposing a troubling lack of will.[56] Legislators also sometimes say they cannot cut off funds for an unconstitutional war because that would amount to stranding soldiers. This argument is largely drawn from a Cold War security context where an almost global security guarantee seemed important for US security interests. In some contexts, the concern may be sound. But not all security dilemmas are like those

---

52   Wayne S. Cole, *Senator Gerald P. Nye and American Foreign Relations* (Minneapolis: University of Minnesota Press, 1962), 80.

53   Robert A. Divine, *The Reluctant Belligerent: American Entry into World War II* (New York: John Wiley & Sons, Inc., 1965), 22.

54   Francis D. Wormuth and Edwin B. Firmage, *To Chain the Dog of War: The War Power of Congress in History and Law* 2nd ed. (Urbana, Il: University of Illinois Press, 1989), 21.

55   J. William Fulbright, "Foreword," in Glennon, *Diplomacy*, xiv.

56   Rostow, "Great Cases," 869, quoting Dean Acheson, *Present at the Creation: My Years in the State Department* (New York: W. W. Norton, Inc., 1969), 414–15. See also Rostow, "Great Cases," 839; Bork, "Erosion," 699.

of the Cold War. Nor should we overlook the costs of the security order that Cold War Congresses built. In many, if not all cases, the soundness of the actual policies that the president and Congress enact should have greater consequence for enemies than the tenor of public conversation. If contentiousness contributes to better-crafted security policies, then contentiousness can also support security. Today we know that the contentiousness of democratic politics may keep the country from entering or sustaining unwise hostilities, hostilities that themselves pose enormous costs to troops.[57] Finally, a refusal to fund continuing operations does not mean leaving troops in the field unprotected. The president continues to bear responsibility for troops even as they withdraw.

A third pro-presidency argument is based on practice. John Yoo is incredulous that many pro-Congress scholars believe "many of the wars of the last half-century . . . were all illegal because they were not accompanied by a declaration of war or its functional equivalent."[58] The State Department estimates that the United States has placed the military into hostilities at least 125 times, and the Congressional Research Service counts 215. Yet the country has declared war only five times.[59] Some of these were legislatively approved by statutes or resolutions; some never formally approved, but were supported by appropriated funds. Given Congress's ultimately decisive control over the military, moreover, this

57 Dan Reiter and Allan Stam, *Democracies at War* (Princeton: Princeton University Press, 2002); Kenneth A. Shultz, *Democracy and Coercive Diplomacy* (Cambridge: Cambridge University Press, 2001); William Dixon, "Democracy and the Peaceful Settlement of International Conflict," *American Political Science Review* 88:1 (1994): 14–33; Bruce Russett, *Grasping the Democratic Peace: Principles for a Post–Cold War World* (Princeton: Princeton University Press, 1994); T. Clifton Morgan and Valerie Schwebach, "Take Two Democracies and Call Me in the Morning: A Prescription for Peace?" *International Interactions* 17:4 (1992): 305–20; Bruce Bueno de Mesquita and David Lalman, *War and Reason: Domestic and International Imperatives* (New Haven: Yale University Press, 1992); Bruce Bueno de Mesquita, James Morrow, Randolph Siverson, and Alastair Smith, "An Institutional Explanation of the Democratic Peace," *American Political Science Review* 93:4 (1999): 791–807; Michael Koch and Scott Sigmund Gartner, "Casualties and Constituencies: Democratic Accountability, Electoral Institutions, and Costly Conflicts," *The Journal of Conflict Resolution* 49:6 (2005): 874–94.

58 John Yoo, "War and the Constitutional Text," *University of Chicago Law Review* 69:4 (2002): 1639–84.

59 Ibid., "The Continuation of Politics by Other Means: The Original Understanding of War Powers," *California Law Review* 84:2 (1996): 167–305, 177. See also Office of the Legal Advisor, U.S. Dept. of State, "The Legality of United States Participation in the Defense of Viet-Nam (1966)," reprinted in *The Vietnam War and International Law, Vol. 1*, ed. Richard A. Falk (Princeton: Princeton University Press, 1968), 583, 597; Congressional Research Service, *Instances of Use of United States Armed Forces Abroad, 1798–1989*, ed. Ellen C. Collier (Dec. 4, 1989), reprinted in Thomas M. Franck and Michael J. Glennon, *Foreign Relations and National Security Law, 2nd ed.* (West Group, 1993), 650.

historic precedent implies some legislative permissiveness toward presidential war. Such long-standing interbranch agreement, presidentialists argue, is decisive of the constitutional question.[60]

The argument based on practice gains most of its force from the Cold War. Within that specific historical context, permissive legislation and legislative quiescence have sustained insularism around the executive's war and emergency powers.[61] Still, the meaning of the Cold War precedent is itself a question to be interrogated. No plausible general theory of constitutional authority tells us that long-standing practice on its own is authoritative.[62]

As importantly, the practice of war does not speak univocally. Prolonged periods of contentious interbranch relationship coexist with long histories of deference. While few wars have been declared, many have been authorized, and even more have been supported with resolutions. Before Truman, no president ever claimed a power to engage troops in large-scale hostilities regardless of Congress's will.[63]

While there may be good structural and functional reasons for presidentialism in war, there are also good structural and functional reasons for legislative war authority. With no outside arbiter, the branches themselves must interpret and enforce the proper meaning of the Constitution's textual war powers regime. Without a textually fixed horizon, with no neutral institution formally empowered to answer the dispute, how can elected officials assess the authority of each branch's constitutional claims?

This book advances a web of alternative standards that, all together, I name the *relational conception* of war authority. I argue that the branches' powerful governance and epistemic capacities can be used to support constructions of constitutional war powers that are well adapted to the security context of their own time. Instead of evaluating whether the branches adhere to determinate textual meaning, we can evaluate them in terms of how well they bring their special institutional capacities to bear

60   Henry P. Monaghan, "Presidential War-Making," *Boston University Law Review* 50:5 (1970): 19–33, 19, 31. See also Emerson, "War Powers Legislation," 53, 72.

61   See Harold Hongju Koh, *The National Security Constitution: Sharing Power after the Iran-Contra Affair* (New Haven: Yale University Press, 1990); Gordon Silverstein, *Imbalance of Powers: Constitutional Interpretation and the Making of American Foreign Policy* (New York: Oxford University Press, 1997).

62   Political practices far more durable than the Cold War may violate the Constitution: consider Southern racial apartheid after the Civil War. For an effort to theorize historic practice in credible ways, see Curtis A. Bradley and Trevor W. Morrison, "Historical Gloss and the Separation of Powers," 126 *Harvard Law Review* (2012). For an illuminating discussion of practice-based interpretive accounts of war powers, see Griffin, *Long Wars*.

63   For a strong repudiation of the practice-based argument for pro-presidency insularism, see Barron and Lederman, "Lowest," 941–1112.

on the problem of interpreting the Constitution's substantive standards about war.

The next sections excavate these standards in two sets. First are the substantive standards pertaining to war, defense, and security. Next are what I call *processualist* standards, which are derived from the branches' structural positions in the constitutional order. The processual standards are for assessing the processes through which the branches deliberate over war powers in practice. Together, these substantive and processual standards form a web for evaluating the branches' politics of war authority which is called the relational conception.

SUBSTANTIVE STANDARDS

The Constitution's text offers a set of substantive standards for disciplining the war power. The preamble commits all institutions to an aspirational standard that they advance the "general welfare" and a system of "common defense." The president vows to "preserve, protect, and defend" the constitutional order. The legislature is granted authority to "declare war." Assessing the branches' fidelity to these concepts is one starting point for analyzing the constitutionality of their behavior.[64]

These substantive terms are important for disciplining any investigation of the contours of each branch's war authority. Consider the meaning of "war," whose declaration is committed to Congress. What is the meaning of this word, or, as the OLC puts it, "war in the constitutional sense"?[65] Does "war" signify any international conflict using military force? Does it mean military action not sanctioned by international law? Does it mean military action that imposes the likelihood of high domestic costs for the United States? Or, is "war" a legal term of art, not necessarily referring to force at all but instead a piece of jargon referring to "the ability of the President to act in a legislative manner"?[66]

One common way of distinguishing between "war" that requires legislative authorization, and conflict that the presidency may authorize, is with reference to scale. Perhaps "war in the constitutional sense" refers to wars that are expensive, time consuming, and pose heavy risks of casualties— big wars. This distinction, though, raises a series of conceptual problems.

64 While preserving, protecting, and declaring are arguably procedures too, I name them substantive standards because constitutional dispute centers on the substantive content of the categories—i.e., what is the meaning of "war" or "defense."

65 E.g., *OLC April 1*.

66 For a discussion of legal approaches to the problem of defining war, see Seth Weinberger, "Presidential War Powers in a Never-Ending 'War'" *ILSA Journal of International & Comparative Law* 13:1 (2006), 11.

First is that the Constitution's explicit commitment of the power to issue letters of marque and reprisal to Congress implies a measure of legislative authority over small as well as big wars.[67] Reprisals were "the most common form of limited and undeclared war" at the time of the founding.[68] Second is a problem of practice: while the polity came to accept small presidential strikes during the Cold War and in the late nineteenth- and early twentieth-century period of imperial expansion, the legislature has not otherwise been friendly to the claim that presidents may unilaterally fight small wars.[69] Third is the problem that wars anticipated to be little and cheap can become big and expensive. Even wars that stay little may be highly consequential for foreign policy, and Article I Section 8 clearly gives Congress a substantial role in foreign policy development. And for good reason: legislatures can be useful institutions for developing sound foreign policy in a complex world. There are good reasons not to accept the distinction between big and little wars as a constitutionally significant dividing line for all contexts.

A second important substantive standard is that of defense, present in the Constitution's preamble and made especially relevant to the presidency through his oath to "preserve, protect, and defend." This oath, along with the fact that the president's war powers are implied, is widely accepted as indicating that a president's use of military force must be for defensive purposes. Perhaps the concept of defense is the right dividing line for adjudicating between legislative and presidential war powers claims.[70] Pro-Congress insularists would interpret this defensive standard narrowly, as a power to "repel sudden attacks"; pro-presidency insularists broaden this standard's scope by arguing that, whatever its content, the president must be the only judge of its meaning. But this way of theorizing the boundary between the two institutions is also, on its own, insufficient. Wars of aggression are now prohibited by international law.[71] Does this mean that the legislature no longer has any constitutional authority over war? In addition, some defensive wars are long, costly, and highly consequential in ways that seem to call for legislative engagement. A purely defensive standard, on its own, implies that Roosevelt needed no authorization to fight Japan in World War II.

---

67   When the Constitution was ratified the power to issue letters of marque and reprisal had come "to signify any intermediate or low-intensity hostility short of declared war that utilized public *or* private forces, although the emphasis on the use of private forces remained." Stromseth, "Understanding," 854.

68   Ibid., 860, citing Bailyn, *Ideological Origins*, 27–29.

69   Stromseth, "Understanding," 885.

70   Turner, "Forgotten," 906–10; Ramsey, *Foreign Affairs*; J. Terry Emerson, "Making War Without a Declaration," *Journal of Legislation* 17:1 (1990): 23–64, 30–31.

71   Stromseth, "Understanding," 897.

While the Constitution's allocation of the authority to make war seems to call for some important distinctions, war, repelling attack, and defensive action are capacious categories whose meaning must be politically constructed. The distinctions between war, hostilities, and police actions, or between repelling attacks, defensive war, and offensive war, are not formal distinctions but rather pertain to the meaning of hostilities which is itself a core political question at stake in the Constitution's allocation of security power. As such, these categories—the distinction between aggressive and defensive bellicosity, for example—should not be understood only as legal or formal categories, but as already politicized in a way that settlement theory hopes to avoid.

To call an account of war or defense "political" is to say, in part, that it rests on deeply contestable judgments about where security resides. That these categories are political does not mean that they cannot be sensibly evaluated. Setting off a nuclear bomb, unprovoked, for aesthetic pleasure clearly does not count as a defensive action. While it was once acceptable to commit genocide to restore honor among city-states, this cannot today be offered as one more option in the policy tool kits of nations.[72] Acknowledging that the content of these terms is contestable, I nonetheless argue for substantive elaboration of categories like "defense" as one standard of constitutional assessment.

While the evaluator's independent assessment of the best meaning of these terms is relevant, recognizing that the operational meaning of these categories is constructed through politics also turns attention to whether these processes of construction can themselves be constitutionally defended. Through what processes should the polity engage these disputes about the meaning of war or defense?

THE STRUCTURAL CONDITIONS OF WAR POWERS

Given the lack of an ultimately authoritative interpreter, it is the branches themselves that must construct useful meaning out of these substantive terms. How should the branches set about the task of generating good answers to these difficult interpretive questions? The relational conception advances a set of "processual" standards for disciplining the branches' political process, no less than the outcomes they generate. But because the processual standards are based on the branches' distinctive governance capacities and structural positions, understanding the processual

---

72 Hans van Wees, "Genocide in Ancient Greece," *The Oxford Handbook of Genocide Studies*, Donald Bloxham and A. Dirk Moses, eds. (Oxford: Oxford University Press, 2010).

standards requires us to take a brief detour into discussing the structural conditions of the branches' war politics.

Departmentalist constitutional theory offers a useful starting point for interrogating these structural conditions. There, political scientists, historians, and academic lawyers have generated a robust body of research that reveals the extent to which the branches regularly interpret the Constitution according to their own lights.[73] One departmentalist literature argues that the Constitution's strategy around war powers amounts to an "invitation to struggle" between the president and Congress.[74]

Departmentalists are correct to note that without a single authoritative interpreter, interpretive struggle (or its endemic possibility) is a defining empirical characteristic of war powers. For all its rich empirical insight, departmentalist scholarship today has not yet developed useful standards for assessing these constitutional politics. While judicial interpreters have theorists like Ronald Dworkin, John Ely, and Justice Scalia to reflect on how judges should interpret the Constitution, the elected branches will find that departmentalist literature gives their institutions little guidance. On what basis should Congress, or the presidency, develop

73   Mark Tushnet, *Taking the Constitution Away from the Court* (Princeton: Princeton University Press, 2000); Susan R. Burgess, *Contest for Constitutional Authority: The Abortion and War Powers Debates* (Lawrence: University Press of Kansas, 1992); Edward Corwin, *Court over Constitution: A Study of Judicial Review as an Instrument of Popular Government* (Buffalo, NY: W. S. Hein, 1938); Neal Devins, *Shaping Constitutional Values* (Baltimore: Johns Hopkins University Press, 1996); Christopher L. Eisgruber, "The Most Competent Branches: A Response to Professor Paulsen," *Georgetown Law Journal* 83: 2 (1994): 347–70; Louis Fisher, *Constitutional Dialogues: Interpretation as Political Process* (Princeton: Princeton University Press, 1989); Louis Fisher, *Constitutional Conflicts Between Congress and the President* (Lawrence: University Press of Kansas, 1997); Scott E. Gant, "Judicial Supremacy and Nonjudicial Interpretation of the Constitution," *Hastings Constitutional Law Quarterly* 24:2 (1997): 359–440; Kent Greenfield, "Original Penumbras: Constitutional Interpretation in the First Year of Congress," 26 *Connecticut Law Review* (1993): 79–144; Michael Stokes Paulsen, "The Most Dangerous Branch: Executive Power to Say What the Law Is," *Georgetown Law Journal* 84: 2 (1994): 217–345; Wayne Moore, *Constitutional Rights and the Powers of the People* (Princeton: Princeton University Press, 1996); Keith E. Whittington, *Constitutional Construction: Divided Powers and Constitutional Meaning* (Cambridge: Harvard University Press, 1999); Steven G. Calebresi, "Caesarism, Departmentalism, and Professor Paulsen," *Minnesota Law Review* 83: 5 (1999): 1421–22; Gary Lawson & Christopher D. Moore, "The Executive Power of Constitutional Interpretation," *Iowa Law Review* 81: 5 (1996): 1267–330.

74   Edward Corwin, *The President: Office and Powers* (New York: New York University Press, 1984); Roger Davidson, ed., *Congress and the Presidency: Invitation to Struggle* (Beverly Hills: Sage Publications, 1988); Cecil Crabb and Pat Holt, *Invitation to Struggle: Congress, the President, and Foreign Policy* (Washington, DC: CQ Press, 1989); Louis Fisher, *Conflicts*; Charles Jones, *The Presidency in a Separated System* (Washington, DC: Brookings Institution Press, 2005). Certain forms of departmentalism are compatible with the settlement thesis. See Gant, "Interpretation," 359–440.

its constitutional understandings? What distinguishes a strong legislative interpretive position from a weak one? Does Congress's independence from the judiciary carry any implications for the forms of reasoning Congress should apply to its interpretive task? Should legislators interpret ambiguities in a way that advances the fortunes of their party? Should the president always interpret so as to advance the primacy of that branch? What if the needs of security conflict with the maintenance of a branch's prestige, as many legislators worried during the Cold War?

The few standards on offer in departmentalist research are reactive to judicial norms, and ill-adapted to the war powers context.[75] For example, departmentalist scholar Dawn Johnsen asks that, to be considered authoritative, a "President's contrary legal views result from a principled, deliberative, transparent process," deliberation that "transcends politics" and offers "candor."[76] Mitch Pickerill's sustained investigation in *Constitutional Deliberation in Congress* operationalizes constitutional deliberation in the legislature as deliberation about the questions the Supreme Court rules on. In the war powers context, where a scanty case law advances tests that are already highly deferential to the elected branches, that standard would render invisible much of the branches' constitutional

---

75 One line of research resists the Rehnquist Court's efforts to enforce standards of "due deliberation" on the legislature that are inconsistent with basic features of legislative governance like strategic interaction, but stops short of articulating what standards should govern legislative or presidential constitutional elaboration. See Philip P. Frickey and Steven S. Smith, "Judicial Review, the Congressional Process, and the Federalism Cases: An Interdisciplinary Critique," *Yale Law Journal* 111:6 (2001): 1707–56; William W. Buzbee and Robert A. Schapiro, "Legislative Record Review," *Stanford Law Review* 54:1 (2001): 87–161; Ruth Colker and James J. Brudney, "Dissing Congress," *Michigan Law Review* 100:1 (2001): 80–144. Paul Brest's hopefully titled canonical work, "The Conscientious Legislator's Guide to Constitutional Interpretation," *Stanford Law Review* 27: 3 (1975): 585–602, asks legislators to apply judicial tests to their own conduct rather than wait for courts to do so. Departmentalists may resist "judicial overhang," a tendency of officials to apply the constitutional reasoning of the courts instead of exercising their own judgment. See Graham K. Wilson, "Symposium: The Most Disparaged Branch: The Role of Congress in the Twenty-First Century," *Boston University Law Review* 89:2 (2009): 331–869, especially Mark Tushnet, "Some Notes on Congressional Capacity to Interpret the Constitution," *Boston University Law Review* 89: 2 (2009): 499–510. Resisting judicial overhang simply opens the question of what positive standards should be used in legislative constitutional elaboration. See Keith Whittington, "On the Need for a Theory of Constitutional Ethics," *The Good Society: A PEGS Journal* 9:3 (2000): 60–66; Jeremy Waldron has called for a "rosy" account of congressional constitutional authority, one that "matche[s], in its normativity, perhaps in its naivete, certainly in its aspirational quality, the picture of courts . . . that we present." *The Dignity of Legislation* (Cambridge: Cambridge University Press, 1999).

76 Dawn E. Johnsen, "Functional Departmentalism and NonJudicial Interpretation: Who Determines Constitutional Meaning?," *Law and Contemporary Problems* 67: 3 (2004): 105–47, 131–32.

deliberations.[77] Later chapters in this book challenge the straightforward relevance of juristic norms to the elected branches' war powers politics.

Instead of emphasizing legal principle, the promising departmentalist research agendas of Neal Katyal, Reva Siegel and Robert Post, and Jack Balkin all emphasize democratic accountability in constitutional interpretation. Katyal calls for Congress to exercise its interpretive powers in ways that are responsive to public opinion.[78] In a series of pathbreaking articles Siegel and Post have defended legislative constitutional interpretation as "a structural mechanism of democratic accountability," and have emphasized the legislature's capacity to "apply constitutional values in a manner that coordinates multiple and potentially competing commitments," as well as the legislature's capacity to gather facts, recognize patterns, draw inferences about social trends, mobilize publics through advocacy, and to legislate in support of constitutional values.[79] But this body of research stops short of translating those capacities into standards according to which Congress can be assessed. So far, the research of these democratically minded scholars calls for the judiciary to respect the legislature's distinctive capacities, rather than elaborating standards that Congress should use to assess its own work.

The fact that the operational meaning of the substantive categories by which the Constitution allocates war authority is constructed in political process suggests that we can assess fidelity not only by assessing whether branches behave in ways that are substantively congruent with the Constitution's terms, but also by assessing whether an interpretive politics is unfolding in ways that are faithfully related to the structural conditions that the Constitution establishes. The design features of the branches suggest

77   J. Mitchell Pickerill, *Constitutional Deliberation in Congress: The Impact of Judicial Review in a Separated System* (Durham, NC: Duke University Press, 2004). Much scholarship defines constitutional deliberation either as deliberation that uses the word "constitution," or as deliberation with reference to the outcomes of judicial decisions or interpretive theories developed for use by the judiciary. For examples, see the outstanding essays in Neal Devins and Keith E. Whittington, eds., *Congress and the Constitution* (Durham, NC: Duke University Press, 2005).

78   Neal Kumar Katyal, "Legislative Constitutional Interpretation," *Duke Law Journal* 50: 5 (2001): 1335–94. See also Jack Balkin's *Living Originalism* (Cambridge: Harvard University Press, 2011), which uses a complex democratic standard to evaluate constitutional constructions.

79   Robert C. Post and Reva B. Siegel, "Equal Protection by Law: Federal Antidiscrimination Legislation after *Morrison* and *Kimel*," *Yale Law Journal* 110: 3 (2000): 441–526; "Legislative Constitutionalism and Section Five Power: Policentric Interpretation of the Family and Medical Leave Act," *Yale Law Journal* 112:8 (2003): 1943–2059; "Protecting the Constitution from the People: Juricentric Restrictions on Section Five Power," *Indiana Law Journal* 78:1 (2003): 1–46. Quotations in text are from: "Policentric," 2026; "Policentric," 2007; "Protecting the Constitution," 14, 16.

a set of governance values that in turn suggest standards for assessing the branches' interpretive work.

Using structural features as a basis for generating interpretive standards is a common move in constitutional scholarship. For example, the judiciary's relative insulation from the electorate and from the process of generating public policy routinely generates the demand that the judiciary reason in ways that bracket the desirability of various public policy options. The existence of a national elected legislature is often thought to imply a constitutional commitment to a democratic or republican form of governance, which suggests a democratic standard for assessing the constitutional politics of Congress.

In fact, the Constitution has a series of design features that act as structural conditions for the ordinary and constitutional politics of national security.[80] Loosely following classical separation of powers theory, three of these conditions are especially worth noting. The first is that each branch enjoys an *independent source of political authority*. No single constituency—the Electoral College, the Senate, state legislatures, or variously configured electoral districts—names the occupant of more than one constitutional office, and officials may not serve in more than one branch. The president and legislators are elected from different geographical bases, at different times of year. The elections of House and Senate members are staggered in time, and their electoral bases differ; the judiciary is composed of officials appointed after a process in which both branches participate.[81] The branches also enjoy independent representational authority in that they do not rely upon one another for continuity in office. Apart from the high barriers of impeachment, officials' continued service is not dependent on the evaluations of rival branches.

80　My articulation of these structural capacities follows the work of Jeffrey Tulis, George Thomas, Reva Siegel and Robert Post, Joseph Bessette, Lawrence Sager, and others. See Jeffrey Tulis, "Deliberation Between Institutions," in *Debating Deliberative Democracy*, James S. Fishkin and Peter Laslett, eds. (Malden, MA: Blackwell Publishing, 2003); George Thomas, *Madisonian Constitutionalism* (Baltimore, MD: The Johns Hopkins University Press, 2008); Siegel and Post, "Policentric," "Juricentric"; Joseph M. Bessette, *The Mild Voice of Reason* (Chicago: University of Chicago Press, 1994), Waldron, *Dignity*, Lawrence G. Sager, *Justice in Plainclothes: A Theory of American Constitutional Practice* (New Haven: Yale University Press, 2004).

81　For conceptions of democratic proceduralism that are not reducible to majoritarianism, see Mariah Zeisberg, "Should We Elect the Supreme Court?" *Perspectives on Politics* 7: 4 (2009): 785–803; Henry Richardson, *Democratic Autonomy: Public Reasoning about the Ends of Policy* (New York: Oxford University Press, 2002); David Estlund, *Democratic Authority: A Philosophical Framework* (Princeton: Princeton University Press, 2008); Christopher Eisgruber, *Constitutional Self-Government* (Cambridge: Harvard University Press, 2001).

The second structural condition is that the branches have *distinctive governance capacities*. The rules that configure the offices—their terms of service, their powers, their existence as a plural or unitary body, the number of members whose decisions are necessary to constitute the judgment of that branch, the policy areas they address—support the branches in performing diverse governance functions. For example, the president and Congress together have a distinctive governance capacity, vis-à-vis the judiciary, in their ability to link the judgments of electoral publics with public policy. They also have the distinctive governance capacity, vis-à-vis the judiciary, to design and carry out public policy. These two capacities do a great deal to explain why war powers has been vested in the two branches; the Court is responsive in only limited ways to electoral publics, and it has limited or no expertise in national security policy.

Congress and the presidency also have distinctive governance capacities vis-à-vis each other. The legislature is structured to enact law that provides for the welfare of a polity with diverse views about politics. Relative to the president, the legislature also provides a platform for the articulation of marginal points of view. Legislatures enjoy a special capacity to clarify the dimensions of conflict that exist in civil society; to harness the intelligence of their members, who may have important experience in security; they also have special capacities to advance broad consensuses and to make general law that accommodates many different points of view.[82] The executive is a unitary office, the most efficient of the three, with the capacity to deliver quick military responses, provide initiative to the legislature, and provide for law enforcement. The executive branch also has diplomatic, intelligence, and consultative capacities that equip it with special forms of knowledge.

Of course, officials face conflicting incentives toward conflicting political goods within each branch. Scholars sometimes represent the relationship between Congress and the Supreme Court as interest-ridden political will squaring off against principled legalism, but Congress is capable of beautiful feats of principle and the Court is loosely responsive to public opinion.[83] Legislative strength sometimes manifests as the delivery

82   Jane Mansbridge, "Rethinking Representation," *American Political Science Review* 97: 4 (2003): 515–28; Harvey C. Mansfield, *America's Constitutional Soul* (Baltimore, MD: The Johns Hopkins University Press, 1991), 124; T. V. Smith, *The Legislative Way of Life* (Chicago: University of Chicago Press, 1940); Bruce G. Peabody and John D. Nugent, "Toward a Unifying Theory of the Separation of Powers," *American University Law Review* 53:1 (2003): 1–64, 22. See also Benjamin Wittes, *Law and The Long War: The Future of Justice in the Age of Terror* (New York: Penguin Press, 2008), on the security value of statutory law.

83   See, for example, Alexander Bickel, *The Least Dangerous Branch* (New Haven: Yale University Press, 1958); Michael Perry, *The Constitution, the Courts, and Human*

of integrated public policy that responds to many different dimensions of concern, but it also sometimes manifests in the public articulation of marginal perspectives on politics. Presidential strength can manifest as quick responsiveness to emerging threat, or it can manifest as strong policy continuity in response to diplomatic needs. The branches have multiple capacities. Nonetheless not every political capacity is represented in this system. The major religious institutions (and hence the distinctive capacity to reason theologically about matters of public concern) are nowhere represented in the interbranch structure, for example.

The exercise of different functions generates a capacity for the branches to advance distinctive perspectives on political problems. Far from being simple platforms for expressing preferences, the structure of each branch can be expected to support the articulation of certain kinds of preferences and certain forms of reasoning over and above others. As each branch carries out its functions, it develops particular forms of expertise both organizationally (such as the executive branch bureaucracy, or Congress's reference service) and informally (i.e., the entrenchment of bargaining attitudes in the legislature versus hierarchical decisional qualities in the executive branch). Congress's assessment of war often focuses more on domestic costs, and presidents are often relatively more alert to war's diplomatic implications. Variation in the branches' capacities can be expected to affect their constitutional positions no less than their policy orientations.[84] We see here a second condition of interbranch relationship: these different capacities condition the perspectives of each branch, and these perspectives may in turn lead the branches to different evaluations of constitutional meaning in service of distinctive political goals.[85]

Rights (New Haven: Yale University Press, 1982); Ronald Dworkin, *A Matter of Principle* (Oxford: Oxford University Press, 1986). For counterevidence, see Barry Friedman, *The Will of the People: How Public Opinion Has Influenced the Supreme Court and Shaped the Meaning of the Constitution* (Farrar, Straus and Giroux, 2009); Robert Mann, *When Freedom Would Triumph: The Civil Rights Struggle in Congress, 1954–1968* (Baton Rouge, LA: LSU Press, 2007).

84 See Jeffrey Tulis, *The Rhetorical Presidency* (Princeton: Princeton University Press, 1987), 41–45; Tulis, "Deliberation"; Morton H. Halperin, *Bureaucratic Politics and Foreign Policy* (Washington, DC: Brookings Institution, 1974); Margaret G. Hermann, ed., *Political Psychology: Contemporary Issues and Problems* (San Francisco: Jossey-Bass, 1986); Philip E. Tetlock, "Accountability: The Neglected Social Content of Judgment and Choice," *Research in Organizational Behavior* 7 (1985): 295–332.

85 Some evidence suggests that public appraisal either reflects, or helps to drive, the distinctiveness of the branches' orientations toward public policy. See H. D. Clarke and M. C. Stewart, "Prospections, Retrospections and Rationality: The Bankers of Presidential Approval Reconsidered," *American Journal of Political Science* 38:4 (1994): 1104–23; Aaron L. Friedberg, *In the Shadow of the Garrison State* (Princeton: Princeton University Press, 2000); David C. Kimball and Samuel C. Patterson, "Living Up to Expectations: Public

Officials who have served in more than one branch reveal how divergent structures can encourage officials to advance divergent judgments on constitutional meaning. Salmon Chase, Secretary of the Treasury for Lincoln, supported the president in issuing paper money during the Civil War to raise money without raising taxes. As an administration official, Chase viewed winning the war as a constitutional imperative. But once appointed to the Supreme Court, and after the war had been won, he argued that the very paper money he had advocated actually violated the constitutional rights of the individual and that security needs could not justify such violations.[86] Earl Warren was a stronger defender of individual rights on the Supreme Court than he had been as attorney general and governor of California, when he advocated Japanese internment as a security measure.[87] As a senator during the Truman administration, Richard Nixon vociferously defended congressional power, but he changed his tune as president. As attorney general for the Roosevelt administration, Robert H. Jackson participated in constructing strong doctrines of executive power, but in the *Youngstown* case, Justice Jackson wrote that a judge could not simply defer to the advocacy of one branch, "even if the advocate was himself."[88] We can interpret these switches as unprincipled efforts to maximize political power. We can also interpret them as the consequence of being exposed to new experiences in new offices, which in turn shaped these officials' judgments of constitutional meaning in context.[89]

Attitudes toward Congress," *Journal of Politics* 59:3 (1997): 701–28; Thomas J. Rudolph, "The Economic Sources of Congressional Approval," *Legislative Studies Quarterly* 27: 4 (2002): 577–99; J. Tobin Grant and Thomas J. Rudolph, "The Job of Representation in Congress: Public Expectations and Representative Approval," *Legislative Studies Quarterly* 29: 3 (2004): 431–45; Miroslav Nincic and Barbara Hinckley, "Foreign Policy and the Evaluation of Presidential Candidates," *Journal of Conflict Resolution* 35: 333–35; James Meernik and Elizabeth Oldmixon, "Internationalism in Congress," *Political Research Quarterly* 57:3 (2004): 451–65; John Mueller, "Presidential Popularity from Truman to Johnson," *American Political Science Review* 64:1 (1970): 18–52; Theodore Lowi, *The Personal President* (Ithica, NY: Cornell University Press, 1985), 16.

  86 *Hepburn v. Griswold*, 75 U.S. 603 (1870).

  87 Earl Warren, *The Memoirs of Earl Warren* (New York: Doubleday, 1977).

  88 Jackson developed legal justification for the destroyers-for-bases deal. Robert H. Jackson, "Opinion on Exchange of Over-Age Destroyers for Naval and Air Bases," *American Journal of International Law* 34: 728 (1940).

  89 There are a variety of ways to conceptualize the mechanisms by which this institutionally rooted pluralism develops. An office may affect an officeholder's preferences and understandings of politics in deep ways. Also, even if institutional position fails to affect officials' deep preferences about public policy, it may make salient different dimensions of a problem, or induce officials to differentially prioritize different outcomes, in ways that generate institutionally induced conflict even among actors whose preferences are congruent. See e.g., William G. Howell and Saul P. Jackman, "Inter-branch Bargaining over Policies

It is important to note the fairly high level of abstraction and the aspirational filter being applied to the distinctive capacities of each of the national institutions. For example, I am reading Congress's constitutional capacities in terms of a general legislative capacity to reflect a variety of political positions in the world, to cultivate diverse responses to dilemmas of public policy, and to integrate those different positions into law. However, another theorist could note the regional basis for legislative representation, and argue that Congress's distinctive capacity amounts to a capacity to reflect and integrate *regional* differences in particular. I pitch the constitutional capacities at a fairly high level of abstraction to allow for a consistent evaluative standard to be applied to these institutions over time. The institutions of Congress, the presidency, and Supreme Court are obviously different in the late twentieth and the early nineteenth century. As only one expression of that difference, the increased mobility of the US population means that an electoral connection to a territorial constituency no longer serves as a single gold standard for assessing legislative representation (if it ever did), and forms of constituency are now expressed in the legislature that would have been inconceivable when the Constitution was written.[90] As we shall see in the case studies, it is possible to get significant analytic traction even with the constitutional capacities of the branches pitched at a fairly abstract level. This methodological choice also has the advantage of keeping the resulting model of constitutional authority more relevant as the branches evolve and develop through time. Still, the contingency of this modeling choice is worth noting. We can also note the loose normative filter I apply to identifying the branches' capacities. The presidency has the capacity to bribe, suborn perjury, and carry out torture; these governance capacities are not included in the model. It is the capacity to contribute a political functionality that is *good* for governance that is the relevant basis for developing normative standards.

The first two conditions are both conditions of separateness. They ensure independence and the basis for mutual criticism. If we consider only them, we might think of the branches as sealed off from one another, each pursuing its tasks in a hermetically sealed universe. The final condition is what brings the branches into relationship. It is their *shared powers*. To be effective, many government decisions, and certainly those of war, require the cooperation of more than one branch.

---

with Multiple Outcomes," available at http://harrisschool.uchicago.edu/About/publications/working- papers/abstract.asp?paper_no=11%2E02+++ (accessed April 7, 2012). It would be surprising if the production of institutionally rooted pluralism happened through only one mechanism.

90   Jane Mansbridge, "Rethinking," 515–28.

While it is frequent for people to speak of the independent branches as systems of "separated powers," Richard Neustadt, among others, has pointed out the inaccuracy of the term, emphasizing that the Constitution constructs "a government of separated institutions *sharing* powers."[91] Clearly the government's power to make war is shared by both the executive and Congress. Government simply cannot make war—raise funds, organize troops, deploy them, communicate with foreign governments, negotiate and ratify peace treaties—without the cooperation of both branches. In fact, all of the sovereign powers of government—the power to regulate commerce, to tax, to convict and imprison criminals—require the participation of more than one branch. The executive can propose legislation, veto bills, call Congress into special session, and adjourn the houses under certain circumstances. Executive orders provide a significant locus for executive "lawmaking," especially with the rise of the administrative state, where so many of the government's activities are conducted under the umbrella of the executive. Congress creates every executive office and agency, establishes lines of authority within the executive branch, and shares in the appointments power. James Madison described this pattern as *"partial agency* in, or . . . *controul* over the acts of each other."[92]

Hence we see a third noteworthy condition: the actual exercise of their powers brings the branches into relationship with one another, a relationship that may activate the conflictual possibilities inherent in their independent sources of authority (condition one) and distinctive perspectives on public matters (condition two). These conditions mean that the possibility for interbranch conflict is both endemic and consequential. Because these conditions, taken together, activate the possibility for interbranch conflict, I name them the "conditions of conflict."[93]

---

91   Richard E. Neustadt, *Presidential Power and the Modern Presidents: The Politics of Leadership from Roosevelt to Reagan* (New York: The Free Press, 1991) (rev. ed. of *Presidential Power*, c1980), 29. Neustadt speaks of "power" (the common commodity of politics) and "powers" (the formal capacities of the various branches) but nowhere of "authority." Neustadt has no distinctive category for political authority derived from convincing normative constitutional argument. I think he would have to call such authority something like "personal influence," thereby neglecting its constitutionalist dimension (see Neustadt, chapter 3, note 1).

92   James Madison, " The Federalist Papers: No. 47," *The Avalon Project*. Available at http://avalon.law.yale.edu/subject_menus/fed.asp (accessed October 19, 2011).

93   I use the term "conditions of conflict" rather than "separated powers" because, in this context, "separated powers" has distracting implications insofar as it implies that each branch is reviewable only by the electorate. This would directly contradict the third condition of conflict. It is the branches' relationship that makes their judgments about the value of one another's interpretive and policy work politically consequential.

This book treats these conditions not only as empirically observable facts about the Constitution's textual order, but also as a set of capacities. The independence of each branch (the first condition of conflict) is formally secured through the Constitution's selection and impeachment provisions, but we can also read independence as a political *capacity* that different presidents or legislatures make varying use of. So, too, the second condition—that the branches are structured to achieve different valuable ends, and may generate diverse perspectives related to those ends—designates a feature of the Constitution's formal design, as well as a capacity that can be exercised more or less successfully. And while the third condition—that the branches exist in responsive relationship—is formally guaranteed through the shared powers, different interbranch systems develop their capacities for responsiveness with more or less success. None of these conditions amount to rules about how Congress or the executive always behaves. They are rather observations about the empirical capacities the constitutional form of the legislature or presidency generates.

Viewing the conditions of conflict as a set of capacities makes it straightforward to translate them into a set of standards for assessing the branches' war powers politics. For example, we can evaluate the presidency on the basis of whether it makes good use of the distinctive intelligence capacities at its disposal (part of the second condition of conflict). In fact, each of the conditions of conflict can be translated into a standard or standards for assessing that branch's processes of constitutional elaboration. The standards that come out of that translation are distinctively constitutional to the extent that the capacities themselves are constitutional ones.

THE PROCESSUAL STANDARDS

This section translates the structural capacities of the branches—the conditions of conflict—into a set of standards for evaluating their war politics. The first condition is the independent political authority of each branch. This is a condition for the dilemma of war authority in the first place. If the branches did not have structural independence, their colliding claims could be settled through enforced deference. Pro-presidency insularists seek to expand the independent capacity of the executive branch into a norm of insularity. Independence-as-insularity means that the president uses his office as a shield against the political demands of the other branches. As for Congress's independence, little theoretic literature has interrogated the meaning of legislative independence at all.

I propose that we translate the branches' structural independence into a norm of *independent judgment*, not a norm of political insularity.

Presidents can, and must, generate independent judgments as to the security politics of the moment; only in this way can the polity fully benefit from the president's special knowledge about security, diplomacy, and threat. Yet these independent judgments can, and must, be politically defended to the other branches. This process of mutual review allows the constitutional system to harness the governance capacities of both branches, not just the presidency, in the war-making system. At the same time, the independence of the office means that a president who believes he must act quickly, without conferring with Congress, to protect security, is free to do so, for security is his special charge. As a representative, he must act to defend the security of the nation. Yet this structural capacity, given by the first condition, cannot be extended into an informal norm of decisional insularity without great cost. Chapter 4 uses the difference between independent judgment and insular judgment as one basis for assessing Presidents Kennedy's and Nixon's war politics.

Congress's structural independence also implies a norm of independent judgment. The link between independent judgment and constitutional authority is intuitively sensible: a bill passed into law because the president plausibly threatens to fire legislators who vote against his policy suffers from impaired constitutional authority, because the first condition (that Congress acts as an independent branch) is what renders legislative assent meaningful. More subtly, legislative independence can also suffer when Congress fails to insist upon the value of its governance contributions in contexts where those are relevant. The processual standard of independent judgment asks that each branch view itself as authorized and equipped to judge the constitutional and policy claims that it confronts while conducting its business. In chapter 5, I argue that the legislature's due regard for its own independence supported the Seventy-Third and Seventy-Fourth Congresses in rendering constitutionally authoritative claims in the war powers system.

The second condition of conflict is that the branches exercise distinctive capacities that predictably generate distinctive perspectives on both policy and constitutional meaning. Because the branches have many, not just one or two, distinctive capacities, this structural condition translates into not one but rather many standards for assessing the policy and constitutional work of each branch.

The first, most obvious strength of the presidency and legislature vis-à-vis the judiciary is their connectedness to policymaking. As they confront security politics every day, officials in the legislative and executive branches acquire knowledge that is useful for making good judgments about foreign policy. This shared distinctive strength partly grounds their actual dominance and normative prominence in security politics relative to the judiciary. We can translate this constitutional capacity into two different standards for processual assessment. The first is that the branches engage in reasoning over public policy that is *sensitive to the security realities they encounter*. Because they are exposed to dilemmas of war and security in their daily governance tasks, they should be equipped to use reality-based assessments about war and security in their deliberations. To what extent are the branches' deliberations premised on reality, rather than fantasy? To what extent are they using their governance capacities to generate the kind of information about the world they need? The extent to which each branch uses, and cultivates, the knowledge available to it; the extent to which deliberative processes incorporate more rather than fewer relevant considerations; the extent to which deliberation is able to clarify relevant alternatives; and a scalar consideration, about the extent to which the branches advance high priorities over and above low priorities—these are all relatively ordinary ways that citizens, officials, and scholars already assess whether the branches engage in politics that are sensitive to policy realities.[94]

I also translate this strength in a way that some will find controversial: namely, that the branches actually *link their arguments about constitutional authority to their substantive agendas for security policy*. In other words, as the Obama administration's OLC did in its reasoning on Libya, the branches should justify their own, and challenge one another's, constitutional positions through reference to the security consequences at stake in one allocation of constitutional war authority versus another. This, after all, is one of their strengths: a capacity to think about the link between security processes and security outcomes. If such expertise is a reason for judicial deference on the war power, then it is also a resource that the president and legislature should use in developing their positions.

This standard directly opposes the common idea that arguments about constitutional meaning should not hinge on policy consequences. There is something questionable about interpreting the Constitution's guarantee of a qualified executive veto into an absolute veto to support a desired policy outcome. The settled, framework dimensions of the Constitution would not do a very good job of enabling secure decision-making if they were manipulable in this way. Policy-based constitutional reasoning for judges is also professionally suspect because and to the extent that judges are professionally insulated from the policy implications of the decisions

---

94   Jane Mansbridge, "Rethinking," 515–28; Jane Mansbridge and Christopher Karpowitz, "Disagreement and Consensus," *Journal of Public Deliberation* 1:1 (2004): 348–64; Richardson, *Autonomy*; Jane Mansbridge, "Self-Interest and Political Transformation," G. E. Marcus and R. L. Hanson, eds., *Reconsidering the Democratic Public* (University Park: Pennsylvania State University Press, 1993). On how publics can judge expert deliberations, see Elizabeth Anderson, "Democracy, Public Policy, and Lay Assessments of Scientific Testimony," *Episteme* 8:2 (2001): 144–64.

they make. However, the war powers controversy occurs within a zone of textual vagueness. It is difficult to read the war powers text of the Constitution only through the lens of a framework when the text seems to settle so little. Also, the national Congress and presidency have strengths not in policy neutrality but in policy development.

A second strength that Congress and the presidency share vis-à-vis the judiciary is the elected branches' relatively tight link to the public.[95] Given recurrent elections, the justifications the branches offer for their policies and constitutional positions play out within a horizon of meaning and interpretability set by the need to justify policy to larger publics. The branches make security and constitutional claims not only to persuade one another, but also to persuade public constituencies that are watching, evaluating, and voting. In fact, the branches are often aware that their success in winning over rivals may depend on their success in mobilizing public opinion. Both branches have resources to woo that opinion.

My view is that translating this strength into a standard for assessment calls for a constitutional theory of democracy. The "public" is not a simple fact but rather a constitutionally created set of offices no less than Congress or the executive. Given how the US Constitution structures its democratic politics, any theory that can speak to the capacities of that public will be extraordinarily complex. Just to begin, there is not only one democratic public. House districts, states, and national electorates are all different publics. The theoretical dilemmas engaged by this particular processual standard are vast. For the purposes of this book, I reduce this dimension to a relatively flat set of observations about a branch's *relationship to an electorate*.[96] This flat standard has only limited theoretical value, and so in turn, it is engaged in only limited ways. For a branch to behave responsively to its electorate is not always the same as for a branch to enact its duties of public representation. I nevertheless note this capacity first, in order to call attention to a feature of the relational conception that is presently underdeveloped; and second, to signal its position within the broader account of constitutional authority the book develops. I also note this capacity because in some of the case studies, the role of the electorate is important for making sense of officeholders' behavior. Assessing Franklin Roosevelt's security politics requires at least some ability to notice the constraints imposed on him by public opinion.

---

95 I thank Josh Chaefetz for his insistence on this point.
96 For work considering the standards of public office specifically in light of maintaining relationships of trust with the electorates, see Dennis F. Thompson, "Constitutional Character: Virtues and Vices in Presidential Leadership." *Presidential Studies Quarterly* 40: 1 (2010): 23–37.

So too, the overwhelming popular support for President Polk's and President Theodore Roosevelt's adventurism cannot be overlooked.

In addition to these are the capacities Congress and president have that are distinctive relative to each other. The distinctive strengths of the presidency are rooted in the hierarchical structure of that branch, as well as in the resources of the executive bureaucracy. For example, the president is able to *command the resources of intelligence, diplomatic, and military establishments, branch-specific research agencies, and consultative forums like the cabinet or National Security Council (NSC).* For presidents to use these resources in their internal processes of deliberation enhances the authority of their resulting positions. In addition, the proper use of executive branch resources implies some degree of careful management of the administration. *Rewarding and elevating subordinates who demonstrate excellence, and dismissing or marginalizing those with less successful job performance*, puts the hierarchical qualities of the executive branch to use in fostering good governance. The branch's hierarchy also supports the president in *experimenting with policy* and in *responding quickly to changing circumstances.*

There is a wide variety of ways for presidents to successfully mobilize the resources of the executive branch. While presidents can gain access to the knowledge of agencies by consulting them, decision-making according to rules and bureaucratic organization is only one model of successful executive branch functioning. Classical realists like George Kennan advocate reliance "on the insight and instincts of the executive or diplomatic professional rather than rules."[97] Presidents Truman and Roosevelt made excellent judgments using informal consultations with a selected core, rather than through rigid adherence to bureaucratic procedure.[98] Allison and Zelikow note three different models of presidential decision-making:

> (1) a "formalistic" or "multiple advocacy" approach with clear structure, division of labor, and well-defined procedures managed by an "honest broker" (the Eisenhower administration is the usual example); (2) a "competitive" or "centralized management" model that encourages competitive advice by allowing overlapping responsibilities and many formal and less formal channels of communication but filters information and advice in a small inner

---

97   Deborah Welch Larson, "Politics, Uncertainty, and Values: Good Judgment in Context," in *Good Judgment in Foreign Policy: Theory and Application*, eds. Stanley A. Renshon and Deborah Welch Larson (Lanham, MD: Rowman & Littlefield Publishers, Inc., 2003): 310. See also Philip E. Tetlock, "Good Judgment in International Politics: Three Psychological Perspectives," *Political Psychology* 13 (1992): 517–39.

98   See, e.g., Larson, "Politics," in *Good Judgment*, eds. Renshon and Larson. Graham Allison and Philip Zelikow, *Essence of Decision: Explaining the Cuban Missile Crisis, 2nd ed.* (New York: Addison-Wesley Longman, 1999), 314–15.

circle of top officials (e.g., the Franklin Roosevelt administration); and (3) a "collegial" or "adhocracy" style which blurs responsibility and formal channels but emphasizes a team identified with the president (as in the Kennedy administration).[99]

There is no need to artificially reduce styles of decision-making to a single rubric.[100] There are many different ways to successfully use the intelligence, diplomatic, and consultative capacities of the executive branch. So then, there are a number of different ways presidents can achieve the full authority associated with this processual standard. In practice, many of the distinctions that arise in this book between presidents who achieve more of this processual authority and those who achieve less pertain less to matters of style and more to an intelligent use of capacities given a particular style. I argue in chapter 4, for example, that the authority of Nixon's constitutional and policy positions on the Vietnam War was undermined by his participation in war deliberations while drunk.

Also, the president does not directly control all of what is required to make good use of the executive branch's capacities. Throughout the book, I speak of the behavior of an entire administration as if it is that of the president, who is, of course, supreme in the executive branch hierarchy. For example I may describe "Obama's" behavior instead of the behavior of the Obama administration. This language obscures the extent to which a president's processual authority relies upon the capacities of a large bureaucracy. For example, Kennedy's handling of the Cuban Missile Crisis benefited from the expertise and good judgment of subordinates throughout the intelligence and military communities. While his oversight and the tone he set supported their skill, presidential hierarchy does not mean that a president can entirely control the executive branch. Constitutional officials work in relationship and are rarely able to single-handedly control the authority available to them.

What are the legislature's distinctive strengths? This question brings us immediately to Congress's major dilemma in being taken seriously as a constitutional agent: the idea that because it does not speak with one voice, it has no constitutional agency. In fact, one strength of legislative governance is precisely its ability to offer a forum for the public expression of divergent lines of reasoning on matters of public concern.

---

99   Allison and Zelikow, *Essence*, 266, citing Richard T. Johnson, *Managing the White House* (New York: Harper and Row, 1974); Roger B. Porter, *Presidential Decision-Making: The Economic Policy Board* (Cambridge: Cambridge University Press, 1982). See also Stephen Hess, *Organizing the Presidency* (Washington, DC: Brookings Institution, 1976), 154.

100   Dawn Johnsen has argued that we should assess presidencies on the basis of transparency, adherence to proper bureaucratic procedure, and the extent to which presidents consult all the agencies available to them. Johnsen, "Functional."

Articulating differences, clarifying grounds of disagreement, and developing multiple solutions to governance problems, which is part of the work of partisanship, enriches the broader decision-making space. A Congress that *creates and expresses divergent paths of reasoning, on both policy and constitutional matters,* is carrying out one of its important governance capacities.

It is no less a legislative strength to integrate multiple preferences into a policy that can win broad support. Hence an emphasis on legislative pluralism is not to artificially deny the authority that can be generated when Congress does manage to speak with strong majorities and to *harness the power of a consensus politics* behind its agenda. Congress does not only represent this consensus politics. The legislature's professional duties also cultivate its skill in *lawmaking*: translating areas of political agreement into statutory or treaty language that can, in turn, guide citizens or state officials. One processual interrogation of Congress pertains to the extent that it crafts law that can provide such effective guidance to others.

Finally, a strength of legislative governance is its capacity to mobilize vast quantities of information through hearings, testimony, research services, and the subpoena power. Congress's ability to *pool and weigh information from multiple sources, and to generate large understandings of public policy on the basis of complex information,* is yet a fourth strength of legislative governance.

When Congress exercises its powers—declaring or authorizing war (whether for defensive purposes or as an instrument of policy), issuing supportive resolutions, challenging presidential agendas, using public hearings to shape dynamics of war authority in practice, advancing interpretive positions on constitutional matters of war—in ways that are connected to its relative governance strengths, it generates more constitutional authority for its behavior. As with the presidency, we should recognize that the legislature has more than one route toward harnessing its distinctive capacities.[101] Given that there are several different ways for the

---

101 See, e.g., Josh Chafetz, "The Unconstitutionality of the Filibuster," *Connecticut Law Review* 43: 4 (2011): 1003–40; David R. Mayhew, "Supermajority Rule in the U.S. Senate," *PS: Political Science and Politics* 36: 1 (2003): 31–36; Neal Kumar Katyal, "Internal Separation of Powers: Checking Today's Most Dangerous Branch from Within," *The Yale Law Journal* 115:9 (2006): 2314–49; Bruce Ackerman and Oona Hathaway, "Limited War and the Constitution: Iraq and the Crisis of Presidential Legality," *Michigan Law Review* 109:4 (2011): 447–518; Seth Barrett Tillman, "Noncontemporaneous Lawmaking: Can the 110th Senate Enact a Bill Passed by the 109th House?" *Cornell Journal of Law and Public Policy* 16:2 (2007): 331–47; Aaron-Andrew P. Bruhl, "Burying the 'Continuing Body' Theory of the Senate," *Iowa Law Review* 95:5 (2010): 1401–65; Gary Mucciaroni and Paul J. Quirk, *Deliberative Choices: Debating Public Policy In Congress* (Chicago: University of Chicago Press, 2006).

branches to express their constitutional capacities, there should be several different ways for them to achieve the full constitutional authority associated with this second condition of conflict. At the same time, that not every political capacity is represented in the constitutional system is one feature that gives the processual standards their disciplining power. The branches have several, but not infinite, different ways to achieve their full processual authority.

The third condition of conflict is the branches' shared powers over war. We can translate this fact of interdependence into a standard about responsiveness. Branches that *accompany their uses of the shared war power with a policy and constitutional position that the other branch may judge*, and that *use their powers in ways that are more rather than less responsive to the positions of their rivals*, generate more constitutional authority for their behavior and for the larger war-making system.

The branches often are responsive to one another's positions even if only for strategic reasons. For example, the presidential veto; speeches and representations to foreign powers; directives about troop movements; and policy proposals are all governance powers that also allow the president to communicate his support, or resistance, to Congress's security visions. So too, the Congress may grant statutory authorization or pass restraining orders; interrogate the president's claims in resolutions, hearings, or floor debate; appropriate funds; retrospectively authorize or condemn presidential conduct; or impeach the president as ways of communicating its policy and constitutional agendas.

The branches also have powers to influence each other's internal politics. With its power to create bureaucracies and confirm nominees, Congress exerts power over the executive branch. The executive, with its powers of nomination, diplomacy, treaty negotiation, the veto, and execution of statutory law, creates agendas that Congress must react to. Agenda creation is a formidable power in part because of its capacity to exploit latent cleavages in the responding agent. Reagan's choice to defend his conduct in the Iran-Contra scandal according to a legalistic standard invited Congress to react in a legalistic way that was poorly suited to its governance capacities, or so I shall argue in chapter 5. On the other hand, sometimes the branches respond to one another in ways that are mutually supportive. President Roosevelt's expansion of the powers of the executive branch was one political trigger for the Legislative Reorganization Act of 1946, when Congress, for the first time, gave itself professional staff.

The concept of responsiveness allows us to capture, and theorize, the difference between a president closing military bases in response to a set of programmatic commitments, versus the president closing military bases to punish legislators. We should be able to notice the difference between a Congress that shuts down war funding because of constitutional disagreement, versus a Congress that shuts down war funding because it believes the security issue has been resolved. Constitutional analysis should be sensitive to the meanings of exercised powers in context.

In the war powers debate, such analytic capacity is especially important because the very heart of the conflict between the relational conception and insular visions concerns the extent to which it is *proper* for the branches to use their bare powers responsively to one another's constitutional positions. *Should* the branches use their bare powers as powers of review and judgment? Or should one branch use its powers to advance its security vision, while the other branch uses its powers only in deferential support? We are hardly equipped to engage this question if we are not able to register, in the first place, the difference between a branch using its powers, and a branch using its powers responsively.

Pro-Congress insularists resist this standard when they argue that presidents should always defer to the legislature's security judgments. But the president may at times perceive a defensive security necessity that Congress has not yet brought into focus. Insofar as the president's threat assessment is a constitutionally responsible one, the president acts responsibly when he exercises his powers in ways that prompt Congress to address the threat he perceives. Pro-presidency insularists also resist this norm when they suggest that requiring the president to justify his actions to Congress would disable him from acting defensively when necessary. But inappropriate deference to misguided legislatures, or a failure to take necessary action, are also proper grounds on which to judge a president no less than his dangerous willingness to seek war. Officials must be willing and able to act in the context of being judged no matter what they do. Insularists try to contain the political costs of their favored institution's use of the war power by enshrining it with a set of insular norms. But the war power is inherently a risky power.

Insularists sometimes forget the difference between facing the burdens of justification and being utterly disabled by criticism. A president unpersuaded by Congress has resources to chart alternative paths. His structurally guaranteed independence makes action possible even in the midst of conflict. And if Congress finds a presidential justification unconvincing, it too has powers for countering his vision. Both will obviously be more effective if they manage to win the other over; but, as the next section argues, the standard of mutual responsiveness prizes, not interbranch agreement, but rather the production of appropriate reasons and well-defended judgments.

Applying these processualist standards will necessarily embed evaluators in controversial terrain. Each of these standards requires a range of assessments that can't be made without reference to at least a few independent substantive judgments about politics. For example, I ask that the legislature "clarify relevant alternatives." No observer can assess whether Congress has "clarified relevant alternatives" without some independent idea about which alternatives are "relevant" in the context Congress faces. At the same time, the criteria of "clarifying relevant alternatives" is a more open and capacious, more proceduralist standard than, say, "delivering a good policy result." To distinguish these institutionally rooted standards from either "procedural" or "substantive" standards of evaluation common in deliberative democratic and legal literatures, I name them "processualist."

The overall standards I advance for evaluating the branches' constitutional politics are both substantive and processual. We first evaluate on the basis of the substantive terms that the Constitution offers on its face: that the president behave so as to "preserve, protect, and defend" the constitutional order; that the legislature maintains authority over "war." These terms give a set of standards for assessing the constitutional politics of the branches. The relational conception directs constitutional evaluators to begin with their own first-order assessments about the best construction of these categories in context.

At the same time, understanding that these categories are political categories, we can use the processual criteria to evaluate the branches' processes of constitutional elaboration in context. When the branches advance a particular vision of the Constitution's war powers order, does their work reflect independent judgments, the use of their distinctive governance capacities, and responsiveness to one another's positions? To the extent that the branches deliberate on the Constitution's substantive terms through a politics that can be defended on processualist grounds, they are developing more, rather than less, authoritative elaborations of constitutional meaning in context.

The rest of the book applies these standards to a series of controversies. Throughout, I will move between arguments *about* the relational conception and arguments from *within* the relational conception. From a scholarly point of view, the effort is to redescribe classical war powers controversies in terms of the relational conception and to thereby demonstrate that the relational conception provides fruitful terms for constitutional analysis. From the point of view of a constitutional participant, I demonstrate how the relational conception can be used in practice by applying its standards to the cases I treat. My description of a branch's "good" or "intelligent" constitutional politics is derived from this second position: the vantage point of a would-be faithful interpreter, applying the relational conception's substantive and processual standards to develop a judgment about constitutional war authority in context.

INTERBRANCH DELIBERATION AND THE
RELATIONAL CONCEPTION

Clearly the Constitution does not create, in theory or practice, one supreme interpreter when it comes to war powers. Instead the Constitution puts the two branches in responsive relationship. The value of their responsiveness is sometimes made explicit in the text. For example, the Constitution provides for a state of the union address and legislative journals, and Article I Section 7 instructs the executive to give reasons for his veto so that the originating house may "enter the Objections at large on their Journal, and proceed to reconsider it." These indicate a constitutional valorization of at least some practices of interbranch reason-giving. The processual standards point to others. When the branches review one another's political behavior, including their interpretive claims, according to the perspectives conditioned by their various distinctive capacities, they embark on a process of *interbranch deliberation* that, I argue, creates constitutional authority for the war powers system as a whole.[102] The centrality of well-conducted interbranch responsiveness leads me to name this a *relational conception* of war authority.

If, when deliberating upon an act of war or security order, the president and Congress reach similar constitutional and policy positions even given the different political functions they are designed to serve, through processes informed by the processualist standards, then there are good reasons for endorsing these conclusions as constitutionally adequate. When the branches come to divergent conclusions, interbranch conflict can result. Does this conflict in and of itself mean one branch is being constitutionally faithless? No. In some contexts, well-structured conflict is linked to the *production* of constitutional authority when that conflict is the result of the branches' excellent use of their differing governance and interpretive capacities. Chapter 2 argues that interbranch contentiousness prior to World War II was consistent with a high level of war authority for the interbranch system that resulted in US entry into the war.

Bruce Ackerman is among those scholars who link the possibility of interbranch conflict to a more robustly defensible representative practice. Ackerman argues that when officials challenge one another's representation of "the people,"

---

102 The concept of interbranch deliberation was pioneered by Bessette, *Reason*, and Tulis, "Deliberation."

the result . . . will be precisely the opposite of each partisan's hopes. Rather than allowing the House or Senate or the Presidency to beguile us with the claim that it, and it alone, speaks in the name of the People themselves, the constitutional separation of powers deconstructs all such naive synecdoches. As it works itself out in practice, the system emphasizes that no legal form can enable any small group . . . to speak unequivocally for We the People.[103]

Ackerman is arguing for the value of some interbranch conflict purely on the grounds of democratic representation. Multiple veto points filter the plausibility of all claims to public authority. But the processual standards don't filter only on the basis of democratic representation. They also filter with reference to the distinctive governing capacities of the branches.[104] The Constitution creates an order that allows officials to develop policy and interpretive judgments that are more, rather than less, sensitive to diplomatic imperatives, information about threats, the interrelationship of multiple security commitments, needs for policy flexibility, and justifiable distributions of cost and benefit. Because the processualist standards do not prize consensus for its own sake, but rather emphasize independence, skillfully conditioned judgment, and responsiveness, these standards allow for assessing the constitutional politics of the branches even when they do not agree.

The portrait of interbranch deliberation I develop here is normative because, as I argue through the chapters, it produces constitutional authority, which is a public good for a constitutional republic. This does not mean that all actors are motivated by good or faithful aims. The relational conception evaluates behavior and language, not the inner hearts of officials. I nonetheless maintain some hopefulness that the realities of power-driven politics can produce outcomes that are normatively justifiable. In the ideal case, officials would vigorously assert the most important constitutional claims at stake, and then the lengths to which

103   Bruce Ackerman, "The Storrs Lectures: Discovering the Constitution," *Yale Law Journal* 93: 6 (1984): 1013–72, 1028–29.

104   See Tulis, "Deliberation," 16; also Pickerill, *Deliberation*, for analysis of how Supreme Court interventions support rights-responsive public policy even in the legislature. The simple checking-and-balancing story or veto point story ignores how institutions shape the particular narrations that structure the delivery of public policy. For exceptions, see Stephen Elkin, *Reconstructing the Commercial Republic: Constitutional Design after Madison* (Chicago: University of Chicago Press, 2006); Bessette, *Reason*; Mark Tushnet, "Some Notes on Congressional Capacity to Interpret the Constitution," *Boston University Law Review* 89:2 (2009): 499–509; Melissa Schwartzberg, *Democracy and Legal Change* (Cambridge, NY: Cambridge University Press, 2007); Henry S. Richardson, "Institutionally Divided Moral Responsibility," *Social Philosophy and Policy* 16: 2 (1999): 218–49.

each branch is prepared to go in pursuit of its claims would provide a rough measure of their importance. Thus in the ideal case, the balance of power between the branches in any particular security dispute would result from political conflict that is driven by how the particularities of the case actually relate to the relational conception's standards.[105] Obviously, many cases are not ideal.[106]

The concept of interbranch deliberation is a lens that directs attention to the claims that the branches make about the merits of the policies they propose, including their positions about the allocation of war authority. (Throughout the book I refer to this combination of enacted security policy judgments, plus an enacted system of interbranch war authority to achieve those ends, as a *security order*.) To the extent that the branches' exchanges mobilize each institution's capacity for high-quality interventions about good ways of constructing a security order given a particular security context, those deliberations are productive of constitutional authority.

The exchanges between the branches encompassed by the concept of interbranch deliberation are comprised by the rhetoric and justifications they offer one another—formal communications (joint resolutions, state of the union addresses, testimony); engagement in the public sphere (speeches, interviews, editorials); and official meetings and discussions. Deliberation also includes the authoritative actions each branch takes in response to the other. Many interbranch exchanges that do not appear to be "deliberative" according to dominant scholarship in deliberative democracy will register as "deliberative" under this model. The concept of interbranch deliberation aims only to highlight the extent to which the rhetoric and authoritative actions of each branch are accompanied by reasons formulated in response to the claims of the other branch and in response to the security context at hand.[107] Of course, an authoritative act not accompanied by any substantive justification whatsoever, in

---

105 Tulis, "Deliberation," 43.

106 A fruitful line of research highly relevant to the relational conception is about the political conditions that support, or threaten, the branches' good use of their capacities. See, for example, Rebecca U. Thorpe, *The Warfare State: Perpetuating the U.S. Military Economy* (Chicago: University of Chicago Press, forthcoming), arguing that certain forms of defense spending in congressional districts deform legislators' judgments about constitutional war powers.

107 This way of conceiving deliberation is looser than even one of the less demanding conceptions of deliberative democracy, that advanced by Jack Knight and James Johnson, in that there is no requirement even that deliberation be conducted through fair procedures. See their "Aggregation and Deliberation: On the Possibility of Democratic Legitimacy," *Political Theory* 22:2 (1994): 277–96. See also James D. Fearon's very stripped-down notion of deliberation as simply "discussing matters before making some collective decision," in

a context that is completely devoid of reason-giving practices, does not count as a deliberative intervention. This is a low bar. A more interesting question is about the extent to which the reasoning the branches offer achieves the processual standards. It is for the observer to say at each step whether each institution demonstrated appropriate regard for reasons that were in fact, or should have been, available; whether they were appropriately responsive to one another; and whether the institutions were applying their own distinctive strengths to the problem at hand.[108]

John Dewey is the philosopher who helps us understand that both behavior and speech can be understood as manifestations of how we apply our intelligence to the world. Elizabeth Anderson provides an elegant description of how Dewey can help us perceive deliberative processes:

> [Dewey] argued that practical intelligence is the application of experimental methods to value judgments and practical precepts. We test our value judgments by living in accordance with them and seeing whether doing so is satisfactory—whether it can provide satisfactory answers to questions like this: Does action in accordance with the value judgment solve the problem it was intended to solve? Does it bring about worse problems? Does it give rise to complaints from others that need to be addressed? Might we do better by adopting different judgments? If we find life in accordance with the value judgment satisfactory, we stick with it; if it fails these tests, we seek new judgments that can better guide our lives.[109]

Expanding the concept of deliberation to include speech, rhetoric, and reasons, but also behavior, fits with Dewey's notion that conduct is as much a matter of practical intelligence as are words.

In short, there are three significant claims here. First is the empirical claim: that, as departmentalists know, the Constitution does structure the political space between the branches so as to place them in a distinctive form of responsive relationship. Second is that we can understand, and evaluate, how well this responsive system develops meaning for the Constitution's *substantive* categories by reference to the *processualist*

"Deliberation as Discussion," *Deliberative Democracy*, ed. Jon Elster (Cambridge: Cambridge University Press, 1998), 44.

108   Elsewhere I locate processualism as a standard already implicit within literatures on deliberative democracy. Mariah Zeisberg, "Democratic Processualism," *The Journal of Social Philosophy* 41: 2 (2010): 202–209.

109   Elizabeth Anderson, *The Imperative of Integration* (Princeton: Princeton University Press, 2010), 89–90, citing John Dewey, "Valuation and Experimental Knowledge," *The Middle Works*, 1899–1924 (Carbondale: Southern Illinois University Press, 1976), 3–28.

standards. And finally, that well-conducted interbranch deliberation can produce constitutional authority for the branches.

Because partisanship, group affiliation, interest group membership, and other politicized standpoints condition whether an observer believes these standards have been achieved, these standards are not neutral benchmarks. Different evaluators will judge these questions differently. In the case studies that follow, the arguments I make about policy and institutional process are easy to fit within different partisan registers. Some of my arguments will be intuitive to many people; I try to show that, in fact, the relational conception can accommodate and explain some common intuitions that are analytically neglected in settlement accounts. In other cases, my arguments will be controversial. Interpretive controversy can be appropriate even over the question of whether a particular deliberative process has been conducted so as to produce constitutional authority. This does not pose a problem for the relational conception. In fact, a central effort of this book is to demonstrate that standards of constitutional authority need not be capable of producing consensus in all instances. The relational conception seeks to focus controversy on questions about institutional performance rather than legal compliance.

THE RELATIONAL CONCEPTION AND CONSTITUTIONAL AUTHORITY

At each step, the more the branches govern and interpret constitutional meaning in accord with the substantive and processual standards of the relational conception, the more constitutionally authoritative is the warmaking system they construct. The relational conception puts the processes of knowledge production and interbranch deliberation at the center of its conception of constitutional authority. The practices of discernment, elaboration, and review at the heart of interbranch deliberation *generate* constitutional authority for acts of war and security orders.

Constitutional authority to use the war power has a stipulated definition here: it is what emerges from the branches' successful navigation of a web of justificatory processes. When the branches mobilize their institutional capacities, develop good understandings of the security needs of the moment, and place themselves in responsive relationship, they generate constitutional authority over war; authority is hence both presumed and created by their interactive processes.

This way of conceiving constitutional authority is unusual. Legal and philosophic scholarship prominently associated with Joseph Raz commonly describes "authority" as content-independent reasons to obey.[110] In other words, for an institution to be authoritative means that others obey it even if they object to what they are told to do. And yet the relational conception asks the branches to respond to, and perhaps even challenge, one another's determinations. While this is an unfamiliar notion of constitutional authority, it is not unusual in the world more broadly. Consider a junior faculty member being advised by his chair. If asked why he treats the chair's advice as authoritative, the faculty member may well answer in a Razian fashion that the chair is empowered to instruct junior faculty. But it would also be perfectly sensible to say that the faculty treats the chair's advice as authoritative because he recognizes that the advice is coherent and informed by the chair's unique perspective on a situation, because the chair has been responsive to counterconsiderations and frames a dilemma in a way that makes good sense, and because the chair offers recommendations of recognizably high quality. We may consider a friend's advice authoritative for similar reasons. In fact, people often consider one another's perspectives authoritative on the basis of assessments that are not entirely content-neutral, but which are also not reducible to following a good idea no matter where it comes from. This way of relating to authority views it as a resource that actors develop for one another.

Authority also means having reason to obey. A second reason for viewing authority in a bimodal way rests upon a view of compliance that is itself bimodal. A soldier either will, or will not, comply with an order to deploy. It doesn't make sense for a soldier to partially deploy in response to a form of authority that is shaky but still intact. To have the option to comply or not comply with a command suggests that authority itself must be bimodal.

But this way of viewing compliance is also limited. When Congress declares war, the president does not face a choice of "obeying" or "not obeying." The president may use that declaration of war as the grounds for an all-out assault on another nation's sovereignty, or he may use it as one more tool of coercive diplomacy. These are only two among many possibilities. When the president deploys troops in a provocative manner, the legislature too faces a large array of possible policy and constitutional

---

110 See, e.g., H.L.A. Hart, *Essays on Bentham* (Oxford: Oxford University Press, 1982), ch. 10; Richard Friedman, "On the Concept of Authority in Political Philosophy," in Richard Flathman, ed., *Concepts in Social and Political Philosophy* (New York: MacMillan, 1973), 129; Joseph Raz, *The Morality of Freedom* (Oxford: Oxford University Press, 1986), 38–69; Joseph Raz, *The Authority of the Law* (Oxford University Press, 2009); Frederick Schauer, *Playing by the Rules* (New York: Oxford University Press, 1991); Thomas Christiano, "The Authority of Democracy," *The Journal of Political Philosophy* 12: 3 (2004): 266–90.

responses. Because the branches are policymaking institutions, the authoritative behavior of each triggers a range of possible responses from the others. Each branch has governance tools that may resist, narrow, closely execute, extend, or intensify the instructions the other branch has communicated.[111] The relational conception asks officials to link their responses to their judgments about each branch's relative authority. Authority here does not function as a fully exclusionary reason. In the US constitutional system, it is rare for commands to be given without reasons, and we expect pushback from agents if or when these reasons are inadequate.[112] Using the word "authority" to signify the presence of content-independent reasons for action is only one way of conceiving how authority functions in our lives.

What do we gain and lose with this way of describing constitutional authority? First, it is, on its face, more consistent with the Constitution's actual strategy of elaborating institutional structure but not defining the boundary lines between war powers. The vagueness present in how the relational conception conceives authority corresponds to a vagueness rooted in the Constitution's own text. Second, this way of describing authority provides a vocabulary for political intuitions that cannot otherwise be accommodated. Consider debate in Congress about whether its own declaration of the War of 1812 was constitutional, given insufficient British hostility.[113] Or consider that, when I discuss this book, some mention the US entry into the Iraq War as a moment of constitutional deficiency.[114] Yet the Iraq War was legally authorized by Congress acting through its regular procedures. No other war powers theory on offer can account for the common intuition that legislative processes may sometimes be so deficient as to actually impair the constitutional authority of legislative assent. Highlighting the role of the processual standards in generating constitutional authority makes these common intuitions more sensible. Through the case studies, I bring attention to common intuitions about American constitutional politics that the relational conception of war authority—but not settlement accounts—can track.

Certain dimensions of this way of conceiving authority may raise empirical skepticism. For example, the branches' exercise of their capacity to develop knowledge about difficult constitutional and security questions is central to their development of constitutional authority. But do

111   See Douglas L. Kriner, *After the Rubicon: Congress, Presidents, and the Politics of Waging War* (Chicago: University of Chicago Press, 2010).

112   Many thanks to Elizabeth Anderson for helping me think through this point.

113   Abraham D. Sofaer, *War, Foreign Affairs and Constitutional Power: The Origins* (New York: Harper Collins Publishers, 1976), 268; Barron and Lederman, "Lowest," 977.

114   See Michael Bressler, "Congressional Dissent During Times of War: How Congress Goes Public to Influence Foreign Policy," *Extensions* (2008): 9–14.

the branches have that capacity? Many commentators seem comfortable grounding presidential war authority in the president's access to security knowledge, but even advocates of Congress may be reluctant to make parallel claims. Imagine this alternative, non-epistemic defense of Congressional authority:

> Congress doesn't know anything about security. Legislators' most developed skills are those of campaigning and bargaining, neither of which is relevant to war. While Congress may contain plural perspectives, a president can convene panels of experts with diverse perspectives to inform his deliberations.
>
> But Congress still has an important role to play. Congress' role is to check against unitary presidential action. Legislators are elected to represent particular districts, whereas the President is elected by the nation as a whole. The President is incentivized to pick policies that will appeal to the national median voter, but passing a bill through Congress requires the approval of a majority of districts. Given simple differences in opinion between districts, the requirement of Congressional action imposes a higher hurdle. At the very least, Congressional approval requires the assent of a broad cross-section of America. Congress is also more directly accountable to the electorate (the House is voted in every two years, while second term Presidents are done).
>
> Blocking the president's path to war by requiring him to go to Congress for approval can be justified in terms of the value of slowing down the decision to go to war and representing the interests of a large cross section of America, not simply the median voter.[115]

This familiar checks-and-balances story grounds legislative authority not in knowledge, but in Congress's capacity to represent the majority of districts and to slow down decision-making.

Some pieces of this account must be rejected as matters of fact. Congress can produce knowledge on security, not simply knowledge about the dynamics of campaigns and bargaining; and Congress is capable of governing, not only campaigning.[116] We also should not assume that

115   Many thanks to David Nickerson for pressing this point.

116   Nelson W. Polsby, "Legislatures," eds. Fred Greenstein et al., *Handbook of Political Science* (Reading, MA: Addison-Wesley, 1975), 257–319. For discussion of legislative process improving the content of security legislation, see Donald R. Wolfensberger, "Congress and Policymaking in an Age of Terrorism," *Congress Reconsidered*, eds. Lawrence C. Dodd and Bruce I. Oppenheimer, 8th ed., (Washington, DC, CQ Press, 2005). See also Richard Fenno, *Home Style: House Members in Their Districts* (Boston: Little, Brown, 1978); Richard Fenno, *Congressmen in Committees* (Boston: Little, Brown, 1973); David Mayhew, *Divided We Govern: Party Control, Lawmaking, and Investigations, 1946–2002* (New Haven: Yale University Press, 2005).

going to war is always the least desirable outcome and that Congress will be less desirous of war than the president. In fact, war may sometimes be an intelligent response to a security problem. To slow war in such cases can spell catastrophe. And Congress has sometimes been more, not less, eager to go to war than the president.[117]

Other pieces of the account must be rejected because they are incompatible with more general theories of constitutional authority. Accounts of authority in particular domains should be consistent with the best understanding of what constitutional authority, in general, consists of. Certain features of the checks-and-balances story fail this test. Locating congressional authority, as a matter of constitutional theory, in its representation of plural interests is unsatisfactory. There is no reason for a plurality of interests to be viewed as more authoritative than the median voter. Pluralism is useful for generating authority when it is used to generate appropriate justifications for public policy; or when it ensures democratic inclusion and impartiality; or when it contributes to political stability. On its own, it has no normative weight. We need a broader theory to explain what pluralism is for, especially when accommodating pluralism undermines other goals like speedy response.

A final concern about this notion of authority pertains to subjectivity and partisanship. The relational conception of war authority fails to incontrovertibly resolve questions of war authority, because its substantive and processual standards are not themselves easy to incontrovertibly apply. Consider Congress's deliberation over the 2001 Authorization for Use of Military Force, which not only authorized open-ended war against "nations," "organizations," and "persons," reaching to those who may have "harbored" those who "aided" the attacks, but also stated that "the President has authority under the Constitution to take action to deter and prevent acts of international terrorism against the United States."[118] For some, Congress's willingness to enact such a massively broad delegation without considering broader Middle East foreign policy or antiterrorism security policy undermines the legislature's claim to deliberative responsibility. For others, Congress's willingness to support the president so broadly demonstrates a responsible sensitivity to the unique dilemmas of fighting nonstate actors. Our own assessments of what was at stake in these decisions partially condition our judgments about whether Congress did a good job in its deliberations.

---

117 Consider Cleveland's threat to veto a declaration of war against Spain. See Clinton Rossiter, *The Supreme Court and the Commander in Chief* (Ithaca, NY: Cornell University Press, 1976), 66.

118 Authorization for Use of Military Force, September 18, 2001, PS 107-40.

The relational conception of war authority cannot resolve many of the political controversies at the heart of the judgments it elicits. But it provides common terms for deliberation that encompass the constitutional values implicitly at stake in these decisions. I demonstrate in the case studies that follow that the relational conception can accommodate common intuitions that cannot be accommodated in settlement accounts which neglect the political dimensions of constitutional authority. Remaining controversy is then focused onto questions of institutional performance rather than legal obedience.

These arguments will be embedded within fields of partisan controversy, but constitutional theorists probably worry more about this partisanship than we need to. Consider that when the Constitution was ratified, basic questions of constitutional authority became partisan questions. For example, the relationship between a sovereign and a preexistent legal order split the Federalists from a wide variety of Anti-Federalist positions. And yet the ratification was a highlight of constitutional deliberation, producing profound statements of constitutional meaning.[119] Even theories meant to guide impartial judicial decision-making fit within fields of juridical partisan controversy. Originalism, natural law, or the Warren-court emphasis on minority participation are all approaches that are recognizably partisan within the field of legal studies. Skepticism about partisanship in constitutional reasoning fits poorly with experience, where deep expressions of constitutional meaning are expressed through and alongside deep partisan divides.

The power to take the actions of war—to fund troops, engage in policies antagonistic to other nations, give speeches that amplify the likelihood of war, place armies in disputed territory, order them to shoot, legally declare hostilities—are dispersed between Congress and the presidency. Many of these institutions' other powers become war powers when used in a context of war. The relational conception of war authority insists that the branches use their powers according to the Constitution's substantive and processual standards. It also insists that the authority to review and judge behavior and rhetoric follows the Constitution's distribution of war powers. When the branches act and judge in ways that summon the governance capacities the Constitution makes available, using their capacities to determine good allocations of constitutional war authority in the context of their own times, then their acts of power become constitutionally authoritative.

---

119 Pauline Meier, *Ratification: The People Debate the Constitution, 1787–1788* (New York: Simon & Schuster, 2010).

CONCLUSION

The war powers literature is marked by a series of conventional controversies. Does a president who uses discretionary power to move the
country toward war undermine legislative war authority? Can Congress
delegate its war power to the presidency? When and how is a president
justified in engaging in independent acts of war? With cases ranging from
the Mexican War to the Cuban Missile Crisis, isolationist resistance to
World War II and the Iran-Contra Investigation, the following chapters
redescribe these basic controversies in terms of the relational conception
in order to show its operation in practice. The aim is to show how the
relational conception illuminates common intuitions and reframes certain controversies, rather than to advance a particular interpretation of,
say, the Korean War. By elaborating the theory through a series of paired
case studies, the book shows that the relational conception can accommodate common intuitions, explain those intuitions, and direct our focus
toward useful new lines of investigation for assessing the ethical behavior
of officials.

The chapters address these controversies not through constitutional
law, but through an analysis of constitutional politics. I use the ordinary resources of political judgment to develop these cases. Histories,
memoirs, journal and news articles, the Congressional Record, and major
scholarly works are all useful and widely available sources for helping
observers and participants understand their own political contexts.[120]
Epistemic priority goes to what can now be seen as most accurate, although it is also relevant to know what was reasonable for the branches
to know at the time. For example, secret letters discovered centuries later
could change the best assessment of a branch's processual authority. It
is congruent with the terms of the relational conception to say "at the
time this behavior seemed constitutionally authoritative, but in fact, it
was not." Ongoing reassessment is one basic feature of ordinary political
judgment.

I use comparative case studies not to investigate empirical variation,
but to address a methodological dilemma of normative work: setting a
standard of assessment. The relational conception inquires into relative
levels of political authority rather than the yes/no judgments of legal
compliance.[121] The bar for assessing the branches is set by the branches'

---

120 See Anderson, "Lay Assessments."

121 The comparative case study approach may not rhetorically enact this central point
vividly enough. The book demonstrates a system of constitutional evaluation that proceeds
within a web of processual and substantive considerations, each of which are scalar, none of

own conduct in formally parallel cases. In addition, the comparative case study method allows for some measure of realism in applying the processual standards. The aspirations the relational conception enjoins are ones that are at least sometimes within reach. And, while the branches' absolute capacities (in terms of their ability to project power) change over time, the relational conception's standards are relative, asking only that the branches make good use of the capacities they do have at the moment.

Chapter 2 pairs President Polk's entry into the Mexican War with President Roosevelt's movement toward World War II and argues, using the relational conception, that while both Polk and Roosevelt behaved independently and made good use of the distinctive capacities of the executive branch, Roosevelt's behavior was more deeply relational in that it was more subject to legislative rebuff. Roosevelt's constitutional authority was also buttressed by a defensive security necessity. After World War II, repelling troops at the border was transparently revealed as an inadequate standard for judging whether a president was using the office's war powers "defensively." Confronted with this transparent destabilization of the category of "defensive," the United States embarked on a project of global institution building to reduce its vulnerabilities. When Truman went to war in Korea without legislative permission, he introduced the idea of an executive branch authorized to make war on the basis of this new, global conception of US defensive interests. The modern war powers debate is structured according to the institutional cleavage of the Korean War.[122]

Chapter 3 introduces the concept of a security order as a way of achieving analytic traction on this Cold War constitutional transformation. We can assess security orders, no less than acts of war, through the lens of the relational conception. The chapter compares the legislative contribution to the construction of the Cold War security order to the legislature's construction of the Roosevelt Corollary to the Monroe Doctrine. I argue that the quality of Congress's participation in the former was qualitatively higher than in the latter. Impressive levels of participation and knowledge, combined with a lengthy deliberative process where the legislature developed a variety of security alternatives, make the legislature's contribution to the Cold War order more constitutionally authoritative than legislative participation in the construction of the Roosevelt Corollary.

---

which can be lexically prioritized for all contexts. But evaluating two cases in relationship to each other is consistent with both threshold and scalar views of constitutional authority. Many thanks to Colin Bird for helping me see this drawback.

122   See Griffin, *Long Wars*, for persuasive historicization of the debate.

Chapter 4 returns to analyzing presidential conduct by showing how presidents can augment their authority to engage in independent acts of war. Assessing Kennedy's behavior in the Cuban Missile Crisis and Nixon's in the Cambodian bombing and incursion, I argue that independent acts of presidential war are more constitutional to the extent that they are interpretable in light of a security order that is itself constitutionally authoritative, and to the extent that they are themselves defensible in terms of the substantive and processual values of the relational conception.

The chapters alternate between assessing presidential, legislative, and presidential authority. Chapter 5 returns to Congress to scrutinize another legislative discretionary power, that of investigations. While the investigatory power is normally conceived as a retrospective power of judgment, chapter 5 construes investigations as both a war power and as a forward-looking tool for developing legislative war authority. The chapter compares the Munitions Investigation of 1934–36 with the Iran-Contra Investigation of 1989, arguing that the former developed far more constitutional authority for the legislature and war-making system than did the latter. The reasons may be surprising: counterintuitively, I argue that Congress's insufficiently developed partisanship undermined the authority of its Iran-Contra Investigation as a challenge to presidential power.

Chapter 6 assesses the connections between the relational conception and a variety of legal approaches to war powers. By placing the relational conception explicitly in dialogue with settlement theories of constitutional analysis; in dialogue with qualities understood as "legal" in a separation of powers system; and in dialogue with the premier judicial war powers expression, that of *Youngstown Sheet & Tube v. Sawyer* (1952), the chapter articulates some of the broader methodological implications of this distinctive form of constitutional theory.

Chapter 2

PRESIDENTIAL DISCRETION AND THE PATH TO WAR

The Mexican War and World War II

Since the founding, legislators have expressed anxiety that the presidency would use its structural independence and discretionary powers to informally usurp Congress's war authority. The president, in carrying out duties like diplomacy, public speeches, and treaty negotiation, can make war more likely. The executive branch's combination of structural independence and discretionary power was at the root of the first postratification exchange on war powers. In the Pacificus-Helvidius debate, officials considered whether President Washington's speech about a treaty with France unconstitutionally undermined Congress's war authority.[1] Both Presidents James Polk and Franklin Roosevelt were later challenged for usurping Congress's war power when they used their office's discretionary powers to make war more likely.

Settlement theory's effort to limit controversy suggests at least two approaches to the problem of presidential manipulation of the grounds for war. The first resists constitutionally assessing the branches for their use of discretionary powers. While a branch's use of discretionary powers—stationing troops, communicating with foreign leaders—may be more or less supportive of the "spirit" of the Constitution, the branches are not constitutionally accountable to one another for their use of core powers. Congress's judgment of a president's use of these powers may then be politically, but certainly not constitutionally, relevant. A second approach accepts that the exercise of a discretionary power may also be an exercise

---

1 Alexander Hamilton and James Madison, *The Pacificus-Helvidius Debates of 1793–1794: Toward the Completion of the American Founding*, ed. Morton J. Frisch (Indianapolis: Liberty Fund, 2007).

of a shared war power, and posits it as constitutionally authoritative insofar as the branches are behaving in mutually consistent ways.[2] One could then argue that Polk's and Roosevelt's actions were subversive of Congress's authority because the legislature was not seeking war.[3] Each of these approaches is misleading.

The first approach is misleading because it ignores the different meanings behind the use of textually granted powers in context. In certain contexts, discretionary powers—moving troops, giving speeches, disbursing appropriations—are simple executor powers, but in a context where they are used to advance war policy aims, they become war powers. When the branches use their powers to advance a constitutional judgment, they become constitutionally responsible for that exercise of power. The capacity to recognize (or interpret) this meaning is critically important in the relational conception. With no outside adjudicator, the process of interbranch deliberation over war happens *only* through the exercise of normal powers. We must be alert to the meanings of the branches' uses of power in context.

The second is misleading because it prioritizes interbranch agreement—that is to say, settlement—over and above high-quality interbranch performance. The relational conception theorizes war authority on the grounds of substantive and processual standards (i.e., independent judgment, use of distinctive governing capacities, and interbranch responsiveness) that are relevant for assessing the quality of each branch's governance. The relevant substantive standard for the presidency is that of defensive security necessity. The president takes an oath of office to "preserve, protect, and defend" the Constitution. He has no explicit powers to engage in war at all, but only powers that are structurally implied. It is the problem of enabling a defensive response that is the basis for any and all of a president's war authority. When discretionary powers are used as war powers, then, the president becomes accountable to a substantive standard of defense. I use the relational conception to argue that Roosevelt's use of discretionary powers for war was more tightly linked to defensive security necessity than Polk's.

---

2 Consider Justice Jackson's *Youngstown* concurrence (1952), where congruence structures the test for analyzing the president's exercise of a shared power. For an argument that this test applies even to the president's textually discretionary powers—inappropriately so, according to the author—see Joseph Bessette, "Confronting War: Rethinking Justice Robert Jackson's Concurrence in *Youngstown v. Sawyer*," *The Limits of Constitutional Democracy*, eds. Stephen Macedo and Jeffrey K. Tulis (Princeton: Princeton University Press, 2010).

3 Arthur M. Schlesinger, Jr., *The Imperial Presidency* (Boston: Houghton Mifflin Co., 1973), 43.

The processual standards ask that a president exercise war powers on the basis of independent judgment, while advancing a perspective developed on the basis of a good use of distinctive executive branch capacities and that he make his policy and constitutional positions subject to evaluation and rebuff. The heart of my case against Polk is based on two standards of the relational conception: the substantive standard of defense, and Polk's failure to advance a policy and constitutional position to Congress for evaluation and rebuff. While both Polk and Roosevelt behaved in ways that were independent and made good use of the distinctive capacities of the executive branch, Roosevelt's behavior was more deeply in accord with the standards of the relational conception.

This chapter does not address executive branch lawbreaking. President Roosevelt did violate statutory law. Whether he was constitutionally permitted to do so is a question about the status of prerogative power in the constitutional system.[4] The relational conception, by contrast, focuses on dilemmas of constitutional authority where the constitutional text itself points in more than one direction. Such behavior is not "without" or "against" the law, as in the classical definition of a prerogative power. It is in accordance with a constitutional text that points in multiple directions.

THE MEXICAN WAR AND WORLD WAR II

The story of the Mexican War is nested within Texas annexation, which was itself characterized by a history of duplicitous executive action.[5] Prior to Texan independence, Mexico's northern boundary had been fixed at the Nueces River, a border ratified by the United States in an 1819 treaty. Texas's defeat of General Santa Anna included a secret agreement, signed while the general was a prisoner, calling for Santa Anna to "evacuate

---

4   On his violations of statutory law see Aaron Xavier Fellmeth, "A Divorce Waiting to Happen: Franklin Roosevelt and the Law of Neutrality, 1935–1941," *Buffalo Journal of International Law* 3:2 (1996): 413–517. A voluminous, high-quality literature engages prerogative in US constitutionalism. Important recent contributions include Benjamin A. Kleinerman, *The Discretionary President: The Promise and Peril of Executive Power* (Lawrence: University Press of Kansas, 2009); Clement Fatovic, *Outside the Law: Emergency and Executive Power* (Baltimore, MD: The Johns Hopkins University Press, 2009); Michael Genovese, *Presidential Prerogative: Imperial Power in an Age of Terrorism* (Stanford: Stanford University Press, 2010); Oren Gross and Fionnuala Ní Aoláin, *Law in Times of Crisis: Emergency Powers in Theory and Practice* (Cambridge: Cambridge University Press, 2006). See also Thomas S. Langston and Michael E. Lind, "John Locke and the Limits of Presidential Prerogative," *Polity* 24:1 (1991): 49–68.

5   For Tyler's machinations see Schlesinger, *Imperial*, 39; Robert W. Merry, *A Country of Vast Designs* (New York: Simon & Schuster, 2009), ch. 4, 127–28.

the Territory of Texas, passing to the other side of the Rio Grande del Norte."[6] Texas used this agreement (later named a "treaty," although Santa Anna had no diplomatic authority and the agreement was never recognized by Mexico) to claim an additional 150 miles of land between the Nueces and Rio Grande Rivers when it achieved its independence in 1836. Mexico, refusing to recognize Texas's independence, told the United States that Texas's annexation would bring war. Into this context, James Polk was elected president on a platform of aggressive territorial acquisitiveness.

Polk entered office with a vision of annexation, and war, in mind. Leading presidential candidates Clay (Whig) and Van Buren (Democratic-Republican) had both opposed Texas's annexation, Clay for worries about the implications of an unnecessary war for slavery politics, and Van Buren for the legal implications of annexation and the lack of a real security threat in an independent Texas.[7] But electorates in both the North and the South supported acquisition. This created an opening in the Democratic Party for a pro-annexation candidate and launched Polk to the presidency.[8]

Polk took a variety of provocative actions once he assumed office, including the alleged dispatching of private agents John Stockton and John Charles Frémont to foment war in Texas and in California; instructions to diplomat Slidell to negotiate with Mexico on the basis of inflammatory terms; secret orders to the Navy's Pacific squadron to occupy the major ports of California in case of war; and finally his deployment of naval units to the Mexican port of Veracruz, and of General Taylor to the Rio Grande.[9] Political debate around his use of discretionary powers focused on one of these decisions in particular—his placement of troops within disputed territory even before the annexation of Texas was legally complete.

Before Texas had ratified its annexation to the United States, Polk sent troops to the Texas coast, assuring the American chargé in Texas that

6 "Treaty of Velasco" (May 14, 1836), *The Avalon Project*. Available at http://avalon .law.yale.edu/19th_century/velasco.asp (accessed July 31, 2011).

7 Merry, *Designs*, 75–76, citing Henry Clay, "Mr. Clay's Letter," *National Intelligencer* (April 27, 1844); Merry, *Designs*, 76–77, citing Martin Van Buren, "To the Editor of the Globe," *Daily Globe* (April 27, 1844).

8 For the story of the nomination, see Merry, *Designs*, ch. 4; also p. 77.

9 For discussions of these actions see George C. Herring, *From Colony to Superpower: U.S. Foreign Relations Since 1776* (New York: Oxford University Press, 2008), 198–99, also citing Paul H. Bergeron, *The Presidency of James K. Polk* (Lawrence: University Press of Kansas, 1987), 73–74; Joseph Wheelan, *Invading Mexico: America's Continental Dream and the Mexican War, 1846–1848* (New York: Carroll & Graf Publishers, 2007), 56; Merry, *Designs*, ch. 9, also pp. 145, 159.

"he intended to defend Texas to the limit of his constitutional power."[10] In June of 1845 he told General Zachary Taylor that his "ultimate destination" would be the disputed territory of the Rio Grande.[11] By mid-October, about six months before war broke out, Taylor's command had three brigades and almost four thousand men—about "half the total strength of the army and . . . the largest force assembled since the War of 1812."[12] Polk ordered them into the territory between the Nueces and Rio Grande. Placing troops into disputed area, Polk had every reason to expect they would be attacked. The on-the-ground sequence that occasioned the attack was an exchange of words between Taylor and the Mexican general Ampudia, followed by Taylor blockading the mouth of the Rio Grande, cutting off supplies to the thousands of Mexican troops on the other side of the river, and pointing his artillery to Matamoros.[13] In late April 1846 US soldiers were attacked and killed. While one historian has charged that Polk maneuvered Mexico into firing the first shot, it is also plausible that Polk was just willing to behave in an intimidating, belligerent way regardless of the possibility of war.[14]

Polk discovered that the troops had been attacked while in the midst of preparing a war message to Congress. Congress had not authorized war with Mexico nor had it declared war or authorized any other belligerent action on behalf of the territory. Nor did Congress's joint resolution for annexing Texas endorse in any way the Rio Grande border. This is not to say that certain forces in each institution did not welcome war: the Senate Foreign Relations Committee had submitted a report on relations with Mexico saying it could, "with justice, recommend an immediate resort to war or reprisals," and the House Foreign Relations Committee had stated that "ample cause exists for taking redress into our own hands," although in the end both recommended peaceful negotiation.[15]

Polk's war message to Congress was based on a defensive claim, stating that "Mexico has passed the boundary of the United States, has

10   Norman A. Graebner, "The Mexican War: A Study in Causation," *Pacific Historical Review* 49:3 (1980): 405–26, 410; Dean B. Mahin, *Olive Branch and Sword: The United States and Mexico, 1845–1848* (Jefferson, NC, and London: McFarland & Company, 1997), 36.

11   Mahin, *Olive Branch*, 36.

12   Jack Bauer, *The Mexican War 1846–1848* (Lincoln: University of Nebraska Press, 1992), 33.

13   Herring, *Colony to Superpower*, 199; Merry, *Designs*, 241, citing Wheelan, *Invading Mexico*, 90.

14   Herring, *Colony to Superpower*, 198. The major revisionist study making this charge is Glenn W. Price, *Origins of the War with Mexico: The Polk-Stockton Intrigue* (Austin and London: University of Texas Press, 1967).

15   Merry, *Designs*, 185.

invaded our territory and shed American blood upon America's soil."[16] The House debate, restricted to two hours, considered the president's war resolution under closed rules. Democrats, many of whom were motivated to increase slave territory, rallied to the war. However, certain legislators raised objections. Elias Holmes argued that, "[w]e know nothing more than that the two armies have come into collision within the disputed territory, and I deny that war is absolutely, necessarily, the result of it." Garrett Davis of Kentucky charged that "[t]he river Nueces is the true western boundary of Texas. . . . it is our own President who began this war."[17] Despite these objections, Democrats added a preamble to the appropriations bill stating that Mexico had begun the war. A vote to send material to the troops thus became an endorsement of Polk's characterization of the conflict.[18] Even as Congress declared war, it also expressed ambivalence about Polk's conduct leading up to the war. An amendment indicating Congress's disapproval of Polk's order to move troops into disputed territory was proposed, and defeated.

In the Senate, Democrats Calhoun and Benton tried to slow the bill's passage, fearing the addition of free, not slave, territory from Mexico. They raised constitutional objections, Calhoun arguing that "the President is authorized to repel invasion without war. But it is *our* sacred duty to make war, and it is for *us* to determine whether war shall be declared or not. If we have declared war, a state of war exists, and not until then," and urging Senators to offer "that high, full, and dispassionate consideration which is worthy of the character of the body and [its] high constitutional functions."[19] Ohio Senator Tom Corwin accused Polk of involving the United States in an aggressive war. Massachusetts Senator Daniel Webster voiced doubts about the constitutionality of Polk's actions because of Polk's failure to consult adequately with Congress. Yet finally the Congress declared war on Mexico with a strong vote of support: 40–2 in the Senate and 173–14 in the House.[20] Representatives Abraham Lincoln, then a freshman, and John Quincy Adams were among the fourteen dissenting House Whigs. Several Whigs in the Senate responded to the roll call "Aye, except for the preamble," and Calhoun declined to vote.[21]

As the war deepened, Whigs escalated their criticisms of Polk. A Whig newspaper argued that the American troops had been in disputed

---

16 James K. Polk, "Message of President Polk" (May 11, 1846). Available at http://www.dmwv.org/mexwar/documents/polk.htm (accessed July 31, 2011).

17 Merry, *Designs*, 246.

18 Wheelan, *Invading Mexico*, 96.

19 Merry, *Designs*, 246–47 citing John C. Calhoun, "In Senate," *Daily Union*, May 11, 1846; see also Wheelan, *Invading Mexico*, 97.

20 Merry, *Designs*, 246.

21 Ibid., 251.

territory, and challenged the constitutionality of Polk's provocation: "The Constitution contemplates that before deliberate hostilities shall be undertaken in any case, a declaration of war shall be made; but in this case a hostile aggressive move was made under the personal orders of the President."[22] On December 22, 1847, Abraham Lincoln introduced the "Spot Resolutions," challenging the president to demonstrate that the spot where hostilities had erupted was really on American soil. One of several congressional resolutions opposing the war, it was never acted upon by the full Congress. A month before the end of the war, a bill praising Major General Zachary Taylor was successfully amended—and passed—with a criticism of Polk for initiating a war "unnecessarily and unconstitutionally."[23] The vote followed party lines, with all Whigs supporting the amendment. Still, the Whig resistance had little consequence, especially as pragmatist Whigs had decided not to back their constitutional criticisms with resistance to war funding.

Roosevelt, too, used the discretionary powers of the presidency to make American entry into World War II more likely. From an electoral point of view, Roosevelt's behavior may have been more troubling than Polk's. Where Polk was elected on an expansionist platform, and whereas the pre–Mexican War Congress had not imposed blocks or restraining orders on executive bellicosity, Roosevelt faced a public weary of war and an isolationist block in Congress that was mobilized, determined, and sophisticated in generating statutory law to restrict the president. Yet while publicly affirming his commitment to nonintervention in Europe, Roosevelt repeatedly used his discretionary powers in a pro-Allied direction to fight what Edward Corwin called "the War before the War."[24]

Congress's resistance to engagement with European conflict—and its fear of presidential manipulation to get the United States into war—was firm in the late 1930s. The Johnson Act of 1934, prohibiting loans to any country behind on its World War I debt, barred support to every friendly country except Finland. The United States responded to Mussolini's invasion of Ethiopia with the Neutrality Act of 1935, which placed an embargo on trading arms with belligerents, an embargo that was deepened again in the Neutrality Act of 1936. In 1937 these terms were again updated to prohibit travel by US citizens on ships of belligerents and to expand neutrality to include civil wars (the Spanish Civil War) as well as wars between nations. And, although the 1937 Act granted the president

22   Daniel D. Barnard, "The Whigs and the War," *The American Review* 6:4 (1847): 331–46, 333.

23   *Journal of the House of Representatives of the United States* (January 3, 1848), 184; see Schlesinger, *Imperial*, 42.

24   Edward Corwin, *Total War and the Constitution* (New York: Alfred A. Knopf, 1946), 22.

the power to allow non–arms trade to belligerents through cash-and-carry provisions (giving the president more scope to aid Britain), the Act also extended the terms of the other neutrality acts indefinitely. The president signed all these acts into law.

Congress was not only legislating neutrality but was also generating a politics highly oppositional to executive maneuvering in support of the Allies. For example, Congress tried to restrain the president by proposing a constitutional amendment to require a national referendum to declare war. Congressman Louis Ludlow believed in the amendment because "[i]t is always possible, as matters now stand, for a president to maneuver congress into declaring war. Members of that body would have to be men of steel and iron if they could stand up and vote for what they believe is right after a president has set the stage for war."[25] In 1937 this amendment narrowly failed passage in the House. Many of Roosevelt's controversial policy decisions encountered outrage or mobilized opposition in Congress. In addition to statutory restrictions, Roosevelt faced a congressional politics skeptical of the value of support for the Allies and careful to design legislation that would limit executive discretion.[26]

But Roosevelt was resourceful in finding discretionary executive power to strategically support the Allies and, in so doing, move the United States closer to war.[27] Roosevelt did this even as he affirmed the value of

25 Ludlow to James A. Crain, January 21, 1935, as cited in Nancy Young, *Why We Fight: Congress and the Politics of World War II* (Lawrence, KS: University Press of Kansas, 2013). One woman, Jeanette Rankin, did vote her conscience against entry into World War II.

26 Isolationists were even successful at amending the Lend-Lease Act (1941)—which essentially repealed US neutrality—to block the president from using US convoys to protect British ships with American munitions. See Bruce Russett, *No Clear and Present Danger: A Skeptical View of the U.S. Entry into World War II* (New York: Harper & Row, 1972), 69, 70, referencing Warren I. Cohen, *The American Revisionists: The Lessons of Intervention in World War One* (Chicago: University of Chicago Press, 1967). In June 1940 Congress amended the Naval Appropriations Bill to bar transfers of military material to foreign governments unless the Chief of Staff or of naval operations could certify it was useless, just after the chief of naval operations testified to congressional committees on the potential value of the ships. See Ian Kershaw, *Fateful Choices: Ten Decisions That Changed the World, 1940–1941* (New York: The Penguin Press, 2007), 215. This statute was the reason the destroyers-for-bases deal was arguably illegal. Legislative sophistication was not accidental. Many key non-interventionists, including William Borah, Hiram Johnson, Burton Wheeler, Gerald Nye, and Arthur Vandenberg, were either in the Senate or on the actual committee during the 1934–36 Senate Munitions Committee Investigation. The committee's revelation of Wilson's small steps toward war fortified the non-interventionists' resolve to constrict the discretionary agency available to the president. T. R. Fehrenbach, *F.D.R.'s Undeclared War 1939–1941* (New York: David McKay, 1967), 4–5, also chap. 6.

27 Important works include: David Reynolds, *From Munich to Pearl Harbor: Roosevelt's America and the Origins of the Second World War* (Chicago: Ivan R. Dee, 2001); Fellmeth, "Law of Neutrality"; William L. Langer and S. Everett Gleason, *The Challenge to Isolation: 1937–1940* (New York: Harper, 1952); Richard Harrison, "A Presidential

neutrality as a paradigm for US security interests. Some of his important uses of executive power to advance intervention include:

- His effort to push war supplies to the democracies, beginning with airplanes. In early 1938 he developed a scheme to build aircraft in Canada with US parts and ship them to France, suggesting that "[i]f London could avoid an actual declaration of war, he might be able to ignore the Neutrality Act and continue arms sales, as he was doing with China."[28] In May and June of 1940 he committed vital military equipment to the Allies.[29] Such transfers would have been, or were (if they happened), illegal until Lend-Lease in 1941. The promises were not illegal, but they did undermine Congress's neutrality policy.
- His request that the British trade use of its Caribbean bases for US action to patrol the waters of the Western Hemisphere, and his strategic timing of that request in 1939, before war broke out, to avoid "awkward questions about unneutral conduct."[30] The British Foreign Office complied. In June of 1939 Roosevelt also approved a series of secret conversations between top US and British naval officials to discuss a coordinated naval defense strategy.[31] None of these behaviors were prohibited, but none were consistent with the legislature's emphatic vision of a neutral foreign policy.
- His coordination of fleet movements with the British in the Far East,[32] and patrols of the Atlantic for U-boats starting in 1939. In the summer of 1941, when Admiral Stark, chief of naval operations, asked for clarification about the proper response to German U-boat presence in the Atlantic, Roosevelt said, "don't ask me that." The fleet commander "simply ordered the fleet to go after any German submarine or raider close by or at 'reasonably longer distances.'"[33]
- The September 1940 destroyers-for-bases agreement, which gave fifty destroyers to the British in exchange for leases on territory in the Caribbean. Some claim that the deal was simply illegal. The 1917

Démarche: Franklin D. Roosevelt's Personal Diplomacy and Great Britain, 1936–37," *Diplomatic History* 5:3 (1981): 245–72.

28   Dominic Tierney, *FDR and the Spanish Civil War: Neutrality and Commitment in the Struggle that Divided America* (Durham: Duke University Press, 2007), 77; see also Barbara Rearden Farnham, *Roosevelt and the Munich Crisis: A Study of Political Decision-Making* (Princeton: Princeton University Press, 1997), 73–74, 109–10.

29   Fehrenbach, *Undeclared War*, 65, 137. On his early efforts to get planes to Britain and France, see Farnham, *Munich Crisis*, 178–86.

30   James Leutze, "The Secret of the Churchill-Roosevelt Correspondence: September 1939–May 1940," *Journal of Contemporary History* 10: 3 (1975): 465–91, 482.

31   Leutze, "Correspondence," 483.

32   Tierney, *Spanish Civil War*, 30–31.

33   Joseph E. Persico, *Roosevelt's Secret War: FDR and World War II Espionage* (New York: Random House, 2001), 120–21.

Espionage Act criminalized exporting vessels of war to belligerent nations. This bar was reinforced with the Walsh Amendment to a naval bill, which barred the transfer of military material from the United States unless it could be certified as surplus and obsolete. Executive branch lawyers issued a series of convoluted statutory interpretations that pressed the grammar of the Espionage Act and Walsh Amendment to their absolute limit.[34] Ultimately the critical legal resource was a claim made on the president's war authority. Roosevelt, supported by Robert Jackson, argued that the president's status as commander in chief gave him authority to execute the trade. Jackson's legal opinion argued that the Walsh Amendment itself was "of questionable constitutionality."[35]

- The imposition of embargos on Japan of iron, steel, and aviation gasoline in December 1940 as a response to Japanese aggression in China and Indochina.[36]
- Secret meetings between US and British military staffs between January 29 and March 27, 1941, establishing key elements of US grand military strategy, eventually leading to the ABC-1 staff agreements prioritizing battle in Europe and the Atlantic, extending American neutrality patrols farther out in the Atlantic, and an agreement that the Navy would assume convoy as soon as it was ready (forbidden by the Neutrality Act of 1939).[37]
- His imposition of sanctions on Japan and notice of intention to terminate a 1911 commercial treaty. These led to a de facto oil embargo, leaving the Japanese the choice to de-escalate in China or go to war with the United States before running out of oil.[38]

Predictable consequences came to fruition in the USS *Greer* incident. A British plane had signaled to the *Greer* that a U-boat lay ahead. The *Greer* began tracking the U-boat and reporting its position to the plane, which dropped depth charges without hitting the sub. The British plane left, but the *Greer* kept tracking. Believing the *Greer* had dropped the depth charges, the U-boat fired torpedoes at the *Greer*, none of which

34 Another problem was possible contravention of Article 6 of the Hague Convention, barring transfer of military materials from neutral to belligerent countries. However, Britain and Spain had not signed the Hague Convention, and Article 28 qualified that the provisions only applied to contracting powers.

35 "Letter from Robert Jackson, U.S. Attorney General, to Roosevelt" (August 27, 1940), *The Public Papers and Addresses of Franklin D. Roosevelt* (New York: Russell & Russell, 1969), 490.

36 This was particularly important in light of Roosevelt's failure to proclaim Japan and China at war. Fellmeth, "Law of Neutrality," 467.

37 Fehrenback, *Undeclared War*, 206, 222–26, 255–56, 259; Kershaw, *Fateful Choices*, 234; Persico, *Espionage* 123–24.

38 Frank Ninkovich, *The United States and Imperialism* (Oxford, UK: Blackwell Publishers Ltd., 2001), 227–28.

hit.[39] It is doubtful this was an intentional attack on US forces, but Roosevelt told the public that the *Greer* had been on a "legitimate mission," and he emphasized "the blunt fact that the German submarine fired first upon this American destroyer without warning, and with deliberate design to sink her."[40] And while he eschewed a "shooting war" with Hitler, he also emphasized that "neither do we want peace so much that we are willing to pay for it by permitting him to attack our naval and merchant ships while they are on legitimate business."[41] Senator Nye called this a "declaration of war by presidential proclamation."[42]

In October of 1941 the destroyer *Kearny* was torpedoed and eleven American sailors killed. Roosevelt insinuated American innocence, claiming that "history has recorded who fired the first shot." Secretary of the Navy Knox reported that the *Kearny* was dropping depth bombs on a submarine that was attacking merchant ships.[43] Public and congressional opinion was by now shifting. In mid-November of 1941 Congress removed all remaining restrictions of the Neutrality Acts at Roosevelt's request, permitting American ships to carry supplies clear across the Atlantic. In late November Roosevelt and his War Council met, and Stimson's notes expressed that "[t]he question was how we should maneuver them into the position of firing the first shot without allowing too much danger to ourselves."[44]

The Roosevelt administration's diplomacy with the Japanese inspired Congress to investigate whether the president had actually incited the Pearl Harbor attack, and the minority report of the Congressional Investigating Committee blamed Pearl Harbor on Roosevelt and core members of his administration. Most historians have rejected the idea that Roosevelt directly anticipated Pearl Harbor. Still, it is clear that Roosevelt

39   Persico, *Espionage*, 124; Russett, *Danger*, 79; Robert Divine, *Roosevelt and World War II* (Baltimore: The Johns Hopkins University Press, 1969), 44.

40   Franklin Roosevelt, "Fireside Chat to the Nation" (September 11, 1941), *The Public Papers and Addresses of Franklin D. Roosevelt, 1941* volume, ed. Samuel I. Rosenman (New York: Harper & Brothers, 1950), 384.

41   "President's Address on Freedom of the Seas," *New York Times* (September 12, 1941): 1, 4. Roosevelt may not have known all the facts of the incident. See Kershaw, *Fateful*, 320.

42   Wayne S. Cole, *Senator Gerald P. Nye and American Foreign Relations* (Minneapolis: University of Minnesota Press, 1962), 195; see also Wayne S. Cole, *America First—The Battle Against Intervention 1940–1941* (Madison: University of Wisconsin Press, 1953), 159–62.

43   See "Army Gives a Hand to Navy on its Day," *New York Times* (October 28, 1941), 4. Roosevelt quote from "We Americans Have Cleared Our Decks and Taken Our Battle Stations" (October 27, 1941), *Public Papers 1941*, 438.

44   Persico, *Espionage*, 142, citing Roberta Wohlstetter, *Pearl Harbor: Warning and Decision* (Palo Alto, Stanford University Press, 1962), 239–40.

consistently used his powers in a pro-Allied direction contrary to the war policy being set by Congress. For this he encountered constitutional criticism, and on more than one occasion Roosevelt expressed worry about impeachment.[45]

DEFENSIVE SECURITY

For evaluating a president's use of war power, the relational conception first advances a substantive standard: whether the president's use of powers is responsive to the defensive security interests of the nation. Of course, the presidency is not a single-minded pursuer of security, and presidents may use discretionary powers—including those of military command—to advance economic or other policy aims, as well as security aims. However, when discretionary powers are used as war powers, the president is accountable to a substantive standard of defense. The president takes an oath of office to "preserve, protect, and defend" the Constitution. The war power is shared with the president only by implication, specifically the intersection between the governance needs associated with a defensive response and the distinctive capacities of the executive office. For these reasons, when the president uses discretionary powers to advance an aggressive war, he should do so with legislative support. The president's own independent war authority is constitutionally disciplined by a defensive standard.

Elaborating the nature of "defense" is not easy. The Mexican War and World War II illustrate that the content of defensive security interests must be politically specified. By this I mean that any concept of defense rests upon a preexistent concept of a nation's core security interests. While the concept of "repelling attack" is often seen as a paradigmatic threat calling for a defensive executive war power, this paradigm was not written into the Constitution's text. Attack itself, as the 1993 bombing in the World Trade Center reveals, cannot be interpreted as a threat necessitating bellicose response without engaging questions like relative military capacity, the significance of the dispute for broad security interests, the costs and likely outcome of military action, and other judgments about national priorities, costs, and resources. Technological advances in

---

45 Herring, *Colony to Superpower*, 524; Farnham, *Munich Crisis*, 106. For some sense of the criticism he faced, see Hamilton Fish, *Tragic Deception: FDR and America's Involvement in World War II* (Old Greenwich, CT: Devin-Adair Publishers, 1983); Leutze, "Correspondence," 478, paraphrasing charges of others; Charles A. Beard, *President Roosevelt and the Coming of the War, 1941* (New Haven: Yale University Press, 1948); Charles Callan Tansill, *Back Door to War: The Roosevelt Foreign Policy, 1933–1941* (Santa Barbara: Greenwood Press, 1952).

war intensify this dilemma as a diplomatic mobilization across the globe may be of more profound security significance, from a defensive point of view, than a skirmish at a border. The Mexican War was triggered by the presence of hostile troops in the boundary areas of the nation, and yet the security stakes of World War II were, I argue, far more significant than those of the Mexican War.

What substantive threat was at stake in the Mexican War? A first possibility, and the one that Polk cited in his message to Congress, was from Mexico. But Mexico itself was extraordinarily weak at the moment, a "dysfunctional" country.[46] Between 1837 and 1851 a series of coups had resulted in sixteen different presidencies.[47] While Polk's war message to Congress emphasized unsatisfactory diplomatic relations and unpaid claims, these were not security threats.[48] Unsatisfying diplomacy did not render Mexico a threat, and the total value of the American claims at stake was less than the cost of a week at war. Many US states were also failing to honor claims the federal government was pursuing. Thefts from American businessmen voluntarily traveling in Mexico do not rise to a defensive security threat.[49] Mexico was no threat to the United States.

What about a threat from European powers, who might opportunistically insert themselves into Mexico's turmoil? President Tyler had pushed annexation of Texas in part over concerns about the "meddlesome British . . . hovering over it with an aim of establishing an alliance of mutual convenience," and foresaw the possibility of Britain undermining US supremacy in the Gulf of Mexico and menacing New Orleans, gateway to the Mississippi.[50] But by the 1840s, the European powers were focused on continental rivalries and internal wars, and "European ambitions in the Western Hemisphere were receding."[51] Polk's own diplomacy brought major concessions from Britain on the Oregon territories, belying the idea of Britain as an ongoing expansionist threat. (Upon resolution of the Oregon question, the *New York Herald* opined: "Now we can thrash Mexico into decency at our leisure.")[52] In fact, the war with Mexico itself posed a security threat. The war cost approximately fourteen thousand casualties.

Finally, a source of threat Polk did not address but that was arguably present in the broader discourses of the time was the need to preserve

46 Merry, *Designs*, 185.
47 Herring, *Colony to Superpower*, 196.
48 Mahin, *Olive Branch*, 73.
49 Graebner, "Causation," 408–409.
50 Merry, *Designs*, 71–72.
51 Herring, *Colony to Superpower*, 177.
52 Quoted in David M. Pletcher, *The Diplomacy of Annexation: Texas, Oregon, and the Mexican War* (Colombia: University of Missouri Press, 1973), 414.

republican institutions through expansion. Expansion was widely supported in both the North and the South. Both sections sought to expand their labor systems—free labor and slavery—in part to protect the political systems they valued. In the North, an emerging class society provoked political anxieties about Europeanization; the longing for California was a longing to extend territory for free white labor. Southerners knew that slavery was most secure in contexts where it was hardest for slaves to escape to freedom—that is to say, where they were kept far away from free borders. Calhoun sought to tie slavery and expansionist policy when he claimed credit for Texas annexation (much to President Tyler's annoyance, for Tyler saw annexation as a national enterprise to extend trade for all the sections).[53] As senator, Calhoun also attached to the Tyler administration's Texas annexation treaty a statement that the rationale for annexation was to protect slavery in the South from British interference. (His doing so caused the issue of Texas annexation to explode in the Senate, and the annexation treaty was voted down 35–16.)[54] All sections were invested, for their own reasons, in territorial growth.[55]

Both sections had ideological resources available to link acquisition with the defense of republicanism. In one expression, an independent free politics depended upon an economic structure of small agricultural production. In southern racialized republicanism, to "survive" meant to extend territory in part to secure slavery by making escape more difficult. Both versions may claim a "defensive" security interest in protecting a certain political economy through the opportunities new land made possible.

Why not interpret this shared interest in preserving republicanism through expansion as rooted in a preservationist, defensive security interest that meets the substantive standard of the relational conception? While Polk never discussed the defensive value of war or expansion in these terms, perhaps this security discourse, readily visible in the larger culture, could nonetheless justify his conduct. I reject this line of reasoning. While all sections may have had an interest in expansion, their reasons for that interest differed in ways that are highly important. Both North and South had interests in expansion, but the nature of those interests was directly repugnant. Because republicanism has such different

53   Edward P. Crapol, "John Tyler and the Pursuit of National Destiny," *Journal of the American Republic* 17:3 (1997): 467–91, 484. See, too, Don E. Fehrenbacher, *The Slaveholding Republic: An Account of the United States Government's Relations to Slavery* (Oxford: Oxford University Press, 2001), 122–24, on Calhoun's efforts as Tyler's Secretary of State to link expansion to slavery.

54   Merry, *Designs*, 73–74.

55   Jesse S. Reeves, *American Diplomacy Under Tyler and Polk* (Baltimore: The Johns Hopkins University Press, 1907).

sectional meanings, using it to assert a common national security interest would be asserting commonality on the basis of a pun.

In addition, some of these defensive interests are in the first place only tenuously related to security. For example, I would reject attributing to any nation a defensive security interest in extending slavery because of the devastating costs slavery poses to the human security of slaves. Even if the nation could have expanded while maintaining the political balance between slave and free states, slavery itself had such devastating costs to human security that its extension cannot be understood as neutral even if it is extended along with free institutions. Security through preemptive territorial expansion is also an insufficient conceptualization of national defensive security because at some point, domestic security must be consistent with stable territories to ensure peaceful coexistence between nations. The drive to achieve security through expansionism is theoretically limitless: many Americans, for example, were convinced that Cuban acquisition was every bit as important to US security as the acquisition of Mexican territory.[56] And yet it is a basic dilemma of political life to achieve coexistence not premised on preemptive aggression. The threats associated with possibly endless territorial encroachments were apparent after the Peace of Westphalia, not only World War II. Of course, my skepticism toward territorial encroachment as a pathway to security certainly relies on twentieth-century experiences, but the relational conception asks us to judge security needs according to our own—the evaluators—best understandings. This means that judgments of constitutional authority in context may shift over time as new and, one hopes, better understandings of the basis of human security emerge.

The extent to which expansion can be justified as a defensive security interest is, under the relational conception, a core standard for assessing presidential war authority. The relational conception tells us that illuminating this question—the nature of the country's defensive security needs at this moment—helps to accurately theorize the constitutionality of Polk's exercise of discretionary war powers.

Roosevelt's claim to be exercising his discretionary war powers according to the needs of defensive security is more plausible than Polk's. By 1940 few believed that the international context was not threatening, although opinion was divided on the best way to meet that threat. Roosevelt's perception of threat had more than one aspect. At first he seems to have been concerned about US survival in a hostile ideological environment. His 1939 State of the Union spoke to ideological isolation.[57]

---

56 Fehrenbacher, *Slaveholding*, 127–28.

57 Roosevelt, "State of the Union Address" (January 4, 1939). Available at http://teaching americanhistory.org/library/index.asp?document=1352 (accessed October 24, 2011).

It is unclear whether the United States ever could have countenanced a Nazi and fascist victory on the scope that Hitler was imagining. Hitler did not imagine the United States would be able to.[58] But Roosevelt also feared for the physical security of the nation, that if the dictators destroyed the European democracies, the United States would have to face them alone. He also feared vulnerability through Latin America, that the Western Hemisphere would be militarily, economically, and politically threatened.[59] The development of the long-range bomber made it possible for Germany to bring war to the Western Hemisphere through Brazil.[60]

Roosevelt's uses of discretionary power meet the substantive defensive standard to the extent that fighting that war was required to maintain domestic constitutional institutions. It is not just that presidents are permitted to use their discretionary powers against the legislature's security vision. Under the relational conception, such defensive behavior is required insofar as it truly is necessary to protect the nation. Deference to Congress cannot insulate a president from constitutional rebuke if that deference imperils the constitutional order. A president who failed to extend himself to protect US security in the face of a threat like Hitler's would, I argue, merit serious constitutional criticism. That Roosevelt's judgment of defensive security need was better than Polk's is one of the controversial conclusions I advance to show how the relational conception enables constitutional evaluation in context.

ASSESSING EXECUTIVE BRANCH JUDGMENT: THE PROCESSUAL STANDARDS

The relational conception also points to a series of processual standards for assessing the president's contribution to interbranch deliberation over war. The first is independence—the structural premise for the very dilemma. The relational conception interprets this independence not as a problem to be overcome, but as a constitutional capacity to act and

58 Hans Louis Trefousse, *Germany and American Neutrality* (New York: Bookman Associates, 1951), 20–21.

59 Farnham, *Munich Crisis*, 159. Cordell Hull, *The Memoirs of Cordell Hull*, 2 vols. (New York: The Macmillan Company, 1948), vol. 1, 496–97 testifies to reports of Nazis organizing the Germans in Latin America, contacting militaries there, and trying to undermine US trade relations. For the foundations of these worries, see Alton Frye, *Nazi Germany and the American Hemisphere, 1933–1941* (New Haven: Yale University Press, 1967); Gerhard L. Weinberg, *The Foreign Policy of Hitler's Germany: Starting the War, 1937–1939* (Chicago: University of Chicago Press, 1980); Hugo Fernandez Artucio, *The Nazi Underground in South America* (New York: Farrar & Rinehart, 1942); Tierney, *Spanish Civil War*, 81–83.

60 Farnham, *Munich Crisis*, 160.

judge. The second processual standard is about whether the president's judgments made good use of the various governance capacities of his branch. And third, the processual standards direct us to scrutinize the extent to which the president made deliberative contributions that were subject to rebuff. The two presidents, I argue, differ most in terms of the third processual standard—the nature of their deliberative contributions to the interbranch system.

The president was certainly exercising independent judgment in both cases—there is no evidence that either was overly deferential to the views of other institutions. To what extent did each presidency manage to meet the other processual standards? While both presidents made good use of their electoral, intelligence, and diplomatic capacities, Roosevelt's policy development made better use of those capacities for the substantive ends of a common defense. This in turn affected the nature of the deliberative contribution he was able to offer Congress.

Let us first consider Polk. One distinctive capacity of the executive branch is its connection to the public mediated by elections, and Polk did fairly well advancing the electorate's desires. His agenda—Texas's annexation, even at the cost of war with Mexico—was a goal Polk brought with him to office. While expansion was a partisan issue between Democrats and Whigs, in 1844 most of the regions had some interest in expansion.[61] The South wanted land to develop its cotton and slavery systems, and to balance the power of the free states. In all regions, the export possibilities of the California territory, especially to the commerce of East Asia, beckoned, and "land-hungry westerners sought territory for its own sake."[62]

Public enthusiasm over expansion dominated the presidential election, and the public identified Polk as an expansionist candidate. However, electoral support for expansion cannot be construed as a sign that majorities approved expansion over and above other goals such as containing slavery. While he was the overwhelming victor in electoral votes, Polk's popular vote was by a narrow margin in part because emerging abolitionist politics split his opponents. If the antislavery Liberty Party had mobilized for Whig Clay, they might have prevented Polk's victory.[63] Also, Polk campaigned promising to be a one-term president, thereby undercutting the value of the electoral mechanism as a tool for the retrospective judgment of the electoral public. Nonetheless, by all accounts,

61   See Fehrenbacher, *Slaveholding* (Feherenbacher, *Slaveholding*, 118), on the stronger expansionist commitments of the South.

62   Herring, *Colony to Superpower*, 181.

63   Ibid., 110–11.

in this divided field, Polk's commitment to expansion was critical for his victory, and to carry electoral judgments into representational office is certainly among the constitutional capacities of the presidency.

At his inauguration, Polk noted to Navy Secretary George Bancroft that two of his four most important presidential ambitions were to acquire Oregon and the California territory.[64] Mexico had already rebuffed US overtures, broken off diplomatic relations in response to Texas's annexation, and clearly viewed US acquisition of that territory as hostile to its core national interests.[65] Polk's resolve to acquire territory in this context implied "a corollary willingness to force the issue through war."[66] The policy of expansion through war was not developed in relationship to the forms of knowledge made distinctively possible in the presidency. Despite broad public support for expansion, some leading presidents and legislators of the time with more governing experience than Polk were reluctant to pursue acquisition at all in part through fear about the political consequences that would be unleashed. It was in fact Van Buren's and Clay's reluctance to pursue Texas annexation that had created space for the relatively obscure former Tennessee governor, Polk, to pursue the presidency.[67] One history of the period expresses confusion about Clay's and Van Buren's failure to endorse expansion, and speculates about their "stubbornness, ideology, ego, nostalgia," but it is also possible that other major officials were simply more aware, or cared more than Polk, about the stakes of Texas annexation for slavery.[68] Both Van Buren and Clay cited a worry about seeing "the existing Union dissolved or seriously jeoparded [sic] for the sake of acquiring Texas," as well as reluctance to enter an unjust war, as reasons for their reticence to join in the public enthusiasm.[69]

Given the goal of annexation, Polk used the capacities of the presidency well. From his thorough diary we know that cabinet deliberations were alert to the prospect of war with Mexico. Polk elicited a variety of viewpoints, including in-party rival Buchanan's in his capacity as Secretary of State, and there is no evidence that Polk sought to manipulate or subvert the counsel that Buchanan or the rest of the cabinet offered him. Polk's confrontations with Buchanan led the president to carefully record

64 Merry, *Designs*, 131.
65 Ibid., ch. 11.
66 Ibid., 132.
67 Ibid., 7–8.
68 Ibid., 110. See Fehrenbacher, *Slaveholding*, 119 on how easily apparent to Van Buren and others were the links between annexation, war with Mexico, and a highly alarming domestic slavery politics.
69 Merry, *Designs*, 109.

his cabinet meetings, and his diaries testify to a relatively robust set of exchanges.[70]

But those exchanges were premised on an opportunistic, not defensive, point of view. When discussing Texas the cabinet inquired into how much territory the country wanted, and how much territory was worth going to war for, rather than the security consequences of war or peace.[71] When he received diplomatic reports that Mexico was "too weak and chaotic to confront the United States... The cabinet was weak, Herrera seemed beleaguered," Polk decided to intensify the bellicosity of negotiations. Polk's discovery that the Herrera government "was in danger of collapse" encouraged the president to put troops in place for military confrontation. When an associate of General Santa Anna proposed that Polk place troops in a threatening position so as to allow Mexico to justify a land settlement to its public, Polk's diplomacy became even more intransigent.[72] Discussions as to the likely value of war with Texas were prominent in cabinet deliberations. Once the war began, Polk also immersed himself deeply in military governance, directing operations from the White House.[73] Some histories argue that the president miscalculated in imagining that war would be over in mere months, but the length of the war was partly a function of Polk's own escalating terms for peace rather than a miscalculation about material dominance. There is no evidence of any real subversion of the intelligence, diplomatic, military, or other epistemic resources of the presidential branch. To the contrary, Polk skillfully used these capacities for war.

And Roosevelt? Roosevelt's use of the constitutional capacities of the executive branch was admirable in several ways. One significant constitutional capacity of the presidency is that of carrying an electoral judgment into representational office. Given that Roosevelt so often advanced security policies that had not been electorally endorsed in his presidential runs, there is serious historical debate as to whether Roosevelt did enough to educate the public about the threat of the Axis powers.[74] His

70   Ibid., 191–92, 213; Milo M. Quaife (ed.), *The Diary of James K. Polk During His Presidency, 1845–1849,* 4 vols. (Chicago: A. C. McClurg & Co., 1910), II, 101.

71   Merry, *Designs,* 203–204, chs. 13, 14.

72   Quotations from ibid., 195, 218. See also pp. 219, 230–33, 239. Ultimately the Mexican government fiercely held onto its territorial claims even in the face of overwhelming US power.

73   Richard Bruce Winders, *Mr. Polk's Army: The American Military Experience in the Mexican War* (College Station: Texas A&M University Press, 1997), 187.

74   Fehrenbach claims that the isolationist success was partly explainable by Roosevelt's failure to publicly advocate his own position. Fehrenbach, *Undeclared War,* 213. See Leo Kanawada, *Franklin Roosevelt's Diplomacy and American Catholics, Italians, and Jews* (Ann Arbor: University of Michigan Research Press, 1982), 54; Farnham, *Munich Crisis,* 88; Kershaw, *Fateful,* 230, 236–38. For a good account of this debate, see Robert Divine,

first clear public demonstration of support for the Allies was not until the destroyers-for-bases deal in late 1940. However, this was before the 1940 election, and so Roosevelt's internationalism was presented before electoral publics in time for electoral judgment. In the wake of France's surrender to Germany, the Republican Party's nomination of Willkie, a prominent internationalist, instead of isolationist frontrunners Vandenberg and Taft, made it clear that both parties had judged the necessity of an interventionist president for governing in the midst of global crisis. Roosevelt campaigned vigorously on the value of his aid to the allies. On October 28, 1940, Roosevelt pointed out that the isolationists had voted against the 1938 naval expansion, and he described the 1939 repeal of the arms embargo not in terms of neutrality but as aid to the Allies.[75] Of course, he continued to assert, "your boys are not going to be sent into any foreign wars," even as he told his speechwriter that if the United States were attacked the war would no longer be foreign.[76] For these reasons, it is plausible to argue that Roosevelt's 1940 reelection developed some electoral authority, but only in limited ways because both candidates failed to consistently describe their security visions, or their stakes, to the electorate.[77]

The Roosevelt administration's excellence in using executive branch constitutional resources is most fully revealed in its formulation of the policy goals themselves. Roosevelt's policy deliberations clearly reveal an aim to provide for security rather than, say, opportunistically exploit world events for American dominance. However, assessing what kind of

---

"Diplomatic Historians and World War II," *Causes and Consequences of World War II*, ed. Robert A. Divine (Chicago: Quadrangle Books, 1969). William Langer and Everett Gleason conclude that Roosevelt often lagged behind public opinion. Those who defend Roosevelt's conduct as a reliable leader, allowing events to educate the public, include Basil Rauch, *Roosevelt: From Munich to Pearl Harbor* (New York: Creative Age Press, 1950), Herbert Feis, *Churchill, Roosevelt, Stalin: The War They Waged and the Peace They Sought* (Princeton: Princeton University Press, 1967), Trefousse, *Germany*, 53; Manfred Landecker, "FDR's Leadership before World War II: The Concept of Anticipatory Reaction," in Thomas C. Howard and William D. Pederson, eds., *Franklin D. Roosevelt and the Formation of the Modern World* (Armonk, NY: M. E. Sharpe, Inc. 2003).

75 Franklin D. Roosevelt, "Campaign Address at Madison Square Garden, New York City" (October 28, 1940). See also Roosevelt's "Campaign Address at Philadelphia, Pennsylvania" (October 23, 1940).

76 Samuel Irving Rosenman, *Working with Roosevelt* (New York: Harper & Brothers, 1952), 242; Wayne S. Cole, *Roosevelt and the Isolationists, 1932–45* (Lincoln: University of Nebraska Press, 1983), 400.

77 Colin Dueck, *Hard Line: Republican Party and U.S. Foreign Policy Since World War II* (Princeton: Princeton University Press, 2010), 51–53, on how Willkie and Roosevelt's campaigns both replicated ambiguities in public opinion, simultaneously emphasizing security strength and isolation from European affairs. Both the Democratic and Republican Parties offered platforms promising nonparticipation in foreign wars.

policy would protect American security was no easy task. To make that assessment Roosevelt made use of the presidency's capacity for flexibility and responsiveness by adopting an experimental approach toward developing policy in a deteriorating global situation. He almost continually exerted himself toward finding solutions to the European crisis. Roosevelt also mobilized, and even developed further, the branch's diplomatic, ambassadorial, intelligence, and administrative capacities.

In the early 1930s the meaning of Hitler's rise was not transparent to Roosevelt and his advisors, or to the other global powers.[78] While there is obvious benefit from the earliest possible recognition of a tyrant seeking world domination, the idea that Hitler could be made content with Germany's pre-1914 position was at least plausible.[79] Roosevelt used this time of uncertainty to experiment with public policy, gathering more information about the domestic and international context at hand. Early efforts to respond to Hitler involved projects for international disarmament, conferences, and diplomacy.

In the early 1930s, Roosevelt also began developing the Good Neighbor Policy, strengthening alliances in the Western Hemisphere. He began supporting US involvement in international peace efforts, and developed and advocated plans for collective security and disarmament.[80] His development of the idea of collective neutrality was triggered by Congress's failure to grant him revisions to the neutrality legislation he sought in early 1936: "Obliged to be neutral, Roosevelt would find a way for neutrals to act."[81] In the mid-1930s he developed plans for countervailing duties on Germany, supportive monetary policy for the French, more disarmament policies including overtures to other nations, a World Diplomatic Conference, and a series of ideas about blockades.[82] Some of these policy avenues lay on repugnant policy premises: for example, international conferences including the dictators, while at the same moment planning

78   Farnham, *Munich Crisis*, 81.

79   Robert Jervis, "Intelligence and Foreign Policy: A Review Essay," *International Security* 11:3 (1986): 141–61, 151; Tierney, *Spanish Civil War*, 28.

80   Sumner Welles, *Seven Decisions that Shaped History* (New York: Harper, 1951), 77–78; Farnham, *Munich Crisis*, 80–85; Richard Harrison, "A Neutralization Plan for the Pacific: Roosevelt and Anglo-American Cooperation, 1934–1937," *Pacific Historical Review* 57:1 (1988): 47–72; Robert Dallek, *Franklin D. Roosevelt and American Foreign Policy, 1932–1945* (New York and Oxford: Oxford University Press, 1995), 43–47, 69; Robert Divine, *Illusion of Neutrality* (Chicago: University of Chicago Press, 1962), 48, 50–51; Arthur M. Schlesinger, Jr., "Franklin D. Roosevelt's Internationalism," in Cornelius A. Van Minnen and John F. Sears, *FDR and His Contemporaries: Foreign Perceptions of an American President* (New York: Palgrave MacMillan, 1992), 3–16; J. Simon Rofe, *Franklin Roosevelt's Foreign Policy and the Welles Mission* (New York: Palgrave Macmillan, 2007).

81   Farnham, *Munich Crisis*, 79, 128–29.

82   See ibid., 59, 63–69; Rofe, *Welles Mission*, ch. 1.

a naval blockade against Germany.[83] These various avenues allowed him to "keep his options open, politically and strategically, while he searched for a policy that would work both domestically and internationally," but at the same time to develop more information about the international context by gauging the reactions of the dictators and the democracies to his proposals.[84] He characterized his famous Quarantine Speech as an effort to communicate this experimental frame of mind. Roosevelt said the speech advanced an attitude rather than a program: "but it says we are looking for a program."[85]

This experimentalism and policy flexibility meant that the president had developed an array of policy possibilities when crisis did come. Barbara Rearden Farnham notes the extent to which Roosevelt's deliberations, in the midst of the Munich crisis, were framed by policies he had been experimenting with for years:

> In the summer of 1938 . . . he resurrected the notion of economic measures against Germany . . . which he had advanced first in 1936 and again during the *Panay* incident. During the initial phase of the crisis, when he believed the democracies would be forced to fight Hitler, he advanced three other policies with a considerable history: a strategic blockade such as he had contemplated as early as March 1935 and which had reappeared in the Quarantine Speech and during the Nine Power Conference and the *Panay* Incident; expanding the democracies' air forces, an idea he had supported at least since . . . January 1938; and the notion that the United States would provide substantial aid to the democracies. . . . Finally, after deciding to intervene directly . . . Roosevelt turned to a number of other ideas he had entertained throughout the 1930s, such as appealing to the ideals of peaceful settlement of disputes and meaningful negotiations, and he resurrected the notion of an international peace conference, which had been in his mind at least since the Welles Peace Plan.[86]

So too, Lend-Lease, the pivotal redirection of the country's energies toward supporting the Allies, was developed on the basis of his reflections after Munich, when he had considered the value the European democracies might have found in the sale or loan of warplanes.[87] This is an elegant expression of one of Roosevelt's good uses of a constitutional capacity of the presidency. Having used the flexibility of his office to experiment with policy and to gain knowledge about the likely responses of foreign

83   Farnham, *Munich Crisis*, 50.
84   Ibid., 82. On Roosevelt's experimentalism, see also Richard M. Pious, *The American Presidency* (New York: Basic Books, 1979), 142, 154–55.
85   Farnham, *Munich Crisis*, 83; Bor, *United States*, 383.
86   Farnham, *Munich Crisis*, 131–32.
87   Kershaw, *Fateful*, 223.

and domestic audiences, at moments of crisis and pivotal policy change, the president was equipped with a variety of already-developed policy resources. It should be noted that Roosevelt's full expression of this dimension of processual authority was related to the length of time he had been in office. By 1942 he had been grappling with gathering threats in Europe for almost ten years.

Of course, Roosevelt's experimentalism is also criticized for giving wavering and inconsistent signals to Hitler and the allies, or for policy drifting.[88] Under the relational conception of war authority, presidential authority can also be bolstered by taking strong, consistent lines toward dictators when that policy is a well-defended security judgment. There is a range of constitutionally authoritative ways to use presidential capacities because the capacities themselves are diverse.

Yet another of Roosevelt's processual strengths was his effective use of diplomatic and intelligence channels. Throughout the lead-up to World War II, his reports from Ambassadors Bullitt, Messersmith, Bowers, and Kennedy, who were warning about cataclysmic war, and his consultations with Secretary Morgenthau, seemed to be robust, energetic, engaged, and truthful.[89] The testimonies of his cabinet members indicate that they believed they were engaged in serious exchanges.[90] Roosevelt was willing to acknowledge mistakes: he told Ambassador Bowers that he had been right all along about the Spanish Civil War.[91] Managing these diplomatic resources during the Spanish Civil War taught Roosevelt about some of the political consequences of fascism in Europe, a lesson representatives in other branches were not exposed to in the same way. The benefit he received from his diplomatic position was not limited to the information he was able to access from others. He also benefited in that his experience with diplomacy and negotiation informed his sense about what kinds of policies would best advance his security goals. For example, witnessing at Munich the meaning that major negotiators for France and Britain

88   Frederick W. Marks III, *Wind Over Sand: The Diplomacy of Franklin D. Roosevelt* (Athens: University of Georgia Press, 1988); Edward M. Bennett, *Franklin D. Roosevelt and the Search for Security: American-Soviet Relations, 1933–1939* (Wilmington: Scholarly Resources, 1985), 192; James MacGregor Burns, *Roosevelt: The Lion and the Fox* (New York: Harcourt, Brace, 1956), 262; Dorothy Borg, *The United States and the Far Eastern Crisis of 1933–1938* (Cambridge: Harvard University Press, 1964); Kershaw, *Fateful*, 188, citing the title of ch. 3 of Warren F. Kimball, *Forged in War: Churchill, Roosevelt, and the Second World War* (London: William Morrow, 1997).

89   On disagreement between advisors, see Farnham, *Munich Crisis*, 98–99. See also Kershaw, *Fateful*, 197.

90   Rofe, *Welles Mission*, 17.

91   Tierney, *Spanish Civil War*, 53.

attached to air power led Roosevelt to orient his domestic efforts toward the massive production of planes.[92]

Roosevelt also ensured that the resources of the executive branch were pursuing the aims he judged important. He was bureaucratically engaged and attentive.[93] He worked to develop branch capacities in preparation for the danger he saw. After German triumph in Western Europe, Roosevelt began building bureaucratic capacity, relying on World War I legislation to create defense agencies and to establish coordinating bureaus for wartime governance.[94] In June 1940 he replaced an "ineffectual" Secretary of Navy with Frank Knox, and replaced an almost-isolationist Secretary of War with Henry Stimson.[95] Roosevelt elevated members of the executive branch whose judgment he saw as sound even if they challenged him: in 1938, several months after General George Marshall challenged Roosevelt "outright . . . at an important meeting," leading those present to believe Marshall had ended his career, Roosevelt promoted Marshall to chief of staff.[96] Marshall's elevation was highly consequential for US strength. Consider only the importance of Marshall's May 1940 prevailing on Roosevelt to reconsider his rejection of a proposal for $657 million for the army, leading Roosevelt to reverse his decision on a critical issue of wartime preparedness.[97]

Roosevelt has a reputation for having fostered confusion within his administration.[98] This confusion was conditioned in part by the range of views of his closest advisors, a range that supported the president's policy flexibility as he was able to "oscillate between options as he chose."[99] He would frequently set offices at cross-purposes and intervene at various levels of the administration to keep watch. He fostered a competitive spirit between his subordinates. However, there is no indication he manipulated intelligence or subverted his advisors' exercise of sound judgment.

The third dimension of the processual criteria is about the extent to which the president positioned his judgments within an interbranch deliberative system. Because war is a shared power, the branches should

92 Farnham, *Munich Crisis*, 74, 94, 162, 169, 178–86.
93 Kershaw, *Fateful*, 305, 306.
94 Ibid., 203; Langer and Gleason, *Challenge*, 478.
95 Kershaw, *Fateful*, 203.
96 Ibid., 205.
97 Ibid.
98 See Pious, *American Presidency*, 240–42; Rofe, *Welles Mission*, 15–17, 20–22; but also Raymond Moley, "History's Bone of Contention," *Franklin D. Roosevelt: A Profile*, ed. William Leuchtenburg (New York: Hill and Wang, 1967), 157.
99 Kershaw, *Fateful*, 206.

make their policy and constitutional judgments available for one another's scrutiny. Constructing a good meaning of "defensive" security in the context of a particular time requires good political judgment. The president, while he may be justified in using discretionary powers to advance his own concept of national security, should also contribute to the broader development of good political judgment by making his concept of defense available to Congress. A president who offers his security vision so as to enable Congress's review and judgment behaves with more constitutional authority than one who does not. This is a pro-Congress position, but not because legislative authority is plenary. Under the relational conception, for a president to maintain deliberative relationship with Congress increases the constitutional authority of his judgments, even if the president and Congress are at odds.[100] Here, I argue that more serious differences between the presidents emerge.

Polk is notorious for his secretive and closed war governance. Consider legislative sentiment on the location of Texas's borders. One of his first acts in office was to reject a Senate request for the Tyler administration correspondence on the February congressional annexation resolution on the grounds of "injury to the public interest."[101] It is also likely he wanted to conceal his own duplicity. Tyler had negotiated Texas annexation through a House, not the Senate, version of the annexation offer after Senator Benton and allies felt they had received a commitment from Tyler to choose the Senate version.[102] Polk had privately assured legislators during this stalemate that, if left discretion to handle the matter on his own, he would renegotiate a treaty with Texas. But when he arrived in office, Polk stood by Tyler's approach, leaving many Democrats feeling betrayed.[103] Tyler's papers would have revealed how thoroughgoing Polk's subversion of his agreement truly was. In his May 11 address to Congress, Polk also misrepresented his participation in the war, claiming that only in January 1846—after Texas agreed to annexation—had he

---

100   An obvious question when Congress and the president are at odds is about executive branch lawbreaking. The relational conception does not take a stand on the Constitution and prerogative power. Restrictive theories of prerogative power will heighten the costs to a presidency of full transparency to Congress when he contemplates legislative opposition, because achieving transparency may impair his practical efficacy (when the legislature finds out his intentions and then statutorily restricts him). Permissive theories of prerogative power imply that if the president presents his case to Congress, and Congress disagrees and bars him statutorily, he retains a capacity to actually violate statutory law in a constitutionally defensible way. At stake is the US Constitution's capacity to align its incentives surrounding the production of constitutional authority with its incentives surrounding effective governance.

101   Wheelan, *Invading Mexico*, 53.

102   Merry, *Designs*, 136.

103   Ibid., 136, 137; Wheelan, *Invading Mexico*, 54.

authorized Taylor to use defensive force. These subversions continued throughout the war.

Polk also failed to rhetorically advance a reasonable defensive security judgment. The security claim that the administration made to justify its bellicosity toward Mexico was about Mexican intransigence and possible British interference and colonization.[104] But prior to Texas annexation, Sam Houston was giving public speeches to overflowing crowds who were applauding Houston's strategic flirtations with the British to get better terms from the Americans.[105] Polk had access to this information, although the general public did not. There was no institutionally specific reason to believe Polk had information about threat that others could not apprehend or make sense of. To the contrary, Polk's privileged information pointed toward a weak and chaotic adversary unsupported by any of the other major colonial powers—information that made war with Mexico more, not less, appealing to him.[106] As recorded in his diary, he also made these goals clear to his cabinet on May 30, 1846: "I declared my purpose to be to acquire for the United States, California, New Mexico, and perhaps some of the Northern Provinces of Mexico," goals that had been a part of "Mr. Slidell's secret instructions," and whose prospect was more favorable "now, with the United States and Mexico at war."[107]

Polk's deliberative framing of the war also subverted legislative judgment over the complex relationship between the Mexican War and sectional politics of slavery. While the legislature was expansionist, it was not likely that Congress would have authorized an aggressive war with Mexico in order to acquire territory. It is clear that Congress would not have endorsed a war of aggression to extend slave territory (one important possible meaning of the war).[108] Deliberations in Congress about the value of an aggressive, expansionist war with Mexico would have put the attendant slavery politics into sharp relief and enabled legislative judgment on the costs and benefits of expansion given sectional divides over slavery.

---

104 Concerns about a British threat in public discourse of the time arguably tracked a worry that British expansion would undermine southern slavery, since by this time Britain was committed to abolitionism in its foreign policy. On the slavery subtext of fears about British expansion, see Fehrenbacher, *Slaveholding*, 120–21.

105 Merry, *Designs*, 152.

106 Herring, *Colony to Superpower*, 200.

107 Richard Bruce Winders, *Mr. Polk's Army: The American Military Experience in the Mexican War* (College Station: Texas A&M University Press, 1997), 187.

108 When Senator Calhoun attached to the Tyler administration's Texas annexation treaty a statement that the rationale for US annexation was to protect slavery in the South from British interference, the issue exploded in controversy and the treaty was voted down 35 to 16. See Merry, *Designs*, 73–74.

The link between expansion and slavery needed serious scrutiny. The intensity of both sections' interests in expansion masked important links between expansion and a dangerous slavery politics. While slavery was a security concern because of the human security of slaves, it could also lead to rebellion or interstate war. Some historians have argued that the expansion made possible by the Mexican War supported the country's movement toward the Civil War.[109] Some contemporary observers feared the link between the Mexican War, expansion, and the increasing intractability of slavery politics. Before annexation was complete, many political officials, most prominently Henry Clay, were linking Texas annexation, war with Mexico, and a possibly disastrous inflammation of the slavery issue.[110] A few slavery proponents also feared the destabilization of the Mexican War: John Calhoun compared Mexico to a forbidden fruit that would kill the Republic.[111] When the war ended, Emerson wrote, "it will be as the man who swallows the arsenic which brings him down.... Mexico will poison us."[112]

Polk and his predecessor Tyler were able to procedurally subsume this politics. President Jackson, wishing to avoid even the risk of challenge, had waited until the day before he left office to recognize Texan independence. Free state opposition kept the first annexation treaty, of June 1844, from garnering a two-thirds Senate approval and split Democrats along North-South lines.[113] But Tyler created a procedural end-run around the Senate by annexing Texas through joint resolution, not treaty. Fidelity to the preestablished constitutional procedure, in this case, would have blocked Texas annexation until the Senate—the chamber with the most at stake in territorial expansion—was able to come to terms with the balance of power implications of that policy. Polk, too, procedurally subsumed legislative judgment by pitching the war as a defensive one and then convincing House Democrats to debate the Mexican War under closed rules allocating less than two hours. This constriction of legislative inquiry at the moment when debate would have been most consequential

109   Arthur Bestor, "The American Civil War as a Constitutional Crisis," *The American Historical Review* 69: 2 (1964): 327–52. See also Bernard DeVoto, *The Year of Decision 1846* (Boston: Houghton Mifflin, 1942), 496; William Wiecek, *Sources of Antislavery Constitutionalism in America, 1760–1848* (Ithaca: Cornell University Press, 1977), 277.

110   Clay, "Letter"; Merry, *Designs*, 120–24.

111   Bill Kauffman, *Ain't My America: The Long, Noble History of Antiwar Conservatism and Middle-American Anti-Imperialism* (New York: Metropolitan Books, 2008), 33. But see also Merry, *Designs*, 67–68, 73–74, on Calhoun's earlier expansionism.

112   Ralph Waldo Emerson, Charles Johnson, and William H. Gilman, *The Selected Writings of Ralph Waldo Emerson* (New York: Signet Classics, 1965), 116.

113   Merry, *Designs*, 113.

kept bellicosity around the Texas question moving forward despite its consequences for slave politics.

Polk failed to deliberatively integrate—or to support the legislature's deliberative integration of—the security concerns of slavery with those of the Mexican War. The politics of slavery was intensifying in the lead-up to war. Northern Whigs, incensed by the possibility of five new slave states along the Rio Grande, "increasingly coalesced behind the politics of abolitionism," in turn pressuring northern Democrats.[114] Southerners perceiving the movement of the Whigs, and the split in the Democratic Party, as fearsome developments began to say that secession might come if annexation failed. There is "no evidence" that Polk considered or reflected upon these developments at all. He seemed to consider slavery "a side issue, something that just got in the way of the important political objectives."[115] While his journals reveal his desire to "put my face alike against Southern agitators & Northern fanatics & ... do everything in my power to allay excitement by adjusting the question of slavery and preserving the Union,"[116] Polk was relatively unsophisticated in calculating the interrelationship between these different policy arenas. In fact, prior to the election Polk's concern was to decouple, rather than integrate, the issues of slavery and expansion "in order to get the full benefit from the annexation emotions emerging within the country."[117]

Congress's unwillingness to consent to a war of acquisition through a prospective, expansionist frame rather than through a retrospective, defensive frame was arguably in part rooted in the political consequences expansion would have for that very institution. Legislative blocks are not always simply obstacles to be overcome. They may also carry valuable information about the consequence of the suggested reform. If the House and Senate had been more insistent upon their institutional prerogatives, or if Tyler and Polk had respected the meaning of these legislative "failures" (failure to do what the presidents wanted the Congress to do), then the legislature would have had more deliberative space to integrate the deep and complex challenge that expansion posed for the balance of power between the states. Given that the issue of slavery and expansion could foster either rebellion or interstate war, such integration of security policy was, I argue, important.

Many histories of the war discuss Congress's failure to deeply involve itself in the conduct of the war, including deliberations over its aims.[118]

---

114   Ibid., 129.

115   This was a perspective broadly shared by Democrats during the Jacksonian ascendancy. See ibid., 129–30.

116   Quaife, *Diary*, 299.

117   Merry, *Designs*, 97.

118   See, for example, Mahin, *Olive Branch*, 183.

What looks like Congress's weakness from the point of view of efficacy in carrying out a public policy was a notable strength in terms of providing information about possible consequences of massive expansion. Slavery politics undermined Congress's ability to achieve a consensus view on the extent of territory to be acquired from Mexico in treaty negotiations. Congress's stalemate in turn gave Polk room to conceal and maneuver around Congress.[119] Polk interpreted Congress's difficulty managing this politics as licensing a zone of pure discretion for himself. By failing to interpret this important aspect of Congress's inability to act effectively, Polk missed a critical contextual signal about the unstable demands of territorial governance.

Polk's constitutional deficiencies are sometimes described only procedurally. Abraham Lincoln argued in the House against "the continual effort of the President to argue every silent vote given for supplies, into an endorsement of the justice and wisdom of his conduct."[120] Lincoln implied that Polk had blocked the Congress from judging the war. Articulating a position that was not Polk's, Lincoln wrote, "Let me first state what I understand to be your position. It is, that if it shall become *necessary*, *to repel invasion*, the President may, without violation of the Constitution, cross the line and *invade* the territory of another country; and that, whether such *necessity* exists in a given case, the President is to be the *sole* judge." Lincoln objected that this would mean allowing the president "to make war at pleasure."[121]

But Lincoln misstated Polk's position. Only after Korea did anyone advance the claim for presidential powers that Lincoln describes here. In fact, Polk sought authorization from Congress after troops had been attacked, and he achieved that authorization through overwhelming majorities.[122] Despite Polk's efforts to procedurally undermine legislative governance, Congress had some opportunity to judge the president when it voted to authorize and fund the war.[123]

---

119   Ibid., 183.

120   Lincoln, "From Speech in the U.S. House of Representatives on the War with Mexico," *Lincoln: Selected Speeches and Writings* (Vintage Books, 1992), 60.

121   Abraham Lincoln to William Herndon, (February 14, 1848), quoted in Gordon Silverstein, *Imbalance of Powers: Constitutional Interpretation and the Making of American Foreign Policy* (New York: Oxford University Press, 1997), 49.

122   See discussion in Silverstein, *Imbalance*, 49.

123   Whigs, remembering the fate of the Federalists after the Hartford Convention pressed their grievances surrounding the War of 1812, decided to support war funding even as they rhetorically opposed the war itself. Conscience Whigs argued that opposition should be thoroughgoing. See Daniel Walker Howe, *The Political Culture of American Whigs* (Chicago: University of Chicago Press, 1984).

Lincoln's procedural criticism, I argue, is better conceived as a processualist one. The problem is not that Congress was procedurally barred from voting on the Mexican War. It is that Polk's conduct framed the problem as one of defense even though the Mexican War was not a defensive war. Polk's "defensive" intervention structured an agenda for Congress that allowed for expansionist policy aims to play out in the legislature without deliberative accountability, and with their complexities receiving insufficient deliberation given their importance. Some legislators were mobilized and ready to debate these links. Legislative authority is at its height in scrutinizing the complex interrelationship of multiple security dimensions, such as those at stake in the relationship between slavery and the Mexican War. Polk's introduction of the issue through an inappropriate defensive frame, and his failure to address the sectional conflict at stake in the Mexican War, meant that his contribution subverted rather than supported legislative judgment over the important security issues at stake.

While a president need not respond to all criticisms of every party faction, the links between slavery and the Mexican War were important enough security considerations to merit fuller deliberation before the fact. Debating the war through the frame of a "defensive" security need supported deliberative evasion by both institutions.

In addition to subverting Congress's opportunity to judge important interrelated policy concerns, Polk also failed to advance a constitutional theory of the presidency to ground his use of discretionary powers. His inaugural made a Jacksonian promise to "assume no powers not expressly granted or clearly implied" in the Constitution, vowed to fight threats to the union, and declared the value of expansionism. Beyond that, Polk simply did not have much of a security policy or constitutional judgment to offer the country. Insofar as he failed to rhetorically develop an adequate constitutional and policy challenge, Polk behaved to subvert rather than challenge the received structures of interbranch accountability. Perhaps this was unsurprising in light of his goals and the powerful public response he was able to evoke. But the consequence was to undermine the constitutional authority available to him under the relational conception. Insofar as Polk used discretionary powers to advance a war that was not defensively necessary, and insofar as this conduct created a pretextual "defensive" framing of the war that subverted legislative judgment on the complex links between the Mexican War and domestic slavery politics, legislative critics were right to charge him with usurping legislative war authority.

Roosevelt's conduct, while it also displayed deliberative gaps, achieved more of the constitutional authority associated with responsiveness than did Polk's.[124] A strength of Roosevelt's relationship with Congress was his activity in communicating a sense of threat. In 1939 he began speaking more frankly to members of Congress, addressing the link between the fate of the democracies and the fate of the United States, even as these exchanges risked exploding into public relations fiascos.[125] In 1939, after Germany invaded Poland and Britain declared war, Roosevelt also committed himself fully to the battle of neutrality revision.[126] He called a special session of Congress, presented his neutrality revisions in person, and extensively mobilized the political resources of the executive branch to achieve what would be the 1939 Neutrality Act. In this effort Roosevelt told Congress he regretted the earlier neutrality acts.[127] But at the same time he insisted "he was reverting to traditional standards of neutrality," emphasized that the United States was "desiring to preserve its neutrality in wars between foreign states and desiring also to avoid involvement therein," argued for strengthening existing legislation to bar American ships from combat zones, and did not suggest that he wished to aid the Allies.[128] Roosevelt hoped to expose that a commitment to neutrality was not consistent with staying out of war, although isolationists viewed these goals as linked. However, he did not challenge the paradigm of neutrality itself. After almost six weeks of debate he achieved important, but still limited, revisions to neutrality.

Roosevelt again mobilized to persuade Congress in May 1940, after Germany invaded the Low Countries and the battle in France began. The president declared an emergency and on May 16, 1940, requested from Congress an immense program for defensive armament. He slipped into this speech a request that Congress not "hamper or delay the delivery of American-made planes to foreign nations which have ordered them, or

---

124   In a few cases, it is clear that Roosevelt actively dissembled, for example presenting false maps, or withholding the precise value of US aid and transfers from Congress in order to avoid controversy. Such moments are troubling from both democratic theoretical and constitutionalist points of view. For discussion of these, see Persico, *Espionage*, 126, 127–28; Tierney, *Spanish Civil War*, 84; Alvah Bessie, ed., *Alvah Bessie's Spanish Civil War Notebooks* (Lexington: University of Kentucky Press, 2002), 16; Fellmeth, "Law of Neutrality," 485.

125   Farnham, *Munich Crisis*, 195.

126   Ibid., 203–11.

127   Franklin D. Roosevelt, "Message to Congress in Extraordinary Session Regarding the 1939 Neutrality Act" (September 21, 1939), reprinted in Franklin D. Roosevelt, *Roosevelt's Foreign Policy, 1933–1941* (New York: Wilfred Funk, Inc., 1942), 194.

128   Quotes are from Herring, *Colony to Superpower*, 518; "Neutrality Act of 1939," *The American Journal of International Law* 34:1, Supplement: Official Documents (January 1940): 44–74.

seek to purchase more planes." The language of Roosevelt's request emphasized the American responsibility to prepare for an attack, and never indicated a plan to enter the war on behalf of the Allies. But Roosevelt also subtly located the US security interest in terms of an imperative to protect "the whole American Hemisphere against invasion or control or domination by non-American nations."[129] Congress acceded as France fell. Roosevelt and the Cabinet began full-out war preparation and Congress joined in, achieving planning for defense production, mobilization of industry, ship and airplane building, plans for wartime monetary policy, and finally instituting the Selective Service and Training Act.[130] It is plausible that the United States would not have been equipped to win the war when it did if it had not started arming then.[131]

By September 1940 Roosevelt's abandonment of neutrality was becoming more clear in the content, but not rhetoric, of his decision-making with the destroyers-for-bases deal. This decision, a clear public manifestation of Roosevelt's partiality, was unilateral, but open, and it happened only months before the presidential election in which he faced internationalist Willkie.[132] After reelection Roosevelt went further, finally in December of 1940 articulating the US security interest at stake in Britain's victory. The address was a call to arms, telling Americans that "[t]he Nazi masters of Germany have made it clear that they intend not only to dominate all life and thought in their own country, but also to enslave the whole of Europe, and then to use the resources of Europe to dominate the rest of the world," and that "[w]e know now that a nation can have peace with the Nazis only at the price of total surrender."[133] Yet even with this level of threat, Roosevelt asked only that the United States send war materiel.

Lend-Lease was the major vehicle for his confrontation with Congress over the security paradigm that would govern US war politics. Despite the Nazi menace he had pointed to, Roosevelt still justified the bill in terms of American neutrality. He emphasized that the goods were to be lent, not donated. His limited aspirations were informed by the extraordinary mobilization of isolationists, for whom this was to be the decisive debate. After some months, some urged him to take action to cut

129 "Address Delivered by President Roosevelt to the Congress" (May 16, 1940), U.S. Department of State, Publication 1983, *Peace and War: United States Foreign Policy, 1931–1941* (Washington, D.C.: U.S., Government Printing Office, 1943), 525–31.

130 Fehrenbach, *Undeclared War*, 96, 123, 155.

131 Ibid., 142.

132 For discussion, see Langer and Gleason, *Challenge to Isolation*, xii.

133 "Radio Address Delivered by President Roosevelt From Washington, December 29, 1940". Available at http://teachingamericanhistory.org/library/index.asp?document=657 (accessed October 24, 2011).

the debate short. But Roosevelt's response was that "he *preferred* a full
and exhaustive debate, so that its conclusion with the passage of the law
by Congress could be seen as a democratic sign of real national unity."[134]
Luther Gulick, who had supported Roosevelt's administrative reorganization efforts, "marveled at his patience."[135]

Months after the passage of Lend-Lease, Roosevelt spelled out the
logic of a new security policy. On May 27, 1941, he proclaimed an un-
limited national emergency and told the nation he would "not hesitate"
to use military force to repel Germany from establishing bases in the
Atlantic. All strikes would be defensive:

> [T]he United States is mustering its men and its resources only for purposes
> of defense—only to repel attack. . . . But we must be realistic when we use the
> word "attack"; we have to relate it to the lightning speed of modern warfare.
> Some people seem to think that we are not attacked until bombs actually drop
> in the streets of New York or San Francisco or New Orleans or Chicago. But
> they are simply shutting their eyes to the lesson that we must learn from the
> fate of every Nation that the Nazis have conquered. . . . [W]e know enough
> by now to realize that it would be suicide to wait until they are in our front
> yard.[136]

On September 11, 1941, Roosevelt elaborated his policy position with
the speech "When You See a Rattlesnake Poised to Strike, You Do Not
Wait Until He Has Struck Before You Crush Him," which brilliantly used
a familiar experience of gathering threat to explain the complex logic of
collective security. The images of a snake about to strike, or a neighbor
lending a hose, provided basic images of threat and solidarity that made
the complex situation Roosevelt saw more broadly intelligible. Here
Roosevelt explicitly claimed authority to exercise defensive war powers:

> My obligation as President is historic; it is clear. . . . It is no act of war on our
> part when we decide to protect the seas that are vital to American defense. The
> aggression is not ours. Ours is solely defense. . . . From now on, if German or
> Italian vessels of war enter the waters, the protection of which is necessary for
> American defense they do so at their own peril. . . . That is my obvious duty in
> this crisis. That is the clear right of this sovereign Nation.[137]

---

134   Luther Gulick, *Administrative Reflections from World War II* (Birmingham: University of Alabama Press, 1948), 42, as cited in Farnham, *Munich Crisis*, 86, fn. 138.

135   Ibid.

136   President Franklin Roosevelt, "We Choose Human Freedom," (May 27, 1941),
Public Papers, 181. ("(May 27, 1941), *Public Papers 1941*, 181.")

137   Ibid.

This was the constitutional premise for Roosevelt's major exercises of discretionary executive power prior to 1941 as well, although the constitutional authority of his behavior was amplified after he articulated its premises to Congress.

A serious limitation of Roosevelt's communication was that, even as he sought to aid the democracies, his communications to Congress continued to rely on a paradigm of neutrality.[138] Does this represent a subversion of his constitutional obligation to foster interbranch responsiveness and deliberation?

To judge this, we should note the difference between public opinion and the legislature. Isolationist legislators were alert and attentive, and they were savvy in interpreting even the limited cues Roosevelt offered. In fact, it is that savviness that made Roosevelt hedge so deeply. Isolationists saw the logic of Roosevelt's choices. In 1939 they correctly predicted that repealing the arms embargo would be followed by an effort to repeal first the cash, and then the carry requirement.[139] In the passage of Lend-Lease they anticipated the need for convoys that Roosevelt in fact seems to have launched.[140] The legislature's sophistication in reading Roosevelt's limited signals makes it difficult to claim that his security paradigm was invulnerable to legislative rebuff. While he did not develop a full vision of a new security policy, the signals he did give were actually rebuffed almost relentlessly.

This brings us to the central dilemma of Roosevelt's experience. Can the relational conception of war authority endorse a president's evasions about his policy and constitutional views, if full transparency is likely to trigger such entrenched political opposition as to make it impossible to provide for public security? Roosevelt's defenders argue that opacity was required because of public ignorance and the mobilization of intransigent isolationists.[141] Critical policies, including aid to Britain, could have been imperiled if Roosevelt had been more vocal about his assessment of global politics. This is how Roosevelt seems to have perceived his own dilemma. How does the relational conception speak to this concern?

---

138 Even as Roosevelt's early orientation toward the conflict was toward helping France and Britain, he criticized neutrality legislation for being overly rigid in a way that amounted to a "complete lack of neutrality." See, e.g., "Press Conference in the White House, April 20, 1938, 2:20 P.M.," and "Press Conference in the White House, April 21, 1938, 9:00 P.M.," as cited in Farnham, *Munich Crisis* 77.

139 Cole, *Roosevelt and the Isolationists*, 411.

140 Herring, *Colony to Superpower*, 526; Reynolds, *Munich to Pearl Harbor*, 127–29.

141 Thomas A. Bailey, *The Man in the Street: The Impact of American Public Opinion on Foreign Policy* (New York: The MacMillan Co., 1948); Robert Endicott Osgood, *Ideals and Self-Interest in America's Foreign Relations: The Great Transformation of the Twentieth Century* (Chicago: University of Chicago Press, 1964), 412.

If circumstances are such that the needs of public security collide with those of interbranch responsiveness, a constitutional official will fail to achieve all of the constitutional authority the office is capable of harnessing. Constitutional authority is dependent upon many features of a context that are outside a single official's control. In these conditions, external social or political conditions make it impossible to harness all of the Constitution's authority. The various dimensions of assessment that the relational conception offers do not necessarily conflict, but in certain political or social contexts, they might create pressures in directions that are repugnant. In these situations we should recognize that the full authority of the constitutional system cannot be achieved, as it can when publics and their representatives are able to maintain robust communication without sacrificing security.

Roosevelt's contributions to the interbranch deliberative system suffered from other gaps as well. The relational conception asks that presidents make their constitutional, as well as security policy, positions available for legislative rebuff. This Roosevelt failed to do. Isolationist legislators were not only resisting an interventionist foreign policy. They also had a constitutional objection, worrying about lawless dictatorship and unreviewable executive power.[142] Isolationists feared an empowered domestic presidency as a security threat of its own, and the civil liberties violations under Wilson during World War I were not reassuring as to the consequences of war for domestic liberties.[143] While their mobilization around constitutional objections have been derided as "only display[ing] their irrelevance,"[144] isolationists were in fact raising important considerations about how new security policy commitments could be achieved without threatening interbranch relationships as they had previously existed. The isolationists were actively bringing into critical focus the emerging dimensions of a new constitutional security order. Isolationists rightly perceived that the kind of security threat Roosevelt was addressing was one that implied vast presidential leadership.

Their concerns were prescient. The new international order heralded by World War II raised obvious questions about how external security obligations would affect the internal relationships of power between Congress and the executive branch. In the 1940 debate over a peacetime draft, leading isolationist Senator Nye prophesied that the legislation

142   Warren Kimball, *The Most Unsordid Act: Lend-Lease, 1939–1941* (Baltimore: The Johns Hopkins University Press, 1969), 163, 171, 176, 179.

143   Julian E. Zelizer, *Arsenal of Democracy: The Politics of National Security—From World War II to the War on Terrorism* (New York: Basic Books, 2010), 37.

144   Alonzo L. Hamby, "World War II: Conservatism and Constituency Politics," in Julian E. Zelizer, ed., *The American Congress: The Building of Democracy* (Boston: Houghton Mifflin Company, 2004), 474–92, 479.

would cast "a yoke of militarism upon us that will not be easily, if ever, cast off."[145] It is difficult to argue that he was wrong. Presidents operating in the post–World War order have found ample resources within the military establishment for lawlessness, violence, and subversion of domestic liberties.

The period from World War II through the early Cold War called for a new constitutional theory of presidential powers in what had become a multilateral world. Lincoln's experience as a wartime president led him to create a new constitutional theory of the Union that could sustain his vision of the presidency and the powers he sought to develop in that branch. So too, such a serious commitment to global security called for a new constitutional theory that could set the terms of relationship between international engagement and domestic constitutionalism. That theory in turn could ground a theory of presidential war powers, including a theory about how these powers would be reviewed. Roosevelt could perhaps have generated a new constitutional theory by attempting to answer the basic constitutional anxiety of the isolationists.

Roosevelt did begin to sketch the outlines of such a theory. In justifying the destroyers-for-bases agreement, the administration developed a novel claim for a form of presidential war authority under the commander-in-chief clause that could even rebut legislative efforts to statutorily restrict the president. Citing *United States v. Curtiss-Wright Export Co*'s (1936) broad language of presidential authority, the opinion argued that to delay by waiting for legislative affirmation, given "present world conditions," was unacceptable.[146] This analysis was an early expression of a theory that the Truman administration would later amplify in its constitutional challenge to the Court and Congress. Roosevelt's January 1944 fireside chat added policy content by giving a broad definition of security; describing security as a human value integrated with economic, social, and moral systems; and presenting the requirements of global security as a relevant problem for the "family of nations."[147] Other elements of his general understanding of politics could have been useful for theorizing a conception of presidential powers in relationship to multilateralism. For example, Roosevelt's conception of democracy was hardly fixated on majoritarian politics, but also emphasized the importance of protecting individual rights, minorities, economic justice, and social inclusion for robust

145 *Congressional Record*, 76th Congress, 3d sess. (1940) 86:10807.

146 Office of the Attorney General, "Opinion on Exchange of Over-Age Destroyers for Naval and Air Bases," *American Journal of International Law* 34:4 (1940): 728–36, 729.

147 Franklin Roosevelt, "Fireside Chat 28: On the State of the Union" (January 11, 1944). Available at http://millercenter.org/president/speeches/detail/3955 (accessed October 24, 2011).

self-governance.[148] This capacious vision of democracy created space for understanding the way multilateral processes can improve constitutional processes domestically.[149] In his January 1944 speech, he also addressed how special interests can capture domestic democratic processes: today this is one important approach for considering the democracy-enhancing capacities of international institutions.[150] Roosevelt addressed the epistemic value of global consultation, noting that "[i]n the last war such discussions, such meetings, did not even begin until the shooting had stopped. . . . There had been no previous opportunities for man-to-man discussions which lead to meetings of minds. And the result was a peace which was not a peace."[151]

Finally, in the limited steps toward global integration that Roosevelt took before his death, he made important preludes to the "bipartisan consensus," a creative form of interbranch review to politically discipline the presidency in a global age. Roosevelt's contribution to the development of the bipartisan consensus was probably more strategic than constitutionalist in its motivations, but an actor need not be motivated by constitutional fidelity to produce policies and processes that the relational conception can endorse. Roosevelt appointed Republican Senator Vandenberg and other elite legislators from both parties to the conferences on the UN Charter because he remembered Wilson's failure with the Treaty of Versailles. His administration supported the development of regular briefings of the SFRC, which ultimately evolved into a mechanism for communicating with elite foreign policy legislators. These opening gestures would pave the way toward a more robust development

148   See Cass R. Sunstein, *The Second Bill of Rights: FDR's Unfinished Revolution and Why We Need It More Than Ever* (New York: Basic Books, 2004). On Roosevelt's development of grand design for postwar international order, see Alexander L. George, "Domestic Constraints on Regime Change in U.S. Foreign Policy," in Ole R. Hosti, Randolph Siverson, and Alexander L. George, eds., *Change in the International System* (Boulder, CO: Westview Press, 1980), 233–62, 244.

149   Robert O. Keohane, Stephen Macedo, and Andrew Moravcsik, "Democracy-Enhancing Multilateralism," *International Organization* 63:1 (2009): 1–31, especially 1–9; Allen Buchanan and Russell Powell, "Constitutional Democracy and the Rule of International Law: Are They Compatible?" *Journal of Political Philosophy* 16:3 (2008): 326–49; Daniel Deudney, *Bounding Power: Republican Security Theory from the Polis to the Global Village* (Princeton: Princeton University Press, 2006).

150   Roosevelt, "Fireside Chat 28"; Keohane et al., "Multilateralism," 5–7; Edward T. Swaine, "The Constitutionality of International Delegations," *Columbia Law Review* 104:6 (2004): 1492–614.

151   "Fireside Chat 28"; Keohane et al., "Multilateralism," 18–20. Also see Alexander Thompson, "Screening Power: International Organizations as Informative Agents," in Darren G. Hawkins, David A. Lake, Daniel L. Nielson, Michael J. Tierney, eds., *Delegation and Agency in International Organizations* (New York: Cambridge University Press, 2006), 229–54.

and articulation of the bipartisan consensus in the early Truman years. Roosevelt's contribution to these limited forms of constitutional review buttressed his claim to war authority, even as his authority would have been yet more buttressed had he articulated in constitutional language the stakes of these political innovations. Roosevelt's rhetorical disengagement with these constitutional challenges meant that he was not yet fully challenging the preexistent order. In this way, the constitutional authority of Roosevelt's war conduct was less monumental than it might otherwise have been.

I have argued in this chapter, using the relational conception, that Roosevelt's conduct leading up to World War II was more constitutionally authoritative than Polk's. Roosevelt used war powers to advance a good conception of defensive security; his security policy was developed in ways that brought the capacities of the executive branch to bear on the question of the meaning of "defense"; and his security vision was made more deeply subject to legislative rebuff. By contrast, while Polk made good use of some of the capacities of the executive branch for making war, he did not use them to construct plausible content for the meaning of "defense." His use of discretionary power was not disciplined by defensive security need, and his action subverted the grounds for legislative judgment by presenting the war with Mexico through a frame that obscured the complex security links between slavery and expansion.

These judgments are controversial, not least because of empirical uncertainty. Making judgments under conditions of large empirical uncertainty is a basic practice of politics. Other interpreters may and will disagree with these substantive and processual assessments of Roosevelt and Polk. Such interpreters would come to different conclusions about the relative constitutional authority of each president's conduct. In a political world governed by the relational conception, constitutional claims, as well as the policy judgments they are linked to, would be challenged vigorously whenever appropriate. This challenge would focus both scholarly and public debate on useful questions of security need and institutional performance as the relevant terms for assessing a president's war authority.

Chapter 3

"UNITING OUR VOICE AT THE WATER'S EDGE"

Legislative Authority in the Cold War and Roosevelt Corollary

A central controversy of war powers today is whether, and under what conditions, the president may directly engage in war without particular legislative authorization. Pro-Congress scholars read Congress's ability to "declare war" as an exclusive power to authorize hostilities, implying that independent presidential war is unconstitutional. This view met a profound challenge in the Korean War, commonly read as the "single most important precedent" for the displacement of Congress in the war powers system.[1] Many see legislative acquiescence to Truman's deployment of troops as a harbinger of constitutional degradation, a turning point in which fast-moving events, widespread fear, and opportunism created an unconstitutional shift in the balance of war authority toward the presidency.[2] Yet we have seen that, by structural implication, the

---

1   Louis Fisher, "The Korean War: On What Legal Basis Did Truman Act?" *The American Journal of International Law* 89:1 (1995): 21–39, 21.

2   Arthur Schlesinger wrote that such vast global responsibilities "overwhelmed the Constitution." Arthur Schlesinger, *The Imperial Presidency* (Boston: Houghton Mifflin Company, 1973), 169. Harold Koh is skeptical that the presidency could "reconcile basic constitutional principles" with the demand to contain communism around the globe. Harold Koh, *The National Security Constitution: Sharing Power after the Iran-Contra Affair* (New Haven: Yale University Press, 1990), 106. Stephen Griffin argues that meeting the global responsibilities of the Cold War required constitutional amendment. Stephen Griffin, *Long Wars and the Constitution: From Truman to Obama* (Cambridge: Harvard University Press, forthcoming), 3, 4 (manuscript). Louis Fisher characterized the period after World War II as "a climate in which Presidents have regularly breached constitutional principles and democratic values." Louis Fisher, *Presidential War Power* (Lawrence: University Press of Kansas, 1995), xi. John Hart Ely contended that the Truman administration's Korean intervention broke with a "long-standing legislative-executive consensus." John Hart Ely,

president must have some powers to engage in hostilities even absent legislative authorization. What is the scope of that power?

War powers literature treats the Korean War as a unique transformative event for broadening the scope of the independent presidential war power. But the Cold War order's combination of legislative acquiescence and independent presidential bellicosity was not unprecedented. Throughout the late nineteenth and early twentieth centuries, presidents and Congresses reworked the Monroe Doctrine into a (Theodore) Roosevelt Corollary that also licensed independent presidential acts of war.[3] Despite Congress's lack of authorization for particular acts of war in both periods, the legislature served as more than a passive onlooker to an out-of-control presidency. Congress participated in creating both the state capacity and a constitutional politics that were permissive of Roosevelt and Truman's conduct. In both contexts, Congress and the presidency tethered a set of distinctive foreign policy objectives to a vision of constitutional authority that empowered the presidency to act independently to pursue those objectives. They created security orders—policy ends and a construction of constitutional meaning that allowed for an empowered presidency to accomplish large national goals.[4] The constitutional dilemmas raised by these orders are similar.

Despite their parallels, the two cases receive very different amounts of attention. Truman's action was quickly challenged. In the early 1950s a "Great Debate" resisted the emergent presidential order, and war powers scholarship today is essentially organized around the constitutional question of Korea.[5] By contrast, constitutional theorists have found little worth investigating in a period when the US president used force countless

---

War and Responsibility (Princeton: Princeton University Press, 1995), 10. See Francis Wormuth and Edwin Brown Firmage, *To Chain the Dog of War: The War Power of Congress in History and Law* (Champaign: University of Illinois Press, 1989), 151. See also Michael J. Glennon, *Constitutional Diplomacy* (Princeton: Princeton University Press, 1991), 80.

3   Walter LaFeber, "The Evolution of the Monroe Doctrine," in *Redefining the Past: Essays in Diplomatic History in Honor of William Appleman Williams*, ed. Lloyd C. Gardner (Corvallis: Oregon State University Press, 1986), 123, 132. Wormuth and Frimage also notice the parallel (*Chain*, 149).

4   Truman and the State Department cited the adventures of Presidents McKinley, Roosevelt, Taft, and Wilson as precedents for presidential war in the Cold War. Undersecretary of State Nicholas Katzenbach, "Hearings before the Senate Committee on Foreign Relations," *U.S. Commitments to Foreign Powers*, 90th Cong., 1st sess., (1967): 126; Jack Werkley, "Truman Says He Can Send Troops to Palestine Without Congress," *New York Herald Tribune* (April 23, 1948).

5   In part this was because of the breathtaking scope and consequence of Truman's constitutional theory of the presidency. See Gordon Silverstein, *Imbalance of Powers: Constitutional Interpretation and the Making of American Foreign Policy* (New York: Oxford University Press, 1997), chapters 2 and 3, 67; Louis Fisher, *Constitutional Conflicts Between Congress and the President* (Lawrence: University Press of Kansas, 1997); David J.

times to organize Caribbean and Latin American affairs to the advantage of the United States and other imperial powers.[6] This, too, may be a reflection of contemporary interest. Congresses of this period debated imperialism, but the period is remarkable for the lack of a sustained challenge to the propriety of independent presidential war. Whether because of the small scale of intervention (from the US perspective), or racism, or from an identification of the nations of Central and South America as "uncivilized," many contemporary officials failed to view these aggressive interventions as acts of war.

In this chapter, I use the relational conception to argue against the quality of the legislature's constitutional construction in the era of the Roosevelt Corollary. Applying the processual standards, I argue that the early Cold War security order was more, not less, constitutionally authoritative than that of the Roosevelt Corollary because its Congresses were able to articulate, challenge, and ultimately ratify its construction of constitutional powers. Applying the substantive standard of defensive war, I also argue that early Cold War Congresses faced a more important national threat, to which broader presidential empowerment for defensive purposes was a reasonable response. For both processual and substantive reasons, then, I argue that the constitutional construction of early Cold War Congresses is easier to defend under the relational conception than the formally parallel, but lower quality pro-presidency construction of the Congresses of the Roosevelt Corollary.

A CONSTITUTIONAL SECURITY ORDER

The president uncontroversially possesses some "defensive" war powers. While this is an implied, not explicit, power, it is uncontroversial in that nobody would deny a president the constitutional authority to repel the attacks of dangerous belligerents at the nation's border, even if Congress had not authorized that action. But importantly, the content of the nation's defensive security interest—that which grounds the president's "defensive" war powers—is politically constructed, through processes that necessarily involve legislative participation. Chapter 2's analysis of the Mexican War and World War II demonstrates that repelling hostile

---

Barron and Martin S. Lederman, "The Commander in Chief at the Lowest Ebb—A Constitutional History," *Harvard Law Review* 121:3 (2008): 689–804, 941.

6   Although see Stromseth's call for "fuller analysis" of the questions these parallels raise. Jane C. Stromseth, "Understanding Constitutional War Powers Today: Why Methodology Matters," *Yale Law Journal* 106:3 (1996): 845–915, 849–51, 887–88.

troops at the border is not the only useful standard for assessing the meaning of "defensive."

The legislature can participate in creating new standards of defense through its construction of a politics that sets priorities and defines vulnerabilities. In both the Cold War and Roosevelt Corollary to the Monroe Doctrine, Congress's weapons decisions, appropriations, treaty ratifications, rhetoric on the floor, and participation in building global institutions were interdependent choices that constructed security orders that were then used to license certain independent acts of executive war authority. After defining a national interest, creating a state capacity to pursue that interest, and constructing an international politics where independent executive acts of war were not only predictable, but actually key ingredients for achieving the kind of foreign policy Congress approved, Congress proceeded to either affirmatively or tacitly ratify particular incidents in which presidents seized the ideological and material tools that Congress had created. The role of Congress in creating these security *orders* has been overlooked by analysis centered on legislative authority for particular acts of war.

The concept of a *security order* is related to the idea of a regime or constitutional order.[7] Stephen Griffin has described a regime order as the "reciprocal relationship among the text of the Constitution, the political and policy objectives of state officials, elites, and the public, and the structure and capacity for action of state institutions."[8] A security order is a combined policy and constitutional construction that specifies and enacts the content of a national security interest; what will be construed as threats to that interest; and a supportive construction of constitutional war authority. The concept of a security order helps make sense of the fact that different regimes in American political development have developed different practices for managing executive-legislative relations in security. It also helps us understand the very different kinds of national interests that have undergirded various conceptions of defense. In contrast to a regime order, I do not mean for the concept of a security order to be temporally bounded. The United States often has multiple security goals and different organizations of security authority to accomplish those different goals; president-legislative relations on European defense, for example, may vary from those associated with the politics of the war on Al-Qaeda.

---

7   Mark Tushnet, *The New Constitutional Order* (Princeton: Princeton University Press, 2004); Karen Orren and Stephen Skowronek, "Institutions and Intercurrence: Theory Building in the Fullness of Time," in *Political Order*, eds. Ian Shapiro and Russell Hardin (New York: New York University Press, 1993).

8   Stephen Griffin, *Long Wars*, 134 (manuscript).

Because a security order is an organizing concept for a particular form of politics, multiple security orders can coexist. The relational conception can be used to evaluate security orders no less than particular exercises of war-making power.

Security orders are not necessarily articulated only in law. For example, the defensive security interest in "repelling hostile troops at the border" has exerted analytic leverage for theorizing presidential powers far beyond its legal expression. Congress can construct national defensive security interests both in its creation of legal architectures and also by mobilizing a politics in which new dimensions of security and vulnerability come to operate as premises, premises that then are reflected in the language of official acts.

Of course, the president, no less than Congress, participated in constructing both of these orders, and it is far more common to assess these orders by analyzing the presidency's often highly visible contributions. For example, one important question is about the extent to which each president's contributions to these new constructions represented either subversions of, or legitimate challenges to, inherited security orders. We can assess a president's deliberative contributions to an order just as we assess the legislature's contributions, by applying the relevant substantive and processual criteria. But this chapter is primarily about legislative, not presidential politics. Whether or not the president is subverting an order, the legislature has an independent power to create security orders, and hence independent responsibilities for its exercise of that power. To these we now turn.

THE ROOSEVELT COROLLARY AND COLD WAR SECURITY ORDERS

To begin analysis, it will be helpful to bring certain features of each case into focus. From the 1890s through the First World War, a series of shocking economic depressions and the closing of the frontier inspired political elites to turn to foreign markets. Opening those markets required controlling the seas, and in pursuit of this control the United States intervened many times throughout Central and South America and the Caribbean. In the Western Hemisphere, this belligerency was justified according to a conception of the Monroe Doctrine reworked by Theodore Roosevelt in his 1904 message to Congress. This did not announce the beginning of the corollary's practical significance, but it was a good formulation of its parameters. Roosevelt invoked a fear that instability in the Western Hemisphere could pave the way for European economic dominance:

Chronic wrongdoing, or an impotence which results in a general loosening of the ties of civilized society, may in America, as elsewhere, ultimately require intervention by some civilized nation, and in the Western Hemisphere the adherence of the United States to the Monroe Doctrine may force the United States, however reluctantly, in flagrant cases of such wrongdoing or impotence, to the exercise of an international police power.[9]

This transformed the Monroe Doctrine from a doctrine of isolation into one of intervention.

Roosevelt was explicit about the constitutional dimension of the power he sought. His invocation of an "international police power" claimed presidential authority to initiate war pursuant, not to authorization either by Congress or by international institutions, but rather to his own conception of global and domestic normativity. The Roosevelt Corollary is conceptually consistent with a number of interventions before 1905: the 1893–94 deployment of warships to Brazil to suppress a European-supported revolutionary moment; Cleveland's incursion into Panama in 1885; and Roosevelt's support for the Panamanian revolution and US acquisition of the Panama Canal Zone in 1903 are all easily decipherable through the Roosevelt Corollary.[10] After this address, presidents went on to cite the corollary as a premise for incursions into the Philippines, Cuba, Nicaragua, Haiti, and the Dominican Republic.[11] It was applied in 1905 when Roosevelt forced the Dominican Republic to accept an American economic advisor as the financial director of that state, and in the formation of a provisional government in Cuba in 1906.[12] As in the Cold War, the president acquired a certain habit of

9 Theodore Roosevelt, "1904 Annual Message to Congress" (December 6, 1904). Available at http://www.infoplease.com/t/hist/state-of-the-union/116.html (accessed June 11, 2012). See also his First Annual Message to Congress (December 3, 1901).

10 Daniel H. Wicks, "Dress Rehearsal: United States Intervention on the Isthmus of Panama, 1885," *Pacific Historical Review* 49:4 (1980): 581–605, 582; Walter LaFeber, *The New Empire: An Interpretation of American Expansion, 1860–1898* (Ithaca, NY: Cornell University Press, 1963), 210.

11 Thomas Andrew Bailey, "A Latin American Protests (1943)," in *The American Spirit: Since 1865*, David M. Kennedy and Thomas Andrew Bailey, eds. (Boston: Houghton Mifflin, 1998), 199. Such incursions were often recognized in terms of the Monroe Doctrine even if the Doctrine was not explicitly cited. See Hiram Bingham, *The Monroe Doctrine: An Obsolete Shibboleth* (New York: Da Capo Press, 1976). For an argument that Taft's dollar diplomacy represented a "radically different" security project than Roosevelt's, see Richard Collin, *Theodore Roosevelt's Caribbean* (Baton Rouge: Louisiana State University Press 1990), 86–87.

12 The approach to World War I featured a highly intrusive projection of American power into Central and South America, but its legitimating source was Wilsonian ideas about law and order rather than Monroe Doctrine commitments to resisting European

intervention, and continued to engage in acts of war on his own initiative, even as the relevance of the particular security aims associated with the Roosevelt Corollary declined. The president also intervened in China to protect markets, but without linking that protection to US security from European affairs (some of these could be construed as interventions outside of any security order, i.e., orderless interventions). By 1934 Franklin Roosevelt had formally repudiated the Roosevelt Corollary.

The imperialist aspiration behind the Roosevelt Corollary was not new; after the Civil War, a restored nation looked outward. Some Roosevelt Corollary interventions had nineteenth-century prequels in which the president's aspiration toward war was disciplined by Congress. For example, in 1892, the president intervened in a dispute between Chile and England. Turning to Congress, Harrison delivered a ringing message reviewing an assault on American soldiers and an "impudent" Chilean response, concluding that Congress, which under the Constitution had the sole power to declare war, should "take such action as may be deemed appropriate."[13] Chile paid an indemnity, and the confrontation was resolved without force. Just a decade later, a supportive politics had developed such that this pattern of facts—Latin American "impudence," a small property claim or strike on the honor of American citizens or military, and the presence of European influence—would be a premise for independent executive bellicosity.

Were these acts of war? While Cold War officials noted similarities, pro-Congress scholars Louis Fisher, E. Corwin, and Arthur Schlesinger have resisted the parallels between the war acts under the Roosevelt Corollary and those of the Cold War on the grounds that the early twentieth-century interventions were "modest in scope."[14] This resistance to the

---

influence (and hence should be construed either as part of a different security order, or as orderless acts). For more on the difference in these presidents' uses of the war power, see James R. Holmes, *Theodore Roosevelt and World Order: Police Power in International Relations* (Washington, DC: Potomac Books Inc., 2006), 83.

13   LaFeber, *New Empire*, 135.

14   Senator Connally made the precedential connection explicit when he stated that "[t]he Atlantic Pact is but the logical extension of the principle of the Monroe Doctrine." U.S. Senate, Committee on Foreign Relations, 81st Cong., 1st sess., *Hearings on the North Atlantic Treaty* (1949), 231. For resistance to the parallels, see Edward S. Corwin, *Presidential Power and the Constitution: Essays* (Ithaca, NY: Cornell University Press, 1976); Louis Fisher, *Congressional Abdication on War and Spending* (College Station: Texas A&M University Press, 2000), 21; Henry P. Monaghan, "Presidential War Making" *Boston University Law Review* 50:1 (1970): 26–27; Schlesinger, *Imperial*. See too Jules Lobel, "'Little Wars' and the Constitution," *University of Miami Law Review* 50:1 (1995): 61–79. Fisher's resistance to the parallel is confusing given his belief that Libyan bombings are "war," regardless of the limited scale of hostilities. Louis Fisher, "Military Operations in Libya: No War? No Hostilities?'" *Presidential Studies Quarterly* 42:1 (2012): 176–89.

formal precedent is ironic, because justifying Roosevelt's acts of war as "small" was the answer early twentieth-century imperialists gave to the pro-Congress advocates of their own time. Using scope to distinguish between legitimate and illegitimate presidential bellicosity not only problematically elevates imperialist arguments of the early twentieth century, but more importantly, begs rather than answers the question of how we should theorize the intersection between presidential and legislative war authority. Are presidents authorized to engage in acts of "minor" war without legislative assent? The framers believed that "repelling sudden attacks" justified independent presidential war. Is scope a better alternative? Why? At stake in these cases is precisely the quality of Congress's judgments about the conditions under which a president should be independently empowered.

If the imperialism of the Roosevelt Corollary was in part inspired by economic turmoil, the Cold War order was characterized by fears about a global communist menace. After World War II, Congress and the president together developed a series of policy pathways for countering communism. One of these relied upon new international institutions, prominently the United Nations and the North Atlantic Charter, which could sustain the political conditions for global liberalism and defend allied countries from communist intrusions. The enemies, first the Soviet Union and then China, were construed as making long-term plans that would be responsive to force rather than diplomacy or negotiation. This new ideology called not only for the creation of long-term global alliances and institutions, but also for military preparedness and executive empowerment to respond to communist confrontations at any moment.[15]

The emergence of an order of executive empowerment was apparent before Korea. When Woodrow Wilson sent troops to revolutionary Russia without authorization from Congress, legislators threatened to cut off funding and convinced the administration to withdraw forces.[16] But in 1948 Truman, after consultation with foreign policy leaders in Congress, claimed power to send US troops to Palestine as part of a UN force without congressional approval. Senator Vandenberg supported this bid,

---

15   Michael J. Hogan, *A Cross of Iron: Harry S. Truman and the Origins of the National Security State, 1945–1954* (Cambridge: Cambridge University Press, 1998): 10–14. Kennan to the Secretary of State, February 22, 1946, U.S. Department of State, *Foreign Relations of the United States, 1946* (Washington, DC: GPO, 1969), 6: 696–709 and X (George F. Kennan), "The Sources of Soviet Conduct," *Foreign Affairs* 25 (July 1947): 566–82.

16   David Foglesong, *America's Secret War against Bolshevism: U.S. Intervention in the Russian Civil War, 1917–1920* (Chapel Hill: University of North Carolina Press, 1995), 71, 251.

which was unopposed by the legislature.[17] Like the 1903 Panama incursion, the Korean War was not a one-off incident. More interventions followed: in Formosa (Taiwan), Vietnam, and Central America.

The president's perspective on the emerging Cold War security order was crystallized in NSC-68, a highly secret document drafted by the National Security Council and promulgated through the White House just months before Korea.[18] The document has been called a "white paper for a new constitutional order."[19] NSC-68 did not call for any alteration to the Constitution, nor did it specifically advocate executive branch empowerment. But it cites the Constitution's preamble as the "fundamental purpose" of the United States, and it articulates a global context that threatens this aspiration. Speaking to the two world wars, Russian and Chinese revolutions, and the recurrent violence of the previous thirty-five years, NSC-68 emphasized the role of the United States as the remaining superpower and the USSR's aspiration to "impose its absolute authority over the rest of the world," while gesturing to the catastrophic possibilities of nuclear warfare.[20] It committed the United States to protecting American values as well as "the material environment in which they flourish" and to changing "the world situation by means short of war in such a way as to frustrate the Kremlin design."[21] Its rhetoric suggests rapid US military buildup as a more durable containment strategy than diplomacy.[22]

17   Schlesinger, *Imperial*, 131; Werkley, "Truman Says."

18   Assessing the full constitutional authority of the Cold War order would require evaluating executive branch processes behind moments like the promulgation of NSC-68. The administration was internally divided over NSC-68's framing of the security context. George Kennan and Charles Bohlen, both of the State Department, and Secretary of Defense Louis Johnson raised concerns that it would "make American policies too rigid, simple, and militaristic" and that it would "bankrupt the country." Secretary of State Acheson overruled these advisors. Walter LaFeber, *America, Russia, and the Cold War 1945–1992*, 7th ed. (New York: McGraw Hill, Inc., 1993), 96, 98.

19   Griffin, *Long Wars*, 90 (manuscript). For more on the elements of the Cold War consensus, see Eugene R. Wittkopf and James M. McCormick, "The Cold War Consensus: Did It Exist?" *Polity* 22:4 (1990): 627–53.

20   "A Report to the National Security Council by the Executive Secretary on United States Objectives and Programs for National Security, April 14, 1950, Washington" (hereafter "NSC-68"), 4.

21   "NSC-68," 13, 9, 12.

22   Ibid., 44–59. The deliberative contribution of NSC-68 is certainly subject to criticism. See John W. Coffrey, "The Statesmanship of Harry S. Truman," *The Review of Politics* 47:2 (1985): 231–52, 246; John Lewis Gaddis, *Strategies of Containment: A Critical Appraisal of Postwar American National Security* (New York: Oxford University Press, 1982), ch. 4.

The Cold War security order was not constructed in a single moment. For example, while Truman's March 1947 speech to Congress laid out many central tenants of the Cold War order, it was the legislative elections of 1948, 1950, and 1952, when Democrats and Republicans competed to perform Cold War ferocity, that solidified the status of this substantive consensus in legislative politics. The question of relative geographic priorities, or the relative importance of military, economic, and diplomatic strength, were worked out over time with Congress.[23]

In addition to this substantive consensus about the nature and location of threat, the Cold War security order also featured two procedural elements. The first was an empowerment of the presidency to act as a first responder to communist disruptions of the global order. The second was the bipartisan consensus, which sought to provide for review of the president without disabling the united political front required to prosecute Cold war aims—to "unite our voice at the water's edge."[24] In exchange for consultation with legislative elites in the formation of public policy, members of Congress would refrain from obstructing presidential initiatives in the legislature.[25] These procedural disciplines depended in part on officials' basic substantive consensus about the importance of the communist threat. Nothing else could inspire presidential contenders, for example, to refrain from publicly challenging one another's foreign policy determinations.[26]

23 Harry Truman, "Special Message to Congress on Greece and Turkey: The Truman Doctrine" (March 12, 1947), *Public Papers of the Presidents of the United States: Harry S. Truman, 1947* (Washington, DC: Government Printing Office, 1963), 176–80; John W. Coffrey, "The Statesmanship of Harry S. Truman," *The Review of Politics* 47:2 (April 1985): 231–52, 241; Julian Zelizer, *Arsenal of Democracy: The Politics of National Security—From World War II to the War on Terrorism* (New York: Basic Books, 2009), 71.

24 The full quote is to "[u]nite our official voice at the water's edge," "Vandenberg to a constituent, January 5, 1950," Arthur H. Vandenberg, Jr., *The Private Papers of Senator Vandenberg* (Boston: Houghton Mifflin Company, 1952), 552, as cited in Philip J. Briggs, "Senator Vandenberg, Bipartisanship and the Origin of United Nations Article 51," *Mid America: An Historical Review* 60:3 (1978):163.

25 Gordon Silverstein emphasizes the difference between influencing policy and controlling it, and the importance of formal delegations of power, especially in a context of judicial oversight. *Imbalance*, 14.

26 Cecile V. Crabb, Jr., *Bipartisan Foreign Policy: Myth or Reality?* (Evanston, IL: Row, Peterson and Company, 1957), 49. The Mackinac Declaration of 1943 united Republican Party leaders for postwar international organization. On the Cold War consensus, see Andrew D. Grossman, "The Early Cold War and American Political Development: Reflections on Recent Research," *International Journal of Politics, Culture, and Society* 15:3 (2002): 471–83; Ole R. Holsti, "The Three-Headed Eagle: The United States and System Change," *International Studies Quarterly* 2:3 (1979): 339–59; Gabriel A. Almond, *The*

MAJOR WAR EVENTS: PANAMA 1903 AND KOREA 1950

The Panamanian intervention of 1903 and the Korean War were pivotal for the public articulation of the content of these respective security orders. Both also established clear templates of intervention within each order.

A watershed moment in the Roosevelt Corollary was the 1903 incursion into Panama. Directly after the Civil War, American leaders had enlarged their claims to the area: President Grant, as well as the House Committee on Foreign Affairs, stated that the canal should belong only to the US.[27] In the early months of the Cleveland administration, in what was to become a military prelude, the president sent a Navy landing force to Panama to pacify a local revolt.[28] Congress was adjourned during this intervention, and when it returned, it attacked the president for his too-early withdrawal from Panama.[29]

Responding in part to domestic pressure, the Senate pressed President McKinley to negotiate and renegotiate a series of treaties between the United States and the United Kingdom over control of the isthmus. The Clayton-Bulwer Treaty, renegotiated in February 1900, broadened US claims to any canal at Britain's expense.[30] Senate agitation seeking yet broader US military access ultimately forced the president to renegotiate that treaty again, resulting in McKinley's Hay-Pauncefote Treaty, which did not forbid the United States from constructing fortifications or require that the canal be kept open in times of war. That treaty also guaranteed that any canal built should never be taken by force. The Senate never specified a domestic enforcement mechanism for that guarantee.

In mid-1902, Congress authorized the president to build a canal in Panama provided a favorable treaty could be arranged with Colombia, but to otherwise turn to Nicaragua. When Colombia rejected the US offer of the Hay-Herrán Treaty, Theodore Roosevelt became incensed. Instead of turning to Nicaragua as required by law, and in violation of

American People and Foreign Policy (New York: Praeger, 1960); Richard Falk, "Lifting the Curse of Bi-partisanship," *World Policy Journal* 1:1 (1983):127–57.

27 Robert Kagan, *Dangerous Nation: America's Place in the World, from Its Earliest Days to the Dawn of the 20th Century* (New York: Alfred A. Knopf, 2006), 305; Thomas A. Bailey, "The Lodge Corollary to the Monroe Doctrine," *Political Science Quarterly* 48:2 (1933): 220–39, 227. For more on the rising tide of American claims, see LaFeber, *New Empire*, 43.

28 Wicks, "Dress Rehearsal," 582.

29 Ibid., 598.

30 Robert E. Hannigan, *The New World Power: American Foreign Policy, 1898–1917* (Philadelphia: University of Pennsylvania Press, 2002), 26.

US treaty obligations to protect Colombian sovereignty in Panama, Roosevelt coordinated military activities with an insurrectionary movement in Panama, backing a coup d'état on behalf of a revolutionary government that was willing to invite the United States into the canal zone. On November 2, 1903, the executive branch sent orders to an American gunboat to "prevent the landing of any armed forces with hostile intent, either government or insurgent."[31] The next day a second American warship docked at Colón and dispatched four hundred Marines to block Colombian claims. On May 6, the United States formally recognized the new Republic of Panama, and the Navy was ordered to form a blockade making it impossible for Colombian vessels to intervene.[32] The Senate quickly ratified a treaty with the new Republic of Panama granting US control of the canal zone. Roosevelt is famous for bragging "I took the canal zone and let Congress debate,"[33] but the legislature in fact largely endorsed his claims and went on to ratify treaties that further entrenched US legal and military control of the area.

Consider now the Korean War. After World War II, having witnessed two major world wars, aware of the threat of nuclear weapons, and perceiving in Stalin the rise of a new totalitarianism, Congress and the executive branch set about building a new global order that could prevent world war and contain global communism. The two major institutions created for these purposes, the UN and NATO, were both constructed with heavy legislative participation. Not only did committee and floor debate on these treaties feature high levels of Senate involvement, but even in their drafting, legislators had been included. The UN Charter, for example, was developed in a set of conferences featuring heavy representation of legislators, most notably Senator Vandenberg, a former isolationist who now spearheaded the movement to contain communism through collective security. The UN Charter, like the bilateral security treaties of the Roosevelt Corollary, did not specify any domestic procedures for authorizing hostilities under the terms of the treaty. Congress resolved this gap by mandating a set of negotiation procedures, highly inclusive of the legislature, in the domestic UN Participation Act (UNPA), specifying that troops would be available to the UN pursuant to a set

31 Dispatch from president to commanders. As cited in Joseph C. Freehoff, *America and the Canal Title: Or, an Examination, Sifting and Interpretation of the Data Bearing on the Westing of the Province of Panama from the Republic of Colombia by the Roosevelt Administration in 1903 in Order to Secure Title to the Canal Zone* (Ithaca: Cornell University Library, 2009) (original ed. 1916), 11.

32 Stephen Kinzer, *Overthrow: America's Century of Regime Change from Hawaii to Iraq* (New York: Times Books, 2006), 61.

33 Peter Irons, *War Powers: How the Imperial Presidency Hijacked the Constitution* (New York: Metropolitan Books, 2005), 97.

of legislatively authorized special agreements. In 1950 no such special agreements had been executed.

In the wake of World War II, a UN Temporary Commission on Korea partitioned North and South Korea. In June of 1950 North Korea invaded South Korea by crossing the 38th parallel: the first major boundary trespass after World War II. To observers who saw a resurgence of the threat of global totalitarianism in both Stalin's ascension, and in the Soviet-China alliance, this plausibly represented a recurrence of Hitler's encroachments. The UN Security Council adopted a resolution terming the attack a "breach of the peace," calling upon the authorities of North Korea to withdraw to the 38th parallel, and asking UN members for assistance. North Korea ignored the Council resolution, and on June 27 Truman ordered American forces to the defense of South Korea.[34] Days later the UN issued a resolution calling for armed resistance. Truman's conduct went beyond what was legally requested by the UN. He intervened before receiving an authorizing UN resolution; bore responsibility for MacArthur's incursion into North Korea, which arguably exceeded the boundaries of both the UN mandate and the Cold War security order; and ordered the US Navy to include Formosa (Taiwan), not just South Korea, in its protective orbit.[35]

Truman was first applauded for his quick and decisive actions. Truman's defenders did not view the intervention as war. From the paradigm set by World War II, the confrontation in Korea looked minor, and given the significance of international law to the dispute, quite possibly could even be characterized as a police action. If the intervention was not "war," then perhaps the Constitution did not require congressional authorization. A few legislative critics had constitutional skepticisms. Led by Senator Taft, a longtime critic of presidentialism and of US responsibility for global security, legislative criticism only intensified as the war proved to be costly, time consuming, and, with the entry of China, dangerous.

As the Republican Party strengthened its position in Congress, and as the Taft wing strengthened its position in the Republican Party, the constitutional and policy debate surrounding the Truman administration heated up. Truman's 1951 proposal to send four divisions to Europe to support NATO reactivated the cleavages of the Korean War, and controversy exploded. The military disaster of Chinese entry into the war, combined with ongoing legislative resistance to presidential war

34 For a good overview of the constitutional arguments of the war, see Charles A. Lofgren, "Mr. Truman's War: A Debate and Its Aftermath," *The Review of Politics* 31:2 (1969): 223–41.

35 Lester H. Brune and Mark Leach, "Congress During the Korean War," in *The Korean War: Handbook of the Literature and Research* (New York: Greenwood Press, 1996), 345.

empowerment, formed the context for the "Great Debate" of 1951. Senators Taft and Kenneth Wherry led the legislature in six months of extensive debates, hearings, and resolutions criticizing Truman's security policy and curtailing presidential authority under the UN and NATO. These were not successful in stemming the movement toward presidentialism. By the time of the Kennedy administration, Congress and the president had found a way to signal legislative assent within the new Cold War security order. Congress would pass broad delegations and resolutions, premised on vast independent presidential war powers, to express both a pro-presidency construction of constitutional war powers as well as its support for particular policies. Its resolutions retreated from the language of legislative empowerment: the Cuban Resolution, for example, resolved to resist the spread of the Cuban Revolution rather than authorized the president to engage in war.[36]

Using the relational conception to analyze the quality of legislative war authority in these two cases means asking about the extent to which the legislature exercised its powers in ways that conform to the processual and substantive standards of the relational conception. Theodore Roosevelt and Harry Truman were not *only* opportunistically seizing power: they were also doing so in response to the legislature's construction of a security order. Can that construction be defended?

DEFENSIVE SECURITY NECESSITY

The Constitution says nothing about the conditions under which Congress may authorize war. The preamble commits the polity to the pursuit of the "general welfare" as well as common defense, and the legislature's empowerment over war is not structurally implied but is textually given, without conditions, in Article I Section 8. These imply that the legislature's power to authorize war is a textually discretionary power. The relevant standard for assessing the legislature's use of this discretionary power is simply the extent to which war furthers the "general welfare" of the nation as a whole, the capacious standard of the Constitution's preamble.

However, what is at stake here is not legislative authorization for particular acts of war, but rather legislative participation in constructing a security order to discipline the presidency in its use of independent war powers. When a presidency exercises independent war powers, that behavior is subject to the standard of defensive security necessity. We have seen that the content of a defensive security standard must be constructed

---

36   For a legislative history of the Cuban Resolution, see Silverstein, *Imbalance*, 80–81.

politically. Hence, one relevant question for assessing legislative deliberations in constructing a security order is about the extent to which the legislature gives reasonable content to the substantive standard of "defense," which in turn serves to constitutionally discipline independent acts of presidential war. When the legislature generates this substantive content, to what extent does it do so in a way that is responsive to the actual security threats of the moment? To what extent does it take cognizance of the presidency's special capacities and limitations in constructing this new order? A construction of defensive necessity that more accurately tracks real threat, and which is more accurately tethered to the president's distinctive capacity to meet those threats, is one that in turn garners more constitutional authority under the relational conception.

Evaluation begins by assessing the objective security threat to which each set of Congresses was responding. What threat was at stake under the Roosevelt Corollary? On first view it is hard to find any threat justifying presidential bellicosity. Certainly Colombia, Nicaragua, Panama, and Haiti, for example, posed no threat to the United States. However, these countries were highly significant for their relationships to transformations in European politics, and for their promise for sustaining US economic development.

With the retreat of British imperialism, the relationship of major European powers to one another was changing. At the same time the United States, having come through the Civil War, was experiencing both new wealth and startling new economic depressions. The United States began to seek a place as a world, rather than regional power. Imperial expansion had been a traditional way to gain international respect and to mark the entrée of a nation as a great power. Weak Caribbean and South American nations were useful territories for performing a broader set of claims about national power to Europe.

Defenders of this US foreign policy argue that elites could reasonably believe that imperial expansion was necessary to achieve a core security interest. Claiming territory before powerful rivals do may create a security buffer. Richard Collin argues that American fears were justifiable "because the introduction of European national rivalries into the New World, combined with the growing instability of Central America . . . would destabilize the entire region."[37] France had occupied Mexico during the US Civil War. Collin cites German expansion in China at Kiaochow in November 1897 and in Shantung Province in March 1898 as giving credible reason for fear.[38] Wilhelm II, the German kaiser, was also demonstrating overt hostility toward the United States, exploring plans

37   Collin, *Caribbean*, xiii.
38   Ibid., 56.

for the occupation of New York City or the establishment of a base in Puerto Rico from which to conduct military raids.[39] Some of these plans were publicly circulated and well received by reviews in the German press, even if they were militarily unrealistic.[40] Collin defends Roosevelt's concern about German encirclement.

While the presidency is not the focus of this chapter, nonetheless I would argue that Roosevelt's sense of threat is implausible. European powers were coming to see that the expenses of colonial governance could outstrip its benefits, and events like Cuban independence were pointing toward declining, not encroaching, European power. US intervention created its own destabilizations in Latin America. Some current scholarship reveals Roosevelt's fears about the Germans to have been implausible, arguably then as now.[41] The discovery by historians working in German archives that Germans sought "mischief," but "were not ready or willing to risk a major confrontation with the United States" is also relevant evidence for assessing the objective security context of the moment, even if elites at that moment did not have access to that information.[42]

On the other hand, nations in South and Central America could be consequential for US economic development. This economic development was itself arguably related to a sense of threat—however, not a threat of foreign powers, but rather a threat to the power of domestic political elites. In the late nineteenth century a dramatic series of depressions generated a radical populist movement, a radicalized labor movement, and a series of strikes and turmoil that frightened elites. The domestic violence associated with labor unrest at this time was real. Theodore Roosevelt came to power as a result of President McKinley's assassination by an anarchist. The Populist movement responded to turmoil by rendering a set of proposals for reform in banking, monetary, and labor policy.[43] Outside the Populist movement, US elites diagnosed the source of unrest not in domestic economic policy, but rather in the overproduction of agrarian materials. Officials' "great fear of domestic violence and radicalism, emerging out of the depression, drove them to the conclusion that imperialism was preferable to domestic reform (and economic redistribution)

---

39 Ibid., 70.

40 Ibid., 73, citing Franz von Edelsheim's *Operations Upon the Sea: A Study* (New York: The Outdoor Press, 1914). That book was itself influenced by Alfred Mahan's *Influence of Sea Power Upon History: 1660–1783* (Cambridge: Cambridge University Press, 1890).

41 Holmes, *Theodore Roosevelt*, 166; Wormuth and Firmage, *Chain*, 148.

42 Collin, *Caribbean*, 98.

43 See Gretchen Ritter, *Goldbugs and Greenbacks: The Antimonopoly Tradition and the Politics of Finance in America, 1865–1896* (Cambridge: Cambridge University Press, 1999).

as a device to quell the danger."[44] Economic tension could be relieved through enhanced access to foreign markets. The consensus that non-Populist elites had on seeking profit through foreign markets, then, was related to the "threat" (to elites) of a mobilized domestic public seeking radical political reform.

This is indeed the language legislatures used to describe the benefits of the policies that enabled Roosevelt's belligerency. While theoretically speaking, one could imagine a German threat (and Roosevelt did imagine one), members of Congress did not deliberate over these treaties in terms of threat at all. They instead described how the treaties would support the nation's material interests. Debate noted the "vast . . . material interests of the people" at stake;[45] the importance of "a proper tribute to this great nation, an American canal,"[46] "which will be of incalculable benefit and advantage to commerce generally and especially in the interest of our own great nation."[47]

While the desire to open foreign markets is a policy goal that may, under some circumstances, be a constitutionally appropriate reason for Congress to authorize war, preservation from the threat represented by a radical domestic politics does not rise to the kind of security consideration that can license independent presidential bellicosity. Such a threat is not a foreign threat but rather a domestic one. Theorizing defense in terms of heading off the threat of domestic reformers—that is, to "defend" a certain set of elite interests in maintaining power and their preferred policies—subverts the consensual foundations of the relationship between representatives and publics. Also, there is no reason to believe that meeting this economic threat required the particular capacities of presidential empowerment. The legislature has a significant role to play in clarifying, judging, mediating, and integrating the diverse political claims associated with economic unrest. While it could, perhaps, be constitutionally acceptable for Congress to decide that domestic economic unrest calls for wars of aggression to expand markets, these are not defensive security interests of national publics beyond representatives themselves. Nor does the pursuit of these officials' interest in power reasonably call for empowering the presidency to wage independent war.

---

44   LaFeber, *New Empire*, xxv. Peter Trubowitz agrees that elites perceived foreign markets as a "safety valve." See his *Defining the National Interest: Conflict and Change in American Foreign Policy* (Chicago, University of Chicago Press, 1998): 34, 36.

45   Sen. Bacon, *Congressional Record*, 58th Cong., 2nd sess. (February 23, 1904), 2245; see also Sen. Depew, *Congressional Record*, 58th Cong., 2nd sess. (January 14, 1904), 758–61.

46   Sen. Quarles, *Congressional Record*, 58th Cong., 2nd sess. (January 19, 1904), 870.

47   Sen. Cullom, *Congressional Record*, 58th Cong., (March 17, 1903), 110.

Responding to this question is critical for evaluating the authority of the security order the president and Congress established. We do so using all of the materials available to condition our judgment today. The relational conception asks observers to assess the actual existence of a threatening context using all of the best evidence of the moment. While it cannot itself resolve substantive disagreement about threat, the relational conception focuses our attention on adjudicating this issue as one element of assessing the authoritativeness of the security order the branches constructed.

The threat of the Cold War is easier to bring into focus. Amazingly, a great deal of war powers scholarship evaluates the Cold War security order without describing the nature and structure of threat that the president and Congress faced in the late 1940s and early 1950s. For most theories, the nature of this threat is of limited or no relevance in assessing the constitutional war claims of the branches. But the threats of the early Cold War were serious, and the Constitution clearly commits its governing officials to the protection of a system of "common defense." A Congress and president that failed to respond to these threats would have merited very serious constitutional criticisms, particularly because the world had just witnessed the devastation of Europe in a war in which nuclear weapons still had not been available. Any semi-aware observer saw that World Wars I and II demonstrated deep instabilities in the international system as well as violence and security interdependence on a scale previously unimagined. The world wars had demonstrated that modern warfare could be total, and that victory in one global war would not guarantee future security. To the extent that maintaining domestic constitutionalism requires a favorable international environment—as the authors of the *Federalist Papers* argued, and as most legislative officials and the public had become convinced after World War II—the failure of officials to develop such a peaceful global environment would merit serious constitutional criticism. This is not to say that US perceptions were not sometimes wrong, or that the United States pursued its security at the lowest possible cost.[48]

---

48 For an argument that the Cold War order was rooted in national security concerns, see Thomas A. Bailey, *America Faces Russia* (Ithaca, NY: Cornell University Press, 1950); Melvyn P. Leffler, *A Preponderance of Power: National Security, the Truman Administration, and the Cold War* (Palo Alto, CA: Stanford University Press, 1993). Respondents to revisionist history include Charles S. Maier, "Revisionism and the Interpretation of Cold War Origins," *Perspectives in American History* 4 (1970), 313–47; Warren F. Kimball, "The Cold War Warmed Over," *American Historical Review* 79:4 (1974), 1119–36; Robert W. Tucker, *The Radical Left and American Foreign Policy* (Baltimore: The Johns Hopkins University Press, 1971).

Many of course claim that the threat from the USSR was overblown, a matter of elites entrenching their interests both domestically and internationally. Those skeptical of a Cold War security problem at the close of World War II may point out that the Soviet economy was in shambles; that its military capability was suffering given the demobilization of the Red Army and a national labor shortage; and that Stalin did not have a secure grip over Eastern Europe.[49] Perhaps it was the US failure to accept the legitimacy of USSR nonparticipation in a global free enterprise economy, or the legitimacy of Soviet power in Eastern Europe, that was to blame for early Cold War fears. This fear itself generated security problems, because it generated internal domestic repression and an impetus for the United States to side with foreign dictators who could repel communist movements. If US security did not require a reworked international system, and more particularly if there was no true threat from Stalin and later China, then this substantive standard of the relational conception gives no justification for the flow of war power to the presidency in the early Cold War. Instead, the relational conception would paint a devastating criticism of the behavior of officials in manufacturing threat—the entrenchment of a "carefully managed antagonism" that served elite interests.[50]

Using the relational conception, I would argue that legislators in the early Cold War were reasonable to perceive threats. The instability of the global environment led to the creation of the UN even before the Cold War began to consolidate.[51] The United States and the USSR had advanced different visions for global affairs starting in the early days of World War I.[52] Economic decline and turmoil could foster the development of communist influence in Europe without a Red Army. Moreover, the USSR's status as an encroaching negative force was revealed in the late 1940s through its resistance to the Marshall Plan and its militant attacks in Eastern Europe, including the Czech coup and the Berlin blockade. Stalin's willingness to rely on actual terror, not simply rhetoric, to achieve

49   Michael Cox, "From the Truman Doctrine to the Second Superpower Détente: The Rise and Fall of the Cold War," *Journal of Peace Research* 27:1 (1990): 25–41; Matthew A. Evangelista, "Stalin's Postwar Army Reappraised," *International Security* 7:3 (1982): 110–38.

50   Cox, "From the Truman Doctrine," 30; see also John Lewis Gaddis, *We Now Know: Rethinking Cold War History* (New York: Oxford University Press, 1997), 34.

51   In Gaddis's words, the two world wars had not only created international power vacuums, but also "a vacuum of *legitimacy*," for the wars "discredited the old forms of diplomacy that allowed war to break out in the first place and that proved so ineffective in ending it." Gaddis, *Now Know*, 4.

52   Ibid., 5.

his aims was worth noting.[53] And after Hitler, it was reasonable to consider that internally oppressive leaders (consider Stalin's internal purges in 1936) who explicitly committed themselves to world governance and had the national resources to make a fighting go at it were to be feared. It also appeared that the threat could be long-standing. Stalin's willingness to conform to international rules or to back down after provoking antagonistic responses from others could be interpreted either as limited ambition, or as the lack of any "timetable for achieving them"—in Molotov's words: "Our ideology stands for offensive operations when possible, and if not, we wait."[54] The collapse of the Chinese National government, and pursuant security alliance between China and the Soviet Union, reasonably sparked new fears,[55] as did the Soviet explosion of its first atomic bomb in 1949.

In the early 1950s, the USSR was also providing North Korea offensive weapons, and US officials suspected coordination between Kim Il Sung and Stalin.[56] For a world conditioned by the precedents of the Japanese takeover of Manchuria in 1931, the 1938 Munich conference, and the American failure to protect Europe until it was almost too late, the Korean crisis was a perfect template for response. Other nations, too, perceived threat and sent troops under the aegis of the United Nations.[57]

I believe that greater empowerment of the presidency was also a reasonable institutional response to this threat. An emerging realist scholarship in international relations theorized presidential or authoritarian power as key to international order.[58] This was only too plausible for legislators

---

53   Ibid., 22–23.

54   As cited in Gaddis, *Now Know*, 31.

55   James A. Fetzer, "Congress and China: 1941–1950," Ph.D. dissertation, Michigan State University, 209, citing Mao Tse-Tung, "On the People's Democratic Dictatorship," *Selected Works of Mao Tse-tung* (Peking: Foreign Languages Press, 1961): 415–16.

56   Soviets also drew up the plan of attack once the decision to attack had been made. James T. Patterson, *Grand Expectations: The United States, 1945–1974* (New York: Oxford University Press, 1996), 209–10. Also see Sergei Goncharov, John Lewis, and Xue Litai, *Uncertain Partners: Stalin, Mao, and the Korean War* (Palo Alto, CA: Stanford University Press, 1994); Bruce Cumings, *The Origins of the Korean War: The Roaring of the Cataract, 1947–1950* (Princeton: Princeton University Press, 1990).

57   Gaddis, *Now Know*, 76.

58   The term "realpolitik" emerged from German political theory of statism in the nineteenth and early-twentieth centuries, e.g., Johann Gottfried Herder, Henriech von Trietschke, Friedrich Meinecke, Max Weber, and Carl Schmitt. For an intellectual history of realism, see Daniel Deudney, *Bounding Power: Republican Security Theory from the Polis to the Global Village* (Princeton: Princeton University Press, 2007), ch. 1. On realist dominance in academic political science in the same period, see Brian C. Schmidt, *The Political Discourse of Anarchy: A Disciplinary History of International Relations* (Albany: State University of New York Press, 1998).

who had seen their own institution stand in the way of what later came
to be seen as a defining war effort of the twentieth century. Isolationist
Congresses had blocked Roosevelt in responding to World War II until
the very last minute. Legislative power became associated with threat.
Finally, one of the critical tools for responding to global communism was
brinkmanship diplomacy—diplomacy backed by a constant readiness to
go to war. Brinkmanship diplomacy was believed to be difficult to control through legislative procedure, as it relies on maintaining secret intentions and rapid decision-making capability. The possible long duration of
military confrontation also made it seem worth enabling the president to
conduct diplomacy with a significant source of military power behind him
in an ongoing way. The legislature had scholarship, historical experience,
and the practical requirements of a new diplomacy, all pointing toward
legislative disempowerment over particular acts of war.

Today we can also see the role of legislatures in maintaining global
peace. Through signaling and other mechanisms, legislative empowerment apparently plays an important role in managing the international
security of democracies.[59] An empowered legislature *and* an empowered
presidency may well have created a more supportive context for global
peace over the long run in the Cold War. If early Cold War legislatures
had been able to apprehend the security value of legislative governance
and relate that value even more effectively to their aims, the war authority they produced would have been yet stronger. But the legislature's judgment at the moment—that direct presidential war empowerment was a
critical guarantor for global security—was reasonable at the time given
the state of security scholarship, their own relevant experience, and their
understanding of the practical requirements of coercive diplomacy.

Noting the importance of the objective security situation is important for one additional reason: the Cold War security context changed
over the years. As it became clear that global communism was not a
single force—and that communist ideology was being appropriated on
behalf of struggles about basic rights of self-determination—and as the
costs associated with alliance with dictators and authoritarians became

59   For example, see Kenneth A. Shultz, *Democracy and Coercive Diplomacy* (Cam-
bridge: Cambridge University Press, 2001); Clifton Morgan and Valerie Schwebach, "Take
Two Democracies and Call Me in the Morning: A Prescription for Peace?" *International
Interactions* 17:4 (1992): 305–20; Bruce Bueno de Mesquita and David Lalman, *War and
Reason: Domestic and International Imperatives* (New Haven: Yale University Press, 1992);
Bruce Bueno de Mesquita, James Morrow, Randolph Siverson, and Alastair Smith, "An Institutional Explanation of the Democratic Peace," *American Political Science Review* 93:4
(1999): 791–807; Michael Koch and Scott Sigmund Gartner, "Casualties and Constituencies: Democratic Accountability, Electoral Institutions, and Costly Conflicts," *The Journal
of Conflict Resolution* 49:6 (2005): 874–94.

more clear, it is arguable that this dimension of the Cold War security order's authority faded over time. It is likely that what could be justified as a reasonable response in 1950 could not be justified in 1980; but a Congress whose security governance capacities had atrophied may have undermined its own capacity to judge those differences. For the relational conception, transformations in the objective security context over time affect the ongoing authority of a security order.[60]

The relational conception does not itself resolve the question of which context was, objectively speaking, more threatening, or in which context direct presidential empowerment was, on the merits, a reasonable response to threat. I have generated arguments about these two cases to demonstrate how the relational conception can be used to think through this set of problems. The contribution of the relational conception is to focus our attention on this question—the objective threatening context itself—as one standard for assessing these security orders' relative, and ongoing, constitutional authority.

ASSESSING LEGISLATIVE JUDGMENT: THE ROOSEVELT COROLLARY

The relational conception also argues that the branches produce war authority when they fully exercise their constitutional capacities in relationship to the security context they actually face. The legislature has the capacity to clarify the grounds of policy and constitutional debate; to assess the costs and benefits associated with different courses of actions; to hold open space for the evaluation of courses of action according to many (not just one) political ideologies; and to make law. These are among the governing strengths that lie behind the processual standards.

In both cases, strong legislative majorities participated in creating the material and ideological tools the president needed to wage independent war. But I argue, through the relational conception, that the legislative contribution to the Cold War security order was more constitutionally faithful than that of the Roosevelt Corollary. Let us look at how the legislature participated in constructing each order and evaluate that participation according to the processual standards.

The legislature in the 1890s began with the decision to create military capacity. It is not the mere fact of a military that can be interpreted as a deliberative contribution, but also what the nature of military

60 Jane Stromseth considers how the rise of a "more complex, and less bipolar, foreign policy outlook" signals greater need for legislative governance. Stromseth, "Understanding," 911.

empowerment reveals about the particular security ideologies Congress is advancing. Not all military establishments are equally good at all kinds of strikes, and different visions of security require different forms of military readiness. The Senate's construction of the "New Navy" in the late nineteenth century is one element of the legislature's contribution to the security order of the Roosevelt Corollary.[61] The modern Navy originated in the Appropriations Act of 1883, but this act only authorized unarmored cruisers equipped for hit-and-run operations,[62] and the ships authorized between 1885 and 1889 were small.[63] In the early 1890s, Congress's naval funding decisions revealed a shift in its orientation toward the European powers.

After 1893, as the landed frontier closed, Americans began to speak to the need for a new commercial frontier across the ocean. Public intellectual A. T. Mahan appealed to the necessity of a merchant marine and battleship navy that could deter European competitors from the oceans, which he described not as protective barriers but as highways. Mahan and his allies in office—William McKinley, Theodore Roosevelt, Henry Cabot Lodge—sought colonial possessions as stepping stones to Asian and Latin American markets. They did not want to "colonize" Latin America or Asia so much as extend markets and secure them with military power.[64] They contemplated that this strategy would embed the nation in war. Indeed, it was the experience of war that partly developed their desire for a navy and for bases: Captain Mahan had been present during a rebellion in Panama and had witnessed the significance of US naval strength only months before he began developing his lectures on sea power.[65]

In a series of important congressional debates between 1889 and 1892, other imperial expansionists came to the same conclusion: military confrontation would be an element of expanding US power. They decided then not to reject this vision of expansion, but rather advocate for a battleship fleet. In 1890 Congress authorized the buildup of the first battleships, vessels that could go far out to sea rather than stay close to the coast for immediate defense.[66] Benjamin Tracy, Secretary of the Navy, invoked the "sole purpose" of defense as justification for the naval buildup, but it was obvious that the content of the nation's defensive

61 Wicks, "Dress Rehearsal," 603.

62 LaFeber, *New Empire*, 123–24.

63 Ibid., 59.

64 Ibid., 91.

65 David McCullough, *The Path Between the Seas: The Creation of the Panama Canal, 1870–1914* (Simon & Schuster New York, 1977), ch. 6.

66 LaFeber, *New Empire*, 124–25.

interests was being deeply reconceived.[67] By 1905 the size of the Navy had approximately quadrupled, and the United States "had become a major naval power."[68] The United States invested far more in a navy than it invested in the military arms that would be necessary to subdue colonial populations (i.e., an army).

A second way Congress participated in constructing a presidency empowered for war was through its bellicose floor rhetoric. In the early months of the Cleveland administration, in what was to become a military prelude, the president sent a Navy landing force to Panama to pacify a local revolt.[69] Congress was adjourned during this intervention, and when it returned it found much to criticize in the president's behavior: it attacked the president as "weak" and "puerile" for his too-early withdrawal from Panama.[70] Through the late nineteenth century, Congress became increasingly emphatic about its desire for the US military to guarantee US access to markets and naval routes. In 1880 the House Committee on Foreign Affairs adopted a committee resolution indicating its "grave concern" over the use of European capital to build the canal.[71] In treaty debates on Panama, "leading members of the Senate," including the chair of the Foreign Relations Committee, Shelby Cullom, "publicly suggested the unilateral appropriation of the canal zone as a 'universal public utility,' with compensation to be arranged after the fact."[72] Senatorial impatience apparently entered as an element of communication in Roosevelt's diplomacy with Colombia.[73]

This rhetoric reached a pitched state in Senate deliberations over the Hay-Herrán Treaty. Senator Morgan, who favored the Nicaraguan route for a canal over the Panamanian one that Hay-Herrán would secure, spoke openly about his view of Colombians as a "degraded, dissatisfied, turbulent, mixed, and filthy" population.[74] This was circulated in the Colombian press. Even as Colombia deliberated over this consensual political arrangement for the canal, members of the Senate created a political context favorable for the United States to achieve its goals by encouraging Panamanian revolution. Senator Cullom spoke publicly about seizing

67   Collin, *Caribbean*, 45, citing Benjamin Franklin Tracy, *House Executive Documents*, 51st Cong., 1st Sess., No. 1, pt. 3, Serial 2721, 3–4.

68   Trubowitz, *Defining*, 38.

69   Wicks, "Dress Rehearsal," 582.

70   Ibid., 598.

71   Thomas A. Bailey, "The Lodge Corollary to the Monroe Doctrine," *Political Science Quarterly* 48:2 (1933): 220–39, 227.

72   Collin, *Caribbean*, 199.

73   Ibid., 216.

74   *Congressional Record*, 58th Cong. (March 9, 1903), 15–16; Collin, *Caribbean*, 219.

the Panama canal from Colombia.[75] In the meantime, what had already been said on the Senate floor rendered the treaty "not only unacceptable but offensive" to the Colombian Senate, which, in a stinging rebuke, unanimously defeated it.[76]

When John Bassett Moore developed a memorandum offering specious legal justification for a unilateral seizure of the canal zone, Roosevelt began to prepare for a November special session to urge Congress to endorse seizure.[77] Even while deploying Marines to Panama in preparation for a revolution, Roosevelt was drafting a message to Congress recommending occupying the zone using the legal justification of the Moore memo.[78] Presidential bellicosity had not been authorized by Congress, but the politics of the moment gave Roosevelt many reasons to believe his policies would be supported.

In addition to supplying military power and bellicose rhetoric, Congress contributed to the legal construction of the Roosevelt Corollary through its creation of treaties that articulated a national interest in the extension of trade throughout Central and Latin America. The Senate requested that the president negotiate these treaties, advised him on negotiations, relentlessly reworked treaty language to broaden the space for US military intervention, and ultimately ratified them. The president then used these treaties to assert a basis for projecting US force.

These treaties were highly consequential. The administration perceived accurately that they were at the basis of the president's capacity to make war, and sent Secretary of War Root on a Latin American goodwill tour in 1906 precisely to persuade nations to sign trade treaties, treaties establishing customhouses, or treaties giving the United States power to oversee the external financial affairs of those nations. All of the military operations conducted under the Roosevelt Corollary were at least pretextually connected to treaties between the United States and the relevant nation. Access to the treaty debates is limited because treaties were customarily discussed in the Senate through private executive session with no floor debate. But in some cases, journalistic leaks led debate to spill out onto the Senate floor, providing some evidence that can serve as the basis for an assessment of how faithfully the legislature exercised its war powers.

A US military presence had been introduced into Panama in the first place through the Bidlack Treaty of 1846, between Columbia and the United States, guaranteeing rights of transit for a railroad crossing the

75 Collin, *Caribbean*, 243.
76 Ibid., 219.
77 Ibid., 252.
78 Ibid., 258.

isthmus.[79] Polk's presentation of the treaty to Congress had emphasized "the danger of entangling alliances," but argued that the treaty avoided entanglements because it did "not extend to the territories of New Granada generally, but [only] to the single Province of the Isthmus of Panama" and would "constitute no alliance for any political object, but for a purely commercial purpose."[80] By the turn of the century, the United States had intervened with force multiple times under the terms of this treaty to suppress Panamanian secession from Colombia. Hence by the turn of the twentieth century, the role of treaties in conditioning the president's use of an independent power to engage in hostilities was already apparent. In the legislative debates around Roosevelt's Panama intervention, these prior interventions in support of Colombian sovereignty were conceived, even by critics of the Panama canal, not as acts of war requiring legislative authorization, but rather as acts guaranteeing neutrality and property rights by securing Colombian sovereignty.[81]

In 1900, domestic resistance to European power pushed President McKinley to renegotiate the Clayton-Bulwer Treaty, which, since 1850, had expressed the United States' and Britain's agreement that any canal would be neutral. McKinley's renegotiation led to a draft in February 1900 specifying that the canal's neutrality would be guaranteed by the United States.[82] The neutrality provision was controversial in the Senate. While we do not have access to full Senate debates, leaks and subsequent events reveal a worry in the Senate that the neutrality guarantee would undermine US freedom in using the canal for its own military purposes.[83] These concerns were apparently inspired by the Spanish American War and the Senate's growing awareness about the value of military bases, given the acquisition of the Philippines.[84] The Senate's concern for security not only exceeded what was conventional for imperial powers (the

79 McCullough, *Path*, 136.

80 James K. Polk, "Special Message to the Senate," (February 10, 1847). Available at http://www.presidency.ucsb.edu/ws/index.php?pid=67954#axzz1veUUAsYn (accessed May 22, 2012).

81 On US intervention under the terms of this treaty, see Collin, *Caribbean*, 237; E. Taylor Parks, *Colombia and the United States, 1765–1934* (Manchester, NH: Ayer Company Publishers, 1970), 218–28; see Senator Morgan's discussion of the enforcement of this guarantee in debate over the Hay-Herrán Treaty. *Congressional Record*, 58th Cong. (March 14, 1903): 92.

82 Hannigan, *New World*, 26.

83 Dwight Carroll Miner, *The Fight for the Panama Route: The Story of the Spooner Act and the Hay-Herrán Treaty* (New York: Columbia University Press, 1940), 97. The Senate Foreign Relation Committee's first report is printed in Sen Docs., 56th Cong., 1st sess., no. 268.

84 McCullough, *Path*, 256–59.

Suez Canal had set the precedent that global transit passages should be neutral) but also went beyond the Navy's own assessment of security need.[85] Nevertheless, the Senate successfully pressed for an amendment to the treaty allowing American military use of the isthmus.

Britain rejected the treaty and President McKinley was charged with renegotiation. McKinley ultimately presented the Senate with the Hay-Pauncefote Treaty, which did not forbid US fortifications or require the canal to be kept open in times of war. That treaty also guaranteed that the canal should never be taken by force.[86] This treaty satisfied the Senate.

Finally, the Senate response to the Roosevelt's administration's Hay-Herrán Treaty with Colombia was highly contentious; both treaty defenders and critics were remarkably bellicose. The Senate was dissatisfied with the treaty even though it granted the United States a "sole and absolute" option to build, collect tolls, exercise police and administrative powers, and intervene militarily in the isthmian region, as well as US control of a canal zone.[87] The Senate wanted more.

Senator John Tyler Morgan, a Democrat from Alabama, spearheaded the opposition. Morgan had been an advocate for the alternative Nicaraguan route and he used the ratification process to attack the president for breaking the law by introducing a treaty differing in some details from the Spooner Act, calling the president's treaty negotiations a "brilliant coup d'etat."[88] Morgan's many amendments would have broadened the scope for US military intervention in the zone. He advocated control of the zone "in perpetuity" rather than for a renewable one hundred-year lease, and the right to use and fortify several surrounding islands.[89] He urged exempting the "acts of citizens of Colombia" (domestic rebellion) from the contours of the security guarantee the United States was reaffirming to Colombia, and advocated specifying that Colombian sovereignty would remain intact "except to the extent . . . provided in this treaty." Morgan's amendments would have specifically provided for US military tribunals in addition to regular courts.[90] And Morgan sought to transform Article XXIII's provision for US armed forces to protect the canal under particular circumstances into a right for the United States "at all

---

85   Naval officials viewed naval power and control of bases in the Caribbean as more crucial for the control of the canal than any provisions about militarizing the canal itself. Ibid., 256.

86   See ibid., 256–59.

87   Hannigan, *New World*, 28.

88   *Congressional Record*, 58th Cong. (March 9, 1903), 22; see also 18–19.

89   *Congressional Record*, 58th Cong. (March 9, 1903), 14.

90   Ibid., 14, 15.

times and in its discretion, to use its police and its land and naval forces for these purposes."[91]

In debate Morgan compared the Panamanian treaty to the (in his view) more favorable Nicaraguan treaty, with its more emphatic guarantee of US powers of intervention.[92] The Senate's debates in executive session apparently featured suggestions that the United States should just go to war "once we have a foothold there under this treaty." Morgan called this "derogatory to our country," but his own suggestions for treaty design hardly suggested a limited scope for the projection of US military power.[93] Senator Cullom, chair of the SFRC and an Illinois Republican, responded to Morgan on the Senate floor. He argued that much of the scope for US military intervention Morgan sought was already implicit in the treaty at hand: while "Colombia agrees to provide the armed forces necessary for the protection of the canal... [t]he United States will determine what are exceptional circumstances and unforeseen or imminent danger. Those terms are susceptible of a very broad construction."[94]

Despite the highly conflictual debate, and despite Morgan's criticism of the president's treaty negotiations on constitutional grounds, Morgan never objected that the treaty would unconstitutionally shift powers to the presidency. His lengthy objections included no concern that the treaty's security guarantee, or his bellicose amendments, would have any implications for the war powers of Congress and the president.[95] Even this fierce critic of the president, one who presented himself as very worried about coups and tyranny, failed to note these obvious gaps in legal draftsmanship. Morgan's arguments in the debate read as an ad hoc effort to spit out frightening words in an effort to achieve a Nicaraguan treaty, rather than any kind of developed criticism. The Senate ratified the Hay-Herrán Treaty without any of Morgan's amendments by a vote of 73 to 5.[96]

By the early nineteenth century, then, the Senate had exercised its treaty authority more than once in the direction of military empowerment, without signaling any concern for how this clearly anticipated bellicosity would affect powers of military control allocated between the branches. (The Supreme Court was performing a similar lack of articulation in decisions that suggested the permissibility of strong presidential empowerment and colonial governance without too stringently focusing

91   Ibid., 15.
92   Ibid., (March 17, 1903), 111, 119–20.
93   Ibid., (March 9, 1903), 22; Collin, *Caribbean*, 219–33.
94   Ibid., (March 17, 1903), 109.
95   Ibid., (March 9, 1903), 22; see also 18–19.
96   McCullough, *Path*, 332.

on legal issues around the separation of powers.)[97] The Senate's ratification of these treaties not only enabled executive bellicosity, but it did so in ways that failed to engage the legislature's distinctive capacity to make law. While the Senate pushed the president to negotiate increasingly interventionist treaties, none of them specified enforcement mechanisms for their military guarantees. The Senate was apparently unconcerned by this lapse in effective legal authority.

It is not that Congress was, in general, unconcerned with implementing legislation. The Nicaraguan treaty that Senator Morgan held as a prized alternative included language emphasizing that construction of the canal would proceed only "after the adoption by Congress of legislation."[98] Legislative critics of the president were aware that treaties could require domestic implementation of legislation, but apparently did not construe these particular elements of the treaties as calling for legislative authority. This is a failing according to the processualist standard: the legislature failed to articulate or respond to a major gap of legal draftsmanship, one with serious constitutional implications.

The fact that the Senate had invited, with its military establishment, bellicose rhetoric, and enabling treaties, the conditions for executive empowerment in war does not mean that Roosevelt's actual acts of war in Panama were well received by all in the Senate. Senate debate after the fact did endorse Roosevelt, but only after challenging him for an abuse of war powers. And yet, even in its anxiety about presidential power, amazingly, the Senate failed to develop a coherent line of constitutional challenge.

After inviting presidential war-making by funding a military, performing bellicose rhetoric, and ratifying enabling treaties, the Senate ratified Roosevelt's Panama conduct in its approval of the Hay-Bunau-Varilla Treaty the president had negotiated with the newly recognized state of Panama. With Republican control of the Senate, it seemed clear the treaty would be approved, even as some of the immediate negative security consequences of the bellicosity were already becoming apparent; the Senate numerous times referred to the real possibility of a war with Colombia.[99] Senate debate over the Hay-Bunau-Varilla Treaty ratified Roosevelt's conduct, but since debate did so little to bring into focus the major policy and constitutional issues at stake in the Panamanian incursion, even the Senate's ratification of the treaty by a vote of 66 to 14 can hardly be read

97 While *In re Neagle* (1890) did not deal with any controversy of foreign affairs, it articulated a theory of independent presidential powers to protect that was highly relevant in international affairs. The *Insular Cases* (1898) also theorized extensive national power in foreign affairs without attending to interbranch relations.

98 Sen. Morgan, *Congressional Record*, 58th Cong. (March 17, 1903), 119.

99 Ibid., 285, 292–93.

as producing any kind of high-quality legislative authority on behalf of this emerging security order.

In these debates the Senate discussed the content of the new treaty as well as the hostile acts behind the treaty. Senators Morgan, Tillman, and Carmack, among others, raised a series of constitutional challenges to the president, and resolutions were put on the floor seeking information about the president's role in the revolution; condemning the president for his violation of the Constitution and of war powers; and condemning the president's violation of international law.[100] Roosevelt's supporters defended the constitutionality of the president's exercise of a purely discretionary power to "recognize" a foreign nation, rhetorically sidestepping the issue of armed intervention.[101] When challenged that deploying Marines to block Colombian ships was hardly an act of "recognition,"[102] presidential advocates argued that the president's conduct was not war because it had been necessary to protect US citizens;[103] it was required by the 1846 treaty's guarantee to protect the rail;[104] or it was required by the "law of exhausted patience."[105] Presidential defenders also argued that it was not an act of war under international law, but rather an act of preventing war.[106]

The rhetorical force of the Senate's retrospective challenge was blunted, however, because presidency critics so deeply failed to take cognizance of the enabling conditions of the president's action. While Senators Morgan and Hoar spearheaded the challenge to Roosevelt, Hoar ultimately backed down, arguing that, despite his ferocious statements of presidential misconduct, there was no war powers violation and he could vote for the treaty.[107] Senator Morgan maintained his opposition, but even while Morgan was willing to criticize the president for unlicensed war, he

100   Sen. Gorman offered Senate Resolution 73. *Congressional Record*, 58th Cong., 2nd sess. (Jan 13, 1904), 703; Sen. Morgan, *Congressional Record*, 58th Cong., 2nd sess. (December 9, 1903), 112; Sen. Stone, *Congressional Record*, 58th Cong., 2nd sess. (January 13, 1904), 702. The resolution submitted by Sen. Morgan was Sen. Res. No. 66, *Congressional Record*, 58th Cong., 2nd sess. (December 19, 1903), 399; Sen. Bacon, *Congressional Record*, 58th Cong., 2nd sess. (January 12, 1904), 614; Sen. Newlands, *Congressional Record*, 58th Cong., 2nd sess. (January 22, 1904), 1033.

101   See *Congressional Record*, 58th Cong., 2nd sess.: Sen. Lodge (January 5, 1904), 459–65; Sen. Quarles (January 14, 1904), 756; Sen. Simmons (February 23, 1904), 2249–50.

102   Sen. Carmack, *Congressional Record*, 58th Cong., 2nd sess. (January 13, 1904), 705–706.

103   Ibid. (January 19, 1904), 867.

104   *Congressional Record*, 58th Cong., 2nd sess. (February 22, 1904), 2203.

105   Sen. Dolliver. *Congressional Record*, 58th Cong., 2nd sess. (January 22, 1904), 1031.

106   See exchange between Foraker and Daniel, *Congressional Record*, 58th Cong., 2nd sess. (January 12, 1904), 616–18.

107   Sen. Hoar, *Congressional Record*, 58th Cong., 2nd sess. (February 22, 1904), 2195.

also relentlessly returned to discussing the value of the Nicaraguan route
and continued to advocate treaties that implied a continued policy of independent presidential war without explaining this discrepancy or even
being challenged on it.[108] Morgan's challenge lacked focus. As long as the
president was seeking the Panamanian route, little of his conduct, from
diplomacy, to treaty negotiation, to deliberations with Congress, seemed
not to violate Morgan's sense of propriety. Morgan's challenges read as a
scattershot effort to criticize the president and the Panamanian route by
any means necessary rather than as a developed constitutional challenge.

The Hay-Bunau-Varilla Treaty included a US security guarantee to
Panama, as well as a guarantee that the United States could exercise "all
the rights, power and authority . . . which the United States would pos-
sess and exercise if it were the sovereign of the territory . . . to the entire
exclusion of the exercise by the Republic of Panama of any such sovereign rights, power, or authority."[109] Despite this language, and despite
some senators' expressed concerns about the president's constitutional
violations, not a single one of them indicated that this language once
again implied presidential enforcement action, and that presidential discretion in enforcement could amount to acts of war. And once again, not
a single senator argued that requiring domestic implementation of legislation might serve to discipline future presidents.

As we shall see, a more serious constitutional challenge, such as that
brokered by the Taft wing of the Republican Party in the early Cold War,
paired a willingness to condemn presidential bellicosity after the fact together with an enduring effort to design treaties and laws so as to restrict
or curtail the space for presidential bellicosity on behalf of an alternative
policy and constitutional vision. The presidency critics' permissive attitude toward the legal, material, and ideological conditions out of which
these military strikes arose rendered their deliberative challenge less focused than it might otherwise have been.

Finally, the Senate's ratification of Roosevelt's conduct did little to
bring into focus an emerging global politics or the consequences of presidential empowerment within that politics. I have already noted the Congress's failure to articulate a defensive security interest of any kind that
could constitutionally justify independent presidential empowerment; it
spoke of the value of the treaties in terms of material advantage and
national pride, not defensive security. The Senate also failed to explicitly

---

108 The alternative Nicaraguan treaty that Morgan advocated guaranteed the US
military power to enter the canal zone "for the protection of life, liberty, and property, and
for the preservation of peace and good order." Morgan, *Congressional Record*, 58th Cong.
(March 17, 1903), 119.
109 McCullough, *Path*, 393.

consider the significance of presidential empowerment for broader relations with Latin America and Europe in general. Certainly Roosevelt was not shy about claiming that legislative governance was an obstacle to good foreign policy outcomes.[110] Congress did not engage his challenge by considering the strengths of legislative governance; nor did it seriously consider presidentialism as such—the needs it served and the risks it entailed—in light of the transforming global context. Among the unconsidered costs of the security order they were constructing was the "enormous" damage done to US relations with Colombia, and indeed all of Latin America.[111] Pro-presidency insularists claim that presidential power enhances the security of international commitments, but here, presidential empowerment did not make commitments secure but rather enabled quick US intervention to protect economic interests in contexts of destabilized politics. Critics of the presidency did not bring this global politics into focus.

The Senate's Panama debates were characteristic of legislative politics for some time. The relatively limited criticisms of presidential empowerment were mostly generated by anti-imperialists, but anti-imperialists lost significantly on the annexation of the Philippines in 1899 and on the Spanish-American War (neither of which centered on the president's independent power to authorize war), leaving them disorganized and marginalized.[112] They toned down their oppositional mobilization, allowing the new construction of presidential powers room to flourish. During this period, the anti-imperialist challenge, centered in the Democratic Party, was generally narrow and poorly coordinated. It also largely failed to address the policy or security premises at stake in expansion, to question the nature of the economic systems driving expansion, or to develop policy alternatives to that of stabilizing domestic radicalism through imperial expansion.[113]

According to historian Robert Johnson, only with the peace progressive movement in the 1920s did Congress become a platform for policy and constitutional challenge of the Roosevelt Corollary. Peace progressives advocated disarmament, condemned interventions in the Western

110   Roosevelt's Speech of March 23, 1911, as covered by the *New York Times* (March 24, 1911).

111   McCullough, *Path*, 386. See also David Healy, "Review: Rough Rider and Big Stick in the Caribbean," *Reviews in American History* 19:3 (1991): 402–407, 405.

112   For their criticisms, see Robert David Johnson, *The Peace Progressives and American Foreign Relations* (Cambridge: Harvard University Press, 1995), 26.

113   See Johnson, *Peace Progressives,* 28–29; Wayne S. Cole, *Roosevelt and the Isolationists, 1932–45* (Lincoln: University of Nebraska Press, 1983), 358–59; Johnson, *Peace Progressives,* 28–29.

Hemisphere, and sought isolation from European politics.[114] By the mid-1920s, a movement suspicious of presidential power and able to articulate the serious security dilemmas of imperial expansion was finally emerging. At this very moment, the antagonisms of the world wars were also leading the presidency's own priorities to shift. Herbert Hoover withdrew troops from Nicaragua and Haiti and generally renounced Latin American interventionism, and by 1934 Franklin Roosevelt had formally repudiated the Corollary.

Senate debates surrounding the Panama treaties were one element of a *politics*, rather than a source of legal authority, for presidential bellicosity. Note that criticizing Congress for its processual failure is not the same as criticizing Congress for failing to challenge the president. In fact, the legislature actively challenged the president by vetoing treaties, amending them into oblivion, or making astounding statements of diplomatic rudeness on the Senate floor. Congresses were in heated conflict with the presidency, but the structure of this conflictual politics did not adequately engage the important policy and constitutional issues at stake in this new construction of presidential power.

ASSESSING LEGISLATIVE JUDGMENT: THE COLD WAR

Congress's contribution to the Cold War security order was vast. Through treaties, foreign aid, floor and committee rhetoric, funding, and legislation, Congress constructed a massive new system of global security and a politics of presidential empowerment. Within the executive branch, at least two ideas about presidential empowerment rivaled one another. One of these emphasized presidential empowerment through collective security mechanisms like NATO. The other emphasized global security through presidential unilateralism in foreign affairs. Both options implied an independent presidential authority to wage war, and the Truman administration self-consciously deployed new constitutional claims about presidential war powers to both the legislature and the Supreme Court.[115]

Within Congress, however, which is the focus of this chapter, the mid-1940s and early 1950s revealed a serious heterogeneity of opinion not only about the security goals of the early Cold War, but also about how to structure war authority so as to support these goals. Congress served as a platform for many different conceptions of the nation's defensive security

114   Cole, *Roosevelt*, 358–59; Johnson, *Peace Progressives*, 2.
115   For example, in the *Youngstown* steel seizure case (1952), as well as in the administration's defense to Congress of its behavior in Korea. See also Griffin, *Long Wars*, 106 (manuscript).

interests, and articulated and developed a variety of points of view about how the Constitution could be interpreted to support the foreign policies those defensive interests implied.

A first element of legislative participation in constructing a new security order was the creation of military capacity. The military buildup of the early Cold War was congressionally sanctioned. While the executive branch produced NSC-68, the "X" article, and other major security statements, it was Congress that appropriated billions of dollars for developing the most sophisticated military in the world with the capacity to quickly wage war almost anywhere. The legislature also strengthened militarism in the executive branch: the 1947 National Security Act centralized a security system under the unified command of the presidency. This act created a system designed for a "strong plebiscitary president" who could contain the challenges not only of the Cold War, but also "cope with new and unknown challenges [like] . . . overt undeclared wars, such as the Korean conflict, and overt creeping wars, such as the Vietnam War."[116] The Act's creation of the National Security Council further enhanced the president's capacity to deliberate strategically.

Congress was also active in building the international institutions whose authority was at stake in the Korean War. It first did so through a series of resolutions announcing its commitment to collective security. While the Atlantic Charter had referenced the value of general security, Roosevelt, wary of Wilson's experience with the Versailles Treaty, and chastened by Republican gains in the 1942 legislative elections, was reluctant to prompt the legislature to act. Senators Vandenberg and Connally led legislative efforts for collective security and they were supported by a new generation of internationally minded legislators. In 1942 a young Representative Fulbright, seeking to enhance the House's foreign policy stature, introduced the Fulbright Resolution supporting the creation of an international institution that could "maintain a just and lasting peace."[117] In July of that year Senators Ball (MN), Burton (OH), Hatch (AL), and Hill (NM) enlisted eight bipartisan teams of legislators to tour the country advocating US initiative on collective security and global policing. Fulbright's resolution, amended to emphasize the constitutional prerogatives of the legislature, passed the House with a bipartisan vote in September 1943 by 360 to 29. In the Senate, Ball, Burton, Hatch, and Hill, none of whom were on the SFRC, also proposed a resolution that was

116 Koh, *National Security*, 101–102. See especially Douglas T. Stuart, *Creating the National Security State: A History of the Law that Transformed America* (Princeton: Princeton University Press, 2008).

117 Philip J. Briggs, "Congress and Collective Security: The Resolutions of 1943," *World Affairs* 132:4 (1970): 332–44, 336.

actually opposed by the State Department for being too specific.[118] The Connally Resolution, a vaguer statement endorsing collective security, and drafted cooperatively by the SFRC and the State Department, instead passed by an overwhelming bipartisan vote of 85 to 5.[119]

The major constitutional controversies associated with the UN Charter came into focus at this time—that is to say, before nations even began drafting it. Opponents of collective security, including Senator Robert Taft, criticized the idea of international policing and raised concerns about the executive authority it implied.[120] Senator Taft proposed an amendment to the Connally Resolution specifying that Congress did not intend to enlarge the president's war authority. Senator Claude Pepper (D-FL) responded to Taft's constitutional worry by developing the distinction between the president's "war power" and a "police power," arguing that while legislative war authority could not be delegated, US troops could still be used as "police forces" to combat small aggressions.[121] Truman was a member of the Senate during this debate. Both of the major UN conferences, the Dumbarton Oaks and San Francisco conferences, like the supportive resolutions on collective security, "dodged" how domestic institutions would be empowered to carry out the security guarantees implied by the UN's power to militarily respond to breaches of the peace.[122] The neglect was not accidental. Congress's insistence on reserving explicit case-by-case war authority to the Treaty of Versailles had been at the core of its defeat.

Despite Taft's criticisms, the support being demonstrated for internationalism in Congress led Roosevelt to capitalize by appointing Senator Vandenberg to the San Francisco Conference for the UN Charter (1945). Other elite legislators were included: Charles Eaton from the House Foreign Affairs Committee; Senator Tom Connally, chair of the SFRC; and

---

118   Cecil V. Crabb, Jr., *Bipartisan Foreign Policy: Myth or Reality?* (Evanston, IL: Row, Peterson and Company: 1957), 47, citing Arthur H. Vandenberg, Jr., *The Private Papers of Senator Vandenberg* (Boston: Houghton Mifflin Company, 1952). For a discussion of this legislative history, see William J. Fulbright, "Foreword," *Constitutional Diplomacy*, ed. Michael J. Glennon (Princeton: Princeton University Press, 1990); Schlesinger, *Imperial*, 119–20; Fisher, "Korean War," 21–39.

119   S. Res. 192, 78th Cong., 1st sess. 89 *Congressional Record* (November 5, 1943), 9222. See also Philip J. Briggs, *Making American Foreign Policy: President-Congress Relations from the Second World War to Vietnam* (Lanham, MD: University Press of America, 1991), 24–28.

120   Geoffrey Matthews, "Robert A. Taft, the Constitution and American Foreign Policy, 1939–53," *Journal of Contemporary History* 17:3 (1982): 507–22, 514.

121   89 *Congressional Record* (October 26, 1943), 8742–43. See also Fisher, "Korean War," 25.

122   Schlesinger, *Imperial*, 119–20.

Sol Bloom, Chair of the House Committee on Foreign Affairs.[123] These members became leaders in Congress's ratification deliberations.[124] Interparty consultation also intensified: before the San Francisco Conference, bipartisan consultation rooted in the Committee of Eight expanded to include members of the House Foreign Affairs Committee, the political leadership of both houses, and legislators with serious interest in the issue.[125]

At Dumbarton Oaks (1944), Senator Vandenberg shared Taft's concerns about how collective security would impact the allocation of constitutional war authority. Vandenberg said he would never consent to granting international delegates "the power to vote us into a *major* military operation . . . without a vote of Congress as required by the Constitution"—in other words, that the legislature should maintain a veto power over UN acts of war. On this occasion, Vandenberg's main interlocutor was Senator Ball, who believed that the new global institution needed to be able to take quick action against aggressors to sustain its authority over time. Ball argued with Vandenberg that such a reservation would be "crippling," that other nations would follow suit, and that the UN would be transformed into "simply a debating society, without power to act, and future aggressors will sneer at it just as Hitler sneered at the League of Nations."[126]

These arguments, advanced vigorously by Ball and other internationalist legislators, ultimately won Vandenberg over. By 1945, with the elections behind him and the end of the war in sight, Vandenberg delivered a highly significant speech on collective security. He suggested a closer working relationship between the president and Congress, arguing that "we can agree that we do not ever want an instant's hesitation or doubt about our military cooperation in the peremptory use of force . . . to keep Germany and Japan demilitarized," and that "there should be no more need to refer any such action back to Congress than that Congress should expect to pass upon battle plans today. The commander in chief should have instant power to act, and he should act."[127] Vandenberg then went on tour to argue the importance of the "automatic availability of force."[128] This was the position he advocated as a participant at the San Francisco Conference.

123 Briggs, "Senator Vandenberg," 165.
124 Jane E. Stromseth, "Rethinking War Powers: Congress, the President, and the United Nations," *Georgetown Law Journal* 81:3 (1993): 597–673, 603.
125 Crabb, Jr., *Bipartisan,* 47 citing Vandenberg, *Private Papers.*
126 Schlesinger, *Imperial,* 119–20.
127 Arthur H. Vandenberg, "American Foreign Policy," 79th Cong., 1st sess., *Congressional Record* (January 10, 1945), 164–67.
128 Schlesinger, *Imperial,* 122.

The North Atlantic Treaty, like the UN Charter and Participation Act, was notable for high levels of congressional participation.[129] In 1948, the year the USSR rejected the Marshall Plan, the Senate passed the Vandenberg Resolution asking the president to develop regional defense arrangements and encouraging "[m]aximum [US] efforts to obtain agreements to provide the United Nations with armed forces."[130] Article 5 of the North Atlantic Treaty specified that an attack on any one of its signatories would be considered an attack on them all. Like the UN Charter, but unlike historic treaties like the Rio Grande Treaty or the Treaty of Versailles, the North Atlantic Treaty did not specifically reserve Congress's role in authorizing acts of war.

The legislature's participation in constructing these institutions demonstrated processual strengths. Legislative deliberations over these treaties do not indicate that the issue of constitutional war powers was ignored. To the contrary, key moments of questioning cleanly illuminated the stakes. During the SFRC hearings on the UN Charter, Senator Millikin questioned Leo Pasvolsky, an administrative official who had prepared the final Charter draft, on domestic war powers. Pasvolsky told the committee it would violate the Charter to include a reservation guaranteeing, in each instance, legislative authority over troops sent to the UN. Pasvolsky labeled the broader question of legislative-executive war relations a "domestic question."[131]

Through the UN and NATO debates the legislature considered a variety of positions on this "domestic question." The main alternatives included a defensive powers view, a delegation view, a police powers view, and a "special agreements" view. Each of these received substantial articulation and development. Not every view can be associated with one legislator; the debates featured flux and change, and the same person would sometimes argue for more than one different conception of constitutional war authority. Nonetheless, the debates clearly featured these several distinct lines of argumentation.

129   See Richard H. Heindel, Thorsten V. Kalijarvi, and Francis O. Wilcox, "The North Atlantic Treaty in the United States Senate," *The American Journal of International Law* 43:4 (1949): 633–65, on the high level of Senate involvement in the development of the North Atlantic Treaty.

130   Briggs, "Senator Vandenberg," 168. The Truman administration was skeptical about the value of troops under direct UN command, implicitly favoring troops under US command in support of UN directives. See Aiyaz Husain, "The United States and the Failure of UN Collective Security: Palestine, Kashmir, and Indonesia, 1947–1948," *The American Journal of International Law* 101:3 (2007): 585–96, for discussion of this history. See also Heindel, Kalijarvi, and Wilcox, "North Atlantic Treaty," 633–65.

131   "The Charter of the United Nations: Hearings Before the Senate Comm. on Foreign Relations," 79th Cong., 1st sess. *Congressional Record*, 197 (1945): 298 (henceforth *UN Senate FRC Hearings*, 79th Cong.).

These diverse constitutional positions were articulated in the context of two overwhelming sources of legislative consensus. The first consensus was a rejection of the pro-presidency insularism view that Truman would ultimately use to justify Korea: that the presidency contained inherent authority to deploy forces whenever he judged necessary. Congress was emphatic that it would maintain some voice in the nation's decisions to apply force.[132]

At the same time, the debates also generated a consensus resistance to using treaty reservations to formalize Congress's role. During the SFRC hearings on the UN, Senator Connally, the committee chair, said he believed that a reservation protecting Congress's authority over each military deployment "would, at least, violate the spirit of the Charter" by failing to recognize the authority of the Security Council. Other senators emphasized that UN effectiveness required the UN to know in advance what kinds of force it could use.[133] During debate over the UN Participation Act and NATO, critics of presidentialism proposed multiple resolutions affirming legislative authority over particular acts of war, and these resolutions were repeatedly defeated.[134]

Outside those two points of consensus, the legislature manifested a variety of perspectives on how the treaties would intersect with domestic war authority. The first involved the president's preexistent power to defend the nation. Senators argued that since the Security Council needed the assent of the executive branch, and since the president already had power to deploy armed force as commander in chief, "there was no constitutional issue."[135] Vandenberg said the president's use of force to back up the Security Council was directly analogous to his domestic constitutional war authority.[136] During SFRC hearings, Vandenberg told the committee that requiring Congress's authority for every use of the armed forces would violate the Constitution's "spirit" because "under the Constitution the President has certain rights to use our armed forces in the national defense without consulting Congress."[137] Senator Austin argued

132   Jane E. Stromseth, "Rethinking," 603, citing 91 *Congressional Record* (July 24, 1945), 8000, 8028 (Vandenberg); 8078 (Millikin); 8107 (Ball); 8076, 8079 (Pepper).

133   *UN Senate FRC Hearings*, 79th Cong., 299; Leo Pasvolsky, special assistant to Secretary of State, *UN Senate FRC Hearings,* 79th Cong., 1st sess. 127 (1945) at 124, Connally's statement in *Charter Hearings* at 127, Vandenberg's in *Charter Hearings* at 125.

134   91 *Congressional Record* (Dec 3, 1945) 11,306; Crabb, Jr. *Bipartisan,* 78; see also Heindel, Kalijarvi, and Wilcox, "North Atlantic Treaty," 633–65; Jane E. Stromseth, "Rethinking," 618.

135   Franck and Patel, "UN Police," 68.

136   *UN Senate FRC Hearings*, 79th Cong., 300. See also 298, 299. On the floor, see 91 *Congressional Record* (July 23, 1945), 7957 as cited in Franck and Patel, "UN Police."

137   *UN Senate FRC Hearings*, 79th Cong., 299.

that the mere fact of creating, and then joining, the UN signified that the United States believed "a threat to international security and peace occurring anywhere on earth constituted a direct threat to the security and peace of the United States."[138] When Senator Wheeler said the Charter would give the president additional power to use force without congressional approval, Senator Connally responded that the bill "does not really give him any more power," because presidential power was already broad.[139] In floor debate on NATO, Senators Watkins and Donnell argued that NATO required the United States to treat an attack on London like an attack on Washington, D.C.[140]

A second view advanced was a delegation view: that in ratifying these treaties, the legislature was delegating its war authority to an international institution that could then delegate it back to the president. Some legislators believed the UN Charter would give the president additional power to use force without congressional approval.[141] But mostly, the legal delegation view was articulated by critics of collective security. Senators Burton and Harlan Bushfield argued that without an amendment guaranteeing congressional approval for each act of war, the UN and NATO would represent unconstitutional delegations.[142] Senator Wheeler called for a constitutional amendment to resolve the delegation problem.[143] Ultimately, Senators Wherry, Wheeler, and Shipstead voted against the UN Participation Act (UNPA) as an unconstitutional delegation of war authority.[144]

A third position was that the construction of these institutions was a singular moment of international law that would allow the US president to police the globe to enforce law, not make war. During the SFRC Hearings, Senator Eugene Millikin argued that the relevant distinction was not one of defensive versus offensive war powers, but between "police powers" and "real war problems" that required congressional authorization. Unlike debates during the Roosevelt Corollary, here the distinction tracked two legal categories of force contemplated in the Charter itself: wars of self-defense (Article 51) and police actions (which must

138   91 *Congressional Record* (July 26, 1945), 8059.

139   Ibid. (Nov 26, 1945), 10, 966, 10, 967.

140   Hearings before the Senate Committee on Foreign Relations, 81st Cong., 1st sess., *Congressional Record* (1949): part I, 276–82, part 2, 518–25 (henceforth *SFRC Hearings*, 81st Cong.).

141   See, e.g., Senator Wheeler, 91 *Congressional Record* (Nov 26, 1945), 10, 966–67; Sen. Austin, 91 *Congressional Record* (July 26, 1945), 8065; see also Senator Scott Lucas, 91 *Congressional Record* (July 25, 1945), 8031.

142   Sen. Bushfield, 91 *Congressional Record* (July 3, 1945), 7156, 7988–89 and 7992 (Sen. Wheeler).

143   See also 91 *Congressional Record* (July 24, 1945), 7988.

144   91 *Congressional Record* (December 4, 1945), 11,409 and 11,393.

be specifically authorized by the UN).[145] The distinction would surface repeatedly in the debates. In the words of the SFRC report, "[p]reventive or enforcement action by these forces upon the order of the Security Council would not be an act of war but would be international action for the preservation of peace and for the purpose of preventing war. Consequently, the provisions of the Charter do not affect the exclusive power of Congress to declare war."[146] In floor debates, others amplified the point. Senator Scott Lucas, who would be Senate Majority Leader at the moment of the Korean War, said the president's war responsibilities could lead him to commit US troops to "carry out faithfully the execution of treaties," even without legislative assent.[147]

The implication is that Congress did not need any special agreements or enabling legislation to allow the president to use force. Instead, the sanction of international bodies would directly trigger a president's independent power to execute the law. Presumably, hostilities outside of this legal sanction would violate the Constitution. The difference between the legal delegation view and the police powers view was the scale of commitment advocates anticipated. A conflict requiring large troop commitments would be "war," even if it was defensive and even if it was authorized by the UN Security Council.[148] At the same time, advocates recognized the difficulty of drawing lines. Senator Millikin said the line between police operations and war was "a no-man's land which has never been eliminated by an acceptable definition."[149] The police power was a key frame legislators used to argue for the constitutionality of the Korean incursion.[150]

Finally on offer was the "special contracts view," ultimately enacted into law after intensive bipartisan interbranch negotiations over the UN Participation Act.[151] The UNPA, the Charter's domestic implementing

---

145   This was the distinction relied upon in the SFRC report on the UN Charter and in the House Foreign Affairs report of 1945. Peter Raven-Hansen, "The Gulf War: Collective Security, War Powers, and Laws of War," *Proceedings of the Annual Meeting* (American Society of International Law, 1991): 1–29, 10.

146   Senate Committee on Foreign Relations, the Charter of the United Nations, S. Exec. Rep. No. 8, 79th Cong., 1st Sess. 9 (1945), at 9; Thomas M. Franck and Faiza Patel, "UN Police Action in Lieu of War: The Old Order Changeth," *American Journal International Law* 85:1 (1991): 63–74, 13, citing Staff of Senate Committee on Foreign Relations, *Report on the Charter of the United Nations*, 79th Cong., 1st sess., Comm. Rep. 1945, 8.

147   91 *Congressional Record* (July 25, 1945), 8022.

148   Stromseth, "Rethinking," 604, 608; see also 91 *Congressional Record* (July 26, 1945), 8065, 8067.

149   Stromseth, "Rethinking," 611, citing 91 *Congressional Record* (July 25, 1945), 8033.

150   Stromseth, "Rethinking," 600; Zelizer, *Arsenal*, 100.

151   Stromseth, "Rethinking," 602–603.

legislation, specified that force would be made available to the UN through special agreements to be negotiated via an elaborate process that would be highly inclusive of Congress. The idea was that limited forces were being delegated to international institutions, but that these could be used for any purpose without legislative authorization. Early debate on this method focused on whether the special agreements would be executed by treaty or by domestic legislation, that is to say, by both houses of Congress. Senator Scott Lucas resisted the administration's suggestion that treaties would be adequate for executing special agreements by emphasizing the House's role in authorizing war.[152] House and Senate discussion both underscored the expectation of legislative inclusion.[153]

The constitutionality of these special agreements, too, was fiercely debated. Senators Vandenberg and Millikin emphasized that US forces acting under UN authority would be "peace forces," not implicating the war power and thereby allowing the legislature to avoid controversies over the location of war authority.[154] These peace forces could be of a large or small scale: it would be "up to *Congress* to determine."[155] Critically, it was the legislature that would decide how much military force it was delegating.

In its articulation of this variety of constitutional positions, Congress manifested one of its processual strengths. These positions were raised and placed in dialogue with each other again and again. Legislators recognized the political implications of the treaties they were being asked to ratify. They grappled with useful constitutional categories for resolving the constitutional dilemma of empowering rapid, guaranteed reenforcement of these institutions' authority in global governance while maintaining a legislative role in authorizing war. The debates over the resolutions, treaties, and implementing legislation featured a steady development of the same set of concerns, demonstrating ongoing concern. And while not every critic voted against the treaties, critics demonstrated a constancy of rhetoric over time that, I argue, heightened their rhetorical impact.[156]

---

152   See 91 *Congressional Record* (July 25, 1945), 8021–24; also December 18, 1945, 12,267. See also the defeat of a proposed amendment to the UNPA in the Senate allowing the president to negotiate special agreements with only two thirds of the Senate at 91 *Congressional Record* (December 3, 1945), 11,296; 11,301; and 11,303.

153   *Participation by the United States in the United Nations Organization: Hearings Before the House Committee on Foreign Affairs*, 79th Cong., 1st sess. 23 (1945); S. Rep. No. 717, 79th Cong., 1st Sess. 5 (1945).

154   91 *Congressional Record* (November 26, 1945), 10,967–68.

155   Stromseth, "Rethinking," 618.

156   Taft criticized the absence of legislative controls, but voted with the majority. But in December 1945, Taft voted against sending delegates to the UN when his amendment to curb the delegate's discretion was rebuffed by the legislature. Through the early 1950s

That these debates featured such a variety of constitutional positions developed so continuously over time puts the administration's confusing and misleading interventions into context. In the midst of debate over the UN, Truman informally pledged not to make agreements about the uses of force without congressional authorization.[157] It was clear this was no legally binding guarantee, and Truman obviously could not bind later administrations. The very need for the informal promise underscored the broad war authority implied by the Charter. During deliberations on the North Atlantic Charter, Secretary Dean Acheson also wrongfully refuted Senator Hickenlooper's suggestion that NATO would require the United States to send troops to Europe.[158] But the administration's view was ultimately one among many advanced in Congress.

Ultimately, the UN Charter was ratified, 89 to 2, in July 1945. The Senate ratified the North Atlantic Treaty on July 21, 1949, with only thirteen dissenting votes, its fundamental security guarantee intact. In other words, both treaties passed with overwhelming support in the midst of sharply critical scrutiny. In its construction of the political conditions for an empowered presidency, Congress was displaying the processual strengths of clarifying relevant options as well as harnessing the power of a broad consensus politics into law.

Some pro-Congress insularists argue that the legislature did not construct a new war powers order, and that its treaties were irrelevant to domestic allocations of war authority.[159] Alternatively, Thomas Franck and Faiza Pael, as well as David Golove, argue that UN Security Council resolutions amount to legal authorization for a president's acts of war even when he acts outside the special agreements mechanism.[160] (Special agreements have never been negotiated.) Both positions evade the constitutional politics the legislature was launching.

Taft consistently offered legal proposals aimed at curbing executive discretionary powers. Matthews, "Taft, the Constitution and American Foreign Policy," 514.

157 Fisher, "Korean War," 28; Edwin Borchard, "The Charter and the Constitution," *American Journal of International Law* 39:4 (1945): 767–71, 767–68. The Truman administration also assured that it would be solicitous of Congress. Theodore J. Lowi, *The End of Liberalism: The Second Republic of the United States* 2nd ed. (New York: W. W. Norton & Co., 1979), 141.

158 Lowi, *Liberalism*, 141.

159 Fisher, "Korean War"; *Long Wars*, 65 (manuscript). The SFRC report on the North Atlantic Charter was emphatic that the treaty would not change the relationship between the president and Congress on war powers. U.S. Senate, Committee on Foreign Relations, "North Atlantic Treaty," Executive Rep. 8, 14, 81st Cong., 1st sess. (June 6, 1949). See also Heindel, Kalijarvi, and Wilcox, "The North Atlantic Treaty," 650.

160 Franck and Patel, "UN Police," 63, 74. David Golove, "From Versailles to San Francisco: The Revolutionary Transformation of the War Powers," *University of Colorado Law Review* 70:4 (1999): 1491–523.

The idea that Congress did nothing to change the received war powers order is belied by legislative history. The UN Participation Act clearly "delegates" war authority with its special-agreements pathway. Once agreements are negotiated, the legal power to commit troops rests with the UN and with the presidency, regardless of Congress's views in each case. This legislative construction, clearly enacted into law, is not consistent with the war powers baseline prior to World War II.[161] Never before had the legislature promised directly and through treaties to make military force available for the enforcement of such broad guarantees.

Nevertheless, nor did Congress create a legal pathway for the president to use troops to enforce global security outside of the special agreements pathway. The UNPA is absolutely clear that no UN forces were to be provided outside of the special agreements provision.[162]

I interpret this moment instead as the construction of a politics of presidential empowerment. The UN Charter and North Atlantic Treaty were not simply treaties, but also core elements of a new security order.[163] The SFRC report on NATO directly addressed a set of political implications that exceeded their legal accomplishment, stating, "our entry into collective defense arrangements in the Western Hemisphere and the North Atlantic area should not be taken by anyone to mean that we do not have a very real interest in the maintenance of peace and security everywhere."[164] Congress committed the United States to the development of global security through collective institutions, and accepted some form of independent presidential war authority (through special agreements, at least) as a tool for securing this policy choice.

With the creation of the UN and NATO, and with the establishment of a powerful military capacity, the Congress created ideological and material tools the president would need to independently wage defensive war on behalf of a largely US conception of global security. In so doing, I argue that Congress created a politics—not just a set of legal enactments—that enlarged the scope of an already-existent independent presidential war

161   See Golove, "Transformation," 1500–501.

162   The House and Senate reports on the UN Participation Act were emphatic that nothing in the act affirmatively authorized the president to provide forces to the Security Council beyond what was provided in Article 43 agreements. See H.R. Rep. No. 1383, 79th Cong., 1st sess. 8 (1945); S. Rep. No. 717, 79th Cong., 1st Sess. 7 (1945). At the same time, see how debates were premised on the fact that the special agreements would vest the UN with a war power. See *UN Senate FRC Hearings*, 79th Cong: 645–52. Section 6, UN Participation Act 59 Stat. 619 (December 20, 1945).

163   The extent to which the security politics of today continues to treat the authority of the UN, or NATO, as critical defensive interests, and the extent to which the president is empowered to use force to protect that authority in the global environment of today are open questions.

164   Heindel, Kalijarvi, and Wilcox, "North Atlantic Treaty," 664.

power to defend core security interests of the nation.[165] By tightly linking US national security to the authority of international institutions and the containment of communism, these treaties and statutes broadened the *meaning* of the president's defensive war authority. The result was not the recognition of an inherent presidential authority to wage war (as Truman argued), or a diffuse delegation of Congress's power to authorize war (as Wherry argued). Unlike the special agreements approach (which was also a constitutional innovation), this construction of presidential independence resulted not from explicit legal authorization, but rather from a *politics* whereby the very concept of defense shifted and a *politics* wherein the legislature would exercise political more than legal forms of interbranch review. The legislature's effort at legal draftsmanship in the special agreements approach foundered when Cold War rivalries made the agreements impossible to negotiate, but at least Congress took on the task of making law and in so doing demonstrated awareness that it was constructing a new order.[166]

The legislature manifested additional processual strengths in the early Cold War when it generated a politics of interbranch review for this new construction: the bipartisan consensus. Unlike the special agreements provision, the bipartisan consensus was never given a single coherent legal form. (Over the course of the 20th century a great deal of security legislation did come to incorporate various provisions guaranteeing ongoing consultation between the executive and legislative branches.) Nonetheless the bipartisan consensus represented an innovative way to generate a form of interbranch dialogue in a security context where public disagreement was seen as threatening.

Vandenberg and Connally took the lead in developing bipartisanship in the legislature, urging the Roosevelt administration to create joint briefing committees and ultimately winning for minority Republicans "the right to be consulted."[167] Postwar consultations requested by Senator Tom Connally between the State Department and the Senate Foreign Relations Committee broadened through the years to include more party leaders from both sides. Ultimately a Committee of Eight, with equal Democrats and Republicans, became empowered by the SFRC to meet weekly to evaluate proposals about the UN before these were circulated to Allied leaders.[168] The effective operation of this inclusive process was behind the overwhelming Senate majorities that supported collective

---

165   *UN Senate FRC Hearings*, 79th Cong, 298–99, 641, 654–55.
166   Werkley, "Truman Says." Some of the Cold War rivalries that stymied negotiations around special agreements were produced by the US presidency.
167   Briggs, "Congress," 334; Briggs, "Senator Vandenberg," 164.
168   Crabb, Jr., *Bipartisan*, 46.

security in the late 1940s, with the UN and NATO charters coming to serve as exemplars for the bipartisan approach.[169]

One signal that the bipartisan consensus represented a new constitutional construction was the shift in norms it heralded about legislative independence. Senator Vandenberg said he believed that becoming a delegate to collective security conferences meant he was no longer "a free agent when I return to the Senate to function in my Congressional capacity."[170] But prior to the Cold War, bringing legislators into policy formulation was a practice to which legislators and out-of-power party members would object.[171] Legislators brought into executive branch deliberations either resigned their congressional seats entirely, or faced constitutional criticism for undermining the independence of the legislature's judgment.[172]

Despite its functional role as a constitutional construction, certain features of the bipartisan consensus make its terms hazy. It was an aspiration toward partisan consensus through elite inclusion that could govern a wide variety of political dilemmas. It was never formally written into law or explicitly debated as a constitutional innovation. Its contours developed through practice, rather than explicit design, with focal cases that included Roosevelt's postwar actions around the politics of collective security, including the UN Charter; the stabilization of Western Europe through the Marshall Plan and weapons assistance programs; passage of the National Security Act of 1947; and the creation and ratification of the North Atlantic Treaty—in other words, "the foundation upon which the policy of containment rested in the postwar period."[173] While the bipartisan consensus has its weaknesses, I believe its strengths are rendered visible in comparison with the legislative politics of the Roosevelt Corollary. Legislators supporting Theodore Roosevelt's adventurism apparently found little reason to consult, negotiate, or bring their distinctive foreign policy capacities into these war questions in any way. The weaknesses of the bipartisan consensus are real, but we should appreciate, too, the element of legislative strength in constructing a norm that could procedurally discipline the presidency at all.

That this politics achieved some measure of the authority associated with Congress's processual standards makes it constitutionally authoritative, I argue, under the relational conception. At the same time, the

169   Ibid., 78.
170   Vandenberg, *Private Papers*, 330–31.
171   Crabb, Jr., *Bipartisan*, 35.
172   E.g., Senator James Bayard and House Speaker Henry Clay's participation with President Madison in negotiations surrounding the War of 1812. Crabb, Jr., *Bipartisan*, 36–39.
173   Crabb, Jr., *Bipartisan*, 2, 226. See also Zelizer, *Arsenal*, 71.

legislature's construction was legally incomplete. The bipartisan consensus was never translated into law as a disciplining standard for presidential bellicosity, and the special agreements provision, which was enacted into law, was never executed. The legislature's constitutional accomplishment would have been even more significant if it had more fully managed to use law to regulate presidential behavior. However, these failures of its lawmaking should not blind us to the constitutional significance of the legislature's mobilization of a new politics around defensive security.

Hence when Truman intervened in Korea, his act—not mandated by the UN and even preceding the Security Council's call for global assistance—was interpretable not as the execution of a legally delegated power, but as an act of domestic defense, on behalf of a set of security interests Congress itself had articulated, reviewable through a politics Congress participated in launching. Truman's behavior was certainly a challenge to the preexistent war powers system, but it was a challenge grounded in a politics the legislature was also creating through processes that can be defended to some degree under the relational conception.

Congress's processual authority in the Cold War order is enhanced too if we consider the quality of its ratification of presidential bellicosity through a contentious process of interbranch deliberation. After Truman acted in Korea, the emerging construction of independent presidential war powers was materially and ideologically supported by Congress despite a high level of legislative pluralism, contentiousness, and focused challenge.

An important open question that arose after the Truman Doctrine, the UN, and NATO pertained to setting relative priorities in achieving global security. After the fall of nationalist China, and in the wake of the Republican failure in 1948 to gain electoral strength from its participation in bipartisanship, a segment of Congress began to challenge the president to pay greater attention to China and East Asia.[174] Debates surrounding Walton Butterworth's September 1949 confirmation for Assistant Secretary of State focused on Truman's China policy.[175] Republican victories in the 1950 elections dispersed Senate power by upsetting committee hierarchies, and Vandenberg's retreat created new opportunities for power in the Republican Party. These forces converged in the Taft wing's development of a sustained policy and constitutional assault on the emerging security order.

This group of legislators pushed Truman toward bellicosity in Asia. The so-called loss of China generated a major partisan divide in a moment

---

174 In 1948 Truman campaigned on a do-nothing Congress, while "claiming most of the work of the 80th Congress as his own." Zelizer, *Arsenal*, 78.

175 Fetzer, "Congress," 1.

when foreign policy was generally being developed in a bipartisan way.[176] The administration's announcement in January 1950 that it had no intention of defending Formosa, and then its placement of South Korea outside of the US defense perimeter, provoked a storm of congressional criticism.[177] This legislative politics importantly conditioned Truman's response to the boundary trespass of South Korea. He was already under domestic attack for an insufficiently bellicose East Asia policy, and North Korea had carried out the first trespass of an internationally negotiated, UN-supported boundary since the close of World War II.[178]

Truman's first response to the incident was to meet with his senior advisors, ask for a draft resolution for Congress, announce that he would address the legislature, and invite the SFRC chair Tom Connally to advise him. Secretary Acheson also met with Connally, Republican Senator Alexander Wiley, Democratic Representative John Kee of West Virginia (chair of the House Foreign Affairs Committee) and briefed congressional leaders.[179] In his meeting, Connally told the President he had independent authority to intervene "as Commander in Chief and under the UN Charter."[180] On June 27 Truman met with a bipartisan group of congressional leaders about his decision and received their "overwhelming support."[181]

When it was announced that Truman had decided to commit troops to Korea, the *New York Times* reported that senators rose and cheered.[182] In the summer of 1950 a previously divided Congress almost unanimously extended the Selective Service Act for another year and approved deficit appropriations for defense.[183] It also enacted the Defense Produc-

176 A policy critique was beginning to emerge from legislators who wanted to link commitments to anticommunism in Europe with ones in China and East Asia. Relevant legislators included Senators Knowland, Judd, Ferguson (R-MI), Wherry, Bridges, and McCarran, and House representatives Lodge (R-CT) and Frances Walter (D-PA). Fetzer, "Congress," chapter 6, 193, 196, 198, 201, 202, 206, 217.

177 Fetzer, "Congress," 217.

178 Gaddis, *Now Know,* 75–76. On links between Korea and WWII, see Ernest R. May, *"Lessons" of the Past: The Use and Misuse of History in American Foreign Policy* (New York: Oxford University Press, 1973) and Yuen Foong Khong, *Analogies at War: Korea, Munich, Dien Bien Phu, and the Vietnam Decisions of 1965* (Princeton: Princeton University Press, 1992).

179 Crabb, Jr., *Bipartisan,* 194–95; David R. Kepley, *The Collapse of the Middle Way: Senate Republicans and the Bipartisan Foreign Policy, 1948–1952* (New York: Greenwood Press, 1988), 56.

180 Robert Ferrell, *Harry S. Truman and the Modern American Presidency* (Boston: Longman Publishing, 1983), 124, as cited by James T. Patterson, *Grand Expectations: The United States, 1945–1974* (New York: Oxford University Press, 1996), 212.

181 Schlesinger, *Imperial,* 131; Kepley, *Collapse,* 87.

182 "Democracy in Action," *New York Times* (June 29, 1950), 28.

183 Raven-Hansen, "The Gulf War," 12.

tion Act to give the president power to mobilize military equipment and commodities for war. The military aspirations of NSC-68 began to shape defense expenditures "many times over."[184] The sole voice in Congress to oppose Truman's Korea decision was defeated in the 1950 election.[185]

This strong material and ideological legislative support happened in the midst of ongoing constitutional and policy criticism. Only a few days after the war began, Taft delivered a major address challenging the president's Asia policy and encouraging Truman to submit a joint resolution authorizing the war, promising his vote. Taft's criticisms were focused: he acknowledged support for the president's general policy, but worried about "the process by which it was achieved."[186] (This did not lead him to actually initiate a joint resolution process himself.) Taft went on to vote war supplies and statutory executive war powers, albeit "reluctantly."[187] The content of the constitutional criticism was one that Senator Taft had been developing since the days of Lend-Lease.

This constitutional criticism was linked to policy disagreement. The constitutional challenge was developed by the Taft wing with the support of Kenneth Wherry, the Senate Minority Leader. They denounced Truman's constitutional position, advocated total war against China, and criticized the UN's involvement in Korea.[188] The elections of 1950 brought Republican gains in the House and Senate, seemingly vindicating the Republican strategy of challenging the presidency on foreign affairs, and the conservative internationalism located in the Republican Party began to gain traction. These conservatives advocated more aggression in Asia (although Taft himself was inconsistent on Korea, sometimes urging escalation, sometimes withdrawal);[189] more powerful resistance to Soviet power in Eastern Europe[190] and a reluctance to engage in diplomacy with Soviets;[191] military reliance on airpower, which was cheaper than the army;[192] intensification of domestic anticommunism programs, including the use of legislative committees as a tool to ferret out subversion in the executive branch;[193] military preparedness centered

184 Patterson, *Expectations*, 214; Brune and Leach, "Congress," 359.

185 Brune and Leach, "Congress," 372.

186 See *Congressional Record* (June 28, 1950), S 9322; 96 *Congressional Record* (June 28, 1950), 9320.

187 Kepley, *Collapse*, 89.

188 Richard Cope, "Kenneth Wherry, Negativist from Nebraska," *Reporter* (April 17, 1951), 10–13.

189 Brune and Leach, "Congress," 368, 369; Zelizer, *Arsenal*, 83.

190 Ibid., 84.

191 Ibid., 85.

192 Ibid., 84.

193 Robert David Johnson, *Congress and the Cold War* (Cambridge: Cambridge University Press, 2005), xvi–xvii; Kepley, *Collapse*, 4.

on the territorial boundaries of the United States;[194] and Congressional empowerment.[195] Conservative internationalists hoped that legislative governance—"its slowness, its conservative outlook, and the presence of many conservatives in positions of power ... would limit the very government they were helping to expand."[196] They also made effective use of the committee structure to intensify domestic surveillance programs, most importantly through the empowerment of the House Un-American Activities Committee.[197]

These critics were pressing for *more*, not less bellicose engagement, but engagement that would be licensed by the legislature in each case. And while some might wish more had advocated for the use of "soft power," liberals led by Senator Claude Pepper (FL) did mount a dwindling resistance to the extension of military aid to undemocratic regimes.[198] This spectrum of policy response was a testimony to Congress's security governance according to its processual strengths: manifesting and exposing the main lines of political cleavage in a polity; developing multiple (not just one) policy alternatives; and linking, albeit often weakly, its constitutional criticisms with its policy agendas.

Internationalist legislators regrouped to pitch their battle again. They believed that the presidential power to move quickly in response to threat was a lodestar for the new international system, the only sure way to guarantee the effectiveness of the nascent international institutions expected to serve as bulwarks against World War III. Senator Paul Douglas reinvigorated the presidential "police power" argument.[199] Wayne Morse, who would later become one of the most vociferous opponents of the Vietnam War, justified Truman's intervention under the commander-in-chief clause. Moderate Republicans like John Foster Dulles, Thomas Dewey, and Henry Cabot Lodge, Jr., as well as many southern Democrats, supported the presidency and headed off any resolutions that would have curtailed its UN and NATO authority. Senator Bricker began introducing amendments that would restrict the extent to which treaties could authorize presidential power in foreign relations, but these repeatedly failed.[200] Congress continued to fund and support the war, and Truman

---

194   Kepley, *Collapse*, 4.

195   Zelizer, *Arsenal*, 85.

196   Ibid., 85.

197   Ibid., 85–86.

198   Griffin, "Long Wars," 137 (manuscript).

199   *Congressional Record* (July 5 1950), 9792–94.

200   Brune and Leach, "Congress," 347–48, see also Gary W. Reichard, *The Reaffirmation of Republicanism: Eisenhower and the Eighty-third Congress* (Knoxville: University of Tennessee Press, 1975).

continued to field hawkish criticism from legislators who believed he was too restrained.

The constitutional controversies of the late 1940s ultimately exploded with the "Great Debate" of 1951. Under attack was the idea that treaties could empower the president to carry out acts of war. When Congress met in January, Senators Taft and Kenneth Wherry led the legislature in six months of extensive debates, hearings, and resolutions criticizing Truman's security policy. Truman's policy was challenged from a wide spectrum: while some criticized him for acting outside of his constitutional powers, other resolutions called for MacArthur to seek "total victory" in North Korea.[201] Moderate Republicans like John Foster Dulles, Thomas Dewey, Henry Cabot Lodge, Jr., and many southern Democrats supported the presidency and headed off resolutions that would have curtailed its NATO and UN authority. The controversy ended with tepid results: a sense-of-the-Senate resolution passed supporting the transference of four divisions to Europe only on the condition that future commitments would be approved by Congress. Richard Nixon (R-CA) was one of the legislators who voted on behalf of legislative authority over troop deployments.[202]

Throughout the early 1950s, various versions of the Bricker Amendment were proposed, each a variation on the theme that treaties and executive agreements could not be constitutionally binding without domestic legislation. The Taft wing noted Vinson's dissent in the *Youngstown* decision (1952), citing his rhetoric of vast presidential powers and warning that this reasoning might be the harbinger of a new and dangerous path.[203] But between 1952 and 1954 the language of the Bricker Amendment became more and more general, vague, and diluted, until finally it was beaten down decisively in the Senate.[204] In January of 1953, Representative Frederic Coudert (R-NY) introduced a sense-of-Congress resolution declaring the requirement of Congressional authorization "in each instance" to the deployment of troops abroad. These efforts were not successful. While critics of an empowered presidency won a few significant debates, keeping expenditures down, limiting the size of forces, and achieving mandates for consultative procedures, dissenters failed to stem the movements toward presidentially run internationalism. Instead,

---

201   Brune and Leach, "Congress," 347–48; Kepley, *Collapse*, 89.

202   Schlesinger, *Imperial*, 140.

203   100 *Congressional Record* (February 3, 1954), 1217.

204   Ibid., 151–52. On the Great Debate, see Raymond Ojserkis, *Beginnings of the Cold War Arms Race: The Truman Administration and the U.S. Arms Build-Up* (Westport, CT: Praeger, 2003), ch 8.

their own claims moderated over the course of the debate.[205] I interpret the Great Debate of 1951, and the series of debates in the early fifties about presidential authority, as a series of ratification moments, where constitutional premises of Cold War internationalism were once again challenged, tested, and politically reaffirmed.

By the end of the Eisenhower administration, a kind of accommodation had been reached. Presidents would seek legislative support, but with the idea that the legislature was supporting a constitutional power that was already the president's. This would allow for ongoing legislative participation in constructing a structured defensive politics—naming enemies, priorities, and focusing attention—while reinforcing the constitutional construction of the independent presidential defensive war powers that had been achieved in the past ten years. When China threatened Formosa in January 1955, President Eisenhower requested that Congress "confirm his authority" to block a Chinese communist invasion. Despite the constitutional objections that had been part of Eisenhower's presidential campaign against Truman, the grounds had decisively shifted: Eisenhower said that while "authority for some of the actions which might be required would be inherent in the authority of the Commander in Chief," congressional action would publicly "establish" that proposition.[206] The response from the legislature was revealing. Eisenhower's deference to legislative power was received with suspicion. Johnson emphasized that "we are not going to take the responsibility out of the hands of the constitutional leader and try to arrogate it to ourselves," and Senator Rayburn suggested that Eisenhower take strikes without consulting Congress.[207] Some legislators actually criticized Eisenhower for seeking Congress's view instead of acting from his own judgment. Nonetheless the authorization he sought was passed. The Formosa Resolution, which named no enemy and empowered the president to use the military "as he deems necessary," committed Congress to the approval of hostilities without knowledge of the context in which hostilities might begin.[208]

The Congress was aware that it was acting in constitutionally innovative ways. Eisenhower's requested Mideast Resolution of 1957 essentially endorsed the deployment of US forces to any nation requesting such aid to resist international communism. This resolution was not an authorization or a declaration of war. Senator Jacob Javits (R-NY) told Congress it represented "a new technique in American policy. It is not a declaration

205   John William Malsberger, *From Obstruction to Moderation: The Transformation of Senate Conservatism, 1938–1952* (Cranbury, NJ: Associated University Presses, 2000).

206   Schlesinger, *Imperial Presidency,* 159–60.

207   Ibid., 160; James A. Robinson, *Congress and Foreign Policy Making: A Study in Legislative Influence and Initiative* (Homewood: Dorsey Press, 1967), 55.

208   Schlesinger, *Imperial Presidency,* 160.

of war; nor are we waiting for a situation to arise when it would be the prerogative of Congress to declare war. It is advance notice that we will combat force with force. In that respect I think it is a new technique in meeting Communist techniques which present us with a new situation, and one which the Senate should adopt."[209] This did not mean Congress had surrendered its war authority entirely. In 1954 the legislature raised such a controversy about Eisenhower placing two hundred mechanics in Vietnam that Eisenhower deferred in order to appease his own party.[210] The legislature was supervising the president to avoid another Korea, but it was not more generally resisting the Cold War construction of independent presidential power. It was the beginning of an age of coercive diplomacy; not simple congressional passivity, but rather congressional participation in a new order of war authority.

The role of the champions of legislative power in generating constitutional authority for the legislature's construction of the Cold War order has been underappreciated. Using the relational conception, I argue that legislative participation in the construction of the Cold War security order was authoritative because the legislature combined strong support and a consensus politics with developed criticism from a wide spectrum of policy and constitutional positions. Internationalists have derided the conservative critics, and the loss of conservative Republicans has been called a "display [of] their irrelevance," the Great Debate "little more than a flurry of protest," or an "emotional outburst," "the last convulsive outbreak of an old nostalgia."[211] But I argue that the legislative partisans were doing important work, enhancing the quality of legislative authority that Congress was able to bestow on the Cold War order by supporting Congress's achievement of governance according to the processual standards.

This analysis says nothing about the presidency's contribution to that order. Moreover, the processualist defense of early Cold War Congresses would have been enhanced if legislators had used their institution's lawmaking strengths to create more rigorous legal structures around their new constitutional constructions. I also believe that Democratic partisans of the presidency in Congress demonstrated a failure of independence

209   Silverstein, *Imbalance,* 87.

210   William G. Howell and Jon C. Pevehouse, *While Dangers Gather: Congressional Checks on Presidential War Powers* (Princeton: Princeton University Press, 2007), 117, 120; Melanie Billings-Yun, *Decision Against War: Eisenhower and Dien Bien Phu, 1954* (New York: Columbia University Press, 1988), 25–27, 54.

211   Alonzo L. Hamby, "World War II: Conservatism and Constituency Politics," in *The American Congress: The Building of Democracy,* ed. Julian E. Zelizer (Boston: Houghton Mifflin Company, 2004), 479; Manfred Jonas, *Isolationism in America: 1935–1941* (Ithaca, NY: Cornell University Press, 1966), 278, 281.

(one of the processual standards) when they simply accepted Truman's claim that authority to wage war was "inherent" in the office of commander in chief. It would have been better for them to argue that it was the legislature's participation in the construction of a new set of core security interests that warranted presidential empowerment on this scale. This alternative claim would have preserved their pro-presidency constitutional position, while at the same time preserving the claim to their own institution's competence. Moreover, these levels of legislative scrutiny did not continue unabated throughout the Cold War, nor were they equally characteristic of every Cold War issue. As the legislature lost its vitality as a forum for deliberation about security, the value of its assent to presidential adventures correspondingly declined. Clearly, there are grounds for processualist criticism of the Cold War order.

An analysis of the full constitutional authority of the Cold War would require us to assess the president's contributions to constructing that order as well. Also, some actions, such as MacArthur's passage into North Korea, or, as chapter 4 argues, Nixon's incursion into Cambodia, may depart from what the Cold War security order licensed.[212] Nonetheless, I argue, using the relational conception, that early Cold War Congresses constructed a politics that was highly supportive of independent presidential war authority and that responded to an objectively threatening context while engaging a relatively impressive set of their distinctive governance capacities.

CONCLUSION

I have used the relational conception to defend, in a limited way, the legislature's construction of the Cold War security order. Early Cold War legislatures were more deeply deliberative; enacted their lawmaking capacity more carefully; demonstrated more of the pluralism that is a hallmark of legislative strength; and premised their judgments upon a more accurate assessment of national defensive security needs than the Congresses of the Roosevelt Corollary.

By contrast, the Roosevelt Corollary emerged from a context in which the legislature had done less to define the content of the security interest at stake. The Corollary was constructed with the legislature's material and ideological participation, but the legislature did not make good use

212   See P. Wesley Kriebel, "Unfinished Business—Intervention under the U.N. Umbrella: America's Participation in the Korean War, 1950–1953," in *Intervention of Abstention: The Dilemma of American Foreign Policy*, ed. Robin Higham (Lexington: University Press of Kentucky, 1975), 119–20.

of its capacities to clarify relevant dimensions of constitutional concern, to challenge or deliberate upon the defensive value of the underlying security policy, to consider alternative policies, or even to make law for the new construction they were creating. The Roosevelt Corollary was premised on security claims that were shaky or nonexistent, and yet were not challenged by Congress. By the time an effective policy and constitutional challenge was developed by the peace progressives, presidentially led imperialism had shifted to using economic and diplomatic, rather than military, resources. While pro-Congress scholars see in the Cold War a unique moment of constitutional decline, and while pro-presidency scholars cite the Roosevelt Corollary as a legitimating influence for the Cold War order, I argue, using the relational conception, that the legislature conferred *more,* not less, constitutional authority to the Cold War order than to that of the Roosevelt Corollary.

Of course, the arguments I make in this chapter are controversial. Indeed, the constitutional authority of the Cold War order is a defining controversy of war powers scholarship. The relational conception seeks not necessarily to resolve that controversy, but rather to focus it differently. Settlement approaches treat the entire post-Cold War order as a massive constitutional violation; imagine a presidency with an inherent power to fight global communism; or implausibly argue for a legal transformation in a context where Congress's law was either underdeterminate or actually resistant to independent presidentialism. The relational conception instead asks us to engage a set of decidedly political and contextual questions about institutional performance in developing meaning for constitutional vocabulary. The analysis is grounded, not in a freestanding legal standard, but rather in a comparison to the formally parallel case of the Roosevelt Corollary. Engaging these questions can help scholars and publics to illuminate the kind of politics that rests behind the difficult struggle to achieve constitutionally faithful security governance.

Chapter 4

DEFENSIVE WAR

The Cuban Missile Crisis and Cambodian Incursion

Consider two independent acts of war of two separate presidential administrations: the 1962 Cuban Missile Crisis of the Kennedy administration, and Nixon's interventions in Cambodia. In the fall of 1962 Kennedy had assured Congress there were no offensive missiles in Cuba, consistent with statements he was receiving from the Soviets and from personal communication from Khrushchev, and consistent with the beliefs of US intelligence. When it became apparent that missiles were being installed, Kennedy kept quiet, notifying allies before he notified the public or Congress. He kept the situation secret while preparing for nuclear war and actually initiating an act of war, a blockade, that was not announced until it was being executed. It is plausible that Kennedy kept the blockade secret for electoral reasons; Republicans were attacking him for failures in Cuba, especially the disastrous Bay of Pigs.[1]

Nixon cited this "finest hour" of the Kennedy administration as precedent for the Cambodian invasion.[2] Nixon's intervention in neutral Cambodia began with bombings in 1969, and then proceeded to ground troops in 1970 and ongoing bombing until late in 1973. All of the interventions prior to the Paris Peace Accords (1973) were publicly justified

---

1 For an argument that the choice of a blockade was a response to domestic political pressures, see Fen Osler Hampson, "The Divided Decision-Maker: American Domestic Politics and the Cuban Crises," *International Security* 9:3 (1984): 130–65.

2 President Richard Nixon, "Address to the Nation on the Situation in Southeast Asia" (April 30, 1970) in *Public Papers of the Presidents of the United States: Richard M. Nixon, 1970* (Washington: Government Printing Office), 139 (henceforth *April 30 Address*). On the implausibility of the precedent to others see Rowland Evans, Jr., and Robert D. Novak, *Nixon in the White House* (New York: Random House: 1971), 245.

as a way to weaken that country's value as a supply line and conduit of soldiers into Vietnam. Nixon, like Kennedy, may have kept his actions in Cambodia secret to evade domestic political pressure—in this case, against escalating the war in Vietnam.

In neither of these cases were the president's acts of war statutorily authorized. Both were justified according to the president's independent war authority, but neither represented a response to an immediate attack or invasion. Both were kept secret from Congress and the public. If we view these two acts according to a settlement model of war powers, they rise and fall together.

However, the relational conception of war authority introduces a new set of terms for evaluating these acts. Applying these terms to each president's conduct, I argue that the relational conception accommodates and explains the common intuition that the acts can be constitutionally distinguished. A first difference arises from applying the substantive standard that a president's conduct be justifiable on grounds of defense. I assess the nation's defensive security interests not in a freestanding way, but rather through the filter of the security order that constructed the president's independent war authority in the first place. While both were responses to threats specified through a Cold War security order, the identification and management of threat in Kennedy's case was more deeply connected to the terms of that order than was Nixon's. The acts can also be distinguished on processual grounds. Kennedy's exercise of war power was more deeply connected to his skillful use of executive branch governance capacities.

THE CUBAN MISSILE CRISIS AND
CAMBODIAN INCURSION

In late summer of 1962, it became apparent to informed observers that the Soviet Union was shipping arms and some troops to Cuba. The Soviet government gave multiple assurances, both through private diplomatic and public statements, that only defensive weapons were being supplied, and the United States stated both publicly and through private diplomatic communication that nuclear weapons in Cuba would be unacceptable.[3] Moscow had never before placed nuclear weapons outside of its

---

3 Graham Allison and Philip Zelikow, *Essence of Decision: Explaining the Cuban Missile Crisis*, 2nd ed. (New York: Addison-Wesley Longman, 1999), 78–80; U.S. Department of State, "Statement by President John F. Kennedy on Cuba, September 4, 1962," *U.S. Department of State Bulletin* 47, no. 1213 (September 24, 1962): 450.

borders.[4] In the face of this possible threat, Kennedy initiated a process to coordinate the views of executive branch intelligence analysts, who concluded that, while the USSR could get "considerable military advantage from placing longer range ballistic missiles in Cuba, or, more likely, establishing a base for missile-launching submarines there," such behavior was very unlikely because of the risk it would introduce into US-Soviet relations.[5]

But the global context was one that made edginess appropriate. The 1961 Bay of Pigs fiasco had led Khrushchev to warn Kennedy about a chain reaction that a "little war" in Cuba could trigger.[6] The two had had an unsuccessful Vienna meeting in June 1961, which Kennedy interpreted as Khrushchev's not taking him seriously. Khrushchev had even threatened war if the United States tried to stop him from blocking Western access to Western Berlin.[7] Confronted with Khrushchev's determination, the United States was working hard to reassure NATO allies of the credibility of its commitments to European defense. At the same time, in August 1961, the United States permitted the Soviets to build the Berlin wall without military confrontation.

As US analysts worked to determine the nature of the military buildup in Cuba, domestic politics became increasingly tense. Both Republicans and Democrats feared the consequences of a weak response to the Cuban situation. Republicans in Congress began to push especially hard, attacking Kennedy for ignoring a building crisis.[8] Congress agitated for a forceful response, and on September 7 granted the president the authority to call reservists into the armed forces.[9] In early October Congress passed a resolution expressing national determination to prevent "the creation or use of an externally supported military capability endangering the security of the United States," and to prevent "by any means necessary, including use of arms, the Marxist-Leninist regime in Cuba from extending by force" its subversive activities in the hemisphere.[10]

But Congress never actually authorized Kennedy to use military force in Cuba absent Cuban use of force or threats. The supportive resolutions that the legislature did pass were focused on using arms to prevent Cuba

---

4   Allison and Zelikow, *Essence*, 78.

5   Ibid., 81; Central Intelligence Agency, "The Military Buildup in Cuba," *CIA National Intelligence Estimate*, no. 13 (September 19, 1962).

6   Allison and Zelikow, *Essence*, 83.

7   Julian Zelizer, *Arsenal of Democracy: The Politics of National Security—From World War II to the War on Terrorism* (New York: Basic Books, 2009), 152.

8   Zelizer, *Arsenal*, 157; Allison and Zelikow, *Essence*, 330, 79.

9   Allison and Zelikow, *Essence*, 79.

10   *Cuban Resolution*, Senate Joint Res. 230. Pub. Law 87-733, 87th Cong., 2nd sess.

from extending communist aims through force, but the weapons buildup was not an actual use of force. Hence the only constitutional authority Kennedy would have for the blockade came from his independent war authority to defend the nation from attack. And importantly, despite this anxious politics, the existence of missiles in Cuba did not constitute an attack, or even an immediate threat. Americans had been living under the threat of Russian missiles for some time. As Kennedy perceived clearly, the USSR already had ample missiles to inflict devastating violence upon the Unites States. Moreover, the material balance of power between the nations was scarcely affected. The USSR's intercontinental ballistic missiles were of doubtful reliability. Many of the long-range bombers that Soviet security depended on could plausibly be intercepted by the United States even without well-developed air defenses.[11] The United States had a far superior strategic nuclear arsenal for striking the USSR, and Kennedy had announced in February 1961 plans to increase these forces.[12]

Although the missiles somewhat enhanced Soviet first-strike capability, this would not affect the strength of the US retaliatory response, and retaliatory response was the primary basis for the Cold War security guarantee. Furthermore, the missiles were attractive targets for preemptive strikes given that they did not have rapid launch capacities (the United States was already considering removing its missiles from Turkey for this very reason).[13] And still, American superiority in the Caribbean, as well as in the global system at large, was "overwhelming."[14] For Allison and Zelikow, the more important danger was US overreaction, "prompt[ing] an explosive countermove against Berlin."[15] Certainly the threat was not cognizable within the founding-era paradigm of threat, that of repelling hostile troops at the border.

This is not to say the threat was not real. As a member of the president's Executive Committee, Robert McNamara also discounted the military significance of the missiles, but understood the threat that the missiles posed for the broader security politics of using US reliability to hold together the European alliance.[16] Kennedy had just assured the public that if Cuba were ever to "become an offensive military base of significant capacity," the United States would do "whatever must be done to

11   Allison and Zelikow, *Essence*, 92.

12   Ibid.

13   Arnold H. Horelick, "The Cuban Missile Crisis: An Analysis of Soviet Calculations and Behavior," *World Politics* 16:3 (1964): 363–89.

14   Allison and Zelikow, *Essence*, 110.

15   Ibid., 112.

16   Ibid., 113.

protect its own security and that of its allies."[17] For the Soviets to quickly and secretly insert missiles into Cuba after such remarks represented a threat to the credibility of US commitments, a cornerstone of the mutual deterrence system. This signified a crisis from within the ideology of a Cold War order whereby international security was thought to be guaranteed by the willingness of the US president to back words with force. Kennedy also perceived the threat in terms of international appearance, rather than material consequence: on the first day of his executive committee deliberations, Kennedy said, "Last month I said we weren't going to [allow it.] Last month I should have said that we don't care. But when we said we're *not* going to, and then they go ahead and do it, and then we do nothing, then I should think that our risks increase."[18] Khrushchev, too, understood the conflict at least in part in terms of international public appearance: he "planned to reveal the deployment . . . with a dramatic visit to Cuba, intending to convey Soviet superiority, both to the United States and to the Soviets' other rival, China."[19] In other words, the Cuban missile crisis was a threat according to a particular security paradigm about international credibility, but it did not itself represent an immediate hostile invasion or even the threat of an immediate hostile invasion. Nor was there any indication that Cuba was preparing to invade another nation. Cuba was altering the balance of power, no more.

Thus, the president's act of war was not in response to the kind of threat contemplated in the founding era as a basis for defensive war powers, nor was it authorized by law. And, while it was certainly more limited than the full-scale use of ground troops that some were advocating (the blockade only applied to offensive weapons equipment, and was not stringently enforced), the blockade was an act of war under international law, as would have been Kennedy's threatened action of backing the quarantine with tougher military action had the Soviets violated the blockade.[20]

This unilateral act of presidential war in the absence of threat of immediate invasion was kept secret from the public and from many legislators until it was actually being carried out. Presidential assistant

17   President John F. Kennedy, "The President's News Conference of September 13, 1962," available at *JFK Link*, http://www.jfklink.com/speeches/jfk/publicpapers/1962 /jfk378_62.html (accessed September 20, 2011).

18   Ernest May and Philip Zelikow, *The Kennedy Tapes: Inside the White House during the Cuban Missile Crisis* (Cambridge, MA: Belknap Press, 1998), 92, in Allison and Zelikow, *Essence*, 335.

19   Aleksandr Fursenko and Timothy Naftali, *One Hell of a Gamble: Khrushchev, Castro, and Kennedy, 1958–1964: The Secret History of the Cuban Missile Crisis* (New York: W. W. Norton and Co., 1998), in Zelizer, *Arsenal*, 155.

20   Zelizer, *Arsenal*, 165.

McGeorge Bundy lied about the presence of Soviet offensive missiles on ABC's *Issues and Answers* on October 14.[21] The president emphasized to the acting CIA director that leaks would be unacceptable, both because he wanted to pacify tensions with Khrushchev but also because of his concerns about the politics of the GOP.[22]

Nixon cited the Kennedy precedent in his justification for the Cambodian incursion, a military encounter also not authorized by law but justified in terms of independent executive war powers. The Cambodian incursion was one of the tail-end military encounters authorized by the presidency in an effort to win the Vietnam War. Having won the election on the basis of a secret plan to end the war, Nixon continued the Johnson-era policies of bombing and intensification. In May 1969 Nixon was announcing a peace plan for Vietnam and the plan of removing American forces.[23] While Nixon had promised "peace with honor" in Vietnam, in no way did he intend to surrender South Vietnam. He actually sought to turn the ground war over to the army of the Republic of Vietnam while continuing to furnish all-out military aid and bombing of communist positions throughout Southeast Asia. Congress, especially the Senate, had different aims.

The public unpopularity of the Vietnam War was, by now, in tension with the aspiration to win the war through escalation. The political foundations of the Gulf of Tonkin Resolution, which were never solid, were weakening. Politicians were bringing to light misrepresentations of the Johnson administration that had been pivotal for the legislature's decision to authorize force. Already by 1965 Senator Fulbright, the chair of the Senate Foreign Relations Committee, had moved into an oppositional stance to the war and begun to seek ways to extricate the United States. Senate ambivalence expressed itself in hearings and testimony unfavorable to the administration.[24]

Nonetheless Nixon sought to end the war on favorable terms. To do so required dominating Hanoi, which was as aware as everyone else that public opinion in the United States had turned. Wishing to press Hanoi, Nixon escalated and extended the war, seeking new avenues to show that he, unlike Johnson, was a force to be reckoned with. Bringing the conflict to Cambodia was one option that had not yet been tried.

Cambodia was ostensibly neutral, but Prince Sihanouk had entered into formal agreements with China allowing them to establish communist

---

21   Allison and Zelikow, *Essence*, 338.

22   Zelizer, *Arsenal*, 158.

23   David W. Levy, *The Debate over Vietnam (The American Moment)* (Baltimore, MD: The Johns Hopkins University Press, 1995), 154.

24   Levy, *Debate*, 50, 73, 146.

bases in Cambodia.[25] The country was also serving as a conduit for supplies for the North Vietnamese army. Frustrated with Hanoi's intransigence, and distressed by the lack of military progress, Nixon secretly began a Cambodian bombing on March 18, 1969, about thirteen months before the Cambodian ground incursion. The administration did not alert the relevant congressional committees, but told "a small handful of cooperative members of Congress," who did not notify their colleagues or the American people.[26] Even the Secretary of the Air Force and Air Force Chief of Staff were not informed of the air campaign.

Despite its ignorance about the Cambodian situation, the Democratic Congress was clear that a Republican president was escalating an unpopular war, and it finally began to take authoritative action on the war after years of seeking to shape public opinion. In mid-December 1969, unaware of Nixon's plans, and probably unaware of the bombing then happening in Cambodia, the Senate prohibited the use of funds to send US troops to Laos or Thailand.

On March 18, 1970, Cambodian President Sihanouk was deposed by the Parliament and replaced with General Lon Nol. It is unclear whether the CIA was complicit in this coup, but the US preference for Lon Nol over Sihanouk was transparent, and the US government apparently did "facilitate [the coup] in various collateral ways."[27] Lon Nol's openness toward the United States created an opening for Nixon to intensify his Cambodian operations. On April 14 Lon Nol made a "general plea" for help against the Communists.[28] Nixon and Kissinger secretly authorized the entry of ground troops into Cambodia in late April 1970. Only four days later, Senator Church held a press conference warning Nixon not to jeopardize "his declared policy of de-escalation."[29]

On April 30, 1970, the administration announced that American and South Vietnamese ground troops had crossed the Cambodian border to attack Communist sanctuaries. The administration had not discussed the matter with any congressional committees, and had confided in only a single member of Congress, Senator John Stennis, chair of the Armed

25   Samuel Lipsman and Edward Doyle, *Fighting for Time (The Vietnam Experience)* (Boston: Boston Publishing Co., 1983), 127.

26   John Hart Ely, "The American War in Indochina, Part II: The Unconstitutionality of the War They Didn't Tell Us About," *Stanford Law Review* 42:5 (1990): 1093–148, 1137, 1138.

27   John Hart Ely, *War and Responsibility* (Princeton: Princeton University Press, 1995), 31.

28   Ibid., 31.

29   Frederick Logevall, "The Vietnam War," in *The American Congress: The Building of Democracy*, ed. Julian E. Zelizer (Boston: Houghton Mifflin Company, 2004), 584–600, 597.

Services Committee.[30] The public response to the Cambodian incursion was massive and hostile. Nixon's announcement triggered the Kent State protests and killings, and a week after those shootings over a hundred thousand protesters converged in Washington to protest both the shooting of students and the Cambodian incursion. Over 4 million people were anticipated for a May 9 demonstration; Nixon tried to contain it by holding another press conference announcing, on the spur of the moment, that ground troops would be removed from Cambodia by June 30.[31] The protest nonetheless spilled throughout Washington, with core staff actually unable to get to their apartments, so cordoned were they by protesters. Kissinger wrote that "Washington took on the character of a besieged city."[32]

Congress took action. The Senate revoked the Gulf of Tonkin Resolution almost immediately, and the entire Congress repealed that resolution in January 1971. The repeal was one of the more moderate policy options available to Congress. Also under consideration, but ultimately defeated, was the McGovern-Hatfield Amendment, which would have required a total troop withdrawal from all of Indochina by December 31, 1971. When the presence of ground troops in Cambodia became known, the Cooper-Church amendment, already in the works, was amended to target only funds spent after July 1, 1971, allowing the Nixon administration room to get out of Cambodia. That amendment was passed into law by January 1971.[33] Even without the Gulf of Tonkin Resolution and even in the presence of such hostile politics, the bombing continued, this time, Nixon claimed, under his direct constitutional powers as commander in chief. The defensive interest that could warrant those independent war powers—other than the recovery of American captives—was never clear. Yet Nixon relied on these powers to continue bombing Cambodia until August 14, 1973, after the Paris cease-fire agreements of January 1973, after the last US ground troops left Vietnam in March 1973, and even after Vietnam released the last known American prisoners of war, in April 1973.[34]

---

30   Ely, *War,* 31.

31   President Richard Nixon, "The President's News Conference of May 8, 1970," *The American Presidency Project.* Available at http://www.presidency.ucsb.edu/ws/index.php?pid=2496 (accessed September 20, 2011).

32   John Prados, *Vietnam: The History of an Unwinnable War, 1945–1975* (Lawrence: Kansas University Press, 2009), 311–212; Henry Kissinger, *White House Years* (New York: Little, Brown, and Co., 1979), 511.

33   Ely, *War,* 31.

34   Ibid., 34; Kenton Clymer, *Troubled Relations: The United States and Cambodia Since 1870* (De Kalb: Northern Illinois Univ Pr; 2007), 131, 137.

Although Nixon justified the Cambodian bombing in terms of securing a just peace, that violence represented an escalation of the conflict
against communism in Southeast Asia. During 1969 and the first part of
1970 alone, more than 105,000 tons of bombs fell on Cambodia, "almost
15 percent of the bomb tonnage dropped on North Vietnam in all of
Rolling Thunder."[35] It is plausible that this level of violence helped create
conditions for Cambodians to overthrow President Norodom Sihanouk,
whose authority was largely premised on his capacity to keep his people
out of the war in Vietnam. Some have argued that the carpet-bombing of
Cambodia helped pave the way for the rise of the Khmer Rouge.[36]

The Cuban missile blockade was an appropriate precedent for Nixon
in one respect: it, too, was unauthorized by law. Congressional approval
for the Cambodian bombing (or incursion) could only be pursuant to the
1964 Gulf of Tonkin Resolution. The relevant pieces of that resolution
are as follows:

> Consonant with the Constitution of the United States and the Charter of the
> United Nations and in accordance with its obligations under the Southeast
> Asia Collective Defense Treaty, the United States is . . . prepared, as the Presi-
> dent determines, to take all necessary steps, including the use of armed force,
> to assist any member or protocol state of the Southeast Asia Collective De-
> fense Treaty requesting assistance in defense of its freedom.[37]

Sihanouk had not requested American assistance. While he may have
tacitly accepted US help, he also tacitly accepted the North Vietnamese
establishment of sanctuaries in Cambodia.[38] Kissinger argued that Sihanouk could not publicly ask for help without weakening Cambodia's
claim to neutrality and weakening his own hold on his office.[39] Nevertheless, the terms of the statute are clear that no matter how good the reasons an official may have for not asking for assistance, the US Congress
had authorized intervention only in cases where the leader of the country
was willing to publicly make known its desire for US help. Lon Nol did
request help, but after the Gulf of Tonkin Resolution was repealed in

35   Prados, *Vietnam*, 295.
36   Ben Kiernan, *The Pol Pot Regime: Race, Power, and Genocide in Cambodia under
the Khmer Rouge, 1975–79* (New Haven: Yale University Press, 2002). For an argument
that bombing helped recruitment but that the Khmer Rouge would have prevailed regardless, see Craig Etcheson, *The Rise and Demise of Democratic Kampuchea* (Boulder, CO:
Westview Press, 1984).
37   *Tonkin Gulf Resolution*, Pub. Law 88-408, 88th Cong., 2nd sess.
38   Clymer, *Troubled*, 98; William Shawcross, *Sideshow: Kissinger, Nixon and the Destruction of Cambodia* (New York: Simon & Schuster, Inc., 1979), 92.
39   Kissinger, *White House*, 252.

1971, the ongoing operations of the war through 1973 could be constitutionally faithful only via independent presidential war authority.

Settlement conceptions of war powers would treat these cases as constitutionally parallel. John Hart Ely, a pro-Congress settlement theorist, argues that authority over war rests in Congress's hands. Hence, from a pro-Congress settlement position, evaluating the Cambodian incursion hinges on one's interpretation of the Gulf of Tonkin Resolution.[40] Ely is willing to interpret the Gulf of Tonkin Resolution as legal authorization for executive bellicosity in Southeast Asia, but he interprets the 1969 bombing of Cambodia as illegal because it was kept secret from Congress, denying the legislature the opportunity to retract its authorization when confronted with the consequences of its security decision.[41] A further implication is that the continued bombing of Cambodia after the Gulf of Tonkin Resolution was revoked was no longer constitutional. However, because Congress was aware of the 1970 ground invasion of Cambodia, Ely argues that the ground invasion was constitutional; for him, the constitutionality of a war act is entirely a function of congressional authorization in a context of full knowledge. (Ely's interpretation of the Gulf of Tonkin Resolution is even broader than his Cambodia position would suggest; he was willing to follow the logic of his position to its full conclusion by arguing that bombing supply lines in China would have been constitutional under the Gulf of Tonkin Resolution if Congress knew about this action and had a chance to block it.)[42] Ely never commented on the Cuban missile crisis, other than a footnote noting his astonishment that Robert Kennedy never considered Congress as a possible source of advice about the crisis.[43] But in all of his work, Ely makes it clear that congressional authorization is what makes acts of war constitutional. According to this standard, the naval blockade of Cuba was unconstitutional.

By contrast, pro-executive settlement theorist John Yoo defends the expansion of the war beyond Vietnam as clearly constitutional because the executive power of the president contains an inherent power to initiate hostilities. Under Yoo's reading, presidential authority is fully adequate to

40   William Rogers, contra Ely, argued that the incursion was unconstitutional because the Gulf of Tonkin Resolution only allowed the president to repel "armed attack," not disrupt supply lines. William D. Rogers, "The Constitutionality of the Cambodian Incursion," *The American Journal of International Law* 65:1 (1971): 26–37.

41   Ely, "American War."

42   See Ely's response to Bork's claim that such action would require additional legislative approval because it would involve "a decision to initiate a major war." Ely, *War*, 32; Robert Bork, "Comments on the Articles on the Legality of the United States Action in Cambodia," *American Journal of International Law* 65:1 (1971): 79–81. 79, 80.

43   Ely, *War*, 222, fn. 20.

the task of initiating war and prosecuting war however a president deems necessary.[44]

Nixon's intervention in Cambodia, and the naval blockade that Kennedy established in the Cuban Missile Crisis, were acts of war under international law. Both presidents undertook these acts without Congress's specific consent—indeed, without notifying Congress. Neither of these acts was consistent with an immediate executive power to defend the nation, unless that power is understood quite broadly, as John Yoo does, in which case both acts are justifiable together. But the relational conception's focus on institutional performance accommodates the common intuition that these cases should instead be distinguished.

A DEFENSIVE SECURITY ORDER: THE COLD WAR

This book emphasizes the political content of defense in the context of war. The Constitution's framers may have understood defense to be self-evident; repelling hostile troops at the border, we have seen, served as a paradigmatic example of threat that could license independent presidential response. The authority of that founding paradigm was based on its status within a consensus politics. Even the idea that the president must respond to forms of peril that would seem to be universally recognized as existentially threatening, for example the occupation of Washington, D.C., by hostile forces, is derived from a consensus politics about what merits defensive war response. The Dalai Lama does not view the hostile takeover of Tibet and the presence of an occupying force within his country as an event meriting defensive war. In fact, conceptions of defensive response all depend on a preexistent conception of the content of the nation's security interest, one that cannot be formally delineated. The content of the nation's core security interests is political, which means that those defensive interests that merit independent executive war action are broadly political questions as well. We are thus asked to assess direct, unauthorized presidential war action on the basis of a political standard of defense. And we are called upon to consider the constitutional resources that are available for behavior that is a far greater appropriation of sovereign authority than any controversial use of discretionary powers.

In the postwar years, a new security order, specifying a new construction of core defensive interests, arose. Chapter 3 argued that the legislative contribution to that new construction could itself be defended

44   John Yoo, "War and the Constitutional Text," *University of Chicago Law Review* 69:4 (2002): 1639–84.

according to the relational conception of war authority. Assuming that the presidential contribution could also be defended (a highly controversial assumption), the branches would have constructed a new and constitutionally authoritative security order. That new order then can serve as a disciplining standard for assessing the president's judgment of the nation's defensive security interests.

The alternative major theoretical resource on offer for assessing independent presidential bellicosity is that of a presidential prerogative power.[45] Prerogative is the power to take independent action where not authorized by law in order to protect the security interests of the nation. In the first instance, it is the president himself who serves as the only judge of the content of those interests. According to John Locke's classical formulation of prerogative, the test of legitimate prerogative powers is correctness; to respond effectively to a true threat is a use of prerogative, but if the president's judgment is wrong, then he has abused his power.[46] In other words, Locke judges prerogative according to an independent standard of the common good. The public is, procedurally speaking, the arbiter of the rightness of the president's judgment, but that judgment, whether expressed through parliamentary action or through revolution, is always only retrospective. The role of public and legislative judgments about security needs is relegated to an entirely post-hoc position. A prerogative power approach to these cases would look, first, to the objective security interests of the nation (as given content by the theorist him or herself), and then to the post hoc judgment of the public. Identifying the content of a polity's defensive security interests, under a prerogative approach, doesn't necessarily require any analysis of preestablished legislative commitments.

By contrast, an emphasis on interbranch relationship invites us to consider how the legislature participates in constructing the content of the national security interest. The concept of a security order is helpful for this. Elaborating the content of a country's core security interest is one kind of governance task well suited to legislatures. That task involves deliberating over vast quantities of information; judging the relationships

---

45   See Oren Gross, "Chaos and Rules: Should Responses to a Violent Crisis Always Be Constitutional?" *Yale Law Journal* 112:5 (2003): 1011–34; Benjamin A. Kleinerman, *The Discretionary President: The Promise and Peril of Executive Power* (Lawrence: University Press of Kansas, 2009); Clement Fatovic, *Outside the Law: Emergency and Executive Power* (Baltimore: The Johns Hopkins University Press, 2009); see also David Gray Adler's discussion of retrospective ratification in "The Steel Seizure Case and Inherent Presidential Power," *Constitutional Commentary* 19:1 (2002): 155–213.

46   See chapter 14, "Of Prerogative," in John Locke, *Second Treatise of Government*, ed. C. B. Macpherson (Hackett Publishing Co., 1980).

between many different scenarios, risks, and possibilities; balancing various costs and benefits; integrating multiple commitments; and relating various partial demands to one another into a broad-based agenda that can serve a broader rather than narrower swath of the public. The idea of a security order also helps to identify the importance of legislative judgment in a prospective, not just retrospective way.[47]

The relational conception does not directly interrogate the defensive security necessity of the war act itself when assessing independent presidential acts of war, but rather interrogates its security necessity as viewed through the filter of an established defensive security order. (The prerogative power, by contrast, is relatively unbounded.) The analytic question is about the extent to which the president has achieved a good conception of the nation's defensive security interests given the existence of a security order that itself can be constitutionally defended.

As I argued in chapter 3, identifying a security order is a matter of identifying a security politics, not only a set of legal authorizations. Yet that politics is held independently to serve as one source of authority for direct defensive presidential bellicosity. Does this concept risk undermining legislative governance by subverting the legislature's capacity to act as a direct authorizing body; or by introducing risk into legislative compromises, with the possibility that officials will go on to interpret those compromises not only as legal delegations but also as licensing orders? In some ways, yes. Compared to a pro-Congress settlement view, the idea of a security politics that can serve as a source of presidential authority for acts of war is relatively undermining of legislative authority. However, given that there will sometimes be contexts in which it is universally recognized that a president should act unilaterally; given his capacity to do so; and given that the content of the security interests that license such behavior is not an apolitical category with one answer for all times, how else shall the executive's control of the military be disciplined? The menu for thinking about how legislative judgments can discipline independent executive acts of war is actually quite limited. The concept of a prerogative power is tethered only to the president's own judgment in the first instance, whereas the concept of a security order at least makes reference to preexistent legislative security determinations. Hence the idea of a security order is a relatively more legislatively centered way of disciplining

47   A legislature's capacity to prospectively discipline a president is especially significant given scholarly and public anxiety that a president's role as first-responder cedes, as a practical matter, the entire sovereign war power to the executive. See Robert Dahl, *Congress and Foreign Policy* (New York: Harcourt Brace and Co., 1950), 58; Andrew J. Polsky, "Collective Inaction: Presidents, Congress, and Unpopular Wars," *Extensions* (2008): 4–8.

independent executive bellicosity than that of prerogative power. That the standard can be manipulated is a feature of any standard that is realistically sensitive to context.

Both Kennedy and Nixon were acting in a Cold War security order. That order identified global communism as a threat demanding containment. Congresses and the presidency together had constructed a security state with the capacity, and perhaps authority, to counter that threat. Alongside this articulation of a substantive security interest in containing global communism was a weakly developed source of political review: the bipartisan consensus. Through the bipartisan consensus, officials sought to provide for review of the president without disabling the united front required to prosecute Cold War aims. Chapter 3 defended the bipartisan consensus as a new constitutional construction. For this chapter, we should note several of its important features. First, the bipartisan consensus sought to subsume conflict at the formal institutional level and express it instead at the informal level of negotiations between foreign policy elites of both parties. Second, a key ingredient of the bipartisan consensus is ongoing study, evaluation, and consultation between the president and foreign policy leaders of both parties in Congress. This was characteristic of the UN Charter and UN Participation Act, European weapons assistance, and the North Atlantic Treaty. For example, Truman and his Republican supporters drew up the concrete program of the Marshall Plan only *"after* all interested individuals and groups had been accorded an opportunity to air their views."[48]

Third, the bipartisan consensus does allow for some action even if the president has not undertaken such inclusive procedures. In the Greek-Turkish aid process, another core instance of bipartisanship, interparty unity was achieved not through ongoing study and inclusive deliberations but rather as a result of bipartisan fear.[49] Nonetheless, even here, aid was characterized by support from the foreign policy elites of both parties. Greek aid in 1947 and the Korean War in 1950 were overwhelmingly approved by both parties in Congress at the moment, but they were nonetheless later cited by Republicans "as foreign policy undertakings that lay outside the area of bipartisan collaboration."[50] Hence it is possible that the bipartisan consensus requires more than agreement between party elites at the moment of action; but no successful case of its operation involves less.

---

48   Crabb, Jr., *Bipartisan,* 70.
49   Ibid., 57, 60, 67.
50   Ibid., 7.

CUBA AND CAMBODIA IN THE COLD WAR
SECURITY ORDER

To assess whether the president's independent acts of war are licensed by defensive security need, we turn to the defensive value of the act from within the terms of a preexistent security order.[51] (Later in this chapter, I will assess the president's conduct under the processual standards of the relational conception.) To what extent was each act of war an act of defense as understood from within this Cold War security order? Answering this question requires, first, examining whether the event recognizably calls for a presidentialist response within the substantive terms of the consensus. We also assess the extent to which the president's behavior was linked to the terms of the procedural consensus of the order, if one exists. There are notable differences between the cases on these dimensions.

The Cuban missile crisis was easily recognized *as* a crisis from within the Cold War consensus. The basic tenets of the Cold War, including the identification of the USSR as a threat, the identification of the United States as the only global power able to resist Soviet influence after the Cold War, the division of the world into geographic spheres of influence, and the positioning of the president as the first responder to Soviet threats, had been ratified repeatedly by Congress in everything from the funding and structuring of the massive Cold War military buildup, to alliance decisions and the structure of foreign aid.[52] According to this system for organizing threat, the USSR's placement of missiles in Cuba was aggressive because they could be launched with little or no warning to the United States, and because the warheads placed Cuba, otherwise within the US regional sphere of influence, explicitly within the Soviet deterrence system. The missiles also increased Soviet missile striking power against the United States "by at least 50 percent," raising the costs of engaging in missile exchange.[53] The United States discovered later that Soviet intentions had been to "develop Cuba into a full-scale strategic base."[54]

The danger represented by the Cuban missiles was not an immediate material threat like that of hostile troops at the border. Nor was it

51   Full analysis would require us to scrutinize the ongoing authority of the order, as well as whether or not a particular act of war is authorized by its terms.

52   See Philip J. Briggs, *Making American Foreign Policy: President-Congress Relations from the Second World War to the Post Cold War Era* (Lanham, MD: Rowman and Littlefield, 1994); Robert David Johnson, *Congress and the Cold War* (Cambridge, UK: Cambridge University Press, 2005).

53   Allison and Zelikow, *Essence,* 96.

54   Ibid., 99.

an attack, or even likely to lead to an attack in the near future. It was a shift in balance of power politics. But given the Cold War ideology—one shared by allies and enemies around the world—it nonetheless had the capacity to end in disaster. This was because of an internationally shared perception about what the missiles could represent in the context of US commitments. Kennedy estimated the odds of disaster as "between one out of three and even."[55] War in Cuba could lead to a Soviet incursion into West Berlin or a strike against Turkish missile bases, "thereby lighting other fuses that could soon lead to thermonuclear war."[56] After the very public failure of the Bay of Pigs, and after the disregard Khrushchev had demonstrated to Kennedy, American and European leaders feared signaling a loss of will, and hence a loss of confidence in the security pledges that sustained the Cold War system.[57] The Soviets were working on these assumptions as well. Khrushchev precisely hoped to "unmask an irresolute America," thereby "drastically reduc[ing] the credibility of U.S. commitments to other nations."[58]

Cold War conflicts were not likely to begin immediately with nuclear strike. Rather, nuclear weapons were at the apex of a ladder of escalating security steps, and in 1962, "governments believed: size matters . . . each side knew that the other side knew that the advantaged party could force events up the escalation ladder to a level at which its advantages counted." In 1962 it was also understood as a "truth" that "the state with significant strategic nuclear advantages would likely be emboldened to pursue its interests more aggressively."[59] The material capacity to ratchet up the ladder of escalations was reinforced by the symbolic importance of strategic nuclear weapons in global politics. Khrushchev could expect important diplomatic benefits from successfully establishing a base in Cuba, even if he was unwilling to translate that deployment into an actual nuclear strike.

Not only did the crisis fall within a Cold War substantive security consensus, but the processes Kennedy used in the lead-up to the blockade also fell within the terms of the bipartisan consensus. Legislators had been pressuring the executive to "do something" about Fidel Castro, a pressure that had conditioned their mild response after the failed 1961 Bay of Pigs invasion.[60] Through the month of August, Republican Senators Kenneth Keating and Homer Capehart, who had access to information from

55 Quoted in ibid., 1.
56 Ibid., 77.
57 Ibid., 89.
58 Ibid., 89.
59 All quotes in ibid., 94.
60 David M. Barrett, *The CIA and Congress: The Untold Story from Truman to Kennedy* (Lawrence: University Press of Kansas, 2005), 2.

Cuban informants and from the CIA, attacked Kennedy for ignoring a building crisis.[61] Republicans in Congress, led by Keating, began mobilizing to make Cuba a significant issue in the upcoming midterm elections. The Republican Senatorial and Congressional Campaign Committee had announced Cuba would be the "dominant issue of the 1962 campaign."[62] Republican concern that the president was underestimating the level of threat in Cuba was not based on thin air: Keating's worry was shared by the director of the CIA John McCone, who shared a "deep intuition stimulated by the discovery of antiaircraft missiles going into Cuba," missiles that "made sense only if Moscow intended to use them to shield a base for ballistic missiles aimed at the United States."[63] This anxiety was translated into bipartisan action. In September the Senate passed the Ready Reserve Bill granting the president authority to call reservists into armed forces without opposition. In the House the same bill was slowed only by Republican criticism of Kennedy's weakness.[64]

Moreover, before the crisis Congress had passed a resolution expressing determination "to prevent in Cuba the creation or use of an externally supported military capability endangering the security of the United States."[65] The legislative history of that resolution demonstrates the Kennedy administration's maneuvers through the terms of the bipartisan consensus. In early September, Senate Majority Leader Mike Mansfield told Kennedy that the Senate Majority Policy Committee was worried about the "domestic-political" implications of the Cuban threat. Mansfield communicated that these Democrats "had discussed a full array of actions, ranging from a quarantine of Cuba to an all-out war that might involve Russia."[66] Republicans proposed a congressional resolution of determination in confronting the Cuban crisis, an effort Congressional Democrats joined. The Senate Foreign Relations Committee and the Armed Services Committee unanimously approved the resolution on September 19, specifying that "the United States would not allow Cuba to develop a military capability that threatened the nation." The full Senate passed the resolution by a vote of 86–1 on September 20, stating that the United States was "determined . . . by whatever means may be necessary, including the use of arms" to prevent a Cuban threat. Congressional Democrats concerned about escalation held back Republican efforts

61 Zelizer, *Arsenal*, 157.
62 Allison and Zelikow, *Essence*, 330.
63 Ibid., 80.
64 Zelizer, *Arsenal*, 160.
65 "Cuba Resolution," *Congressional Quarterly Weekly Report* 21 (September 1962): 1565; "House Passes Cuba Resolution, 384–87," *Congressional Quarterly Weekly Report* 28 (September 1962): 1691.
66 Zelizer, *Arsenal*, 160.

to pass a direct legal war authorization.[67] In September Kennedy invited congressional leaders, including Republicans, to a bipartisan meeting to discuss information related to Cuba.[68] By late October the president was narrowing in on a strategy, and on October 22 he reported to congressional Democrats and Republicans, suggesting his orientation was toward a quarantine rather than a military strike.[69] In that briefing, Republicans criticized the administration's response and advocated immediate all-out military action against the missile sites. The most vigorous and aggressive proponent for military action, Chairman of the Armed Services Committee Senator Richard Russell, chastened Kennedy: "you have told them not to do this thing. They've done it. And I think that we should assemble as speedily as possible an adequate force and clean out that situation."[70] In Executive Committee deliberations, the president revealed that he feared impeachment if he did nothing to counter the Cuban missiles.[71] None of these represent congressional authorization of Kennedy's act of war. But Kennedy was clearly acting within the terms set by elites of both parties.

Finally, after the crisis was over, the bipartisan consensus largely held. Eisenhower "boasted that Republicans deserved credit for having pushed the president to stand up to the Cubans."[72] Some Republicans attacked Kennedy for not being forceful enough—hardly evidence that the war authority he did use was not sanctioned by both parties. When Republicans and some southern Democrats kept challenging the president, arguing that he had ignored important CIA warnings, and objecting to the dismantling of US missile bases in Turkey, the Senate authorized an investigation. The investigating committee included war hawks, and their findings nonetheless "concluded that Keating's charges were unfounded."[73] Hence the bipartisan consensus held up both in the legislature's preliminary and retrospective judgment.

A major problem for Nixon in using the needs of the Vietnam War to justify the Cambodian incursion was the imperiled politics of the war itself, and its escape from the grasp of the bipartisan consensus. The Cambodian incursion was in response to the defensive needs surrounding troops already deployed to Vietnam. But the decade before Nixon's Cambodian incursion had featured serious challenges not only to the value of the Vietnam War within the Cold War system, but also to central

---

67   For background and preceding quotations see ibid., 161.

68   Ibid., 159.

69   Ibid., 166.

70   *Voices from the brink.* DVD. Produced by Stephen Phizicky (Canadian Broadcasting Corporation, 2001).

71   Allison and Zelikow, *Essence*, 113–14.

72   Zelizer, *Arsenal*, 170–71.

73   Ibid., 172.

premises of the Cold War order itself.[74] The contentiousness of the security politics around the Cold War order is clear to any curious observer.

Legislative skepticism about the value of South Vietnam for prosecuting Cold War aims was apparent in the early days of the US escalation of its military commitment to that country. In the early fall of 1963, a core group of legislative doves began to sharply interrogate the Kennedy administration about the long-term success of the Vietnam War. They suggested using Diem's repressions as an excuse to exit. Senators Fulbright and Mike Mansfield made emphatic private objections: Mansfield was an especially important voice because he was deeply informed, and had in the 1950s been convinced that Vietnam was important in the struggle against communism.[75] While by 1964 Johnson had bipartisan support in some sense (Democrats John Stennis and Gale McGee, and Republicans including Karl Mundt, John Tower, and minority leader Everett Dirksen), Senate foreign policy leaders from both parties (Mansfield, Fulbright, and Russell) were expressing doubts to the administration about the value of the war and pointing to the benefits of withdrawal.[76] They kept these deliberations quiet, according to the terms of the bipartisan consensus, and in deference to the electoral strategies of a Democratic president heading into a campaign. Nonetheless their doubts were privately expressed and conditioned the strategic terms of Johnson's war engagement by encouraging him toward gradual, not abrupt, escalation.[77]

The terms of the bipartisan consensus direct us to look to informal negotiations between elites as a source of constitutional authority. This means that examining the contribution that the Gulf of Tonkin Resolution made to the constitutional landscape requires us to scrutinize not only its legal language, but also its politics. The bipartisan consensus holds elite, interparty consensus to be one buttress for the authority of acts of war in the Cold War system. Hence, we should assess the legislative politics surrounding the Gulf of Tonkin Resolution to see whether it featured such informal elite consensus.

On this front, the almost unanimous passage of the Gulf of Tonkin Resolution (only two votes opposed) belied the level of consensus actually existent in the legislature. The Johnson administration's guarantees to use bipartisan consultation procedures, and Fulbright's supposed inside knowledge about the administration's true intentions, were pivotal

---

74   The extent to which this tumultuous politics was actually reflected in security legislation is limited. The Cold War order was commited to suppressing formal expression of dissent. Democrats' firm control of both branches through the Johnson presidency also stymied efforts to block the presidency.

75   Logevall, "Vietnam War," 587, 588.

76   Ibid., 586.

77   Ibid., 588, 585.

for the bill's passage.[78] Fulbright not only shepherded the Resolution through, but also headed off an effort by Gaylord Nelson to amend it to avoid "direct military involvement" in the region.[79] Legislators had some reason to trust that these informal promises would be kept. Congress had passed similar resolutions to undergird Eisenhower and then Kennedy's coercive diplomacy while allowing the president to avoid war.[80]

Still, Senate debate expressed skepticism about the value of war and about the likely consequences of authorizing it. Julian Zelizer notes that "many legislators from each party, all regions, and various ideological backgrounds . . . expressed deep reservations about the measure."[81] Republican John Cooper "spoke for many" when he cautioned against deeper involvement.[82] This doubt came from predictable sources like the liberal Frank Church, but also from unpredictable ones like conservative Democrat George Smathers, who said "he was having trouble finding legislators who thought 'we ought to fight a war in that area of the world.' "[83] Even hawkish Democrat Richard Russell was warning Johnson about South Vietnam.[84] That Democratic legislators were days from the Democratic convention, and facing an election, made them reluctant to challenge Johnson.[85] But again in December 1964 and through January 1965, the "entire Senate Democratic leadership" privately warned Johnson about deepening US involvement in Vietnam and publicly predicted the onset of a serious legislative debate, one that never took place in part because of administration pressures.[86]

As casualties rose, Senate foreign policy leadership expressed doubts about the assumptions upon which Vietnam was premised. The Sino-Soviet split belied the idea of a monolithic global communism. The idea that the fall of South Vietnam would inevitably lead to the fall of Thailand, Indonesia, and the Philippines became suspect; and legislative

---

78 Zelizer, *Arsenal*, 187.

79 Logevall, "Vietnam War," 590.

80 Ibid. In 1955 when the People's Republic of China gave signals it was contemplating an attack on Taiwan, Congress passed a strong resolution and the president sent US naval forces to the region as a symbol of American resolve. The Chinese did not attack. Two years later, Congress passed another joint resolution authorizing the president to use military force in the midst of brewing Middle East tensions, and again the situation was defused without casualties to deployed US forces. The Cuban Missile Crisis was yet another precedent for the positive consequences that could come from brinkmanship. All of these form a relevant security context for the Gulf of Tonkin Resolution.

81 Zelizer, *Arsenal*, 187.

82 Logevall, "Vietnam War," 589.

83 Zelizer, *Arsenal*, 183.

84 Ibid., 184.

85 Logevall, "Vietnam War," 590.

86 Ibid., 591.

dissidents interrogated whether it was useful to support authoritarian or even totalitarian governments in the name of containment. The Senate Foreign Relations Committee, under the leadership of Senator Fulbright, held hearings in 1966 featuring the testimony of George Kennan himself who denied the relevance of domino theory for Vietnam. The Tet Offensive in 1968 brought renewed criticism, including Fulbright and half the members of the SFRC characterizing the Gulf of Tonkin Resolution as an "overreaction obtained by misrepresentation."[87] The president was facing immense pressure to disengage and to reframe American security interests.

Once again in 1968, after the Tet Offensive, the legislature called for "fundamental reevaluation of foreign policy and a more active attempt at gaining a negotiated settlement."[88] But once again, election strategy, Johnson's announcement he would not seek reelection, and the April onset of negotiations in Paris kept Congress quiet. Still, the SFRC did conduct investigations that sowed doubts about Johnson's representation of the Tonkin Gulf incident.[89] This was hardly a context in which the *politics* either of containment or of the value of the Vietnam War was robust. Johnson had decided not to run again in part because of war opposition; antiwar Robert Kennedy had won a major victory in the California primary but then was assassinated; Nixon himself ran in part against the draft, trying to show commitment to ending conflict in Vietnam.[90]

This hostile politics was apparent to candidate Nixon. The legislature became more oppositional in its use of its formal powers once the presidency switched parties, cutting military appropriations and proposing limits on presidential war powers.[91] Shortly after Nixon's elections, Senate doves including Mansfield, Cooper, Jacob, George Aiken, Frank Church, Stuart Symington, Phil Hart, and others met to agree "on a critical proposition"—if not to stop the war, then at least to contain it. They wished to highlight "the Senate's constitutional obligations toward foreign policy," and thereby "shrink the war."[92] Their strategy was to do so with a series of amendments that would restrict further US military involvement. In December 1969 their efforts bore fruit when the Senate approved Cooper and Church's defense appropriations amendment to prohibit US funds for American ground forces in Laos or Thailand by

87   Levy, *Debate*, 146.

88   Logevall, "Vietnam War," 595.

89   John Finney, "Tonkin Inquiry by Fulbright to Call McNamara," *New York Times* (Jan. 31, 1968); "Excerpts from McNamara's Testimony on Tonkin," *New York Times* (Feb. 25, 1968).

90   Zelizer, *Arsenal*, 217.

91   Ibid., 220–21.

92   Logevall, "Vietnam War," 596.

a vote of 78–11. Ironically, Cooper had sought to include Cambodia in the bar but Senator Mansfield persuaded him to remove this language in order to avoid offending the neutral Sihanouk—even as US bombings were actually being carried out in that nation.[93]

This was the political context Nixon faced when he began the bombing of Cambodia. Four days after Nixon's secret decision to send in ground troops, Church was discussing the expansion of a new Cooper-Church Amendment to cover Cambodia and warned Nixon not to "open a 'new front' and jeopardize 'his declared policy of de-escalation.'"[94] Cooper and Church softened this amendment by extending its deadline and adding a disclaimer about the president's constitutional authority to protect soldiers, for which they were criticized when the amendment was passed in June 1970.[95] This was by no means a politics of ongoing support for the Vietnam War, to say nothing of its extension to new, unauthorized areas. Elite legislators from both parties, the leaders of the foreign policy establishment, were taking oppositional political action within the procedural guidelines of the Cold War security order. From Kissinger's point of view, it was a "collapse of foreign policy theory."[96]

The politics of Vietnam and Cambodia do not suggest that Nixon was operating within a zone of bipartisan consensus, unless we interpret the bipartisan consensus solely in terms of formal votes and direct authorizations. Bipartisan anxiety about Vietnam and Cambodia was not formalized until the early 1970s. However, the Cold War security order precisely warns against looking only to formal votes as a signal of consensus. The very point of the Cold War order was to cover dissensus at the formal, institutional level and instead register it through interpersonal interactions between party and foreign policy elites. Nixon's conduct was far outside the field of what those informal negotiations could contain. Instead of taking his cues from within the terms of the bipartisan consensus, Nixon came into office "determined to resist these trends," according to Kissinger.[97]

Bipartisan hostility to Nixon's Cambodian incursion asserted itself retrospectively as well. In June 1971 the Senate passed a "sense-of-Congress" resolution from Senate Majority Leader Mike Mansfield urging an end to the Vietnam War. A coalition spearheaded by Fulbright and Republicans John Sherman Cooper (KY) and Jacob Javits (NY) moved to limit the executive branch's power to make war. That effort culminated

93   Ibid., 597.
94   Ibid.
95   Ibid.
96   Quoted in Zelizer, *Arsenal*, 240.
97   Zelizer, *Arsenal*, 221.

in passage of the War Powers Act by Congress in the fall of 1973 over President Nixon's veto. In 1971 Senator Fulbright began hearings on proposals relating to ending the war, and Congress became quite strict about American behavior in Cambodia.

By 1974 Congress had imposed massive restrictions on funding in aid to Cambodia—a ceiling of $377 million against which every expenditure, military or food, had to be counted.[98] From the early 1970s onward, almost all aid bills for Cambodia emphasized that no "commitment" was implied (Nixon had argued that preexisting American commitments required the United States to prolong the war).[99] By 1973 both houses of Congress had cut off funding for bombing operations. Cambodia had become the focal point for legislative efforts to disengage from Vietnam, and in March 1974 military aid to Cambodia was cut off completely.[100] As the BBC reported, Kissinger vainly "had pleaded with the Senate not to rebel against the government" while he was trying to negotiate a settlement.[101] Nixon's ordering of the bombings was considered as an article of impeachment, but the charge was ultimately dropped.

Legally, none of this represents a repudiation of Nixon's conduct: it is plausible that Congress could endorse behavior that it would not want to extend into the future. But the politics of the situation was clear. Nixon's behavior was outside the terms of the bipartisan consensus both in the lead-up to the Cambodian incursion and in retrospect. To be clear, the suggestion is not that the bipartisan consensus cannot abide dissensus of any kind. Certainly it can. But to lose the support of the foreign policy leadership across party lines prior to, during, and after a major act of war undermines that act's claim to authority under the terms of the Cold War security order.[102]

98   Kissinger, *White House*, 514.
99   Ibid., 516.
100   Johnson, *Congress*, 188–89.
101   BBC, "US Senate Stops Cambodian Bombing," *BBC News*, (May 31, 1973). Available at http://news.bbc.co.uk/onthisday/hi/dates/stories/may/31/newsid_2481000/2481543.stm (accessed September 21, 2011).
102   It is worth observing that Nixon's failure was arguably linked to the legislature's failure according to the terms of the relational conception. The bipartisan consensus deemphasized the importance of formal legislative authorization and arguably, over time, weakened the legislature's sense of independence (the first condition of conflict). While chapter 3 defended the authority of the Cold War security order according to the relational conception, that order nonetheless has constitutional weaknesses. Over time, legislative deference to executive war governance arguably weakened the legislature's experience of its own intelligence and constitutional capacities, undermining in turn the value of legislative acquiescence over time and introducing the risk that a legislature would fail to act independently to translate its political ambivalences into restrictive statutory law. The president's failure to base the exercise of his powers upon a robust security order was, I would argue, linked to a legislative failure to use its procedures to authoritatively register the extent of elite division

ASSESSING EXECUTIVE BRANCH JUDGMENT

The relational conception of war authority also asks us to assess all uses of war authority according to the extent to which the branch makes good use of its constitutional capacities—the processual criteria. The differences between the cases on this front are important. Kennedy's conduct in the Cuban missile crisis made better use of the constitutional capacities of the executive branch than did Nixon's Cambodian incursion. Kennedy benefited deeply from his office's resources, and then advanced his policies in a coherent way for legislative judgment. By contrast, Nixon's use of executive independence was highly insular. He resisted coherent political justification, and in so doing evaded serious engagement with and reliance upon the policy making capacities at his disposal.

A few words about the electoral authority behind President Kennedy may be useful. In the 1960 presidential campaign, Kennedy had promised a more active foreign policy in which the United States would participate in "counterinsurgency" against communist guerrillas and support developing nations in resisting communism. Kennedy displayed considerable political awareness, and in many moments framed the moment as a "serious political challenge."[103] This led him to an elaborate use of bipartisan consultation procedures. In September, Kennedy invited the congressional leadership, both Republicans and Democrats, to share information about Cuba in order to "undermine Republican claims that the president was withholding information."[104] At the same time, he also sought to protect his freedom of discernment.

One of the heated Republican attacks against Kennedy was that he did not respond quickly enough to the gathering threat. However, Khrushchev's intentions were idiosyncratic and hard to interpret. Intelligence estimates viewed it implausible that missiles would be introduced into Cuba given the confrontation that could ensue. Llewellyn Thompson, an American ambassador who has been called one of the best to the USSR ever, simply could not understand or make sense of Khrushchev's position on Berlin.[105] Overwhelming US strength in the Western Hemisphere and the absolutely devastating consequences that Khrushchev could face from the excursion made it plausible that the threat was not as large as Cold warriors warned. And the threat of overreaction was serious as

---

and discord, that failure itself being at least partly a result of the ongoing operation of the bipartisan consensus through time.

103   Zelizer, *Arsenal*, 158.
104   Ibid., 159.
105   Allison and Zelikow, *Essence*, 102.

well. In a nuclear context, the value of deterrence and containment had to be weighed against the value of preserving space to de-escalate. Kennedy made good use of the branch's capacities by staying in close touch with his intelligence and diplomatic networks without reacting so as to escalate a situation whose meaning was not yet transparent to him. Kennedy did respond quickly when verified information made it clear that a response was necessary. Days after his September meeting with congressional leaders, the CIA reported to him that it had verified multiple surface-to-air missile sites being built in addition to patrol boats carrying short-range missiles. Kennedy responded by asking Congress for stand-by authority to call up 150,000 men from the Ready Reserve, mentioning the possibility of amphibious operations.

The deliberations within Kennedy's Executive Committee in the critical days before the blockade are legendary.[106] Kennedy took full advantage of the Committee's deliberative resources. The ExCom developed a series of alternatives that encompassed a full spectrum of possible responses, from ignoring the incident to full-out nuclear war.[107] Despite Kennedy's awareness of the political threat he faced—an awareness that led him to sensitivity in his dealings with Republicans in Congress—ExCom deliberations put to the side the domestic political consequences of various proposals. In addition, Kennedy used the presidency's hierarchical resources effectively. According to historian Sheldon Stern, Kennedy's decision to pair the blockade with a secret Turkish base trade resisted his ExCom's unanimous opinion toward bellicosity.[108] Kennedy's decision to override the advice of every single member of his executive committee may well have been buttressed by his experience with the Bay of Pigs, where the Joint Chiefs had been so encouraging of a program that ended in disaster. That experience had led Kennedy to scrutinize the Joint Chiefs' perspectives more carefully, especially their continued recommendation for "decisive intervention" in Cuba.[109]

106   Allison and Zelikow (1999); Gregory Herek, Paul Huth, and Irving Janis, "Decision Making During International Crises," *The Journal of Conflict Resolution* 31:2 (1987): 203–26; David Welch, "Crisis Decision Making Reconsidered," *The Journal of Conflict Resolution* 33:3 (1989): 430–45; Gregory M. Herek, Irving L. Janis, and Paul Huth, "Quality of US Decision Making During the Cuban Missile Crisis," *The Journal of Conflict Resolution* 33:3 (1989): 446–59.

107   Allison and Zelikow, *Essence*, 110–20.

108   Sheldon M. Stern, *The Cuban Missile Crisis in American Memory: Myths versus Reality* (forthcoming: Stanford University Press, 2012), as reported in Fred Kaplan, "What Robert Caro Got Wrong," *Slate.com*, available at http://www.slate.com/articles/news_and_politics/war_stories/2012/05/robert_caro_s_new_history_of_lbj_offers_a_mistaken_account_of_the_cuban_missile_crisis.single.html (accessed May 31, 2012).

109   George C. Herring, *LBJ and Vietnam: A Different Kind of War* (Austin: University of Texas Press, 1994), 27.

After deliberations had concluded Kennedy reflected on the political irony of the situation—he had chosen the blockade, an option advocated by one of his fiercest Senate critics. Kennedy's dry response: "I guess Homer Capehart is the Winston Churchill of our generation."[110] Kennedy's worry about protecting Democrats from GOP attack was not so powerful as to prevent him from choosing a policy option advocated by a partisan rival. Kennedy was able to focus his advisors' deliberations on the best way to resolve the crisis on its own terms—how best to rebuff Khrushchev without escalating to catastrophe.

Kennedy's processual authority also benefited from the skillful use of the intelligence capacities at his disposal. The discovery of the missiles in the first place was no easy matter. Missile discovery was a result of the use of new and profound intelligence capacities developed through the Eisenhower administration and used effectively by Kennedy's subordinates.[111] The ability to track ships coming into Cuba, and the capacity to analyze the likely contents of these ships, helped intelligence analysis raise red flags. While intelligence analysts were also receiving suggestive CIA reports, these reports were treated skeptically, because of both the CIA's role in the Bay of Pigs and the concern that the Republican director of the CIA McCone was distorting his findings to support a hard-line anticommunist agenda. The president responded to these concerns by productively engaging them. During McCone's honeymoon vacation, Kennedy instructed the NSC to independently investigate McCone's concerns.[112] The Defense Department then provided Kennedy with further photographs and analysis confirming McCone's worries. The Kennedy administration's response: to "accelerat[e] its analyses into what could happen if the situation deteriorated."[113] The executive branch took McCone's worries more seriously when it confirmed that ideology did not seem to be distorting his assessment of the intelligence.

Kennedy's clarity about the nature of the threat in Cuba—political more than material—helped him use the military very successfully. Allison and Zelikow have characterized the Navy's Atlantic Fleet as carrying out a "virtuoso" performance in the blockade.[114] Kennedy maintained close involvement in the operational details of the embargo, at times directly intervening to instruct ships to avoid confrontation and to manage the signals they gave. His excellent use of the discernment capacities of the executive branch—correctly perceiving the threat in terms of inter-

110   Zelizer, *Arsenal*, 165.
111   Allison and Zelikow, *Essence*, 217–76.
112   Zelizer, *Arsenal*, 157.
113   Ibid., 157.
114   Allison and Zelikow, *Essence*, 231.

national appearance rather than material confrontation—supported his military success.

Nixon's uses of executive branch resources were almost as legendary in their subversion as Kennedy's were outstanding.[115] To begin, it is worth mentioning a few aspects of Nixon's troubled relationship with the electorate. Quickly upon Nixon's taking office it became clear that his policy thrust was in "the opposite direction" from the campaign's implications that he would negotiate a solution.[116] But Nixon had been an intense Cold warrior during his entire career, and had spent the "mid-1960s attacking Lyndon Johnson for not doing enough." Historian John Prados speculates public desperation might have been responsible for its trusting attitude toward his promises to end the war. Melvin R. Laird, Nixon's Secretary of Defense, has stated that the true plan was to "batter Hanoi into conceding defeat."[117] Henry Kissinger, Nixon's chief diplomat, had outlined the terms of a negotiated settlement plausible at that very moment in an article in *Foreign Affairs*.[118] But after the election, Prados believes that Nixon's desire to publicly demonstrate strength, and the galling fact that his political opponents supported a negotiated settlement in Vietnam, made Kissinger's settlement proposal "unpalatable." Kissinger's article was "quietly discarded" and is not referenced in his or Nixon's memoirs of the moment.[119]

Beyond reversing his campaign promises, Nixon also demonstrated contempt for ordinary processes of mobilizing public opinion. The administration's lobbying effort against the repeal of the Gulf of Tonkin Resolution and Cooper-Church Amendments involved placing FBI wiretaps on legislators. When State Department employees organized a petition campaign to support Cooper-Church, Nixon tried to fire everyone associated with the effort before coming up against the bar of civil service regulations.[120] He referred to the protestors as an "insurrection," and compared himself to Lincoln, stretching the law to save the nation from domestic insurgency.[121] At the same time, Nixon undermined communication channels between the White House and public: he reported the

115   In fact, Nixon's subversions may have started before the elections. There is evidence that Henry Kissinger may have actually undermined ongoing negotiations conducted by the Johnson administration by "contacting the South Vietnamese and assuring them they would get a better deal with Nixon in office." Zelizer, *Arsenal*, 218.

116   Prados, *Vietnam*, 290.

117   As cited in Prados, *Vietnam*, 288.

118   Henry Kissinger, "The Vietnam Negotiations," *Foreign Affairs* 47: 1 (1969): 211–34.

119   Prados, *Vietnam*, 299, citing Kissinger, "Negotiations."

120   Prados, *Vietnam*, 369.

121   Ibid., 302. On his coordination of internal illegal tactics to counter domestic protest, see Stanley I. Kutler, *The Wars of Watergate: The Last Crisis of Richard Nixon* (New

response to the "silent majority" speech as "electric," while in fact presidential aides had been put to work orchestrating a letter-writing response to Nixon.[122]

Such effort to circumvent processes of public justification was characteristic of Nixon's management of the executive branch. When, despite the administration's efforts toward secrecy, a *New York Times* journalist discovered news of the Cambodian bombings, including accurate reports of targets and accurate numbers about amounts of bombs dropped, Nixon became incensed, placed "blistering calls," and illegally tapped the phone lines of his subordinates to ferret out the leak.[123] But the journalist had simply found the story in the Thai press and confirmed its details,[124] and Nixon's hysterical reaction alienated staffers. After his April 30 speech on Cambodia, none of the cabinet secretaries called to offer support; in response, Nixon "ordered that they not be allowed to use the White House tennis courts."[125] Such petty retaliation could hardly support a professionally productive atmosphere.

Nixon's administration used the independence of the executive branch not for steady leadership but rather for insular and impetuous decision-making. He apparently viewed the structural independence of the executive office as an opportunity to wage war in a manner disconnected from political constraint. By the end of his first year, Nixon was "bragging to aids that Hanoi had underestimated 'the man' . . . and 'the time'—he still had three more years left in his first term."[126] His chaotic use of the resources of the executive branch was perhaps amplified by the security approach he took, that of Madman theory—to make the Chinese and North Vietnamese believe he would do absolutely anything to win the war.[127] Signaling strength was a core element of Cold War ideology, but in Nixon's case this approach may have simply created permissiveness around chaos and policy incoherence. This was reflected in both Nixon's willingness to rely on collapsed and deformed deliberative contexts, and his willingness to subvert the procedures of the executive branch to avoid resistance to politically unrealistic aspirations.

For example, Nixon's original hope in introducing troops into Cambodia was to batter Hanoi into negotiations. Yet his announcement that US troops would be out of Cambodia by June 30 was generated "on the

York: W. W. Norton & Company, 1990), 96–101; J. Anthony Lukas, *Nightmare: Underside of Nixon Years* (Athens: Ohio University Press, 1999), 33–37.

122   Prados, *Vietnam*, 313.
123   Ibid., 296.
124   Ibid., 295.
125   Clymer, *Troubled*, 107.
126   Prados, *Vietnam*, 308.
127   Ibid., 290–92, 305–306.

spur of the moment" in hopes of quieting domestic protests.[128] The announcement constrained General Abram's troops without any consultation with that general himself, undermining Nixon's ability to consider the decision in the context of his larger Cambodian strategy. Nixon's subordinates testified to his speedy, rather than coherent, decision-making: "Nixon was forever firing off orders [that] . . . often demanded extreme measures. Some White House officials adopted the technique of sitting on certain Nixon orders for a day or two, then asking the president whether he really wanted those things done."[129] Some of Nixon's subordinates simply began to ignore certain instructions of his. When Kissinger was instructed to tell Soviet Ambassador Dobrynin that the president "was out of control on Vietnam," subordinates "quietly torpedoed" the order.[130]

Histories of Nixon's presidency testify to the limits of the administration's policy deliberation, which did not consider the costs of escalation and repeatedly ignored even considering policy speculation about withdrawal.[131] This is despite Nixon's own characterization, in his memoirs, of escalation as "an option we ruled out very early."[132] The extent to which Nixon conducted his policy reviews on the basis of a collapsed sense of the options available is illustrated by the very first review he conducted upon taking office. Kissinger was charged with presenting a range of options and eliciting the knowledge and differences of opinions among D.C. agencies, military, and diplomatic posts in order to structure a broad assessment of Vietnam policy. Daniel Ellsberg's first draft of the report presented a strange set of choices, with "compromise" presented as a policy, and withdrawal denigrated as an option "with no advocates within the U.S. government." Ellsberg's original paper offered four alternatives for escalation. The draft also specified that escalation was a repeat choice, and that each step of failed escalation would bring renewed pressures. To this draft, Kissinger added two options on invading North Vietnam (at steep cost), and presented a withdrawal option "modified to a partial pullout, leveling off at about 100,000 troops, *excluding* a full U.S. withdrawal."[133] He also added an introductory section specifying that the aim was not disengagement or an end to the war, but rather "ensuring the withdrawal or destruction of North Vietnamese forces in the South and of National Liberation Front infrastructure and forces"—in

128   Ibid., 373.
129   Ibid., 297. For more on how Nixon's subordinates saw his behavior, see Walter Isaacson, *Kissinger: A Biography* (New York: Simon & Schuster, 2005), 260–62.
130   Prados, *Vietnam*, 311–12.
131   Ibid., 302–303, 307.
132   Ibid., 302, citing Richard Nixon, *RN: The Memoirs of Richard Nixon* (New York: Simon & Schuster, Inc., 1990), 430.
133   Emphasis in original. For quotations, see Prados, *Vietnam*, 288–89.

other words, victory.[134] Kissinger also deleted the warnings about pit-falls of escalation.[135] The final draft thus specified a goal at odds with Nixon's publicly expressed commitment, presented a collapsed range of alternative policy options, and a confused articulation of the goals that compromise could help achieve. This draft troubled some advisors, including Morton Halperin, who raised concern about the excluded option of a simple unilateral withdrawal. Halperin has testified that Kissinger, by contrast, was concerned that the draft included no "win" option, which made Halperin "quite nervous . . . because I thought it was a mistake, fundamental mistake, and that it would recreate the illusion that we could somehow win this war."[136]

The paper also contained contradictory assumptions. For example, officials believed that Hanoi was engaging in diplomacy at that moment "because of its military defeat at Tet," and yet the "the documents contained a clear sense the DRV could maintain its strength in the field over the foreseeable future, and no expectation that Hanoi might offer the concessions . . . of a defeated power."[137] Even the characterization of the Tet Offensive of 1968 as a military defeat was odd, given that the paper also spoke to lowered levels of North Vietnamese defections.[138] In terms of a time frame for victory, the paper communicated that optimists estimated over eight years, and pessimists thirteen years or more, to pacify the situation, but "the options section of the paper was framed by the need to achieve an outcome in two years." Nixon emphasized this constraint in his meeting with the NSC.[139]

Nixon's conversation with the NSC, premised on this review paper, never chose any of the options presented. But the conversation did make vague reference to the path Nixon would choose: "avoid a political settlement in Paris; push Hanoi by vigorous near-term military action, combined with Soviet leverage; and play for time with the public by projecting an image of openness to talks, pulling out a few troops, and dealing with the draft."[140] It was also during this transitional period that Nixon began questioning what could be done in Cambodia, asking the Joint Chiefs the day after his inauguration about stopping supply lines through that country.[141]

---

134   Prados, *Vietnam*, 288–89.

135   Ibid.

136   As cited in Larry Berman, *No Peace, No Honor: Nixon, Kissinger, and Betrayal in Vietnam* (New York: The Free Press, 2001), 47.

137   Prados, *Vietnam*, 288–89.

138   Ibid., 291.

139   Ibid.

140   Ibid.

141   Ibid., 292.

The choice to bomb Cambodia was controversial within the executive branch. Operation Breakfast was originally proposed as a military strategy that would help block supply lines and destroy enemy troops, but Kissinger encountered challenges from staff members like Richard Sneider, NSC aide to Kissinger for East Asia, who worried about dispersing the North Vietnamese even further and doubted the bombings would be able to remove the enemy command. These concerns bore out.[142] At the same time, others in the executive branch challenged the president to be more bellicose. Such challenges, according to Kissinger, were frequently effective in moving the president rapidly, which Kissinger attributed to Nixon not liking to appear "less tough than his advisers." In an "advisory" NSC meeting that happened after Nixon had already decided on the first round of Cambodian bombings, he encountered some doubts. But Vice President Agnew challenged the president, arguing that "discussion was irrelevant" if the president was not going to attack all Cambodian sanctuaries at once, and calling any lesser bellicosity "pussyfooting." Kissinger claimed that Nixon then moved his position toward the middle of the group, and then "scolded" Kissinger for not warning him about Agnew.[143]

Unlike Kennedy, Nixon did not use controversy among his advisors as an opportunity to investigate the underlying factual premises that were generating disagreement. Instead, Nixon subverted his own consultative processes. Two of Kissinger's assistants, Tony Lake and Roger Morris, resigned on April 29, 1970—before the incursion was made public—both because of their deep alienation from the administration and also to protest the Cambodian bombings. Their formal letter of resignation cited "grave reservations about the value of using U.S. troops in Cambodia." In a personal letter to Kissinger, they wrote that the administration would "dismiss the critics for their motives or manliness . . . ridicule them with the catch phrases of the Right" rather than "recognizing the validity of the problems, however they are raised, and leading an effort to resolve them."[144] Little did they know this atmosphere of ridicule and alienation was backed with a repeated willingness to wiretap internal consultants, rather than seek out the factual basis for their concerns or indeed elevate those staffers who had demonstrated good judgment. Morris and Lake

---

142   Seymour M. Hersh, *The Price of Power: Kissinger in the Nixon White House* (New York: Simon & Schuster, 1983), 54; also Jeffrey Kimball, *Nixon's Vietnam War* (Lawrence: University Press of Kansas, 1998), 136.

143   All quotations from Kimball, *Nixon's Vietnam*, 203–204.

144   Berman, *No Peace*, 75. William Watts resigned as well. See too Seymour M. Hersh, "Kissinger and Nixon in the White House," *Atlantic Monthly* (May 1982); and Isaacson, *Kissinger*, 276–78, on the resignations.

also worried because they heard regular phone conversations between Kissinger and Nixon in which Nixon was actually drunk, discussing policy. One Nixon aide overheard the intoxicated president telling Kissinger they would have to "nuke" Vietnam.[145]

Intimidating key assistants out of the administration was inconsistent with the processual standard that presidents elevate those who perform well. After the bombings, Sneider's concerns bore out. Vietnamese Communists dispersed into Cambodia, and soon after the MENU bombings the French began to report that "the area of Cambodia under control of the North Vietnamese and the Viet Cong had actually increased; roads that had been traveled without difficulty only a few weeks earlier were now closed."[146] Sneider, by now, was being wiretapped.[147] By contrast, the fact that military advisors like General Abrams had assured that Operation Breakfast, the first on the MENU sequence, would wipe out enemy forces did not stop the military from continuing to recommend new targets or apparently lead Nixon to change his estimate of the value of their advice.[148]

The Cambodian incursion raised skepticism among many in Nixon's cabinet. Secretary of State William Rogers and Secretary of Defense Melvin Laird objected repeatedly. White House aides John Ehrlichman and Charles Colson also worried about the domestic and international response to the incursion.[149] Of course, a president need not surround himself with staff who challenge him. But a president seems more likely to achieve the benefits of either an authoritarian or conflictual management style if he is transparent with staff about his expectations surrounding dissensus. Nixon instead publicly endorsed but privately co-opted dissent, fostering confusion and alienation. While Nixon publicly claimed to value internal challenge, his actual behavior was often to fire subordinates who were critical.[150] By 1970, worried about the political implications of the level of internal opposition he faced, Nixon conducted a series of lengthy meetings intended to induce questioning staffers "to get

---

145 Berman, *No Peace*, 6, 76. Brandishing nuclear weapons was one part of the "Madman" strategy. Kissinger's strategy was to posture with nuclear weapons to "convert the prospect of total destruction into daily leverage." Jeremi Suri, "Henry Kissinger and American Grand Strategy," in Fredrik Logevall and Andrew Preston, eds., *Nixon in the World: American Foreign Relations, 1969–1977* (New York: Oxford University Press, 2008): 67–84, 76. See also Kimball, *Nixon's Vietnam*, 204.

146 Clymer, *Troubled*, 96.

147 See Hersh, "Kissinger and Nixon."

148 Clymer, *Troubled*, 95.

149 Prados, *Vietnam*, 364.

150 Famously, Secretary of the Interior Walter Hickel. For discussion, see Clymer, *Troubled*, 109.

their hands wet with the Cambodia preparations, ensuring they could not disassociate themselves later," including Rogers and Laird.[151]

Confusion permeated executive branch decision-making structures on Cambodia. Nixon had already tried to arrange a back channel to give military orders around Laird. The order Nixon issued for the incursion created yet a new set of decision-making channels, finally precipitating an "open revolt among NSC staffers, some of whom fundamentally objected, [and] wrote papers explaining their reasoning," even threatening to resign if the invasion continued.[152] After believing that he had overcome Rogers's and Laird's objections, Nixon began issuing orders through this new channel, only delaying them slightly to allow Rogers to testify to Congress that no decisions had been made. On April 30, Nixon publicly announced his decision as US troops were crossing into Cambodia.[153]

These process failures had consequences for the success of the policy chosen. For example, a key expressed aim of the bombings was to support the morale of troops, but the secrecy Nixon ordered was so tight that few troops knew what was happening. B-52s received new missions while airborne and were directed to Cambodian targets that had been pre-approved under a "double billing" procedure that allowed for falsified paperwork indicating that attacks were occurring in South Vietnam.[154]

Nixon's willingness to dismiss his advisors' objections was also unfortunate. The ground troop incursion was targeted at an enemy command center in the far south of the country. Laird and Rogers had argued that this center could not be caught, but Nixon dismissed their concerns and Senate committee staff in Saigon were told that its capture was one of the main justifications for the incursion. As it turned out, when the incursion began, "Hanoi and Liberation Front leaders . . . had already been put on notice by the Lon Nol coup, and there are indications the main camp had moved across the border, a short way into Vietnam." Ultimately, the key "success" of the strike was a seizure of weapons and equipment, but these seem to have been surplus after a major arms upgrade. As soon as a week after the strike, "the subject would not even be mentioned."[155]

Despite the fulfillment of Laird's predictions, Nixon treated him not as a source of wise counsel whose authority should be elevated, but rather ordered an FBI wiretap on one of Laird's aides and two senior officials in the State Department on the day of Kent State. A week later, two more

151   Prados, *Vietnam*, 364.
152   Ibid., 364.
153   Ibid., 364.
154   Berman, *No Peace*, 50.
155   All quotations from Prados, *Vietnam*, 365.

departed NSC staffers who had objected to the incursion were put on the wiretap list.[156]

CONTRIBUTIONS TO INTERBRANCH DELIBERATION: SECRECY

A third category of processual standards pertains to whether each branch makes its judgments vulnerable to repudiation by the other branch. Asking that presidents make their policies transparent to allow Congress to rebuff their positions is not the same as the procedural demand in the bipartisan consensus that elite partisans in both parties be included in policy formation. Rather, the relational conception requires Congress as a whole to be put on notice about the president's security judgments so it may offer its institutional judgment on the matter at hand. Also, unlike the bipartisan consensus, the relational conception is not premised on the value of interbranch *agreement* about policy options, but rather on the value of interbranch *deliberation* about those policies.

Both presidents wanted to conceal their actions to avoid political interference. Kennedy, for example, tried to keep the warnings he was receiving from the CIA quiet, in part due to worries about his Republican opposition. He judged that the information he was receiving did not signify a threat, and wished to avoid both public hysteria (which could trigger security consequences of its own) and Republican opposition.[157] Importantly, in Kennedy's case, preserving secrecy supported the president's capacity to formulate an independent and distinctive presidential judgment. To immediately publicize the missile buildup when it was not clear what the executive branch's judgment on the situation was could have significantly limited the scope of Kennedy's deliberations. Kennedy's opponents were primed and eager to set a belligerent course with Cuba. Kennedy had reasonable grounds for fearing that once the placement of Soviet missiles was made public, and his deliberations were exposed, the political winds would be so strong that he would be unable to develop a distinctive perspective of his own. His secrecy was related to the imperative of independently developing a proposal for action. Kennedy thus forestalled the judgment of the other branches (the third condition) in order to shore up his capacity to develop an independent judgment grounded in his branch's distinctive perspective (the first and second conditions).

156 Ibid., 371–72. See also Kimball, *Nixon's Vietnam*, 136.
157 Zelizer, *Arsenal*, 158.

Once Kennedy had developed a judgment, Congress and the public were alerted. While the president's constitutional authority according to the third condition of conflict would have been enhanced had he been transparent to the full Congress sooner, his use of secrecy to protect the political space he needed to come to a developed judgment of his own enhanced the constitutional authority available to him under the processual standards associated with the second condition of conflict. Like Roosevelt, Kennedy was embedded in a political context that made it unlikely he could achieve the full authority connected to each dimension of the relational conception's standards at the same time.

By contrast, Nixon's secrecy is most plausibly interpreted as a direct effort to evade judgment itself. He told a few legislators, including Richard Russell and John Stennis, but they did not alert any of their colleagues.[158] Kissinger explained the administration's "reticence" with reference to the desire to "avoid forcing the North Vietnamese, Prince Sihanouk, and the Soviets and the Chinese into public reactions," which could have pushed Cambodia further into the arms of the North Vietnamese.[159] But the decision to keep the bombings secret was made directly after Laird and Wheeler warned that "those who knew about the messages regarding the bombings might make trouble."[160] Kissinger's premise that the United States sought to preserve Sihanouk's hold on his office is also inconsistent with published allegations that the CIA planned to assassinate Sihanouk and supported the pro-American coup that ultimately deposed him.[161] But most importantly, the Nixon administration's efforts to shield the news from domestic audiences went beyond "reticence." The bombing coordinates, for example, were falsified, violating the Uniform Code of Military Justice.[162] Nixon then refused to acknowledge American combat operations in Cambodia for a year. When he announced the ground incursions in 1970, Nixon simply lied about prior US involvement in Cambodia, claiming that "for five years neither the United States nor South Vietnam has moved against these enemy sanctuaries because we did not wish to violate the territory of a neutral nation."[163] The lies extended not just to the public and almost all of Congress, as well as the relevant

158   Prados, *Vietnam*, 294.

159   Henry A. Kissinger, *Ending the Vietnam War: A History of America's Involvement in and Extrication from the Vietnam War* (New York: Simon & Schuster, Inc., 2003), 66.

160   Prados, *Vietnam*, 293.

161   Ely, "The American War," 1143, citing Shawcross, *Sideshow*, 122; John Prados, *Presidents' Secret Wars: CIA and Pentagon Covert Operations from World War II Through the Persian Gulf War* (Ivan R. Dee, 1996), 303.

162   Prados, *Vietnam*, 294.

163   Nixon, *April 30 Address*.

congressional committees, but also to even the Secretary of the Air Force and Air Force Chief of Staff.[164]

Even after the revelation of troop presence in Cambodia to domestic audiences, Kissinger and Nixon refused to acknowledge the significance of their intervention, with Kissinger arguing that "it was not a bombing of Cambodia, but it was a bombing of North Vietnamese in Cambodia."[165] In 1971, when Congress began to investigate Cambodia more seriously, Pentagon officials told the Armed Services Committee that no B-52 bombing raids had happened in Cambodia prior to the incursion of ground troops in 1970. Senator Hughes exposed in 1972 this major scandal of the false coordinates.[166] When Hughes conducted hearings, one of his first witnesses, former Major Hal Knight revealed that "when he asked his superior officer from whom the Air Force needed to conceal the bombing raids, the response was, 'Well, I guess the Foreign Relations Committee.'"[167]

Far from accompanying his acts of war with a deliberative contribution that would equip the legislature to judge his war authority, Nixon acted to confuse Congress. It was not even clear that the *president* supported a security vision that could render meaningful an intervention in Cambodia. Nixon's own public statements had seemed to offer a foreign policy vision that would preclude expanding the scope of conflict. None of his speeches gave any hint of his Madman theory, rather emphasizing de-escalation and the limited nature of the war.[168] In 1969 Nixon had started making serious public commitments to de-escalate the war, remove American combat troops, and promote "Vietnamization." He also announced the Nixon Doctrine that year, emphasizing that foreign nations would have direct responsibility for their own defense but that the United States would supply assistance when requested in accordance with treaty commitments.[169] Under this doctrine, Cambodia's neutrality

164 Ely, "American War," 1137, 1138. See also U.S. House Committee on the Judiciary, "Statement of Information: Hearings before the Committee on the Judiciary, House of Representatives, pursuant to H. Res. 803, a resolution authorizing and directing the Committee on the Judiciary to investigate whether sufficient grounds exist for the House of Representatives to exercise its constitutional power to impeach Richard M. Nixon, President of the United States of America. May–June 1974," 93rd Cong., 2nd sess. (1974): 6–7; Prados, *Vietnam*, 300.

165 Shawcross, *Sideshow*, 28.

166 Johnson, *Congress*, 187.

167 Ibid., 188, citing U.S. Senate, Armed Services Committee Hearings, *Bombing in Cambodia*, 93rd Cong., 1st sess. (August 16, 1973): 9.

168 Prados, *Vietnam*, 309.

169 See President Richard M. Nixon, "Nixon's Address to the Nation on the War in Vietnam, November 3, 1969," *Watergate.info*. Available at http://watergate.info/nixon /silent-majority-speech-1969.shtml (accessed September 21, 2011).

should have protected it from interference at least until Cambodia itself requested assistance.

It is plausible that Nixon sought secrecy around Cambodia because of the military significance of public opinion. Nixon viewed domestic protest about Cambodia as itself posing a security problem because he felt it heightened the belief of enemies that they need only outlast an unpopular president.[170] In some ways his position was like Roosevelt's: seeking to mollify to maintain the political space necessary to take the action he wanted to take. But whereas Roosevelt's conduct was nonetheless highly interpretable by the legislature, Nixon's effort to mislead the public coincided with highly duplicitous relations with Congress. In this, Nixon's behavior resembled Polk's more than Roosevelt's. In all three cases, the processual authority of the presidents was diminished to the extent that they failed to communicate to Congress their relevant policy and constitutional arguments for legislative response.

Nixon did present some constitutional defense of his conduct. William Rehnquist, then of the Office of Legal Counsel, issued an opinion justifying the Cambodian incursion. That opinion invoked the Supreme Court's *Youngstown* decision, distinguished Cambodia from the domestic problem at stake in the steel seizure, cited past presidential conduct of independent military strikes as authoritative, and actually rejected Congress's authority to prohibit the president from acts of war without declaration.[171] In other words, Nixon leaned on Truman's claims about executive empowerment.

Although Nixon offered a constitutional argument, just as Senator Morgan's constitutional criticism of Roosevelt does not mean the legislature was engaging in a focused constitutional challenge to the Corollary, so too, the simple fact that the administration issued a constitutional opinion does not render Nixon's behavior a constitutional challenge. Nixon was not challenging a preexisting order so much as repeating its official relevance even while departing from some of its core tenants— such as bipartisanship—in practice. If these departures had been justifiable in terms of the security context of the times, and conceived in ways that made use of distinctively executive-branch governing resources, it would be more plausible to claim that Nixon's deviations amounted to a "challenge" rather than subversion. Instead, I argue that the administration's failure to articulate in a steady and ongoing way, to Congress, a

170   Robert Jervis, "Foreign Policy and Congressional/Presidential Relations," *The Constitution and National Security: A Bicentennial View*, eds. Howard E. Shuman and Walter R. Thomas (Washington: National Defense University Press, 1990), 46; Nixon, *RN*, 382.

171   Memorandum from William H. Rehnquist, Assistant Att'y Gen., Office of Legal Counsel, to Charles W. Colson, Special Counsel to the President (May 22, 1970), regarding "The President and the War Power: South Vietnam and the Cambodian Sanctuaries."

policy and constitutional judgment that could license his behavior; and his failures to mobilize executive branch capacities to inform his sense of policy goals, and to advance those goals to Congress, blocks interpreting him as an innovating challenger. Posing a constitutional challenge requires advancing a coherent policy and constitutional agenda. This, I argue, Nixon did not do.

Using the relational conception, I argue that we can explain and enrich the common intuition, which I share, that Kennedy's use of executive branch war powers in the Cuban Missile blockade was more constitutionally authoritative than Nixon's in Cambodia. Because of the relationship of these acts of war to a larger, constitutionally authoritative Cold War security order; and because of the varied quality of each president's engagement with the distinctive governing capacities of the executive branch, the relational conception can constitutionally distinguish these cases despite settlement premises to the contrary.

Chapter 5

LEGISLATIVE INVESTIGATIONS AS WAR POWER

The Senate Munitions Investigation and Iran-Contra

The relational conception's emphasis on war as a political question leads to scrutiny of the processes by which interbranch understandings of war, defense, security, and authority are constructed. Through what processes do the branches form judgments about the security and constitutional controversies of the moment? One important tool Congress uses to hone its judgments and confront those of the president is legislative investigations. While investigations serve many functions, their capacity to serve as a site for the development of an informed institutional judgment is highly relevant to the work the relational conception assigns the branches. Scandals about the president's use of the war power pose important questions to Congress about its own authority. What was the nature of the abuse? According to what evaluative standard could misconduct be identified? What does Congress's effort to hold others to account indicate about the legislature's conception of its own war authority? Could the legislature defend its conception of its own war authority against countervailing paradigms? On what terms?

Legislators obviously approach investigations, and any other exercise of power, with a variety of purposes. After McCarthyism and Watergate, many have come to view investigations as processes for discovering the truth about "what happened" in official abuses of power. Indeed this is one of the organizing frames in both the Munitions and Iran-Contra Investigations. Legislators asserted that they wanted to know how the United States became involved in hostilities that amounted to possible constitutional abuses.

The legislature's articulation of any abuse necessarily implies some conception of the legislature's own role in holding other branches to account. Whether that conception is explicit or implicit, Congress's judgment amounts to a deliberative contribution that can be analyzed from within the terms of the relational conception. To the extent that the legislature's identification of a constitutional abuse—and hence its advocacy for a proposition about Congress's and the president's relative war authority—is tethered to a deliberative space that harnesses Congress's distinctive institutional capacities, Congress's advocacy is of greater, rather than lesser, constitutional authority. The processual standards for legislative war governance are capacious, but they are not all-inclusive. In this chapter, I apply the processual standards to argue that the Senate Munitions Investigation achieved greater constitutional war authority for the legislature than did the Iran-Contra Investigation.

The Senate Munitions Investigation of the 73rd and 74th Congresses, and the Iran-Contra Investigation of the 100th Congress, exposed competing judgments about security policy and interbranch war authority. The Senate Munitions Investigation tried to show that business's illegal conduct was behind US entry into World War I. It did not prove its hypothesis, but the investigation deeply structured the context within which President Roosevelt had to manage entry into World War II. It radicalized participating Senators toward neutrality and developed the leadership of the isolationist movement, contributing to Roosevelt's difficulty with Congress during the lead-up to war. The 1987 Iran-Contra Investigation also investigated lawbreaking, this time in the executive branch. It exposed massive constitutional transgressions and weakened the Reagan presidency. But what began as an effort to reassert legislative authority was whittled down to a few criminal convictions and pardons. The operative interbranch allocation of war power was left intact.

In both investigations, the legislature made its conclusions available for rebuff through the reports it generated. In this chapter I apply the processual standards associated with the first condition of conflict (independence) and the second (perspectives forged on the basis of a branch's distinctive capacities). This chapter also demonstrates the complexity of legislative independence. While both investigations demonstrated some independence in their very willingness to confront the executive branch, I argue that the Munitions Committee displayed a deeper form of independence because it also stood up, in rhetoric and behavior, for the value of distinctively legislative forms of security judgment. While the Iran-Contra Investigation was willing to confront the executive branch, it did so using reasoning and argumentation borrowed from the judiciary. It communicated its own insecurity about the value of independent legislative judgment and achieved less of the processual authority associated with this standard. Sharp contrasts also emerge in the extent to which each investigation took advantage of its constitutionally distinctive governance capacities, for example, the ability to develop constitutional judgments that are linked to policy ones and the ability to assess complex information to make retrospective and future projections.

Both investigations were highly conflictual and inflected by partisanship and institutional rivalry. But through its hearings, the terms of the Munitions Investigation broadened and deepened to support the Senate's capacity to mobilize defensible interpretive judgments about its own war authority given the context of the moment. However, the Iran-Contra Select Committee saw its deliberative space narrow over time. What started as an inquiry into one of the most serious constitutional transgressions of the twentieth century collapsed into a spectacle of criminal trials and convictions set aside. Congress did not bring the security needs of the moment into focus, nor did it develop a point of view about how its governing strengths could be engaged to meet those needs. Relative to the Nye Committee, I argue, using the relational conception, that this highly conflictual process failed to generate constitutional authority for the Congress.

INSULARISM, THE RELATIONAL CONCEPTION, AND INVESTIGATORY POWERS

Investigations are rarely treated as a form of security power.[1] From a settlement point of view, we ascertain which branch has war authority by turning to the Constitution's text or its law on explicit security matters. This drives a scholarly focus on the meanings of the "commander-in-chief" and "declare war" clauses. But many constitutional powers can become war powers when they are used to advance a security agenda.

When it is evaluated, Congress's investigatory power is often assessed in terms of practical efficacy.[2] When a normative standard is applied, it is often that of fairness.[3] But constitutional authority is not a simple mat-

---

1   Important exceptions are Cecil Crabb, Jr., *Bipartisan Foreign Policy: Myth or Reality?* (Evanston, IL: Row, Peterson and Company, 1957), 11, and Douglas L. Kriner, *After the Rubicon: Congress, Presidents, and the Politics of Waging War* (Chicago: University of Chicago Press, 2010).

2   Joel D. Aberbach, *Keeping a Watchful Eye: The Politics of Congressional Oversight* (Washington, DC: Brookings Institution, 1990); Les Aspin, "Why Doesn't Congress Do Something?" *Foreign Policy* 15 (1974): 70–82; James M. Lindsay, "Congress, Foreign Policy, and the New Institutionalism," *International Studies Quarterly* 38: 2 (1994): 281–304; Matthew D. McCubbins and Thomas Schwartz, "Congressional Oversight Overlooked: Police Patrols versus Fire Alarms," *American Journal of Political Science* 28:1 (1984): 165–79, 176.

3   E.g., Michael B. Rappaport, "Replacing Independent Counsels with Congressional Investigations," *University of Pennsylvania Law Review* 148:5 (2000): 1595–633; Deborah

ter of procedural fairness or of practical efficacy. A legislature may be efficacious, but behaving atrociously. An investigation may be fair but lack content. The relational conception views investigations as one of Congress's war powers when they are used to advance positions about the Constitution's allocation of war authority or to advance war aims. We can judge investigations by applying the substantive and processual standards of the relational conception.

From the point of view of the relational conception, constitutional fidelity requires a security order that fits the security imperatives of the moment together with the constitutional capacities of the branches. The branches themselves bear primary responsibility for constructing an allocation of war authority that responds to this need. Investigations are a space where the branches can develop articulations of these given or possible security orders. Any security order premised on shaky processes of discernment and judgment creates for its officials only shaky forms of constitutional authority. If both branches behave in accord with the relational conception, then the constitutional authority behind the security order as a whole is enhanced. War authority in such a case is *produced* as a result of the excellent interpretive politics of each branch. For example, I believe that the war authority produced in the lead-up to World War II was robust, because that system was comprised of a president who offered powerful and well-defended security judgments in relation to a legislature that, as I shall argue, also offered powerful and well-defended security judgments. The development and clarification of alternative possible security orders made the decision toward presidentialism and internationalism after World War II a more constitutionally authoritative choice. This is the case even though neither branch was especially efficacious at achieving its ends until they started working together. By contrast, I argue that the war authority produced in Iran-Contra was weak and flimsy; an incompetent and criminally abusive executive branch was met by a legislature that seemed incapable of defending its prerogatives or articulating the significance of the security breaches at stake.

Chapter 1 emphasized that the standards of the relational conception are political. As such we can expect partisanship and other forms of partial group affiliation to play a role both in organizing the claims that the branches are willing to make, and in organizing interpreters' assessments of those claims. This chapter notes some of the diverse roles of partisanship in supporting processes of interbranch deliberation. Some scholarship associates divided government with more frequent interbranch war

---

L. Rhode, "Conflicts of Commitment: Legal Ethics in the Impeachment Context," *Stanford Law Review* 52:2 (2000): 269–351; Wayne Morse, "Toward Fair Investigating Committees," *Contemporary American Culture* 8:3 (1954): 26–34.

challenges.[4] I assess quality, not quantity, and in these cases partisanship seems to have had multiple effects (not only one) on the quality of the legislature's war judgments.

THE SENATE MUNITIONS INVESTIGATION AND IRAN-CONTRA

The Munitions Investigation (often called the "Nye Investigation" for its prominent chairman) proceeded from the spring of 1934 until February 1936. Its aim was to investigate the role of the munitions industry in the US entry into World War I. A widely circulated "merchants of death" hypothesis specified that business interests had manipulated the public into war with propaganda, bribes, and lobbying.[5] Progressives centered in the Democratic Party hoped that this exposé would help their effort to nationalize the munitions industry. The investigation had bipartisan support, and while its chair Gerald Nye (ND) was a progressive Republican, Democrats held a strong majority in the 73rd Congress that was strengthened in 1934. Nye himself had been seated in the Senate thanks to Democratic support.[6] This was an effort to achieve a Democratic policy goal by conducting an investigation into the conduct of a war under Democratic President Wilson.

The resolution makes it clear that the investigation had a governing hypothesis about the munitions industry, and that the investigation's purpose was to consider the best way to craft a set of desired policy outcomes. The resolution announced that "the influence of the commercial motive is one of the inevitable factors often believed to stimulate and sustain wars" and specifically charged the committee to investigate how munitions makers promoted sales.[7] Its hypothesis of decisive business support

4   For an excavation of some of the multiple links between partisanship and interbranch war challenge, see Kriner, *Rubicon*.

5   The "Merchants of Death" thesis (after a book by that title) presented a major contemporary hypothesis about the cause for US entry into World War I that fit well with the general antiwar and antibusiness sentiment of the early 1930s. The investigation was broadly supported outside the Senate. See Wayne S. Cole, *Senator Gerald P. Nye and American Foreign Relations* (Minneapolis: University of Minnesota Press, 1962), 66. Scholarship on the merchant of death hypothesis includes Charles Callan Tansill, *America Goes to War* (Boston: Little, Brown and Company, 1938); Charles Seymour, *American Neutrality, 1914–1917* (New Haven: Yale University Press, 1935).

6   Matthew Ware Coulter, *The Senate Munitions Inquiry of the 1930s: Beyond the Merchants of Death* (Westport, CT: Greenwood Press, 1997), 13.

7   The authorizing resolution asked the committee to "inquire into the desirability of creating a Government monopoly in respect to the manufacture of armaments and munitions and other implements of war." S. Res. 206, 73rd Cong., 2nd Sess. (February 28, 1934).

leading to US entry into World War I was not borne out after eighteen months of hearings.[8] Yet the committee did make two broader findings. It discovered that the structure of the US economy supported the emergence of groups whose legally defensible yet ethically shaky lobbying and business activities supported bellicosity. And it discovered that the executive branch, not business, served as a fulcrum for US entry into war.

The Munitions Investigation is widely viewed as failed on at least three counts. First, it failed to demonstrate its governing hypothesis. While some bribery scandals were uncovered, hearings mostly featured seemingly respectable businessmen plausibly defending their normal business practices. Second, the policy effort linked to the investigation failed. A proposal to nationalize the munitions industry never even made it to the floor.[9] Moreover, while contemporaries believed that the Munitions Investigation strengthened the power of the isolationist neutrality group in Congress, that group repeatedly failed to enact its most preferred policy outcomes.[10] Finally, the security vision that grounded the investigation—an isolationist neutral America—was set to fade through the experience of World War II. The investigation's hypothesis failed. The efforts of its members to keep the United States out of World War II failed. And the content of the isolationist neutrality vision was repudiated or abandoned.

However, many of the committee's "failures," from the point of view of its own efficacy, were successes for the larger public. Discovering that business corruption did not seem to undergird US entry into World War I probably helped prepare the public for entering World War II. The movement toward nationalizing the munitions industry was ill timed given the impending war, and so that movement's failure was beneficial for the

---

8   The very first report conspicuously omits the merchants-of-death hypothesis, instead noting "connections" among shipbuilding, banking, and raw materials interests and the US Navy. U.S. Senate, Special Committee to Investigate the Manufacture and Sale of Arms and Other War Munitions, *Munitions Industry, Naval Shipbuilding, Preliminary Report of the Special Committee on Investigation of the Munitions Industry*, 74th Cong., 1st Sess., 1935. S. Rept. 944, pt. 1, 4–9 (henceforth *Munitions Report*, pt. 1). The third report acknowledged that the evidence did "not show that wars have been started solely because of the activities of munitions makers," U.S. Senate, Special Committee to Investigate the Manufacture and Sale of Arms and Other War Munitions, *Report on Activities and Sales of Munitions Companies*, 74th Cong., 2nd Sess., 1936. S. Rept. 944, pt. 3 (henceforth *Munitions Report*, pt. 3), 8.

9   Paul A.C. Koistinen, "The 'Industrial-Military Complex' in Historical Perspective: The Interwar Years," *The Journal of American History* 56: 4 (1970): 819–39, 833.

10   On strengthening the isolationist core, see Cordell Hull, *The Memoirs of Cordell Hull* (New York: Macmillan, Co., 1948), I, 404. On the failures of the committee, see James A. Perkins, "Congressional Investigations on Matters of International Import," *American Political Science Review* 34: 2 (1940): 284–94.

nation's security profile at that moment.[11] More importantly from the point of view of the relational conception, the committee demonstrated its willingness to assert the independent value of its perspective on the security politics of the moment. Its self-confident view of its own strengths supported its willingness to develop positions on security matters. One of the most important positions it developed concerned the problem of military-industrial links. Ironically, this aspect of the committee's work actually helped war planning in World War II by making the links between industry, government, and private citizens more transparent.[12] But its apprehension of the military-industrial complex also exposed troubling forms of political leverage that still call out for scrutiny. In addition, although the committee did not achieve the policy results it wanted, the constitutional authority of the security order that did arise after World War II was enhanced because relevant alternatives to internationalism had been articulated and developed in the lead-up to that war. The isolationist vision did not turn out to be well suited to the security needs of the moment, but that the nation grappled with a major foreign policy alternative enhances the constitutional authority of the construction that ultimately prevailed. As a result, I use the relational conception to argue for the "failed" Munitions Investigation as a constitutional success.

The Iran-Contra Investigation did not fare so well. Its task was to investigate a controversy that exploded in 1986 when a Lebanese magazine ran a story about US arms sales to Iran.[13] These arms sales were contrary to a major diplomatic effort led by the president to enact a worldwide arms embargo on Iran after the State Department's designation of that country as a "terrorist state." It was the very success of this embargo that accounted for the Iranian desperation for arms. New outrages soon appeared: the weapons sales were payoffs for the release of hostages. And money from the arms sales was supporting the war efforts of the Nicaraguan Contras, contrary to a prohibition Congress imposed through the Boland Amendment. It seemed that President Reagan and a few National Security Council staff were orchestrating multiple dangerous and covert foreign policies. Those few individuals were able to harness a "virtual private army of ships and planes," using a network of

11   John Edward Wiltz, "The Nye Committee Revisited," *The Historian* 23:2 (1961): 211–33, 233, citing Murray S. Stedman, *Exporting Arms: The Federal Arms Export Administration, 1935–1945* (New York: Kings Crown Press, 1947), pp. 126–36; Earl A. Molander, "Historical Antecedents of Military-Industrial Criticism," *Military Affairs* 40:2 (1976): 59–63, p. 62; also see John Edward Wiltz, *In Search Of Peace: The Senate Munitions Inquiry, 1934–36* (Baton Rouge,: Louisiana State University Press, 1963), p. 145.

12   Wiltz, *Nye Revisited*, 233.

13   Sean Wilentz, *The Age of Reagan: A History, 1974–2008* (New York: Harper Collins Publishers, 2008), 211.

false bank accounts funded by foreign governments and private citizens, operated by mercenaries and retired military officers, and able to carry out large illegal arms transfers as well as actual acts of war.[14] The immediate question concerned lawbreaking in the executive branch. All three branches conducted investigations. The judiciary convicted eleven of the leading participants of crimes, but most of those ultimately had their sentences set aside or were pardoned by George H. W. Bush. Some of the major players in the scandal went on to serve in high public office, their reputations untarnished.[15]

A striking feature of the Iran-Contra controversy is how quickly it was transformed from one of the most significant scandals of the twentieth century to a simple moment of a weakened presidency. Both Republicans and Democrats knew the conduct of Iran-Contra was impeachable. The executive branch had not just broken a few regulations but was actually running multiple covert foreign policies, some of them prohibited by law, all of them poorly conceived and executed. Radical Iranians had been armed; powerful incentives were created for hostage-taking; and, of great significance under the Cold War security ideology, the credibility of US positions was thrown into international doubt. In addition, Democrats had just regained control of the Senate while maintaining their majority status in the House. It is hard to imagine more propitious circumstances for impeachment.

Moving to establish an investigating committee, Senator Byrd (D-WV) emphasized that the goal was "to develop the truth, the whole truth and nothing but the truth—the full facts."[16] Byrd also specified the importance of a legislative inquiry for considering "improvements" that could be made to the foreign policy process.[17] An investigating committee was appointed with careful sensitivity to bipartisan balance. The hearings opened with spirited aspirations: Committee Chair Inouye (D-HI) invoked links between checks and balances and "sound policy based on reasoned and open discourse," the importance of restoring the "constitutionally mandated relationship" between the branches, and even the possibility that the legislature had not been "vigilant enough" in protecting its constitutional prerogatives.[18] But the momentum of the scandal turned dramatically when the committee summoned Oliver North, a NSC staff

14   Ibid., 215.

15   Ibid., 242.

16   *Congressional Record*, 100th Cong., 1st Sess., 1987 (January 6, 1987): 274. Importance of the "facts" emphasized by Arlen Specter, *Congressional Record*, 100th Cong., 1st Sess., 1987 (January 6, 1987): 277.

17   *Congressional Record* 100th Cong., 1st Sess., 1987 (January 6, 1987): 281.

18   U.S. Congress, *Joint Hearings Before the Senate Select Committee on Secret Military Assistance to Iran and the Nicaraguan Opposition and the House Select Committee*

member at the heart of these operations. Instead of meekly apologizing, North attacked the investigating committee and seized the opportunity to articulate a breathtaking theory of executive war-making powers. It soon became apparent that North's understanding of executive power was ascendant within the Republican Party.[19] Republicans on the investigating committee joined North in articulating a conception of war authority according to which the transgressions amounted to "political" missteps, but were not constitutional violations. This vigorous defense, together with Reagan's position late in his last term, headed off impeachment. The committee's final report was split into a bipartisan majority statement and a Republican minority statement. Both reports offered weak policy recommendations, few of which were enacted.[20]

Congress can enhance its war authority when it uses investigations to apprehend the security needs of the moment and to consider the intersection between those needs and its own capacities. At this task I argue that the 100th Congress failed. While the investigation did uncover many facts, the majority report failed to assemble those facts into a cogent story about the nature of the security threat the scandal represented. Neither the majority nor minority report excavated useful policy-relevant content. The majority report failed to engage the security problems at stake in the abuse or the security claims that motivated the president's use of war power.[21] The minority report, animated by a strong ideology

---

to *Investigate Covert Arms Transactions with Iran*, 100th Cong., 1st sess. (hereafter *Iran-Contra Joint Hearings*) (May 5, 1987), 2–3.

19   Stephen Skowronek, "The Conservative Insurgency and Presidential Power: A Developmental Perspective on the Unitary Executive," *Harvard Law Review* 122:8 (2009): 2070–103. See also L. Gordon Crovitz and Jeremy A. Rabkin, eds., *The Fettered Presidency: Legal Constraints on the Executive Branch* (1989); John G. Tower, "Congress versus the President: The Formulation and Implementation of American Foreign Policy, Foreign Affairs," *Foreign Affairs* 60:2 (1981): 229–46.

20   On congressional oversight of the intelligence community, see Loch K. Johnson, "*The Contemporary Presidency*: Presidents, Lawmakers, and Spies: Intelligence Accountability in the United States," *Presidential Studies Quarterly* 34:4 (2004): 828–37, and Marvin C. Ott, "Partisanship and the Decline of Intelligence Oversight," *International Journal of Intelligence and Counterintelligence* 16:1 (2003): 969–94. But see Jack Goldsmith, *The Terror Presidency: Law and Judgment Inside the Bush Administration* (New York: W. W. Norton & Company, 2007) on the legalized accountability mechanisms pervasive in the intelligence community after Iran-Contra.

21   The executive summary on pages 12–18 lays out a series of major security criticisms. These could have formed the backbone of a revamped report. U.S. Senate Select Committee on Secret Military Assistance to Iran and the Nicaraguan Opposition and U.S. House of Representatives Select Committee to Investigate Covert Arms Transactions with Iran, *Report of the Congressional Committees Investigating the Iran-Contra Affair with Supplemental, Minority, and Additional Views*, 100th Cong., 1st Sess., 1987. S. Rept. No. 100-216, H. Rept. No. 100-433 (hereafter *Iran-Contra Report*).

of executive power, was rather more focused on the substantive security outcomes it sought, but also failed to defend legislative capacities even where those were relevant. Framing the president's transgressions as "mistakes in judgment, and nothing more," the minority report also resisted framing Reagan's security judgments as constitutionally transgressive.[22] The majority and minority reports agreed on one major premise: neither viewed Congress as empowered to hold a president constitutionally accountable for "political" transgressions.

In elaborating the details of how these investigations managed to bolster or weaken the war authority of Congress, I refer to an important contrast: that between "interested" and "disinterested" investigation. The *Federalist Papers* use the term "disinterested" as praise; the word signifies a willingness to follow one's trail of reasoning wherever it might lead.[23] I use it to indicate reasoning that is not seeking any particular policy outcome. While such reasoning is useful in some contexts, it turns out that the disinterestedness of certain legislators in the Iran-Contra hearings seemed to be an important ingredient in that committee's failure to mobilize a defensible judgment about the security politics of the moment. The extent to which legislators were *interested* in achieving substantive policy outcomes seemed importantly related to the legislators' success or failure in generating war authority under the relational conception. The relational conception explicitly endorses the branches' linking their constitutional deliberations to concrete policy judgments, so this is not a surprising finding.

SENATORIAL INDEPENDENCE

The relational conception translates the structural independence of each branch into a processual standard of independent judgment. Assessing the constitutional politics of each branch means, in part, scrutinizing the extent to which the branch is making independent judgments rather than simply deferring to the reasoning and conclusions of its rivals. For the legislature, independence means not only a willingness to judge the presidency but also a willingness to assert the value of its own forms of governance. A modern threat to legislative independence is less a worry about insularity (as for the presidency) and more a worry that Congress

22 *Iran-Contra Report* (minority report), 437.

23 See, e.g., its invocation of men with "interested . . . views" who suffer from "honest errors of minds led astray by preconceived jealousies and fears," "false bias," and "[a]mbition, avarice, personal animosity, party opposition, and many other motives not more laudable than these." John Jay, "Federalist 1." Available at http://thomas.loc.gov/home/histdox/fed_01.html (accessed June 11, 2012).

will fail to insist on the value of its governance capacities even when these do have value.[24]

The two investigations varied tremendously on this front. Both investigations sought answers about lawbreaking. But the Munitions Investigation sought answers about lawbreaking on behalf of a forward-looking political agenda. In their statements and choices about how to structure the hearings, it is easy to see that these senators viewed themselves primarily as legislators. Even when focusing on individual criminal acts, they emphasized the policy implications at stake: the committee's third report stated that it was "not particularly interested in the bribery per se . . . but was concerned with what such bribery and corruption really meant in terms of social costs to this country and to all the countries of the world."[25] By contrast, the senators of the Iran-Contra Investigation seemed to understand themselves as inquisitors or judges, oriented toward exposing personal wrongdoing by individuals.[26] These different self-understandings permeated the structure of each set of proceedings and deeply conditioned the deliberative space of each investigation.

The Munitions senators revealed this self-understanding in how they structured the investigation, which began in the first place as part of a broader mobilization in Congress and civil society to take the profit out of war. Given this policy aim, committee membership was stacked with legislators with preexisting commitments toward pacifism or the restriction of war profits.[27] Once assembled, the investigating senators chose Stephen Raushenbush as chief investigator and director of the staff. Raushenbush was a World War I veteran and a progressive Christian activist with a background in public policy who understood his task as that of "shap[ing] . . . a preliminary for a constructive action."[28] He en-

24   See Jeffrey Tulis, *Democratic Decay and the Politics of Deference* (Princeton: Princeton University Press, forthcoming).

25   *Munitions Report*, pt. 3, 120.

26   This may be a result of the Democratic Party's arguably weaker discursive power in security politics at that moment. The identification of the Republican Party with "strength" may—this is speculative—have led Democrats to feel that legal rather than substantive policy claims would bear more political fruit. See Zelizer's discussion of the strength of the Republican Party in reclaiming security after World War II in *Arsenal*, chs. 4, 5, 6. Even in the context of impeachments, a quasi-judicial function, I would interpret legislative judgment as usefully distinguishable from the judgment that courts exercise. The Constitution explicitly distinguishes impeachment trials from trials at law. The standard of "high crimes and misdemeanors" is one that, I would argue, encompasses political as well as legal failure. See, e.g., Keith E. Whittington, "Bill Clinton Was No Andrew Johnson: Comparing Two Impeachments," *Journal of Constitutional Law* 2:2 (2002): 422–65.

27   See Coulter, *Munitions*, 22, 25, 26, 27.

28   Ibid., 48. See also Joan Cook, "Stephen Raushenbush Dies at 95; Had Key Role in War on U-Boats," *New York Times* (July 5, 1991), D8; Coulter, *Munitions*, 8, 29.

couraged the senators to conduct hearings in light of their desired policy results rather than as a simple interrogation of business. The committee obtained the background material it needed to scrutinize its policy goals: documents it obtained from the State Department, Navy, and various firms compose one of the most complete records of the structure of the US political economy of the twentieth century, "probably the best look historians will ever get of the modern armaments industry."[29] Hearings were timed to support legislative mobilization on security issues, and Nye launched a public speaking schedule, coordinated with the various stages of the investigation, to publicize its results. The structure of the final reports reflects this policy-oriented focus: six reports were issued on the structure of the munitions and financial industry, the structure of the US armaments, and political choices around neutrality and war.

Perhaps the Munitions Investigation senators' willingness to interrogate the interlocking parts of the political economy of war was related to their high estimation of the value of legislative governance. Both proceedings encountered constitutional challenges on national security and individual rights grounds. The Munitions Investigation was undeterred by these. For example, Irénée DuPont accused the committee of damaging national defense through its investigation. According to DuPont, legislative governance weakened a country's war posture, and he emphasized that only an "absolute monarch" could wage war effectively.[30] Senator Clark told DuPont that he "would like to disabuse your mind of the idea that you are running this investigation. You are merely a witness."[31] Another lobbyist criticized the committee on Fifth Amendment grounds, resisting the committee's decision to hold "'ex parte' hearings where witnesses had no opportunity to be represented by counsel" and arguing that the Fifth Amendment was there "to protect citizens against inquisition."[32] None of the legislators seemed affected by this criticism, and the hearing did not slow.[33] When Bernard Baruch, an important mobilization advocate for the earlier War Policies Commission, publicly attacked the Nye Committee for its lack of patriotism, Senator Vandenberg (R-MI) asserted his confidence in the committee's capacities, citing the tremendous value of the "type and extent of information which our present Munitions Committee has enjoyed."[34]

---

29   Coulter, *Munitions*, 3.

30   *Munitions Hearings*, pt. 17, 4198; see also resistance to the legislature's tax policies in *Munitions Hearings*, pt. 29, 9059–62, and Coulter, *Munitions*, 58.

31   Coulter, *Munitions*, 51, citing *Munitions Hearings*, pt. 10, 2320-44.

32   Coulter, *Munitions*, 69, 70, and citing *Munitions Hearings*, pt. 18, 4635.

33   Coulter, *Munitions*, 70, citing *Munitions Hearings*, pt. 18, 4635.

34   Koistinen, *Planning*, 289–90. Vandenberg's assurance about the value of the committee's investigations seems to have been shared by all committee members, for the final

This institutional self-confidence kept the senators going in the face of security and individual rights challenges, and even led the investigating senators to scrutinize the constitutional text itself. They wondered whether their desired policy outcomes would require constitutional amendment.[35] The committee refused to allow its deliberations to be limited in scope either by a legal framework for identifying lawbreaking, or by an imagination that was overly determined by the constitutional text itself. Their willingness to allow their judgments on security needs to affect their evaluation of the constitutional structure represents a serious moment of constitutional reflexivity: a congressional committee, confident and assertive in the value of the form of judgment that its institution made possible, turned its legislative gaze upon the constitutional order itself to evaluate whether it could sustain the hopes of the American public.

The Democratic Iran-Contra investigators did not similarly embrace the task of legislative policy formation. Although they too sought to restore proper interbranch war relationships, they imagined doing so as inquisitors or jurors. The investigation did not announce itself as linked to any effort to advance any particular policy. Instead, the chief counsel stated that it was their "principal purpose" to "replace secrecy and deception with disclosure and truth."[36] Using the famous idiom of Watergate, legislators repeated that they wanted to know "who knew what when," and to hold President Reagan to account. The legislators chose Arthur Liman, a lawyer and former federal prosecutor, as the chief of staff. His assistants were a lawyer and a district judge, neither of whom had experience in foreign affairs. The legislators apparently aspired to a standard of disinterestedness.

While the Iran-Contra Committee subpoenaed many records, the scope of its effort was restricted to records and memos to pin down the exact locations of suspected wrongdoing. Legislators did not seek broader policy-relevant information that would be necessary to form a sense of the broader security context or to form security policy judgments. They did not gather information on normal foreign-policy processes or relationships between the CIA, State Department, and other foreign policy departments. Neither did they gather records about the history of the NSC or the relationship between NSC intelligence and the intelligence of other agencies. They neglected to gather records on Iranian intelligence to scrutinize the administration's claim that moderate Iranian factions could

---

report received unanimous endorsement from a committee that, although stacked, was diverse, "a remarkable achievement for a committee whose members ranged from traditional Republicans to populist, even radical, Democrats." Koistinen, *Planning*, 290.

35   Coulter, *Munitions*, 101; *Munitions Report*, pt. 2, 3–4; pt. 4, 3–7.

36   Mr. Neilds, *Iran-Contra Joint Hearings* (July 7, 1987), 10.

improve their position with access to weapons. Nor did they gather information on the security consequences of US involvement in the war in Nicaragua, or even the history and consequence of the struggles between the Sandinistas and Contras. Committee records do not reveal the state of the foreign policy, intelligence, and covert-operations community in the executive branch at the time of Iran-Contra. Congressional documents are "largely silent" on the fundamental question—"just what was U.S. policy toward Iran and the Persian Gulf during the 1980s?"[37] Instead, the majority report emphasized its desire to articulate "the truth," which it believed could be expressed through a narration of facts and timelines. Apparently the Iran-Contra Committee did not understand the legislature's capacity to form broad judgments on security policy as relevant or useful to its confrontation with the president.

The Iran-Contra senators' failure of independence is also reflected in their ignorance or contempt for the value of legislative judgment itself. Instead of independently asserting the value of legislative judgment, Iran-Contra senators sought to discipline their proceedings and rebut challenges with procedures and forms of reasoning suited to the judicial branch. The committee claimed it wished to replace deception with truth and oriented itself toward truth-relevant virtues like impartiality, fairness, objectivity, and nonpartisanship—in other words, disinterestedness. More than one member of the committee explicitly disavowed that its purpose was to consider policy.[38] Seeking fairness, co-chair Senator Inouye, who had served on the Watergate Committee, allowed North to appear with his attorney despite the immunization of North's testimony. Inouye also allowed for limits on how long North could be questioned. Despite these safeguards, the majority party backed down on its questioning almost completely when accused of partiality.[39] Even a cursory look shows how deeply the effort to achieve hearings that were "fair and objective" and not "merely political" conditioned almost every moment of the proceedings.[40]

That senators imagined themselves as disinterested agents does not mean they had the official capacity to carry out that role. While they

37 John Canham-Clyne, "Business as Usual: Iran-Contra and the National Security State," *World Policy Journal* 9:4 (1992): 617–37, 627.

38 Representative Hyde, *Iran-Contra Joint Hearings* (July 13, 1987), 194, agreeing with Senator Inouye that "the business of the Select Committee is not policy." See also Chairman Inouye and Sen. Lee Hamilton's opening statements, *Iran-Contra Joint Hearings* (May 7, 1987), 3, 6.

39 For more discussion, see Michael Lynch and David Bogen, *The Spectacle of History: Speech, Text, and Memory at the Iran-Contra Hearings* (Durham: Duke University Press, 1996), 54.

40 Lynch and Bogen, *Spectacle*, 55.

would frequently announce their impartiality, testifying to "no direct knowledge of many of the covert actions that North described in his testimony," in fact some of the legislators were actually informed about and even implicated in the controversy.[41] As much as the co-chairs Senator Inouye and Rep. Hamilton (D-IN) sought to borrow judicial authority, they were also politicians who stood to gain from Reagan's exposure. By premising the value of the investigation on their disinterestedness, these senators communicated insecurity, positioning their substantive knowledge about the foreign policy process as a liability that could produce bias rather than as a benefit that could illuminate.[42] Democratic senators demonstrated a failure of independence in not even aspiring to one of the greatest strengths of congressional investigations: the opportunity to develop the implications of a particular security ideology to render a political judgment.

At the heart of the legislature's claim to war authority is its capacity to develop defensible judgments about the security needs of a moment. Its assertions on behalf of its own authority, then, are political, not only legalistic, insofar as they are premised on judgments about how to achieve policy outcomes whose value is contestable. Yet the senators of the committee failed to embrace this political resource for their authority. This is evident in their response to challenges. At one point, North spoke of the "strange process" of testifying to a legislature:

> It's sort of like a baseball game in which you are both the player and the umpire . . . in which you call the balls and strikes and where you determine who is out and who is safe. And in the end you determine the score and declare yourself the winner. From where I sit, it is not the fairest process.[43]

Instead of forthrightly rejecting the analogy of Congress as an umpire and asserting the need for legislative judgment, the senators capitulated to North's logic and insisted on their own fairness and neutrality. When Senator George Mitchell (D-ME) pressed upon North that "every American, whatever his or her position, must obey the law," North agreed, then stated that he

---

41   The statements of the chairman and vice chairman emphasized the "bipartisan spirit" of the Committee's deliberations and their success in rising above partisanship. *Iran-Contra Report*, 637. See also Lynch and Bogen, *Spectacle*, 27.

42   See Harold Koh, *The National Security Constitution: Sharing Power after the Iran-Contra Affair* (New Haven: Yale University Press, 1990), 18, on the incongruity between the capacities of Congress and the self-presentation of the investigating legislators.

43   Oliver North, *Iran-Contra Joint Hearings* (July 7, 1987), pt. 2, 190.

believe[d] that the President's policy was within the law, that what we did was constitutional in its essence, that the President's decisions to continue to support the Nicaraguan democratic opposition [were permissible]. . . . Certainly there are folks who can argue the constitutionality of Boland.

North rejected Mitchell's equation of statutes with the law. Mitchell's response was to restate the "unremarkable" fact that every American must obey the law. He continued questioning North as if trying to corner him into an admission of personal wrongdoing.[44] But by the end of the testimony, Mitchell was actually pleading with North to tolerate political disagreement:

> I now address a plea to you. Of all the qualities which the American people find compelling about you, none is more impressive than your obvious deep devotion to this country. Please remember that others share that devotion and recognize that it is possible for an American to disagree with you on aid to the Contras and still love God and still love this country as much as you do.[45]

Moments such as this—of which there were many—made it seem as if it was North's esteem that was at stake, rather than the identification of a security breach. Despite this solicitous attitude, the chairs of the committee were vociferously criticized for their bias.[46] While some believe the investigation failed because it was "blocked," the hearings reveal a committee that was tepid in defending the value of its own judgments and the relevance of its own authority.[47]

The legislature's lack of independence was also manifest in two dichotomous premises about judgment it adopted, both of which make any legislative role in foreign policy transparently dubitable. These premises were advanced by the president's critics and his defenders. The first premise opposed "truth" to "ideology," falsely implying that legislators could access "truth" without the filters of politics, and that truth is irrelevant for the defense of ideological positions. Since pluralism in a legislature guarantees that different positions will be easy to identify as "ideological," in the sense of not universally endorsed, strong oppositions between truth and ideology undermine the ground on which the legislature stands

---

44 Ibid., 31–32.
45 Ibid., 46.
46 Lynch and Bogen, *Spectacle*, 53, citing Haynes Johnson, *Sleepwalking Through History: America in the Reagan Years* (New York: Anchor Books, 1992), 363.
47 Lynch and Bogen, *Spectacle*, 5.

to judge at all. But ideological positions can be assessed, and doing so requires facts, which investigations are amply suited to exposing.

The second binary contrasted what was "constitutionally required" with what was "politically permissible." The Republican minority report treats constitutional matters not explicitly resolved by the text as only political, as policy disagreements not rising to the level of constitutional disputes. It accurately identifies the controversy over Iran-Contra as premised on different "views about the proper roles of Congress and the President in foreign policy,"[48] and says that the basic issues of Iran-Contra are not legal but rather "have to do with the policy decisions themselves, and with the political judgments underlying the way policies were implemented."[49] The report also argues that "[i]f Congress, after the fact, disagrees with [the president] . . . the appropriate remedy is a political and not a legal one."[50] The legal issue, the minority report claims, is a settled one: even in the realm of a shared power, "the rule of law cannot permit Congress to usurp judgments that constitutionally are not its to make."[51]

The minority report uses the contesting political judgments at stake in Iran-Contra not as a reason why the legislature, a political branch, *should* be involved but rather as a reason for legislators to *abstain* from judging Reagan. The logic is that because judgments about Iran-Contra are related to judgments about foreign policy and institutional competencies, the conduct of Iran-Contra does not raise constitutional problems. It repeatedly calls the administration's transgressions "mistakes in judgment, nothing more," and emphasizes that the president's judgments were debatable, implying that legislatures should not judge a president for abuses that are "debatable."[52] While the relational conception sees the problem of mistaken judgments, debatable security policy, and constitutional controversy as normal elements of working out the content of any justifiable security order, the minority report maintains that these features disable legislative governance entirely.

The advantage of these binaries for pro-presidency Republicans was obvious. They were able to counter the Democrats' insistence on discovering "truth" by accusing Democrats of being partisan and ideological. Since truth could not be discovered in the midst of an ideological struggle, and since the legislators' judgments of Reagan were undeniably shaped by their political judgments about the policies Reagan was carrying out,

---

48   *Iran-Contra Report* (minority report), 438.
49   Ibid., 442.
50   Ibid., 546.
51   Ibid., 457.
52   Ibid., 437, 499, 441.

these logics framed the investigation as *merely* a political challenge rather than as *importantly* a political challenge.

The committee's majority report did not challenge these binary logics but rather ceded the ground to pro-presidency Republicans by distancing itself from Congress's own political judgments. Continuing the rhetorical tone set by Democrats in the hearings, the voice of the majority report is "objective, bipartisan, and collaborative."[53] It does not directly tell us that US funding of the Contras would serve as a "convenient pretext" for the Sandinistas to violate the human rights of Nicaraguans, but rather that some "members voiced concern" about that possibility. The reasons for not supporting the Contras are relayed as the preferences of "those who supported these views."[54] The report does not speak directly to the military incompetence of the Contras, but rather states that the "image of Contra military capability cultivated by North was arguably at odds with reality."[55] The report does not frame Congress's judgments about Contra funding as a warranted judgment by the legislature as a whole, as the passage of a statute permits rhetorically. Instead it frames Congress's decisions in terms of the concerns of some members. These qualifying and distancing rhetorical moves keep the report from making a political case. The majority report speaks of Congress as if it were a collection of individual members, instead of an authorizing collective that could be politically interpreted.[56]

The rhetorical strategy of the hearings and majority report distanced Congress's lawmaking function from the necessity of political judging that validates governance through congressional power. The majority report justifies congressional war authority in terms of advancing the will of the people and as required by the constitutional text and law.[57] The report did not respond to Republican criticisms of legislative governance, nor does it anywhere defend the worth of legislative judgment for achieving good security outcomes. In addition, the committee did not take advantage of its bipartisanship to fuel a truly energetic look at US security policy toward Iran and Central America. Instead, the committee seemed

---

53 Lynch and Bogen, *Spectacle*, 157.

54 *Iran-Contra Report* (majority report), 33.

55 Ibid., 49.

56 Treating Congress as a group of individuals makes sense for many research purposes, but the formal processes and official rhetoric of collectivities also licenses interpretating Congress—no less than the Supreme Court, presidency, or a governing university committee—as a collective agent. See Margaret Gilbert, "Modelling Collective Belief," *Synthese* (1987) 73: 185–204; also her "Remarks on Collective Belief," in *Socializing Epistemology: The Social Dimensions of Knowledge*, ed. Frederick Schmitt (Lanham, Md: Rowman and Littlefield, 1994), 235–53.

57 See *Iran-Contra Report* (majority report), ch. 25.

to understand its task as one of avoiding upsetting its witnesses and the Republican Party. The committee majority was relatively unprepared to stand up for the value of legislative governance and legislative strength.

Ironically, during the hearings it was the Republicans who were relatively more vocal in defending Congress. Republican Senator Warren Rudman (R-NH) became incensed at North, telling him that although Rudman had supported aid for the Contras, North was wrong to attack Congress because "like it or not, this Congress represents the people."[58] Rep. Hyde (R-IL) told North that he was "bothered" by North's contempt for the legislature.[59] Other Republicans in the hearings emphasized the negative security consequences of the Iran-Contra affair.[60] Despite these few assertions of institutional pride, the minority report failed to relate Congress's institutional strengths to the legislature's claim to war authority and attacked the majority report's "aggrandizing theory of Congress's foreign policy powers."[61] Its chapter on Congress consisted of a series of criticisms about the instability and lack of secrecy it claimed was characteristic of that branch. Despite their relatively greater emphasis on achieving good security outcomes, the Republicans failed to show how *legislative authority* could be useful for advancing the security outcomes they sought. The value of legislative governance for good security policy was simply left unasserted by anyone.

Of course, a vibrant and pluralistic deliberative space in a legislature may well mean that some members will advocate for the primacy of the executive branch on security grounds. The Cold War security order, discussed in chapter 3, was constructed in part through legislative advocacy for the executive branch. But interbranch deliberation requires, at a bare minimum, that some officials assert their institution's value and articulate their institution's reasonable claims to policy competence. Preferably a variety of legislators would articulate a variety of claims illuminating different elements of what is at stake in war governance. Beneath the substantive debates lurks the more basic constitutional question: why should any of these controversies be decided by a legislature? Neither the majority nor minority report developed the idea that legislative strengths could improve security outcomes. Congress's claim was not rendered. In short the legislature was left without an advocate. It was this failure of institutional self-articulation, as much as North's combative tone, that undermined legislative judgment in the hearings and reports.

---

58 Wilentz, *Reagan*, 239.
59 *Iran-Contra Joint Hearings* (July 8, 1987), pt. 2, 196.
60 Ibid., 194–95.
61 *Iran-Contra Report* (minority report), 437.

THE PROCESSES OF LEGISLATIVE JUDGMENT

The legislature can be assessed with reference to processual values beyond independence. Its distinctive strengths, for example, include the capacity to develop and evaluate multiple policy alternatives; the capacity to generate and engage complex policy-relevant information; and the capacity to make constitutional judgments that are sensitive to policy judgments. The Munitions Investigation certainly sought to judge the relationship between the abuses it saw and the need for structural reform. The committee was aware that its investigations would allow it to interrogate harms that were subtle and insidious rather than direct. It was alert to patterned interactions and circumstantial evidence that revealed structures that inclined the country toward bellicosity. This capacity to focus on implicit links and patterned outcomes is a comparative strength of a congressional investigation, with its capacity to mobilize information that touches on many dimensions of a policy problem simultaneously.

By contrast, the Iran-Contra Committee failed to bring the many policy options at stake in the scandal into focus and failed to interrogate the institutional conditions that had sustained this presidential abuse of power. They focused on lawbreaking rather than insidious influence and this blocked the senators' sensitivity to patterned outcomes that fashioned the security context they sought to judge. Their reliance on legal norms of assessment was doubly unfortunate because the hearings ultimately intruded upon the courts' actual legal processes, such that convictions had to be set aside over concerns about tainted juridical process. Because the 100th Congress relied on a legalistic standard of accountability, this failure to achieve many legal convictions meant that Congress was left with no public claim to its war authority at all.[62]

The investigations differed greatly in the depth of scrutiny they applied to the substantive security problems at stake. As the Munitions Committee came to see the inadequacy of the lawbreaking frame to explain how business interests supported US entry into the war, the investigating legislators broadened their focus. They turned toward examining the general structure of economic mobilizing for war. What were the normal processes of contracting and bidding? How did munitions makers keep

---

62   Lawrence Walsh's report bemoans the "public confusion" that resulted when those who, like North, had been convicted had their verdicts set aside on appeal for tainted process. Lawrence E. Walsh, "Final Report of the Independent Counsel for Iran/Contra Matters," vol. I: Investigations and Prosecutions (United States Court of Appeals for the District of Colombia Circuit: August 4, 1993, Washington, D.C.), Part X, "Political Oversight and the Rule of Law."

profits up during peacetime? How did the military procure its supplies and how did the nation tax wartime profits? These questions led them to insights into the role of executive power in the security order of the time. It was by examining the normal political economy of the time, not only lawbreaking, that legislators developed their constitutional objections.

The findings of the Munitions Investigation were substantial. Senators discovered vast collusion among shipbuilders in bidding for naval contracts. Legislators discovered how the regulations surrounding "vital equipment" shielded munitions makers from complying with labor regulation. The senators plunged themselves into the details on cost-plus contracts and on the handling of surplus, discovering choices made to support private industry rather than the general public.[63] They went into the thickets on tax policy, revealing the importance of setting wartime tax policies before a war actually started.[64] The committee conducted a detailed investigation into policy surrounding munitions nationalization, including consideration of whether publicly owned munitions would create an incentive for armament to maintain worker's wages.[65]

Their hearings with Morgan and Co. amounted to one of the most complete inquiries into the finance system of the early twentieth century. The committee discovered J. P. Morgan's role in precipitating an exchange crisis in 1915, which had the effect of maneuvering the US government into supporting the British sterling. While the committee did not find criminal lawbreaking, it was attentive to evidence indicating that munitions makers had been the primary investors recruited by Morgan to support British and French currencies.[66] The committee read this as circumstantial evidence that the efforts of financiers and munitions makers were linked; that both viewed alliance with the British as in their interests, regardless of the costs to US neutrality. The committee's interrogation of these financial practices reveals a focus not on particular legal transgressions, but on the complex way that systemic influence can create conditions for war. Their discoveries were illuminating to businessmen themselves. In discussion about the Treasury Department's bailout of Allied securities and willingness to waive normal financial standards to make loans to Allied powers, J. P. Morgan confessed that the committee's understanding of events eclipsed his own.[67]

The committee also exposed information about munitions makers

63   See Coulter, *Munitions*, 72, 83, generally chs. 3 and 4.
64   Ibid., 68: See, e.g., U.S. Congress, Senate, Special Committee Investigating the Munitions Industry, *Hearings*, 73rd and 74th Cong. (US Government Printing Office: Washington, D.C., 1935) (henceforth *Munitions Hearings*), pt. 18, 4543–58.
65   *Munitions Hearings*, pt. 36; Coulter, *Munitions*, 64.
66   Coulter, *Munitions*, 110.
67   *Munitions Hearings*, pt. 27, 8235–36.

working to block disarmament and negotiations to end conflict, to evade laws and treaties, and to play belligerents off each other. Again they focused on systemic influence: that munitions manufacturers evaded treaties episodically, and in ways that did not leave smoking guns, did not deter the committee from noticing patterns. For example, they noted that US aircraft companies had supplied material to Germany that was useful for either "commercial or military purposes," but could well have been in violation of the Versailles Treaty and "kept the German explosives companies very much alive and informed regarding new patents and secret inventions";[68] that the ignorance of munitions makers and banks of massive arms sales to rebels in Brazil by a retired army lieutenant against relevant treaties was utterly implausible;[69] that an arms race between Bolivia and Paraguay had relied on American loans obtained under suspicious circumstances and then diverted, leaving local banks liquid for more financing;[70] that payoffs to foreign officials were common and indeed that "practically all business of this type was conducted along [those] lines," as courts were reluctant to investigate payoffs to government officials;[71] that agents would arrange contracts with false buyers to avoid neutrality restrictions;[72] that companies would manipulate belligerents by threatening that limited materials were available and that they should purchase supplies first lest their opponents buy out stocks;[73] that a lack of legislation barring long-term loans by warring countries invested banks and corporations in the military victory of one side, allowing military defeat to produce financial panic, and allowing for the establishment of "heavy capital commitments whose immediate earning power is ultimately dependent on the continuance of belligerent purchasing power, which itself becomes ultimately dependent on the borrowing power of the belligerent in the American money market;"[74] and ultimately that the committee was "impressed by what might be called the semidiplomatic character of the influence sometimes exercised by munitions firms."[75] The

68 *Munitions Report*, pt. 3, 255.

69 Ibid., 115–19.

70 U.S. Congress, Senate, Special Committee Investigating the Munitions Industry, *Munitions Industry Industrial Mobilization*, 74th Cong., 2nd sess., 1936. Senate Report no. 944, pt. 5 (hereafter *Munitions Report*, pt. 5), 4.

71 *Munitions Report*, pt. 3, 118.

72 See *Munitions Hearings*, pt. 1, 218–22, especially p. 221; see also *Munitions Report*, pt. 3, 177.

73 *Munitions Report*, pt. 3, 9.

74 Koistinen, *Planning*, 273–74; U.S. Congress, Senate, Special Committee Investigating the Munitions Industry, *Munitions Industry Existing Legislation*, 74th Cong., 2nd sess., 1936. Senate Report no. 944, pt. 5 (hereafter *Munitions Report* pt. 5).

75 *Munitions Hearings*, pt. 3, 119–20.

first report said that if the naval companies weren't having conversations about bidding, then "there was telepathy."[76]

The committee examined the history of mobilization from 1916 to 1918, noting "the basic dynamic of wartime economics: lacking the experience, information, and personnel for planning the economy, Washington relied on businessmen to design, staff, and operate the mobilization structure," a choice that "had enormous potential for rationalizing and maximizing production" but also "created great opportunities for abuse."[77] They inquired into excess profits taxes and price controls and concluded that procedures for forming new corporations made it too easy to evade tax laws in times of war.[78] They considered the meaning of war profits and bonuses for munitions employees in light of the sacrifices being asked of soldiers, and inquired into whether patriotism could take the place of financial incentives, finally deciding it could not.[79] They developed radical and comprehensive legislation for economic mobilization, including proposals to conscript managers in a firm (while leaving private ownership in control), control commodities completely, a power for the president to close securities exchanges, and plans for tax policy and mobilization agencies. They recognized that these policy proposals might require constitutional amendment, but also emphasized that some measure of legislative control over war could be achieved through "exceptionally harsh legislation" before the outbreak of war. In this way the senators hoped to reduce the political attractiveness of war and "discourage talk of war as antidote to the depression."[80] This attentiveness to the relationship between politico-economic structures of warfare and the actual outbreak of hostilities was replicated throughout the hearings, most notably in their neutrality strategy. Their investigations led them toward a legislative strategy of deeply constraining presidential and business discretion before the logic of escalating hostilities could determine outcomes. Their focus was an exceptional demonstration of the way legislative power can be used to interrogate the security context within which war arises or does not.

The committee members were sensitive to the foreign policy and structural implications of their discoveries. Many of their questions were premised upon the link between the political economy of the interwar years and the security profile of the nation. At times the hearings led them to

76 *Munitions Report*, pt. 1, p. 18.
77 Koistinen, *Planning*, 266. See also *Munitions Report*, pt. 2, 73–79.
78 E.g., *Munitions Hearings*, pt. 15, 4330–35.
79 Coulter, *Munitions*, 55.
80 Koistinen, *Planning*, 273–74. See also *Munitions Hearings*, pt. 15, 4339–40.

explicitly discuss the meaning of defensive war in the context of military preparedness.[81] Investigating senators viewed defense preparedness itself as a possible threat, especially if preparedness required fomenting hostilities in other countries to keep a domestic weapons industry intact. The committee observed that the military did not always have good judgments about security: the "economic welfare of corporations loomed much too large in the navy's decisions," which in turn created security problems insofar as "modern navies were by nature offensive as well as defensive and . . . threatened to trigger or exacerbate an arms race."[82] Most importantly, the committee observed that the United States had repeatedly violated its own commitment to neutrality in the lead-up to the war. The Morgan effort to support Allied currencies was the most blatant of many examples. The fifth and sixth committee reports laid out the full case that the United States had behaved in unneutral ways, in part as a result of economic ties toward the Allies: "a distorted and biased application of neutral rights for the Allies vis-à-vis the Central Powers; unwise, if not illegal, insistence upon rights of American citizens and ships in war zones; questionable policies concerning British merchant ships" created conditions pushing the United States into war.[83]

With astounding prescience, the committee also stumbled into the dangers of the military-industrial complex. The concept is sometimes credited to Eisenhower's 1961 speech or Harold Lasswell's 1941 article on "The Garrison State," but the concept was embedded within the discoveries of the Munitions Investigation well before World War II.[84] The first signs of a military-industrial complex appeared when the committee discovered the lengths the War Department was willing to go to support the domestic munitions industry. Hearings on Electric Boat showed that Navy officers were strong "supporters of Electric Boat's sales efforts." Senator Clark's (D-MO) questioning revealed that an admiral was serving as a representative for negotiating a loan to Peru for armaments,[85] and the committee discovered an active duty naval officer advising Colombia while being paid by private munitions firms.[86] Senators worried about the "personal as well as contractual" ties that linked retired military officers to firms that did business with the military, noting lobbying organizations comprised of members of the military together with military

81 Coulter, *Munitions*, 40.
82 Koistinen, *Planning*, 258.
83 Ibid., 293.
84 Harold B. Lasswell, "The Garrison State," *The American Journal of Sociology* 46:4 (1941): 455–68.
85 Coulter, *Munitions*, 39.
86 Koistinen, *Planning*, 261.

contractors.[87] The committee also discovered a practice of naval officers taking positions in private contracting firms after leaving the military. The committee exposed coordinated lobbying efforts: in some cases the Navy would lobby on behalf of private interests, and private interests would lobby on behalf of the Navy. These efforts were sometimes followed with the Navy awarding contracts to those same interests.[88]

Military officials justified these links in terms of military preparedness. In fact, the committee discovered that "[i]t was official military policy to encourage and assist the export of munitions so as to ensure existing productive capacity in the event of war" and that the War Department cared more about "smooth functioning of the procurement machine rather than . . . profit limitation."[89] The committee unveiled the War Department's solicitation of US munitions sales abroad, and even that the War Department was willing to leak state secrets to promote these sales.[90] The committee also began to apprehend ties being formed between the executive branch and various economic interests, and the effects those ties could have on war policy. Contemporary scholarship confirms that, as the Munitions Investigation was discovering, these emergent links were laying the groundwork for a full expression of the power of the military-industrial complex during the Cold War.[91] These links would become important in the Iran-Contra controversy.

The committee did not have the benefit of a pre-articulated concept to describe what it was seeing. Despite this conceptual lacuna, it did not hold back from describing a patterned set of political relationships that it referred to as an "unhealthy alliance" between the business and military establishment.[92] Consider this articulation:

> [L]eaders in government, business and finance . . . watched the growth of militarism in the pre-war years. Militarism meant the alliance of the military with powerful economic groups to secure appropriations . . . for a constantly increasing military and naval establishment, and on the other hand, the constant threat of the use of that swollen military establishment in behalf of economic interests at home and abroad of the industrialists supporting it. It meant the subjugation of the people of the various countries to the uniform,

---

87   Koistinen, "Interwar," 832, citing *Munitions Report*, pt. 1, 220–21; *Munitions Report*, pt. 3, 10–11, 159–217; *Munitions Hearings*, pt. 36, 11972–2043; pt. 37, 12399–443, 12501–28, 12766; see also *Munitions Hearings*, pt. 27, 12414–15.

88   Coulter, *Munitions*, 39, 56–57.

89   Ibid., 52; Koistinen, *Planning*, 264.

90   *Munitions Report*, pt. 5.

91   Koistinen, "Interwar," 839.

92   *Munitions Report*, pt. 3, 12; *Munitions Hearings*, pt. 27, 8158; Cole, *Nye*, 87; Wiltz, *Nye Revisited*, pp. 226, 227; Molander, *Antecedents*, 63.

the self-interested identification of patriotism with commercialism, and the removal of the military from the control of civil law.[93]

It was in discovering the military-industrial complex that the legislators turned their gaze to a constitutional criticism of the presidency. The military-industrial complex was politically consequential because it undermined domestic and international efforts toward peace, including disarmament and embargo goals that had been set by the legislature. But it was also constitutionally consequential, because it was oriented toward simultaneously increasing executive power while compromising the integrity of executive branch judgments.

The hearings revealed instances of executive branch judgments that the legislators viewed as deformed. Some executive branch officials had taken to advocating military spending as a response to economic depression.[94] Links between the executive branch and business led administrative officials to exercise bad judgment with systemic pernicious effects.[95] The committee seemed worried that the entire economic structure of the country would become tilted toward bellicosity. The effects of this influence extended internationally as well. The committee found not only that the major munitions companies were working to undermine the Geneva Naval Conference, but also that the Navy and War Departments were helping them.[96] In that 1927 conference, some parts of the executive branch were working to undo the efforts of others. Senators also found that the munitions firms, together with the War and Navy Departments, and occasionally helped by the Commerce and State Departments, were concertedly undermining the aims of "every major national and international effort between 1919 and 1932 to embargo, control, and halt the manufacture and trade in arms and to reduce the level of international armaments" without a single exception.[97]

Discovery of the military-industrial complex was highly significant for the separation of powers regime. It meant that business interests affected the nation's security profile through the lever of the executive branch. It also meant the executive branch was able to influence the US security context not only through formal processes of lawmaking but also through its

---

93 *Munitions Report*, pt. 5, 8.

94 At times the link between military spending and the depression was explicit: the committee discovered that Public Works Administration funds were being spent on the armed services. Koistinen, "Interwar," 832, citing *Munitions Report*, pt. 3, 3–12, 15–17, 159–204; Cole, *Nye*, 76, 79–81; Wiltz, *Munitions*, 81. Also see *Munitions Hearings*, pt. 37, 12409–37, 12502–26, 12766; *Munitions Report*, pt. 3, 204–207; Wiltz, *Munitions*, 116.

95 Koistinen, "Interwar," 831.

96 *Munitions Report*, pt. 3, 6–7; Koistinen, *Planning*, 263–64.

97 Koistinen, *Planning*, 263–64.

decisions to support and develop certain patterns of influence within the armaments and finance industry. Finally, it meant that executive branch proposals had to be received with skepticism. Hearings had revealed that the War Department was a participant in the military-industrial complex and was developing legislation to allow the president to control national resources in the event of war—a power that "would allow the president to name printer's ink . . . as [an] essential [commodity] and thereby require newspapers to have a license in order to use [it]." The lieutenant colonel who was testifying "agreed that the president would probably be able to censor the press."[98] The committee's fifth report raised the specter of an imperial presidency, manipulating conditions toward war, conditions that in turn not only continued to narrow the president's own possible policy courses but also defused the sources of political opposition.[99] The broadening of the committee's focus from simple lawbreaking toward scrutinizing the basic structures of economic mobilization led it step-by-step into an understanding of the possibilities inherent in the executive branch for creating conditions for war.

This discovery ultimately ended political support for the investigation. In his questioning of finance groups, Senator Clark came to perceive that Wilson had been highly responsive to pressure from US business to support British fiscal health.[100] That pressure had led Wilson to suppress his complaints about British violations of US neutrality. The committee also found evidence indicating that, contrary to testimony he had given to Congress, President Wilson knew about secret treaties between the Allies for the postwar order. Senator Clark revealed this information on the floor of the Senate, where he was challenged by Tom Connally (D-TX) and defended by Senator Nye.[101] The committee's willingness to criticize a Democratic president led southern Democratic Senators to withdraw their support for the committee's funding, and the investigation closed. However, the investigating committee's discovery about executive power had already become consequential for Congress's war authority. In this case, bolstering Congress's war authority had some practical effects that are positive from the point of view of legislative partisans: the leadership core of those advocating legislative governance was strengthened, and pro-neutrality isolationist senators had been educated about where legislative authority could be most effective for maintaining neutrality—curtailing executive discretion before hostilities erupted.

98   Coulter, *Munitions*, 55, citing *Munitions Hearings*, pt. 16, 3931–33.
99   *Munitions Report*, pt. 5, 81–82.
100   *Munitions Hearings*, pt. 27, 8252–56, 8272–77.
101   Coulter, *Munitions*, 116.

In the lead-up to World War II, isolationists faced a sophisticated political opponent in Roosevelt. But isolationist legislators had themselves already developed a sophisticated awareness about the constitutional politics of war that supported their launching one of the most formidable challenges to executive power that any Congress has mustered before the outbreak of war. A major consequence of the Munitions Investigation was to strengthen the power of the isolationist, neutrality bloc within Congress by giving them political opportunities, developing their core leadership, and developing their sophistication in using statutory language to achieve the effects they wanted.

The committee reports reveal the limitations, as well as the power, of congressional judgment. The investigating senators emphasized how activities of business and the executive branch could together create a web of conditions leading to war. But the final reports did not emphasize another set of conclusions that had become apparent in the hearings: the role of the legislature in the military-industrial complex. The committee report section entitled "relations of munitions companies with departments and officials of the United States Government" did not discuss how legislators on key congressional committees worked to sustain the web of interests that supported belligerency, although the committee's hearings had revealed the importance of such connections.[102] Historian Matthew Coulter suggests that "[t]he hope for enactment of the committee's recommendations made it good politics to avoid alienating fellow members of Congress."[103] The senators' willingness to de-emphasize legislative parochialism reveals the institutionally induced partiality of even this very robust mobilization of legislative judgment. The "distinctiveness" of the judgment of any one institution includes limitations as well as strengths.

The Iran-Contra Investigation, by contrast, is marked by a paucity of policy-relevant material; it stayed trapped within the idiom of personal culpability. Senators' intense focus on personal wrongdoing obscured the larger security questions at stake in Iran-Contra, leaving Congress ill equipped to defend its claims. The investigation did create a historical record of what had happened, a real accomplishment given the complexity of the affair. But gathering material for historians is a different task than developing legislative judgment on the underlying security issues. The Iran-Contra Committee did not inquire into crucial domains of policy needed to reach substantive and constitutional judgments on the security issues at stake.

---

102   *Munitions Report*, pt. 4, 159–218. But see the discussion in *Munitions Report*, pt. 3, 159–218, on congressional lobbying.
103   Coulter, *Munitions*, 128.

Consider the Boland Amendment, which prohibited the use of US funds to support the Nicaraguan Contras. Partisans of the executive argued that the president was justified in violating Boland because Congress's Contra policy was so weak and vacillating. North argued that Congress was the real "villain" for its failure to consistently support the Contras.[104] Throughout the 1980s, the content of Congress's Contra judgment had shifted repeatedly, ranging from strong military support in the early 1980s to absolute bars on funding—but only for twelve months—in the late 1980s. Imagining that such flux would be ongoing, the executive branch argued that this movement in the legislature created a presidential responsibility to keep the Contras strong for the moment when Congress would inevitably change its mind again.

Was the executive branch right that it had an obligation to keep the Contras strong? Investigating senators might have started by scrutinizing the content of the executive's own policy judgment. The Contras themselves were militarily inept, limited in their ability to forment a full-scale insurgency, and perpetrators of war atrocities in Nicaragua.[105] In fact, although the Sandinistas did lose power in 1990, this was a result of diplomacy and peaceful organizing to defeat them through elections.[106] These peaceful forces were already at work in 1989. Congress could have used its hearings to spotlight whether such efforts were likely to bear fruit. Instead, the committee announced that the hearings would be neither pro- nor anti-Contra.[107] Divorcing the policy and constitutional questions in its investigatory procedures left Congress unable to judge the link between the two. For example, Congress was specifically unable to judge whether its vacillation on Contra funding was or was not a reason to disempower the legislature.

It certainly was possible to defend Congress. Many of Congress's shifts on the Contras were not only driven by the flux of partisanship, but were also a result of Congress's responsiveness to new information about the war in Nicaragua.[108] Contra funding could be justified for different reasons: Congress had repeatedly considered whether the best reason to support the Contras involved support for the overthrow of the Sandinistas,

104 Wilentz, *Reagan*, 236, 237.
105 William L. LeoGrande, *Our Own Backyard: The United States in Central America, 1977–1992* (Chapel Hill: University of North Carolina Press, 1998), 413–17.
106 Wilentz, *Reagan*, 242.
107 *Iran-Contra Joint Hearings* (May 5, 1987), 3.
108 The majority report discusses the legislative history of funding for the Contras in seven paragraphs, but devotes many pages to whether and when relevant findings authorizing covert actions were signed. See *Iran-Contra Report*, ch. 2. On p. 34, the majority report does represent Congress's legislation as an effort to clarify and make coherent the administration's reasoning on the Contras.

blocking weapons flow to El Salvador, or providing humanitarian assistance. At least some of Congress's movement over Contra policy related to its effort to sift through the importance of these various purposes. In fact, the strict language of the Boland Amendment was the result of a deliberative process whereby Congress tried to regulate the executive only to see that that looser language failed to block the CIA's participation in a covert scheme to mine Nicaraguan harbors.[109] Congress's movement on the Nicaraguan Contras was in part a result of learning. Legislators on the investigating committee could have defended Congress's movements in terms of an interpreted coherent goal to support democracy in Nicaragua, a goal that would lead to shifting tactical judgments at different moments. Individual Democrats did sometimes describe their own voting changes as responsive to new information and new contexts. The passage of a law gives legislative partisans rhetorical permission to describe it in terms of the judgment of the whole legislature. Yet the majority report fails to interpret or defend Congress as a whole.

The majority report instead handed responsibility for Congress's movement to the presidency, describing the legislature's Contra policy as simply replicating "the internal contradictions" of Reagan's own vision.[110] This lamely depicts Congress as an echo chamber for the president, and then weakly asserts that the problem with transgressions is that "there is no place in Government for law breakers."[111] The chapters on the Contras go on to list a series of legal transgressions without discussing the security consequences of those breaches in Nicaragua or for US interests more broadly.[112] This kind of defense of Congress implicitly concedes the primacy of executive judgment. Once that has been conceded, though, the mandate that the president follow the law—repeatedly emphasized in the majority report—becomes formalistic. For judges to assert the primacy of the law is for judges to assert the foundations of their institutional empowerment. But for legislators to do so, in a context where the Constitution does not give determinate answers on the question of war authority, is for them to beg the question. If the legislative process does not improve the quality of the nation's foreign policy responses, then given an unclear set of textual requirements, why shouldn't the executive simply act on the basis of his own judgments rather than solicit Congress's approval?

109   Theodore Draper, *A Very Thin Line: The Iran-Contra Affairs* (New York: Hill and Wang, 1991), 23.

110   *Iran-Contra Report* (majority report), 33.

111   Ibid., 19.

112   Ibid., chs. 2 and 3.

To be sure, Congress's deliberative process over funding for the Contras was inadequate. The legislature's permissive attitude, sloppy draftsmanship, and shifts in orientation toward the Contras had indeed created space for the president to pursue a policy that was at odds with the administration's publicly stated objectives.[113] The Munitions Investigation came upon the same discovery when it saw how discretionary statutes allowed President Wilson to maneuver the country out of a neutrality posture. But having actually stated the policy it hoped to achieve, the Munitions Committee was able to face that failure of legislative governance squarely. The value of the policy outcome they sought gave the senators a benchmark for evaluating the legislature's conduct. Never having taken up the question of what policy the legislature should aim for, the Iran-Contra Committee was ill prepared to consider Congress's efficacy in achieving those aims.

The committee also ignored pressing questions about whether the security establishment in the executive branch was well designed for achieving the security goals Congress sought. The most blatant failure was its refusal to interrogate the structure of the National Security Council. The NSC operates in an unusual location. While it is, literally, an advisory council for the president, Eisenhower had reorganized its supporting staff as personal adjuncts to the president, rather than as support for the Council itself. During the Kennedy administration the NSC staff had gained an operational capacity, allowing the president to pursue foreign policy goals without the knowledge of the State Department or other relevant agencies.[114] This structure creates the opportunity for the executive branch to carry out secret aims that do not take advantage of the full resources of the executive branch.[115] The majority report did specify that the "NSC staff should never again engage in covert operations" and that "operations should never be delegated . . . to private citizens in order to evade Governmental restrictions."[116] But a great deal of security is provided in ways that rely upon private agents. Collecting intelligence, for example, is a security function that relies on the information private agents are willing to provide; building weaponry relies on private capital. General language about nondelegation does not capture the nature of the abuse in Iran-Contra. Not interrogating the usual function of the NSC or of private agents in their relationships to the State or Defense Departments meant that senators lost the opportunity to figure

113   Ibid., 34.
114   Draper, *Line*, ch. 1.
115   Robert Jervis, "Foreign Policy and Congressional/Presidential Relations," in *The Constitution and National Security: A bicentennial View*, ed. Howard E. Shuman and Walter R. Thomas (Washington DC: National Defense University Press, 1990), 48.
116   *Iran-Contra Report* (majority report), 18, 17.

out the meaning of the Iran-Contra abuses within a larger security structure, or to highlight the nature of the outrageous abuses with precision. Ironically, many of the resources that North and McFarlane leveraged, including ex-military private consultants, businesses with vested interests in arms races, and systems of international finance that concealed rather than exposed the links between agents in different countries, first became visible during the Munitions Investigation. Yet the members of the Iran-Contra Committee apparently found nothing in particular worth exploring in the role of these powerful nonstate actors.

Also ignored was the substantive security context within which the executive was operating. No testimony called forth experts on the Middle East to talk about Iranian politics, the existence or lack of moderate factions, the content of the US interest in the Iran-Iraq War, or the plausible consequences of arming radical members of the Revolutionary Guard. Nor was the Nicaraguan War discussed in any detail. The executive asserted that harassing the Sandinistas was required by US Cold War commitments to keep its sphere of influence free from communism. Yet the experience of Vietnam had revealed long ago that not all communist movements represented the incursion of Soviet domination. What was the nature of the Sandinista movement? What kind of alternative did the Contras represent? The hearings and legislative report nowhere interrogated these questions. Senators who signed the majority report were also apparently uninterested in the security consequences that could have flowed from the way North, Secord, and Poindexter treated the Iranians. North sold weapons to the Iranians for prices far above what he was buying them for from the CIA. Some of the money went to North, Secord, and others involved in the operations and some went to the Contras. The legislative hearings and reports focus on North's personal transgression in skimming this money for personal use. But what are the foreign policy implications of deceiving a nation of major strategic importance?

Congress even failed to discuss why trading arms for hostages is a bad idea.[117] Investigators may have taken it as too obvious to be worth mentioning, and Reagan himself had been publicly arguing against such a policy for some time. The committee hearings and reports chose to gesture broadly toward the problem instead of amplifying the perception of harm. The Republican minority report discusses the problem of hostage-trading in terms of Reagan's overriding "compassion" and mentions the security risk that accrued from the high official position of one of the

117   Muhammed Q. Islam and Wassim N. Shahin, "Economic Methodology Applied to Political Hostage-Taking in Light of the Iran-Contra Affair," *Southern Economic Journal* 55:4 (1989): 1019–24.

hostages.[118] The majority report implicitly cooperates with this narrative when it introduces Reagan's role in terms of his being "moved" by the experiences of the hostages' families.[119] But the report does not consider the security consequences of a hostage-trading regime, nor does it examine whether a final tally of three hostages freed, one killed, and three more taken represents a compassionate security outcome worth tens of millions of dollars of military aid to Iran.[120]

Finally, and most spectacularly, the committee failed to develop an institutional point that should have been devastating for those who, like North, based a theory of presidential unilateralism upon a set of structural premises about executive branch capacity. The minority report is almost an ode to the power of the executive branch to act "quickly and decisively," distinctively positioned to be publicly accountable in foreign policy because of its hierarchical qualities.[121] Yet what was manifestly clear from Iran-Contra was that the executive branch had become unglued from itself and incoherent in its striving. In trying to avoid accountability to Congress, the very hierarchical systems within the executive branch that ensured decisiveness had become ragged. The State Department was pursuing an embargo on Iran that other executive-branch agents were undoing. North was directing CIA agents over whom he had no bureaucratic authority. Secretary of Defense Caspar Weinberger was actually told by the White House that he was not on the distribution list for certain intelligence reports on Iranian arms sales issued from the Defense Department itself.[122] Nor did the theoretical decisiveness of the executive branch mean that the president was always aware of what his subordinates were doing.[123] Yet in theory, it is this hierarchical and unified structure that serves as a core premise for executive branch war authority.

Iran-Contra reveals how the branches' responsive relationship can support the development of their distinctive institutional capacities. North and Poindexter were motivated to subvert the hierarchical integrity of the executive precisely to create trails of plausible deniability and thereby avoid accountability to Congress. The minority report recognizes that the presidency's hierarchical organization is a core condition of that

118   *Iran-Contra Report* (minority report), 437, 519, 529.
119   *Iran-Contra Report* (majority report), 166.
120   Tally from Wilentz, *Reagan*, 242.
121   *Iran-Contra Report* (minority report), 460.
122   *Iran-Contra Joint Hearings*, 218 (testimony of Caspar W. Weinberger, Secretary of Defense). See also Graham Allison and Philip Zelikow's use of the experience as a classic counterexample of "quality decisionmaking," *Essence of Decision: Explaining the Cuban Missile Crisis* 2nd ed. (New York: Addison-Wesley Longman, 1999), 268–70.
123   *Iran-Contra Report* (minority report), 447, 505.

branch's war authority. Yet neither the minority nor majority report label the subversion of that hierarchical structure as a constitutional wrong.[124] Nor do they consider that accountability to Congress is one way to repair that constitutional wrong and recreate the executive branch's claim to authority.

As a result of this failure to develop policy content, participants were left only with the question of whether the executive or legislative branch has ultimate control over US bellicosity. Stripped from the investigations was an elaboration of the context that would have been necessary, under the relational conception, to judge the best answer to this question. Iran-Contra represents a case where an executive branch that has lost control of the sources of its own war authority was met by a legislature that has also lost touch with the sources of its authority. A deeper investigation into the security problems at stake in Iran-Contra might well have helped both branches prepare for post–Cold War security order, with a special emphasis on the nature of US interests in the Middle East. Such conversations needed to happen. As the Cold War ended, the United States needed a new security ideology to locate and identify threats and situate the branches' responsibilities to one another in a new security order. I argue, using the relational conception, that the Iran-Contra Investigation produced only minimal amounts of constitutional war authority and hence degraded the constitutional order at large.

PARTISANSHIP AND BIAS

I have argued that the committees differed greatly both in the independence they were willing to assert, and in their actual exercise of the distinctive governing capacities of the legislative branch. In the case of the Munitions Investigation, the self-confidence of senators may have been supported by the committee's political aims, or as I call it here, its *interestedness*. The Munitions Committee was not representative of the core of Congress or even of Democrats. While many Democrats wished to nationalize munitions, the committee was stacked with agrarians for whom nationalizing munitions was only the first step toward reorganizing much broader US economic structures.[125] Some scholars worry that such bias

---

124   See Secretary George Shultz of the State Department testifying that he learned about crucial dimensions of Iran-Contra policy through legislative investigations, not the executive branch. *Iran-Contra Joint Hearings* (July 23, 1987), 4–9.

125   Koistinen calls the committee the "triumph" of neo-Jeffersonians. Koistinen, *Planning*, 257. But by 1934 the agrarian vision had become an outlier in American politics. See Gretchen Ritter, *Goldbugs and Greenbacks: The Antimonopoly Tradition and the*

on investigating committees undermines fairness and representativity.[126] Indeed, this bias meant that committee members encouraged, rather than restrained, one another with the unsurprising result that the committee's conclusions moved outside the consensus position of Democrats or of Congress on issues of economic and military mobilization.[127] None of the committee's recommendations on altering the political economy of war even received floor consideration. And yet this lack of representational congruence, in the context of an investigating committee, mobilized a critical strength of legislative governance. The nonhierarchical pluralism of legislatures fosters the development of challenges to consensus positions from the margins. The second processual standard—that an institution form its perspective through processes that are informed by its distinctive strengths—asks Congress to form judgments through processes that articulate multiple alternatives. The construction of a deliberative space that manifested multiple security and constitutional positions enriched the constitutional authority of Congress's later conclusions on interbranch war authority.

We saw in the Munitions Investigation that the committee's representational disconnect with the whole Congress allowed it the space to develop conclusions that departed from what the rest of Congress would endorse. The senators' willingness to develop judgments about the implications of the evidence they saw, even if those judgments departed from the median position of the floor, meant that the Munitions Investigation enriched the deliberative space of the legislature as a whole. By contrast, the Iran-Contra Committee distanced itself from the policy positions at stake and hence distanced itself from the grounds for judging comparative institutional competencies at all. The investigation's task was not to get lost in the trails of plausible deniability, but to use legislative strengths to construct a judgment about the security politics at stake in the moment. The aspiration towards *disinterestedness* that was characteristic of the Iran-Contra Investigation seems to have led senators to shy away from engaging the institutionally rooted ideological contest at stake in Iran-Contra.

A critical worry threading through the Iran-Contra Investigation concerned partisanship. Rather than accepting partisanship as a feature of

Politics of Finance in America, 1865–1896 (Cambridge, UK: Cambridge University Press, 1997). See also Coulter, *Munitions*, ch. 6.

126   Roger H. Davidson, "Representation and Congressional Committees," *The Annals of the American Academy of Political and Social Science* 411 (1974): 48–62; James A. Perkins, "Congressional Investigations of Matters of International Import," *The American Political Science Review* 34:2 (1940): 284–94.

127   Koistinen, *Planning*, ch. 14; Cass Sunstein, "Deliberative Trouble? Why Groups Go to Extremes," *Yale Law Journal* 110:1 (2000): 71–120.

legislative governance, senators worried that partisanship would undermine the constitutional authority of the proceedings.[128] This did not mean they succeeded in behaving impartially. The committee reports largely featured Democrats asserting Reagan's guilt according to a legal standard, and some pro-presidency Republicans defending the administration with reference to a pro-presidency vision of war authority. Despite its anxieties about partisanship, the legislature continued to manifest the diverse perspectives that are characteristic of nonhierarchical assemblies.

What do we make, then, of the role of partisanship in conditioning the judgments of legislators over the question of executive bellicosity? Comparing the two cases reveals that partisanship's relationship to high-quality legislative judgment is not univocal. Partisanship had crosscutting effects on the dynamics of war authority.

Note first that partisanship was organized in many different ways in each case. The partisanship of some 1934 Democratic legislators led them to resist the power of a Democratic president in service of a partisan, even factional, policy goal. The partisanship of 1934 southern Democrats, however, led them to shut down an investigation that risked the legacy of a beloved former president. In 1989 the partisanship of Democrats led them to shy away from confronting Republicans about the security politics of the moment, and to neglect developing a serious security agenda of their own. Partisanship also led some Republicans in the 1980s to articulate strong visions of what security outcomes they sought, and what institutional order would be necessary to achieve those outcomes. Then again, in 1989, partisan calculations arguably led yet other Republicans to sacrifice their institutional honor and even some of their substantive partisan priorities (such as isolating Iran and refusing to negotiate with terrorists) rather than abandon a Republican president. In all cases partisanship calculations were certainly at play, but the meaning and content of those calculations was different enough that partisanship itself can only be an unstable explanatory referent. Organized pluralism can have many different kinds of implications for how the branches will develop their war authority. The work of this book is to excavate what the relational conception will endorse, not the likelihood that any particular partisan alignment will or will not generate endorsable constitutional positions.

The important cleavage emerging in these cases is between interested and disinterested partisanship. The Democrats of the Munitions Investigation were deeply motivated to achieve a set of concrete policy goals. When it became apparent that one way of achieving those goals—demonstrating deep and widespread corruption—would not pan out, they

---

128 *Iran-Contra Report* (minority report), 439, 442, 511.

broadened their perspective and shifted tactics. Would they have been motivated to develop a larger vision on US entry into the war had they not been interested in achieving a set of factional policy goals? In this case, interested partisanship seems to have been a source of strength in cultivating the war authority of Congress.

The pro-presidency Republicans of Iran-Contra also displayed an interested form of partisanship. The Republican Party had been developing an expansive theory of executive power for some time. Republicans were ascendant in the executive branch, and were advocating a set of substantive security policies that required a strong presidency. Pro-presidency Republicans in Congress took advantage of these ideological resources, seizing the opportunity to advocate for the executive branch to a public whose attention was focused. Democrats, however, apparently had no substantive security agenda or institutional agenda at stake. They did not seem to have policy or institutional conclusions that the Iran-Contra abuses could highlight. It was unclear whether the episode was politically useful to Democrats at all except as a way to embarrass Reagan. Whereas much commentary focuses on the problem of partisanship in investigations, the problem with Iran-Contra was that the partisanship of Democrats was too disinterested in policy and the partisanship of Republicans was too disinterested in legislative governance. The legislature's policy judgments were never defended and its constitutional claims were insufficiently developed.

From the point of view of the relational conception, linking legislative authority to neutrality represents a more worrying move than the existence of partisanship or bias. Legislatures are not institutionally well equipped to achieve neutrality. But legislative governance does have the capacity to provide a public platform for divergent points of view; to access information from a wide variety of sources, including academic, public policy, and personal experience; and to create integrated public policy that is representative of the diversity of judgments, regions, and interests that are characteristic of a democratic politics. Partisanship is one element of how this diversity is publicly represented. Had the Iran-Contra Investigation been willing to self-confidently assert the strengths of legislative judgment, or had it even been aware of what those strengths are, it might have achieved some of the benefits plurality can bring. Perhaps the committee could have achieved a deep articulation of a possible new security order, even if one that could, for the moment, only be endorsed by one party or faction within a party. Perhaps the committee would have exposed a variety of competing judgments on the relationship between new security goals and legislative governance strengths. The fruitful possibilities of pluralism are multiple. The Iran-Contra Committee availed itself of few of them.

While we know that partisanship alignments play some role in structuring the extent and nature of interbranch challenging, this chapter stops short of articulating any general relationship between partisanship and appropriate constitutional judgment. Partisanship is one of many sources of partiality and pluralism, and we see that although it was deeply at play in these cases, it was not at play in one univocal manner. I have argued that the Democrats of the Munitions Investigation who were *interested* in achieving policy reform were able to enhance the constitutional authority of their branch; the Democrats of the Iran-Contra Investigation, who aspired to impartiality, saw the authority of their branches' constitutional claims atrophy. Chapter 6 broadens these considerations to reflect in a more general way upon the "political" nature of the relational conception of war authority.

Chapter 6

THE POLITICS OF CONSTITUTIONAL AUTHORITY

The pattern that the Constitution sets in its war politics is not unique. The Constitution does not draw clear boundaries between legislative and executive powers in a variety of policy areas.[1] Many of the Constitution's substantive terms are also underdeterminate; and it protects rights whose provisions, in some circumstances, conflict with one another (for example, the right to a fair trial can conflict with guaranteeing a free press).[2] From impeachment, to the debt crisis, to appointments, to governance overseas, a vast universe of constitutional problems is handled not through judicial supervision or adherence to determinate text but rather as a result of legislative—executive interactions in ordinary politics.

The relational conception is a specific theory of war authority. But because its characteristic features are shared in other constitutional policy domains, its broader methodology is relevant for other domains of constitutional policy as well. This conclusion considers the way of constitutional theorizing—which I call a *political* method—at the heart of the relational conception, and especially the way this political method intersects with legal methods familiar in constitutional studies. The effort is to uncover some foundational premises of the relational conception as an aid to those who might like to apply the relational conception to other questions in the war powers debate; or who may wish to extend its methodology to other, similar constitutional policy areas; or who may

---

1 See M.J.C. Vile, *Constitutionalism and the Separation of Powers*, 2nd ed. (Indianapolis: Liberty Fund, 1998). For a discussion of power-sharing between the branches, see Walter Murphy et al., *American Constitutional Interpretation* (New York: Foundation Press, 2003), 81–94.

2 "Underdeterminacy" refers to legal text that constrains but does not fully fix a legal outcome. See Lawrence B. Solum, "On the Indeterminacy Crisis: Critiquing Critical Dogma," *University of Chicago Law Review* 54:462 (1987): 462–503.

even wish to use the insights of the relational conception to theorize the relationships between the elected branches and the judiciary.

What is the methodology of this book? The relational conception starts by identifying the relevant substantive terms at stake in the Constitution's allocation of power; then identifies the institutional process(es) harnessed to give content to that substantive vocabulary; theorizes the terms on which these different processes are related to one another, if there is more than one (i.e., the terms of interbranch relationship); develops standards related to those institutional processes; and then assesses moments of constitutional politics in terms of those relevant substantive and processual standards. This method enables a normative analysis of constitutional politics in light of constitutional ideals.

This method varies dramatically from traditional legal modalities of constitutional assessment, but it is not an antilegal method so much as one that transcends and embraces the "legal."[3] With this methodology, the translation of substantive terms like "free press" into a set of constitutional policy commitments by the judiciary is not the sine qua non of constitutional enforcement. For the judiciary to develop fair and impartial interpretations of the meaning of the "free press" is really just one more episode of an empowered institution constructing policy enactments of constitutional significance by applying its distinctive governing strengths to the task at hand. Academic legal evaluation of judicial decisions is not the lodestar of constitutional studies, but is the effort of professional audiences to apply the disciplines of legal reasoning to an institution whose claim to authority is, in part, premised on its distinctively legal capacities.

In reframing the context of the "legal," this method also reframes the significance of settlement theory that has been discussed throughout the book. In the case studies, I have advanced the relational conception against settlement accounts of constitutional war powers. But this does not mean that the relational conception denies the value of settlement. Rather, the

---

3   For discussion on the redescription of legal processes in broadly political terms, see Howard Gillman, "Martin Shapiro and the Movement from 'Old' to 'New' Institutionalist Studies in Public Law Scholarship," *Annual Review of Political Science* 7:1 (2004): 363–82; Martin Shapiro, "Political Jurisprudence," *Kentucky Law Journal* 52:2 (1964): 294-345; Martin Shapiro, *Law and Politics in the Supreme Court: New Approaches to Political Jurisprudence* (New York: Free Press of Glencoe, 1964); Rogers Smith, "Political Jurisprudence, the 'New Institutionalism,' and the Future of Public Law," *American Political Science Review* 82:1 (1988): 89–108; Mark Graber, "The Non-majoritarian Difficulty: Legislative Deference to the Judiciary," *Studies in American Political Development* 7 (1993): 35–73; Keith Whittington, "Legislative Sanctions and the Strategic Environment of Judicial Review," *ICON* 1:3 (2003): 446–74; Howard Gillman, *The Constitution Besieged: The Rise and Demise of Lochner Era Police Powers Jurisprudence* (Durham, NC: Duke University Press, 1993).

relational conception contextualizes the value of settlement. Insofar as settlement theory claims to be an exclusive account of constitutional order, then, the relational conception dislodges its core premises. The first section engages this contextualization of settlement values. The next section explores "unsettlement," conflict-producing accounts of constitutional authority, arguing that while the relational conception does not evade conflict, neither does it seek it. The relational conception instead seeks governance that is consistent with the explicit and implicit values manifest in how the Constitution allocates war authority. Bringing this into focus is important because the relational conception's orientation to conflict can be relevant for policy beyond war powers.

The conclusion then proceeds to interrogate the "political" qualities of the relational conception. While settlement theory has been most emphatically developed as a legal theory, some accounts of legal authority call upon the judiciary to proliferate, not to resolve interpretive conflict; and some political constructions of constitutional meaning, like the Cold War's construction of independent presidential war powers, are deeply settled as a matter of fact, even as their legal pedigree may be challenged.[4] In other words, the fact that the relational conception is not a settlement account doesn't mean on its own that it is "political." The second part of this conclusion considers the "political" content of this method of constitutional theorizing with reference to a constellation of qualities often named "political" within a separated powers system (for example, partisanship).

The third part of the conclusion considers one of the premiere legal expressions of constitutional war powers: the Supreme Court's *Youngstown Sheet & Tube Co. v. Sawyer* (1952) decision. In practice, legal analysis of the US Constitution's war powers often pivots around this tremendously important judicial expression. What light does the relational conception shed on our understanding of *Youngstown*? Exploring the points of contact between *Youngstown* and the relational conception also helps to ground an investigation about how one might extend this book's methodology to areas of core judicial competence like protecting rights.

CONTEXTUALIZING SETTLEMENT

From a settlement point of view, constitutional authority is linked to constitutional determinacy. That determinacy may be provided by the text (two senators per state) or by settled institutional processes (judicial

---

4 See Stephen Griffin, *Long Wars and the Constitution: From Truman to Obama* (Cambridge: Harvard University Press, forthcoming).

supremacy in elaborating the meaning of equal protection, or presidential supremacy on the contours of defensive war). The view that constitutional authority is coterminous with determinacy is prevalent in normative and conceptual work on constitutions. In Jon Elster's words, "the constitution should be a framework for action, not an instrument for action."[5]

At the same time, a great deal of political science, historical, and legal scholarship, noticing recurrent contestation over the very terms of institutional empowerment, treats constitutional war powers as an "invitation to struggle."[6] The departmentalist research referenced in chapter 1 has exposed a disconnect between the empirics of many domains of constitutional governance, and dominant normative and conceptual theories about constitutional authority. In the area of war powers most particularly, while it is true that the president and the Congress do advance legal claims at times (consider the OLC's precedent-based reasoning in its opinion on Libya), to the extent that those claims are enforced it is through the work of elected and motivated political actors rather than neutral juridical ones.[7] One response to the disconnect between these premises of normative constitutional theory and the empirics of war powers controversies would be to condemn most of war powers politics as unprincipled, unjustifiable, unconstitutional. Another approach might accept practical outcomes as constitutionally authoritative no matter their content.[8] Both responses, practically speaking, accept the assumption that authority in a constitution is coterminous with its capacity to resolve. The relational conception does not reject the idea that constitutional authority is sometimes enacted through textual or institutional

---

5 Jon Elster, *Ulysses Unbound: Studies in Rationality, Precommitment, and Constraints* (New York: Cambridge University Press, 2000), 100.

6 See, e.g., Susan R. Burgess, *Contest for Constitutional Authority: The Abortion and War Powers Debates* (Lawrence: University Press of Kansas, 1992); Roger Davidson, ed., *Congress and the Presidency: Invitation to Struggle* (Beverly Hills: Sage Publications, 1988); Cecil Crabb and Pat Holt, *Invitation to Struggle: Congress, the President, and Foreign Policy* (Washington, DC: CQ Press, 1989); William Howell and Jon Pevehouse, *While Dangers Gather: Congressional Checks on Presidential War Powers* (Princeton: Princeton University Press, 2007).

7 Caroline D. Krass, "Authority to Use Military Force in Libya," *Office of the Legal Counsel* (April 1, 2011). Available at http://www.justice.gov/olc/2011/authority-military -use-in-libya.pdf (accessed January 29, 2012).

8 Mark Tushnet, "The Political Constitution of Emergency Powers: Some Lessons from *Hamdan*," *Minnesota Law Review* 91:5 (2007): 1451–72; John O. McGinnis, "The Spontaneous Order of War Powers," *Case Western Reserve Law Review* 47:4 (1996): 1317–29 and "Constitutional Review by the Executive in Foreign Affairs and War Powers: A Consequence of Rational Choice in the Separation of Powers," *Law & Contemporary Problems* 56:4 (1993): 293–325.

settlement; but it rejects the idea that constitutional authority *necessarily* involves settlement.

In so doing, the relational conception resists an idea that is hegemonic in constitutional studies. Theorizing constitutional authority in relationship to settlement is rooted in a highly developed legal tradition, and echoes of this tradition are notable in the politics surrounding the Constitution's ratification. Alexander Hamilton argued for constitutional settlement to solve economic coordination problems between the states.[9] He would have seen the state governments eliminated entirely, arguing instead for "a compleat sovereignty in the general Government."[10] To support the idea that "two Sovereignties can not coexist within the same limits," Hamilton offered in the *Federalist Papers* terrifying examples of how state resistance to national interpretive power could undermine economic flourishing, disrupt the Union, undermine rights, and promote anarchy.[11] After ratification, Hamilton maintained that complete and undivided interpretive authority was essential to the very nature of law, and hence to constitutional functioning.[12]

The settlement thesis has also been invoked by the Rehnquist Court and judicial supremacists committed to the idea that constitutional functioning requires constitutional settlement, a "fixed" Constitution, which in turn requires a strict interpretive hierarchy, with judges at the top.[13] And the premises of settlement theory infuse the constitutional theoretic literature in odd places; for example, Adrian Vermeule and Eric Posner valorize constitutional "showdowns" between the branches, but do so because interpretive dispute can "reduc[e] transaction costs and uncertainty in later periods."[14]

Frederick Schauer and Larry Alexander made the conceptual parameters of settlement theory explicit in a seminal 1997 article on judicial

9   "The Federalist Papers: No. 15," *The Avalon Project*. Available at http://avalon.law .yale.edu/subject_menus/fed.asp (accessed October 19, 2011).

10   See Hamilton's intervention of June 18 in James Madison, *Notes of Debates in the Federal Convention of 1787 Reported by James Madison* (New York: Norton, 1969), 132.

11   Ibid., 131–36; "No. 15," *Federalist Papers*.

12   Alexander Hamilton, "For the Bank (February 23, 1791)," at the *The Avalon Project*, http://avalon.law.yale.edu/18th_century/bank-ah.asp (accessed October 19, 2011); and Alexander Hamilton, "Report on Manufactures," at the University of Chicago Press, *The Founders Constitution*, http://press-pubs.uchicago.edu/founders/documents/v1ch4s31.html (accessed October 19, 2011).

13   Raul Berger, *Government By Judiciary: The Transformation of the Fourteenth Amendment* (Cambridge: Harvard University Press, 1977), 291. See also Emily Sherwin, "Ducking Dred Scott: A Response to Alexander and Schauer," *Constitutional Commentary* 15:1 (1998): 65–71; *City of Boerne v. Flores*, 521 U.S. 507 (1997).

14   Eric A. Posner and Adrian Vermeule, "Constitutional Showdowns," *University of Pennsylvania Law Review* 156:4 (2008): 991–1048.

supremacy.[15] They emphasized that constitutional officials must "subjugate their constitutional judgments to what they believe are the mistaken constitutional judgments of others." They insisted specifically that officials must "conform [their] actions to [Supreme Court] decision[s]."[16] Such conformity would require that officials even abstain from behavior "inconsistent with the general resolution of a constitutional question extending beyond the boundaries of a particular case."[17] The deference required by this canonical expression of settlement theory is broad enough to condemn Lincoln, who did not interfere in Dred Scott's particular case but who stated that, as senator, he would not extend Taney's logic through statutory law.[18] (Note that, despite Schauer and Alexander's use of the concept to ground juridical authority, the settlement thesis does not logically require judicial supremacy. Alexander Hamilton argued for deference to national, as opposed to state, institutions. This makes it easy for settlement premises to travel into arenas like war authority where the courts are not active players. Pro-Congress insularists, for example, claim legislative constitutional supremacy on war.)

If settling foundational political questions so as to create "frameworks" is *the* core function of a constitution, then constitutional fidelity is a matter of enacting that settlement into political life. The result is an implied constitutional virtue for officials: deference to a supreme interpreter. While all constitutional theorists believe that interpreters should "defer" to the Constitution's meaning, settlement theory also claims that interpreters should defer to the claims of a single privileged interpreter. Since the crucial function of a constitutional order is to resolve foundational political questions, officials should think twice before arousing controversy about the meaning of the Constitution. Instead, officials should conduct themselves in ways that respect entrenched settlements—by, for example, carrying out the census every ten years, resisting the urge to criminalize unpopular speech, and most importantly, obeying the decisions of whichever institution is supreme in the interpretive hierarchy—frequently in the US case, the Supreme Court, but in war powers, the president or Congress. Settlement theory hence offers both a position

---

15 Larry Alexander and Frederick Schauer, "On Extrajudicial Constitutional Interpretation," *Harvard Law Review* 110:7 (1997): 1359–87. Larry Alexander qualifies some of the strong claims made in that piece with his "Constitutional Rules, Constitutional Standards, and Constitutional Settlement: *Marbury v. Madison* and the Case for Judicial Supremacy," *Constitutional Commentary* 20:4 (2003): 369–78.

16 Alexander and Schauer, "Extrajudicial," 1360, 1362.

17 Ibid., 1365.

18 Ibid., 1382; Sherwin, "Ducking," 65–71. See also Thomas Emerson "The Power of Congress to Change Constitutional Decisions of the Supreme Court: The Human Life Bill," *Northwestern University Law Review* 77:129 (1982): 133–42.

about the function of a constitution, and a metaprinciple about the deferential attitudes that constitutional fidelity enjoins.

The relational conception is premised on an awareness of the textual underdeterminacy of the Constitution's war powers text. From a settlement perspective, underdeterminacy is a constitutional problem. If the function of a constitution is to resolve foundational political questions, then vague text may be viewed as a failure of draftsmanship or as a navigable roadblock on the way to achieving settlement. We have seen scholarship premised on the settlement model arguing that the Constitution's seeming vagueness on the question of war authority is actually blessedly resolvable through original intent, consensus, or other interpretive methodologies. Those with less faith in these methodologies, but still committed to settlement theory, argue that the Constitution essentially requires nothing particular of public officials in the domain of war powers; anything goes.

Framework metaphors notwithstanding, it is obvious, and we see in the cases of this book, that many officials link their interpretations of constitutional meaning to the policy outcomes they seek. Senator Morgan challenged Roosevelt's Panamanian incursion because he wanted a Nicaraguan, not Panamanian, route for the isthmian canal. Republican efforts to achieve Cold War strength through an empowered presidency arguably shaped the judgment of some senators on the Iran-Contra Committee as to the meaning of executive power.[19] These "political" constitutional understandings, where textual meaning and policy outcomes are interdependent choices, determine the resolution of disputes between the branches because the branches themselves are the judges of their own claims. The dichotomy that the framework analogy introduces between settled and binding constitutional meaning, and unsettled discretionary political choice, may seem odd to those who notice the framework itself becoming the occasion for partisanship and challenge. The theoretical question is about the status of this interpenetration: is it suspect?

But the reasons to recontextualize the claims of settlement theory go beyond any observance that political actors often don't behave faithfully to its ideals. That is true of any theory with normative implications.

---

19   See U.S. Senate Select Committee on Secret Military Assistance to Iran and the Nicaraguan Opposition and U.S. House of Representatives Select Committee to Investigate Covert Arms Transactions with Iran, *Report of the Congressional Committees Investigating the Iran-Contra Affair with Supplemental, Minority, and Additional Views*, 100th Cong., 1st Sess., 1987. S. Rept. No. 100-216, H. Rept. No. 100-433 (minority report), 442, 444, 483–87, 490. This is not to say that policy goals determine an agent's constitutional reasoning. Senator Taft supported many of Truman's aims, but mounted a constitutional challenge to inherent presidential war powers presumably on the basis of a more general concern to limit executive power outside of the space of their policy agreeement.

Settlement theory's problems are more profound. The first is empirical: settlement theory fails to recognize that the Constitution's text valorizes interpretive conflict as well as resolution. The second is conceptual: settlement theory fails to recognize that the costs of interpretive conflict are empirically contingent. Sometimes, interpretive conflict brings benefits to a constitutional polity. By treating conflict as essentially and intrinsically undermining rather than as contingently so, settlement theory treats what is an empirical problem as a conceptual one. The third is normative: settlement theory's presuppositions fail to accommodate some of the appropriate political demands constitutions must engage, especially the need for both consolidation of and critical resistance to constitutional institutions.

The settlement view exaggerates the extent to which the Constitution's text does settle matters of interpretive controversy. The Constitution resolves the number of legislative chambers, the president's qualified veto power, and the length of terms of office. Highly relevant to the war powers debate, it settles where the power to appropriate funds ultimately resides. Its explicit language on these structural matters makes it appropriate to speak of these parts of the text as enacting a settlement function. The Constitution also claims to be the supreme law of the land, and many associate legalism with settlement.

However, the US Constitution supports interpretive conflict as well as interpretive consensus. Not all of its language is explicit. Not all of its provisions even logically cohere.[20] The Constitution announces multiple goals, but does not mandate any consistent hierarchy or relative priority among them. It could have done so. Jefferson urged a more articulated First Amendment, one specifying that the freedom of speech did not extend to false facts "affecting the peace of the confederacy with foreign nations."[21] This proposal was rejected. The ratified First Amendment does not designate the relationship of the freedom of the press to security. The preamble never indicates the relative priority of national prosperity to national security. The Constitution is silent on many questions such as these. It also establishes multiple branches, each of which engages in tasks demanding robust practices of constitutional interpretation. For example, the Congress must consider on its own whether it is properly exercising powers that are delegated to it. In designing social service programs like Medicare, Congress must consider whether its use of power

20   Walter Murphy, "An Ordering of Constitutional Values," *Southern California Law Review* 53:2 (1980): 703–60.
21   Jefferson to James Madison, 28 August 1789, *Papers of Thomas Jefferson* 15:367; as cited in Robert W. T. Martin, *The Free and Open Press: The Founding of American Democratic Press Liberty, 1640–1800* (New York: New York University Press, 2001), 114, and fn. 111 on p. 199.

respects the Constitution's federal design. Even Congress's decision to let the Court have the final word on, say, the permissibility of environmental regulation amounts to an interpretive position.

This structure predictably generates interpretive pluralism, but the Constitution's text never specifies a single supreme interpreter to order that pluralism. Contrast this to South Africa's Constitution, which specifies that the Constitutional Court is "the highest Court in all constitutional matters" and that it "makes the final decision whether a matter is a constitutional matter."[22] Certain features of the US Constitution support interpretive contentiousness, and careful scholarship must inquire into the significance of these textual choices.

A second problem with settlement theory is that it imagines the costs of conflict as intrinsic, rather than empirically contingent. Schauer and Alexander argue that settlement is necessary for social coordination, for peace, and for the protection of rights.[23] In fact, it is likely that there are links between settlement and coordination, peace, and rights. But the link between interpretive settlement and these other goals is in all cases empirical, and as an empirical relationship, subject to variance.

Consider the claim that settlement is linked to social coordination. Law's capacity to solve some coordination problems—deciding when a legislature shall reconvene, or the contours of a trade regime—is well known, and the benefits of resolving such problems can be more important than arriving at exactly the right solution. Alexander and Schauer write that this provides "content-independent reasons for the existence of the state, of law, and of the obligation of obedience to the law."[24]

Yet law's capacity to resolve coordination problems is empirically variable. For law to serve this function it matters very much what the content of the law is and what field it seeks to regulate. In international law, the proliferation of international legal institutions may undermine coordination as powerful nations face expanded opportunities for forum shopping.[25] Some forms of law worsen coordination problems by making new resources available to powerful actors to deflect compliance costs.[26]

22   South African Constitution, Chapter 8, Section 167.3 (a) and (c) (1996).
23   Alexander and Schauer, "Extrajudicial," 1359, 1371–77, and their article "Judicial Supremacy: A Reply," *Constitutional Commentary* 17:3 (2000): 455–82, are the most significant academic statements of these reasons. Hamilton also argued for settlement for these reasons. Also see Sherwin, "Ducking."
24   Alexander and Schauer, "Extrajudicial," 1374.
25   See Daniel W. Drezner, "The Tragedy of the Global Institutional Commons," *Back to Basics: State Power in a Contemporary World*, Martha Finnemore and Judith Goldstein, eds. (New York: Oxford University Press, 2013).
26   Scholarship in administrative, corporate, and environmental law demonstrates how command-style law can introduce coordination problems, as manipulation of over- and underinclusive rules and lengthy legal processes becomes one more way for regulated groups

The content of the law and the context within which it operates is relevant for understanding whether law will solve coordination problems. The relationship between law and coordination is empirical and hence contingent.

Settlement theory also posits an essential relationship between settlement and peace. John Marshall raised the specter of war brought about by nondeferential behavior in *McCulloch v. Maryland*, the awful possibility that, as Keith Whittington has phrased it, "too many constitutional interpreters . . . might uncompromisingly press their claims to the point of disunion and war."[27] To avoid this, Marshall called for a "peaceful and quiet" way of interpreting the Constitution. The Court's *Cooper v. Aaron* decision (1958) raises the specter of anarchy as a reason for deference, and the frightful imaginary of chaos was raised again in *Bush v. Gore* (2000), a decision Judge Richard Posner defended as necessary to head off the "crisis" of interpretive uncertainty.[28] In the war powers context we have seen pro-presidency settlement theorists advance these claims today.

Yet factors other than interpretive hierarchy enable peaceful society. In the US constitutional order, a representative structure that requires huge coalitions for political action to happen at all; the inertia of previous practices; electoral and other incentives for institutions not to challenge each other too frequently; and stable ideological frameworks all promote stability and peace.[29] When the branches use their shared powers as weapons against one another, they create political costs to conflict, and in the hands of appropriately sensitive officials, the third condition of conflict (shared powers) can restrain conflict from escalating even as it

---

to shift costs and evade compliance. For essays on the empirical relationship between law and coordination, see Gráinne de Búrca and Joanna Scott, eds., *Law and the New Governance in the EU and the US* (Oxford and Portland, OR: Hart Publishing, 2006); Jay Sigler and Joseph Murphy, *Interactive Corporate Compliance: An Alternative to Regulatory Compulsion* (Westport, CT: Greenwood Press, 1988); Orly Lobel, "The Renew Deal: The Fall of Regulation and the Rise of Governance in Contemporary Legal Thought," *Minnesota Law Review* 89:2 (2004): 342–470; Jon Cannon, "Choices and Institutions in Watershed Management," *William & Mary Environmental Law and Policy Review* 25:2 (2000): 379–428. "New governance" models especially abundant in the areas of environmental and administrative law seek "collaborative governance" and "responsive regulation" in part to achieve stronger coordination benefits.

27   Keith Whittington, "Extrajudicial Constitutional Interpretation: Three Objections and Responses," *North Carolina Law Review* 80:3 (2002): 773–851, 786.

28   Richard A. Posner, *Breaking the Deadlock: The 2000 Election, the Constitution, and the Courts* (Princeton: Princeton University Press, 2001), 4.

29   Keith Whittington lists an array of mechanisms by which political stability is maintained. Whittington, "Extrajudicial," 807. See also Peter C. Ordeshook, "Constitutional Stability," *Constitutional Political Economy* 3:2 (1992): 137–75.

sustains the production of conflict in the first place.[30] Even significant disputes can often be contained through participants' unwillingness to face the costs of conflict. In some cases that unwillingness may be a problem. Congress's reluctance to face the costs of conflict reinforced the endurance of a Cold War presidentialist security order in contexts where more assertive legislative governance would arguably have been advisable. And some settlements may generate bellicosity. Some argue that the settlement of Cold War presidentialism proliferated war by removing the constraint of legislative review.[31]

Good constitutions are marked by their designers' sensitivity to differences in how institutions characteristically manage conflictual processes. James Madison advocated political settlement between the states and national government, but not as a general rule for interbranch disputes. He did not believe that interbranch dispute was dangerous because no one branch can "consummate its will, nor the Gov. to proceed without a concurrence of the parts," and so "necessity brings about an accommodation." States, with their own militias and governments, with the capacity and the imagination to form divided political orders, are different. Hence Madison perceived a special need to settle the question of federal authority.[32] In the war powers context, it is likely that vigorous interpretive dispute about the powers of the presidency could be dangerous in certain contexts (1942) but protective in others (mid-1980s). This nuanced view, which looks to the differential costs of conflict in different contexts, is only available to those who recognize the empirical contingency of the relationship between institutional orders and peace.

Finally, settlement theorists claim that settlement is essential for the protection of rights. Alexander and Schauer claim that uncertainty about free speech rules is a deterrent to speech, thereby undermining liberties.[33] The Court has also argued that, "if Congress could define its own powers by altering the Fourteenth Amendment's meaning, no longer would the Constitution be 'superior paramount law, unchangeable by ordinary means.' . . . [U]nder this approach, it is difficult to conceive of a principle

---

30   Jessica Korn, *Power of Separation: American Constitutionalism and the Myth of the Legislative Veto* (Princeton: Princeton University Press, 1996), 37.

31   Theodore H. Draper, "Presidential Wars," *New York Review of Books* (Sept. 26, 1991), 64.

32   Letter from James Madison to Edward Everett (Aug. 28, 1830) in James Madison, *James Madison: Writings 1172–1836*, 2nd ed. (New York: Library of America, 1999), 842, 845. On his incomplete response, see Jenna Bednar, "The Madisonian Scheme to Control the National Government," *James Madison: The Theory and Practice of Republican Government*, ed. Samuel Kernell (Stanford: Stanford University Press 2003): 217–42.

33   Alexander and Schauer, "Extrajudicial," 1376.

that would limit congressional power. . . . Shifting legislative majorities could change the Constitution."[34]

Yet in fact, despite the Constitution's codification of Congress's powers, and despite the allure of settlement theory over time, the content of how officials have interpreted Congress's powers or any other rule has necessarily been subject to shifts. Such shifts have sometimes been problematic, but in other cases, like *Brown v. Board of Education*, protecting rights has required transformation.

To remain politically meaningful, property rights must mean something different in a postindustrial era then they could in an agrarian past.[35] The proper relationship between free speech and national security may have a constitutionally best answer, but that answer may well vary with context, and so require fresh reasoning in new circumstances. Given the fact of representative institutions, new conflicts will continue to emerge that engage constitutional values at a high level of generality. Achieving the level of specificity that settlement would require could undermine the Constitution's capacity to provide a vocabulary for engaging these new conflicts. In some cases, constitutional governance is achieved not through resolution but by inducing actors to frame their disputes and judge their processes through constitutional language.

The special contribution of constitutional framers is not only to codify rights, but also to design institutions skillfully (institutions perhaps including, but not limited to, the courts). One governance task of these institutions will necessarily include that of creating new understandings of fundamental rights in response to changing circumstances. The best way to foster this articulation process is an empirical problem, not only a conceptual one. In all three of these domains, settlement theory evades the empirical dimensions of its own argument.

A final problem is settlement theory's neglect of the political requirements of institutional maintenance, which is no less important for the success of an ongoing constitutional order than rights are. Consider first the importance of institutional consolidation. New constitutional orders face a very basic problem: will these institutions, designed in abstract, function in reality? Will officials occupying those institutions advance their goals in ways that support the ongoing vitality of the institutions, or will the institutions become only symbols of what could have been? Established constitutional orders face a similar problem in terms of

---

34   *City of Boerne v. Flores*, 521 U.S. 507 (1997), 19. Also see Walter Berns, *Taking the Constitution Seriously* (New York: Simon and Schuster, 1987), 171–90.

35   Lawrence Lessig, "Understanding Changed Readings: Fidelity and Theory," *Stanford Law Review* 47:3 (1995): 395–472.

adaptation. Will the legislature be able to adapt itself to the demands of governance in the modern era? How can the executive branch continue to energetically advance a focused foreign policy given the proliferation of security bureaus in the twentieth century? When the Constitution establishes institutions, achieving their faithful consolidation and transformation over time is necessarily a constitutional problem.

Alexander and Schauer approach this problem of consolidation as one of coordination. Like other positivists, they argue that law—and so the Constitution—should settle the question of the "ultimate rule of recognition."[36] The Constitution should tell us (or should be read so as to tell us) whom the primary interpreter is, or what the nature is of the type of argument that can resolve constitutional dispute. Alexander and Schauer write as if resolving coordination problems will on its own secure the practical authority of a constitutional order.

But a too-rigid demand that the Constitution's "final word" be legally identifiable can crowd out space for other practices that support institutional consolidation. We need not always know how political questions have been resolved for them to be resolved. Some constitutional questions can be handled by Congress, others by the Court. In seeking a single way to identify when the Constitution has "spoken," settlement theory rules out the possibility that different circumstances, arguments, institutions, or officials may play unforeseen but constitutionally unobjectionable roles in dissolving important interpretive questions.

Institutional consolidation can also require the development of new institutions (for example, political parties, a Federal Reserve, a Congressional Research Service, or a National Security Council) in ways that support the animating logic of the constitutional order. For example, the settled contours of judicial interpretive authority—a key example of a valuable settlement, according to Schauer and Alexander—did not spring from the text, which is silent on the relationship between the Court's interpretations of constitutional meaning and those of other institutions. That coordination problem has rather been approached politically, and norms of judicial supremacy on certain issues have emerged as the Court has proved itself useful to other political actors over time.[37] Allowing space for institutions to consolidate means allowing space for the possibility of trust-building, and hence risky, behavior over time. Settlement theory ignores the possibility that leaving some coordination problems

36 Alexander and Schauer, "Extrajudicial," 1370.
37 Keith Whittington, *Political Foundations of Judicial Supremacy* (Princeton: Princeton University Press, 2007).

open can create precisely that space which is essential for the consolidation of formal political relationships.[38]

Settlement theory also ignores the critical aspects of institutional maintenance. Maintaining institutions requires ongoing criticism of their performance and, where they perform badly, resistance and reform. If that critical resistance is interpretively rooted, then Schauer and Alexander would interpret it as an indication of constitutional failure. This has very troubling implications in the war powers context. If Lincoln should have extended the logic of *Dred Scott*, and if Congress should not have enacted statutes at odds with *Dred Scott*'s reasoning, then perhaps Congress should only support—never undermine—a president's claim to war authority. Then presidential proclamations would be enough to effectuate the crucial settlement function as it pertains to war, where coordination, peace, stability, and rights are all at stake. Pro-presidency settlement theorists argue for exactly these conclusions. In such a case, the settlement thesis requires other officials not to resist a war proclamation that they judge unconstitutional. Achieving settlement depends not upon the decision any one institution makes, but upon the decisions of others not to resist that decision.[39]

And yet if Congress is never to resist unconstitutional war proclamations, then presumably it also lacks the constitutional basis, not to mention motivation, to scrutinize the executive-branch processes that produce such outcomes; for example, the role of the NSC or the military industrial complex in guiding presidential judgment. When we see that the settlement thesis can easily ground an imperative that citizens and officials—even other elected officials—set aside any worries about being governed by institutions that generate policy and constitutional results they find abominable, some costs of settlement theory for institutional maintenance become more apparent.

Settlement theory tries to evade this problem by offering a sharp distinction between ordinary politics (where democratic governance and contestation can happen unimpeded), and interpretive dispute (a problem whose solution involves interpretive hierarchy and deference). But in war powers, interpretive politics cannot be so neatly cabined away from

38   See Günter Frankenberg, "Tocqueville's Question. The Role of a Constitution in the Process of Integration," *Ratio Juris* 13:1 (2000): 1–30. Short and flexible constitutions are associated with constitutional longevity; solving too many problems at the textual level is associated with constitutional failure. Zachary Elkins, Tom Ginsburg, and James Melton, *The Endurance of National Constitutions* (New York: Cambridge University Press, 2009).

39   See Mark Graber, "Settling the West: *Bush v. Gore* and the Annexation of Texas," in Bartholomew Sparrow and Sanford Levinson, eds., *The Louisiana Purchase and American Expansion 1803–1989* (Lanham, MD: Rowman & Littlefield Publishers, 2005).

ordinary politics. The Fulbright and Stennis hearings over the Vietnam War—neither of which was especially deferential to the president—had both policy and constitutional dimensions.[40] What if Congress, in its resistance to a president's unconstitutional war declaration, refuses to allocate funds to support his military adventurism—or refuses to ratify a treaty—or refuses to confirm a nominee? Are these disputes of "normal politics," or are they interpretive disputes? They are both. Interpretive claims intersect with the decisions officials make within ordinary politics. To claim that settlement is so important that interpretive losers should always give up the game entails serious costs for the possibilities of ordinary, no less than constitutional, politics.

FROM SETTLEMENT TO UNSETTLEMENT?

Because it sometimes valorizes interpretive conflict, some view the relational conception as grounded in an essentially conflictual view about constitutional authority. But it is not. Such views are certainly available in the literature. Settlement theory has met with intellectual resistance from a set of scholars perhaps best named "unsettlement" theorists. Noticing the benefits that interpretive conflict can sometimes provide, unsettlement theory argues that the value of constitutional politics lies precisely in its capacity to destabilize interpretive communities and invite political conflict. In fact, unsettlement theorists argue that constitutional fidelity can be evaluated in terms of how well participants *destabilize* expectations about what the Constitution means.

Unsettlement theory, in orienting itself toward the *presence* of interpretive conflict as an essential signal of constitutional fidelity, adopts a reactionary view that simply mirrors the problematic formal structure of settlement theory itself. Constitutional authority is not always associated with conflict, any more than it is always associated with settlement. While unsettlement theory is a minority position, engaging it reveals the extent to which the relational conception truly departs from formalistic models of constitutional authority. The relational conception does not resist interpretive conflict, but neither does it seek it.

---

40   The implication of the Fulbright hearings was that presidential aggrandizement should be restricted, while the Stennis hearings urged escalation, confrontation with China, and even implied a unilateral presidential power to commit the nation to nuclear war. See Joseph A. Fry, *Debating Vietnam: Fulbright, Stennis, and Their Senate Hearings* (Oxford, UK: Rowman & Littlefield Publishers, Inc., 2006); on the effectiveness of these hearings see also Frederick Logevall, "The Vietnam War," in *The American Congress: The Building of Democracy*, ed. Julian E. Zelizer (Boston: Houghton Mifflin Company, 2004).

Unsettlement theorists argue that, far from resolving fundamental political questions, the function of the Constitution is to start dispute or endlessly replicate it.[41] Larry Kramer and Louis Michael Seidman tell us that the purpose of the Constitution is to proliferate—not resolve—political questions on almost every issue to which it addresses itself.[42] Kramer emphasizes the importance of citizens "feel[ing] entitled to disagree" with the determinations of government institutions, and more importantly, "to act on our disagreement."[43] There is no need for this contentiousness to be channeled through any particular set of institutions. Kramer instead points toward strategies of resistance to judges, including impeachment, slashing the Court's budget, ignoring its mandates, shrinking its jurisdiction, packing its membership, or giving it burdensome duties.[44] (His idea about the location of constitutional interpretation is court centered.)

Like settlement theory, unsettlement theory posits a strong conceptual divide between fundamental and ordinary law. It is precisely because the Constitution is fundamental law that it *cannot* achieve the certainty and predictability that we should expect from ordinary law.[45] Because constitutionalism is not ordinary law, Kramer emphasizes the role of popular groups, acting through any institution whatsoever (legislatures,

---

41 The unsettlement thesis developed by Kramer and Seidman is different from the idea that constitutional commitments often involve the unsettlement of unjust practices. From the First Amendment to the Fourteenth, the gap between certain constitutional commitments and lived realities has made the Constitution a radicalizing, not just stabilizing, force. At stake is not whether settled meaning should destabilize practices, but rather whether constitutions should be read so as to settle the meaning of rights, or the powers of institutions, in the first place. Hendrik Hartog, "The Constitution of Aspiration and 'The Rights That Belong to Us All,'" in *The Constitution And American Life*, ed. David Thelen (Ithaca, NY: Cornell University Press, 1988), 356; Michael Kent Curtis, *Free Speech, "The People's Darling Privilege"* (Durham, NC: Duke University Press, 2000); see too Roberto Mangabeira Unger, *The Critical Legal Studies Movement* (Cambridge: Harvard University Press, 1983), 44.

42 Both have theoretical pedigrees in the work of Roberto Unger. See Louis Seidman, *Our Unsettled Constitution: A New Defense of Constitutionalism and Judicial Review* (New Haven: Yale University Press, 2001), 56–58; Louis Seidman, "Ambivalence and Accountability," *Southern California Law Review* 61 (1988): 1571–1600; Larry Kramer, *The People Themselves* (New York: Oxford University Press, 2004), 241–44. Some premises of unsettlement theory are drawn from the resistance thread of democratic theory. See Bonnie Honig, *Political Theory and the Displacement of Politics* (Ithaca, NY: Cornell University Press, 1993); Chantal Mouffe, *The Democratic Paradox* (London: Verso, 2000); more recently, Bryan Garsten connects this agonism to the American constitutional tradition in *Saving Persuasion: A Defense of Rhetoric and Judgment* (Cambridge: Harvard University Press, 2009).

43 Kramer, *People*, 231.

44 Ibid., 249.

45 Ibid., 185.

conventions, the executive branch, state institutions, or even mobs) in unsettling judicial pronouncements of constitutional meaning.[46]

Unsettlement theory makes mistakes that mirror those of settlement theory. Unsettlement theorists argue for links between conflict and democratic inclusion, and conflict and stability, as necessary relationships rather than as empirically contingent ones. In addition, unsettlement theory mistakenly treats constitutional language as semantically empty, leaving theorists seriously underequipped to engage crucial questions of authority in a text-based politics.

While settlement theory emphasizes the importance of deference, unsettlement theory emphasizes the importance of contentiousness for achieving inclusive political community and political stability.[47] Kramer and Seidman view a main threat to community in terms of silencing. Community is threatened when a citizen feels that political events "cannot" be considered according to his or her own particular interpretations; that his or her own idiosyncratic interpretations will never be either adopted or considered by powerful decision-makers. While democracy theorists are well known for offering dialogic views of constitutional authority, most of them hold the value of dialogue in balance with other significant goals.[48] Unsettlement theory is unique in emphasizing that the *main* threat to constitutionalism is for the particular perspectives of members to be authoritatively considered out of constitutional bounds. This threatens inclusion, but they say it also threatens peace, because such silencing tears from the voiceless any reason to maintain their loyalty.[49]

Unsettlement theory is correct when it recognizes that people who care deeply for some political outcome, and see no possibility of that outcome's realization, could consider themselves to have a reason to disrupt their political allegiances. Crosscutting alliances are valuable for just this reason: loyalty to a polity can be increased when few publics feel they are losing every time on every issue. This is a condition for legitimacy in the sociological sense. The ideal of inclusion is also normative, not just strategic. Democracy requires inclusion regardless of whether or not citizens

---

46   Ibid., 237.

47   Ibid., 215, 227, 228, 242, 247. Seidman, *Unsettled*, 152.

48   Bruce Ackerman, "Constitutional Politics/Constitutional Law," *The Yale Law Journal* 99:3 (1989): 453–547, 477; Sanford Levinson, *Constitutional Faith* (Princeton: Princeton University Press, 1988), 193; Cass Sunstein, "The Republican Civic Tradition: Beyond the Republican Revival," *Yale Law Journal* 97:8 (1998): 1539–90; more recently see Miguel Schor, "Constitutional Dialogue and Judicial Supremacy," *Suffolk University Law School Research Paper 10-66; Drake University Law School Research Paper No. 12-02* (December 23, 2010). Available at SSRN: http://ssrn.com/abstract=1730202 or http://dx.doi.org/10.2139/ssrn.1730202 (accessed January 10, 2013).

49   Seidman, *Unsettled*, 97.

are willing to tolerate their own subordination. The repeated losses of one group may be signals that not all are being treated with equal concern.[50]

Unsettlement theory is also correct to emphasize that conflict can play an ordering role in constituting a community of equals. At least one constitutional theorist believes that "sustained public argument about the meaning of equality and other ideals might plausibly be regarded as the essence of democracy."[51] But for conflict to play the role of enhancing democratic community, it matters very much what kind of conflict is at stake. No liberal constitution could, in this day and age, credibly leave the question of women's suffrage unsettled. A polity can engage some disagreements without discrediting the entire notion of community. But to entertain others, like the legal protection of slavery, mocks the very notions of consent and community upon which unsettlement theory relies. The relationship between interpretive conflict and inclusive political community is contingent.

So too, while settlement theory says that resolving core issues is necessary for stability, unsettlement theory says the opposite: resolution threatens stability by alienating those who disagree.[52] This is not always true. Opponents to women's suffrage accepted the legitimacy of the 19th Amendment although it did not conform to their preferred outcome. The relationship of settlement or unsettlement to stability is an empirical, not only a conceptual, question.

A second mistake of unsettlement theory is its emphasis upon the semantic emptiness of constitutional words. This emptiness generates a corresponding deep skepticism about the possibilities of justification. For Kramer, popular constitutionalism means that the validity of any constitutional position whatsoever "depend[s] ultimately on popular acceptance."[53] It is hopeless to design institutions that can find good answers to difficult questions, because the notion of "good answers" is a red herring.[54] Kramer asks us not to inquire as to whether any particular interpretive position, such as the outcome in *Brown v. Board of Education*, is consistent with the Constitution's core values; instead we are to discuss the extent to which "change[s] in legal philosophy" turn past cases into

---

50   Ronald Dworkin, *Freedom's Law: the Moral Reading of the American Constitution* (Oxford: Oxford University Press, 1996).

51   Christopher Eisgruber, *Constitutional Self-Government* (Cambridge: Harvard University Press, 2001), 35. On the ordering function of conflict, see Don Herzog, *Household Politics: Conflict in Early Modern England* (New Haven: Yale Univeristy Press, 2012), ch. 4.

52   Seidman, *Unsettled*, 38; Kramer, *People*, chs. 8 and 9.

53   Kramer, *People*, 189. See also Larry Kramer, "Fidelity To History—And Through It," *Fordham Law Review* 65:4 (1997), 1632–56.

54   Kramer, *People*, 237.

"anomal[ies] that need to be overruled."[55] Instead of justification, we are to seek congruence.

Seidman also emphasizes the emptiness of constitutional language. He argues that constitutional loyalty cannot stem from a general commitment to liberal democracy: "democracy is also a contested constitutional settlement, and a truly unsettled constitution must attack it as well."[56] Rather, he believes that loyalty is a direct function of whether a polity enacts one's preferred policy positions.[57] However, any substantive commitment will alienate some people. So, he says, constitutions can achieve full loyalty only by being construed as basically empty. Seidman argues that the US Constitution achieves this value neutrality, because its powerful categories of liberty and coercion, public and private, are analytically bankrupt. We should celebrate this bankruptcy, he says, for it allows constitutional rhetoric to "provide powerful support for virtually any outcome to any argument."[58] Such neutrality—the neutrality of the analytically bankrupt—generates political inclusivity.[59]

Understanding constitutional language as semantically empty creates important problems for any broader theory of authority in a text-based politics. What does it mean for citizens or officials to regulate themselves according to the terms of a senseless document? Unsettlement theory cannot bring into focus the self-understanding of constitutional participants who view themselves as governed through and by a text that bears meaning. Although the values of national prosperity, security, and liberty are contested in their applications, those struggling to achieve these values do not understand them as meaningless or empty. The idea that the constitutional commitment to equal protection amounts to a constitutional commitment to "lalala," to choose an analytically bankrupt concept, makes the puzzle of constitutional authority more, not less, confusing.

Neither settlement nor unsettlement theory is willing to embrace the values that the Constitution actually announces for itself in judging constitutional fidelity. Nor are they willing to recognize the benefits of some of the interdependent ways that public and official interpretations of text intersect with the effort to achieve various substantive goals.

The Constitution's own text specifies the goals the constitutional order seeks. The preamble tells us it seeks to "establish justice, insure domestic

---

55   Kramer, "Fidelity," 1639.

56   Seidman, *Unsettled*, 58.

57   Ibid., 16. Contrast this with Alexander and Schauer, who argue that a commitment to constitutionalism as an abstract proposition is often enough to guarantee a participant's acquiescence to disagreeable outcomes.

58   Seidman, *Unsettled*, 10–11.

59   Ibid., 56. Unger makes the connection between loyalty and "negative capability" (a capability fostered by unsettlement rights) as well. Unger, *Critical*, 93.

tranquility, provide for the common defense, promote the general welfare, and secure the blessings of liberty to ourselves and our posterity." (It does not say that it aims to worship and glorify God, preserve the natural rights of families, or inculcate racial pride.)[60] If the Constitution prioritizes a "common defense," then can we say the polity is being faithful when everyone within that polity uncontroversially cooperates with suicidal political decisions? It seems also problematic to argue that a polity is being faithful if *dissensus* makes it impossible to achieve a common defense. Constitutional authority is produced, in part, through governance that is effectively related to accomplishing constitutional ends. Clearly, the Constitution contemplates that its own institutions and guarantees are sensibly related to the accomplishment of these goals.

The Constitution's preamble implicitly offers a metaproposition, which is that interpreters should evaluate proposed interpretive approaches, like all exercises of power, in light of the contribution they will make to these basic goals.[61] Despite this, settlement and unsettlement theory ask us to evaluate constitutional fidelity without scrutinizing whether proposed interpretive orientations actually do in practice promote justice or domestic tranquility. They evade the interdependence that is implied in the preamble between the Constitution's textual commitments, such as the commitment to a bicameral legislature, and certain practical goods, like the blessings of liberty. Neither an emphasis on settlement and resolution, nor an emphasis on controversy and contentiousness, can make sense of the US Constitution's aspiration to govern a polity in pursuit of ends like justice, freedom, a common defense, economic prosperity, and the general welfare.

The view of constitutional authority working in the background of the relational conception is consistent with the large contours of political thought associated with James Madison, and which others have referred to as Madisonian constitutionalism.[62] From the point of view of the relational conception, while both settlement and unsettlement have roles to play in achieving constitutional authority, they should be understood as

---

60 On the significance of constitutional silence, see Gary Jeffrey Jacobsohn, "The Sounds of Silence: Militant and Acquiescent Constitutionalism," Steven Kautz, Arthur Melzer, Jerry Weinberger, and M. Richard Zinman, eds., *The Supreme Court and the Idea of Constitutionalism* (Philadelphia: University of Pennsylvania Press, 2009).

61 See Sotirios Barber's important work on this theme. Sotirios A. Barber, *On What the Constitution Means* (Baltimore: The Johns Hopkins University Press, 1983), and *Welfare and the Constitution* (Princeton: Princeton University Press, 2005).

62 George Thomas, *The Madisonian Constitution* (Baltimore: The Johns Hopkins University Press, 2008). Madison resisted this approach for the problem of war powers. See his statement in Helvidius no. 2, Alexander Hamilton and James Madison, *The Pacificus-Helvidius Debates of 1793–1794* (Indianapolis: Liberty Fund, 2007).

tools or devices rather than as essential features of constitutional order. The Constitution's internal tensions, far from generating either a crisis or bulwark of legitimacy, can be read as a sophisticated way of disciplining and directing the political judgment of variously situated officials. In the particular domain of war powers, the Constitution's text does not settle the question of which branch may authorize hostilities. Instead, it disciplines the judgment of constitutional officials so as to produce better rather than worse answers to the question of war authority given the security context at hand. The underdeterminate substantive categories of the Constitution's text—war, defense—combined with the political capacities that the structure of its branches makes available, are resources that can enable the skillful judgment of officials.

The relational conception is "political" in part because of the challenge it lodges to settlement theory's aspiration to theorize constitutional authority in relatively formal ways. Rather than either resisting or privileging interpretive conflict as a formal indicator of authority, the relational conception views both settlement and conflict as, in many cases, rooted in the multiple ways constitutional text and institutions themselves intersect with a complex political reality. I argue that the more central question for analyzing constitutional authority is to consider whether operative policies appropriately translate the Constitution's values into the political context of the moment. This is one important way that the relational conception offers a "political" rather than a formal or legal conception of constitutional judgment. This brings us to a second set of ways in which the relational conception is "political": not in its comparative resistance to formalism, but in how it is linked to a cluster of concepts described as "political" within a larger interbranch system.

THE RELATIONAL CONCEPTION AND THE POLITICAL

The relational conception tracks a cluster of qualities that are theoretically associated with the distinctiveness of the political. A prolific scholarship in constitutional theory engages the distinction between "law" and "politics." Other work seeks to delineate differences between "political," and, say, "bureaucratic" or "analytical" modes of decision-making. Given the complexity of the political world and the embeddedness of legal, political, and bureaucratic orders, these distinctions are usefully understood as schematic rather than rigidly accurate. This section explores how the relational conception is "political" by considering that war authority is judged by electoral branches; that the branches develop and evaluate constitutional claims in ways that are at least partially responsive to governance needs; that their reasoning is grounded in the relatively open web that is characteristic of public policy justification; that their constitutional positions are inflected by partisanship and other forms of affiliative reasoning; and that the method of the relational conception prioritizes judgment that is relatively resistant to precedent-based reasoning and yet can be, when done well, nonetheless ethical. All of these qualities are associated with the "political" in constitutional theoretic literature.

First, the relational conception is "political" because the question of war authority is committed to the electoral branches, not to the judiciary, for management. A canon of legal judgment is that no agent ought to judge its own case. This is core to the legal establishment of judicial review in *Marbury v. Madison*; a more recent expression by Justice Kennedy in *Boumediene v. Bush* (2008) states that, "[a legal] test . . . must not be subject to manipulation by those whose power it is designed to restrain."[63] While judges may override this canon on behalf of other considerations (as when they rule on their own jurisdiction), its pervasiveness in judicial rhetoric signals its special place in the legal field. In the war powers context, however, constitutional judgment is pervasively exercised by the very institutions whose powers are thereby regulated. The branches are both the creators of, and the audience for, authoritative claims about the power to initiate war. They are, of course, often partial to their own interests and claims: Arthur Schlesinger notes with skepticism the long-standing "habit" of "assuming the superior virtue . . . to the branch where one's own power lay."[64]

But what does it mean to say that the branches are partial to their own claims? What kinds of claims are they making? A second way in which the relational conception is "political" is in its recognition and valorization of the branches' practice of offering claims not derived, in the first place, from a need to neutrally judge between contending advocates, but rather forged in relationship to the practice of governing with public policy.[65] The responsibility to provide governance is a mode of engagement oriented toward directing the positive exertion of state capacity and energy, not just elaborating limits.[66] The branches are charged with the work of security governance. They must decide and carry out policies pertaining to how institutions will distribute vital goods like security, on what terms, and at what costs. The branches should be expected to elaborate constitutional meaning in a way that supports their effort to

63 553 U.S. 723 (2008).

64 Schlesinger, *The Imperial Presidency* (Boston: Houghton Mifflin Company, 1973), 295–96.

65 Barbara Rearden Farnham theorizes the "political" mode of judgment as characterized by a "concern to act." *Roosevelt and the Munich Crisis: A Study of Political Decision-Making* (Princeton: Princeton University Press, 1997), 128–29, 240, 79–85.

66 See Barber, *Welfare*.

achieve the governance tasks the Constitution commits to them. Electoral responsiveness also means that their work is evaluated by publics who can be expected to have relatively less interest in evaluating the complex constraints of legal analysis; but yet who seek some policy outcomes. In short, the agents and audiences for these constitutional claims are oriented primarily toward acting, toward governing, and their constitutional claims are often linked to this imperative.

The case studies reveal how new constitutional constructions can emerge in response to new governance responsibilities. Consider how the branches' effort to construct international institutions after World War II drove them to reconstruct the breadth of presidential war powers. Theorizing the constitutional limitations of this transformation was relatively secondary to the process of constructing, in the first place, policies and institutions that could protect US security after World War II. The branches' constitutional agency was expressed not only in the Taft wing's challenge to Truman's advocacy for inherent presidential powers, but also in the president's and legislature's effort to provide for security by constructing relatively open global institutions in the first place.[67] The branches exercised constitutional agency both in their creation of new public policy and institutions, and in their practices of review.

The concern for providing governance and the concern for constructing limits are both forms of interpretive work under the relational conception. Even in the review or checking function of constitutional politics, it is often concerns about governance that drive interpretive claims. It was Congress's opposition to the war policies of Vietnam that supported legislative challenges to the existent regime of presidential war powers. The Nye Committee's investigation of the economy of war led it to a series of constitutional judgments that were deeply informed by its concern for a set of security policies it viewed as dangerous. The priority of the concern to deliver good governance is in practice and, for the relational conception in theory, an engine of constitutional construction.

Valorizing the link between governance and the development of constitutional claims is repugnant to a deep strand of constitutional theory. Arthur Schlesinger's magisterial *Imperial Presidency*, for example, criticizes "the common fallacy" of "converting political into institutional questions," and rebukes the Congresses of the 1970s for "devising theories of exclusive congressional power because they disagreed with the international projects of . . . Presidents."[68] Pro-presidency settlement theo-

---

67   See G. John Ikenberry, "Constitutional Politics in International Relations," *Liberal Order & Imperial Ambitions* (Malden, MA: Polity Press, 2006): 111–42 on links between domestic and international constitutionalism.

68   Schlesinger, *Imperial*, 295–96.

rist Glen Thurow writes that the powers between the branches should be "divided on principle, and not according to the prudential considerations of the moment."[69] And yet the relational conception insists on prudential considerations of the moment also having a role to play in constructing the constitutional institutions, statutory regimes, and policy decisions at stake in the provision of security.

A third characteristic of "political" governance pertains to the kind of reasoning that goal-seeking officials characteristically rely upon. Officials are charged with achieving multiple goals at once (security and prosperity, liberty and accountability) without any kind of necessary hierarchy or priority between them. Policymakers may well seek to achieve all ends at once, "seeking multiple payoffs" rather than making sharp trumping choices.[70] But if policymakers cannot achieve all ends at the same time, then the calculus according to which trade-offs occur may vary from context to context. It is no less constitutionally faithful for that variance to be set by the relative importance of those ends in context, as it would be for those ends to be adjudicated according to a lexical priority or other rule-bound form of constraint.[71] Indeterminacy, cross-cutting values, trade-offs, and a relatively open framework for decision-making is basic to public policy reasoning. Values need not be hierarchically ordered for reasoning to be sensible, whether in the field of public policy or of constitutional argumentation. And the branches have good tools for judging the relative importance of these ends in context: they benefit from unusual capacities. No other institutions can call so deeply upon the articulation of public values that happens through the electoral process; mobilize access to research, intelligence, and diplomatic tools for empirical assessments; and draw upon the cultivated skills of officeholders themselves.

Just as the ends of governance vary from context to context, so too, the very standards according to which it is reasonable to assess public policy and constitutional process may vary from one context to the next. Standards advanced in the book—for example, that the branches make

69   Glen E. Thurow, "Presidential Discretion in Foreign Affairs," *Vanderbilt Journal of International Law* 7:1 (1973): 17–92, 75.

70   Alexander George, "Adaptation to Stress in Political Decision Making: The Individual, Small Group and Organizational Contexts," in *Coping and Adaptation*, eds. G. V. Coelho, D. A. Hamburg, J. E. Adams (New York: Basic Books, 1974), 184–85. For work that associates the pursuit of multiple values at the same time with a characteristically political mode of engagement, see Barbara Rearden Farnham, "Impact of the Political Context on Foreign Policy Decision-Making," *Political Psychology* 25:3 (2004): 441–63, 446; Barbara Rearden Farnham, *Munich Crisis*, 242, 25.

71   See especially Dennis F. Thompson, "Political Theory and Political Judgment," *PS* 17:2 (1984): 193–97 on the complex, contingent quality of political judgment.

their positions available for rebuff—may be of different significance in different moments. Transparency was arguably a more important priority after the scourges of the Vietnam War than in the lead-up to World War II. In short, the multiplicity of constitutional governance ends is matched by a multiplicity of disciplining standards enabling context-sensitive judgment. The relational conception of war authority constructs a web of justificatory priorities rather than a set of argumentative hierarchies.

What about the relative autonomy of the "constitutional" in this large political field? Some might wonder if the link between an observer's policy and constitutional judgments is a little too tight to call the reasoning of the relational conception any form of "constitutional" reasoning. The many ways of interpreting the Constitution's substantive values, as well as the relative openness of even the processual standards, in which there are multiple routes toward achieving full processual authority, may indicate to some observers that the relational conception does not limit constitutional officials as much as one might hope. Is this "open web" of justificatory process so open that it fails to limit constitutional officials at all? Can any observer simply claim that their preferred policy and constitutional outcome is what the relational conception endorses? In what sense is the political judgment of the relational conception *also* a constitutional judgment?

The relational conception is a more fluid approach to constitutional judgment than many are used to. Nonetheless, the relational conception does provide discipline. For example, I criticized Senator Morgan for challenging the constitutionality of Roosevelt's use of war powers in Panama even while advancing a Nicaraguan treaty that would have licensed the very same conduct. The problem was not that Morgan's constitutional judgment was so directly a function of his policy preference, but rather that Morgan failed to consider that the relationship between institutional empowerment and particular policy outcomes is a bit looser, and more complex, than that. *Why* would it be a constitutional violation to use the war power in one context but not in the other, and how would or could a legislature enforce such particular judgments while at the same time independently empowering the president? Morgan did not seem to recognize this question at all, and so failed to bring the central dilemma of constitutional war powers—shaping institutions to achieve good policy results, where "good" is defined with reference to the Constitution's own standards—into focus in the legislature.

There are a great many wars and security orders that will be constitutionally authoritative in terms of the relational conception, but which theorists or members of the public may find repugnant according to their own ideas about legitimate violence. A Roman Catholic adherent to just war theory—or a left wing Naderite seeking a Department of Peace to "establish nonviolence as an organizing principle of American society"—nonetheless can acknowledge that early Cold War Congresses did a better job in their constitutional deliberations than Congresses of the Roosevelt Corollary, even if both the Catholic and the Naderite reject the value of the Cold War order for their own particular reasons.[72] Despite their different conceptions of justice, both the Naderite and the Catholic should see that early Cold War Congresses considered a broader range of policy and constitutional positions and subjected those proposals to a more focused constitutional challenge.

The key substantive terms of the relational conception—"war" and "defense"—are capacious categories, but not all-inclusive. The processual standards introduce another source of discipline because constitutional institutions are empowered to consider good constitutional outcomes with a form of epistemic bias that is induced by the distinctive capacities of their branch. Such bias means that the best answer to a pressing security and constitutional problem from the point of view of the relational conception is not the same as a hypothetical best answer untethered to this particular pattern of institutional disciplining.

It is worth recognizing, too, that highly limited theories of constitutional authority—theories that aim to generate "one right answer," for example—achieve determinacy within the theory at the cost of amplifying conflict between interpretive positions in larger political and academic debate. Controversy over war powers will continue as long the structural and political conditions for interpretive controversy are in place. Constitutional studies can either seek to "resolve" the question with a theory, which would then take its place within a pantheon of interpretive theories all of which claim to resolve the same question differently, or can—in the strategy of the relational conception—accommodate this controversy within an interpretive theory, and in so doing shed light on its animating features.

A fourth way in which the relational conception is "political" in a separated powers system pertains to the link between reasoning under the relational conception and partisanship (one kind of affiliative reasoning).[73] There are at least two important links between partisanship and the relational conception. The first is the link between the relational

---

72 Matthew Albracht, "Why Progressives and Conservatives Should Support a Department of Peace," *Common Dreams* (May 12, 2004). Available at http://www.common dreams.org/views04/0512-09.htm (accessed June 9, 2012).

73 On the importance of "acceptability" for "political" reasoning, see Barbara Rearden Farnham, *Munich Crisis*, 238, 25; also see Farnham, "Political Context," 444–45. On partisanship as a vehicle for communicating acceptability, see Nancy Rosenblum, *On the Side of the Angels: An Appreciation of Parties and Partisanship* (Princeton: Princeton University Press, 2008).

conception, and the simple fact of irreducible difference and plurality in human judgment—what I call "deep partisanship," referring to the fact that to take a position, any position, is to be a "partisan" of that position, given that not all humans take the same position on any matter. The second important link is that between party organization, and the actual processes of war powers politics.

Deep partisanship refers, not necessarily to ideologies generated by political parties, but also to the irreducible way in which what is best for a polity is subject to dispute. In deliberative democratic literatures, partisanship often refers simply to the fact that humans differ on matters of politics: a partisan position is one that takes a stand on what is good "for . . . the association as a whole, as this benefit is identified through a particular interpretation of the common good."[74] Judgments about the common good are contestable. The best elaboration of war powers in context is subject to partisanship because all political argumentation is subject to difference.

There is no reason to believe that deep partisanship need threaten the quality of public reasoning. To the contrary, the links between this form of partisanship—partisanship as difference—and deep deliberative process are increasingly recognized.[75] Jonathan White and Lea Ypi argue, for example, that any justificatory process relies not just contingently but essentially upon deep partisanship because of the role that comparing alternatives plays in the very process of justification.[76] The process of justification requires comparing one alternative to another; it is people who differ, interacting with and confronting one another in the world, who create these alternatives and carry out the social process of comparison.[77] Applying standards of justification accurately in a complex social world also requires such integration of complex information that reducing the burdens of judgment through reliance on the cues of affiliated groups (like political parties, but not limited to them) can be a sensible strategy for distributing the social work of judgment.

Beyond deep partisanship, there is also the question of the role of parties in government. Deep partisanship is not the same as the ideologies of organized political parties, but political parties do contribute to public controversy about war authority. This brings us to a second question

74 White and Ypi, "On Partisan Political Justification," *American Political Science Review* 105:2 (May 2011): 381–96, 382.

75 Archon Fung, "Survey Article: Recipes for Public Spheres: Eight Institutional Design Choices and Their Consequences," *Journal of Political Philosophy* 11:3 (2003): 338–67; White and Ypi, "Partisan," 381; Nancy Rosenblum, *Angels*; Russ Muirhead, "Can Deliberative Democracy Be Partisan?" *Critical Review* 22 (2010): 129–57.

76 White and Ypi, "Partisan," 385.

77 Ibid., 385–86.

about partisanship: the role parties in government play in developing actual security orders.

Here again we see a relatively superficial set of links, and deeper ones. Superficially, arguments advanced in politics that are consistent with the terms of the relational conception should end up located within a partisan map. For claims to be politically relevant in the context of electoral competition organized by parties is for them to appear somewhere on a partisan map.

At a deeper level, patterns of partisan organization in government should affect the actual processes of justification that lie at the foundation of constitutional authority. Many scholars notice that presidents tend to have greater latitude when their party controls Congress, and that legislative constraint is associated with divided government. A body of empirical work demonstrates the practical role partisan divides, as well as institutional ones, play in cultivating interbranch contestation over matters of war.[78]

At the same time, the implications of this research for any present ethics of office are complicated because partisanship is organized differently in different times, implies different goals to different officials within a particular context, and often embraces multiple, not one, security ideologies.[79] In some contexts partisanship serves as a relatively tight way to reference ideological affinities, but in other contexts it refers more accurately to organizational affiliation. Some Democrats challenged President Johnson's Vietnam policies in an effort to compete for party leadership, but other Democrats tried to defuse challenges to him in order to protect his electoral success. During the mid-nineteenth century, Whigs were divided on the security value of the Mexican War.

Nor is the empirical relationship between partisanship and the frequency of interbranch challenge as straightforward as it might appear. In some cases, major party systems don't produce security disputes but are produced by them. The first partisan alignment, that of Federalists versus the Democratic-Republicans, was fostered by a split on the value of good relations with the British monarchy. This policy dispute took on constitutional dimensions in the Pacificus-Helvidius debate between James Madison and Alexander Hamilton. In other contexts, in-party

---

78 William G. Howell and Jon C. Pevehouse, *While Dangers Gather: Congressional Checks on Presidential War Powers* (Princeton: Princeton University Press, 2007); Douglas L. Kriner, *After the Rubicon: Congress, Presidents, and the Politics of Waging War* (Chicago: University of Chicago Press, 2010); Daryl J. Levinson and Richard H. Pildes, "Separation of Parties, Not Powers," *Harvard Law Review* 119:8 (2006): 2311–86; Logevall, "Vietnam."

79 On the role of leadership in mediating between multiple ideological currents that exist within a party, see Colin Dueck, *Hard Line: Republican Party and U.S. Foreign Policy Since World War II* (Princeton: Princeton University Press, 2010).

fights determine whether the branches challenge one another. Some legislators have been willing to challenge presidents of their own party, either in an effort to assume that leadership, or to protect what the challengers deemed to be more fundamental party commitments. The major constitutional challenge of the early Cold War system was mobilized by conservative Republicans (Knowland, Taft, and later John Bricker) challenging first Truman, a Democrat, under unified Democratic Party control, but then continuing to challenge Eisenhower even after the 1953 elections brought Republicans control of both branches. Chapter 3 argues that this in-party challenge was a critical resource for the authority of Cold War presidentialism. The constitutional challenge over Vietnam began as a Democratic challenge to a Democratic president in a context of unified party control; many of Fulbright's significant opposition activities took place under the Johnson presidency.[80] Finally, a party need not have control of Congress to mount investigations that pose serious problems for a president. Some important interparty challenges have happened in the context of unified interbranch partisan control.[81] Opposition to US entry into World War I, upon which developed a constitutional argument against the League of Nations, was mounted by Republicans (La Follette, Sr., Lodge, and Borah) in a Senate controlled by Democratic President Wilson's party. Isolationist senators challenged a Democratic President Roosevelt in the context of unified party government in the prelude to World War II. Both institutional, and partisan cleavages, structure the constitutional processes of war.

Beyond partisanship, another way the relational conception can be understood as "political" relates to the limited place it gives to precedential reasoning. Many observers associate legal judgment with the justification of decisions in terms of the past. Mark Tushnet described law as primarily a retrospective judgment: "Judges have to explain what they are about

---

80   For more discussion on this theme, see David R. Mayhew, *America's Congress: Actions in the Public Sphere, James Madison through Newt Gingrich* (New Haven: Yale University Press, 2002). Senator and Democratic Majority Leader Mike Mansfield approached Nixon with the idea of exiting the war by blaming it on Democratic presidents. Richard Nixon, *RN: The Memoirs of Richard Nixon* (New York: Grosset & Dunlap, 1978), 399. It was a bipartisan coalition that was ultimately successful in pushing the Senate to limit executive war-making powers. The efforts of Fulbright and Republican Senators John Sherman Cooper (KY) and Jacob Javits (NY) culminated in the passage of the War Powers Resolution in 1973 over Nixon's veto. For more discussion of these congressional politics, including the entanglements between partisanship and constitutional advocacy, see Robert D. Schulzinger, "Richard Nixon, Congress, and the War in Vietnam, 1969–1974," in *Vietnam and the American Political Tradition: The Politics of Dissent*, ed. Randall B. Woods (Cambridge University Press 2003).

81   More recently, see Michael Bressler, "Congressional Dissent During Times of War: How Congress Goes Public to Influence Foreign Policy," *Extensions* (Spring 2008): 9–14.

to do in part by showing that it is consistent with what other judges have done in the past," a feature that creates a "status quo bias."[82] Ronald Dworkin posits that "law[s] . . . license coercion because they flow from past decisions of the right sort."[83] William Scheurman has argued that temporal presuppositions are a premise of separated powers: while the legislature can be simultaneously slow-going and future oriented, the executive will be "expeditious," or present oriented, and the judiciary backward-looking.[84]

Of course, precedential reasoning permeates all of politics if only because past decisions generate "ideological frames" that are then subject to broader use.[85] Nixon cited Kennedy and the Cuban Missile Crisis as precedent for the Cambodian incursion, and the Obama administration cited Clinton interventions in Haiti and Bosnia as precedent for Libya. Legal decisions also create precedent in this broad sense: just as Nixon cited Kennedy, Oliver North cited the Supreme Court's *Curtiss Wright* decision's lofty rhetoric on presidential powers.[86]

But unlike legal theories of constitutional authority, the relational conception creates no special role for precedent-based reasoning. Certain features of its structure even resist precedential judgment. For example, the priority it gives to the intersection between the constitutional capacities of the branches and the security context of the moment calls for decidedly presentist forms of justification. The relational conception prioritizes good judgment in the particular context over and above consistency across cases.

This is not to say that precedent may not work for presentist reasons. Trevor Morrison and Curtis Bradley discuss precedent as a cue, a way for officials to reassure publics that they are behaving reasonably and so to cultivate trust.[87] To the extent that security contexts truly are parallel, relevant precedents may also help officials arrive at good judgments

82   Mark Tushnet, "How Courts Implement Social Policy," *Tulsa Law Review* 45:4 (2010): 855–62, 862.

83   Ronald Dworkin, *Law's Empire* (Cambridge: Harvard University Press, 1986), 93.

84   William E. Scheurman, *Liberal Democracy and the Social Acceleration of Time* (Baltimore: The Johns Hopkins University Press, 2004), xvii.

85   Charles Epp, "*Law's Allure* and the Power of Path-Dependent Legal Ideas," *Law and Social Inquiry* 35:4 (2010): 1041–51, 1044.

86   *United States v. Curtiss-Wright Export Corp.*, 299 U.S. 304 (1936). *Testimony of Oliver North, Iran-Contra Investigation: Joint Hearings before the House Select Committee to Investigate Covert Arms Transactions with Iran and the Senate Select Committee on Secret Military Assistance to Iran and the Nicaraguan Opposition*, 100th Cong., 1st sess. (1987), pt. 11, 39. On the difference between stare decisis and precedent in this broader sense, see Jeb Barnes, "*Law's Allure* and an Interbranch Perspective on Law and Politics," *Law and Social Inquiry* 35:4 (2010): 1029–40.

87   Bradley and Morrison, "Historical Gloss."

more quickly and thereby preserve cognitive efficacy. In these two ways, precedential judgment, like any other cue, may be helpful for mediating the social processes of judgment. (The risk is that, when a security context changes, the presentist value of precedent as a cue is undermined. Whatever precedential value early Cold War experiences achieved—for example, presidentialism in the Korean War or the Formosa Resolution— atrophied over time as the objective security context transformed.) To the extent that the relational conception values precedent, it is as a cue for enabling good judgment on security and institutional politics of the moment.

This valorization of presentist forms of judgment resists the idea that constitutional analysis is coterminous with rule-based reasoning. Herbert Weschler's classical formulation insists that judicial outcomes "must be genuinely principled, resting with respect to every step that is involved . . . on analysis and reasons quite transcending the immediate result that is achieved."[88] An aspiration toward fairness across cases and rule-based ethical reasoning is embedded within legalism as a method. Rule-based reasoning can protect officials charged with difficult decisions by "displac[ing] vague public expectation as the criterion by which the performance of governments and government officials would be judged. . . . [W]hen the rule of law is clear and the program nevertheless fails, we would then have a basis for changing the law rather than vilifying the responsible individuals."[89] This orientation toward rule-bound decision-making fits poorly with the flexibility, experimentation, partisan deliberation, and competitive challenge of the relational conception.

But importantly, not all ethical behavior is rule bound. Sound moral or ethical agency does not always manifest in terms that are internally coherent, principled, and rational. Some philosophers would eschew crosscase consistency as the primary solvent for ethical decision-making.[90] In the case of security, it is hard to call a series of policy choices that result in massive destruction of human life "ethical" simply by reference to

88   Herbert Wechsler, "Toward Neutral Principles of Constitutional Law," *Harvard Law Review* 73:1 (1959), 1–35, 15.

89   Theodore J. Lowi, *The End of Liberalism: The Second Republic of the United States*, 2nd ed. (New York: W. W. Norton & Co., 1979), 299.

90   Nomy Arpaly, *Unprincipled Virtue: An Inquiry Into Moral Agency* (New York: Oxford University Press, 2003). Arpaly cites the example of Huck Finn acting against his own best judgment to protect his friend Jim (pp. 9–10). See also Nel Noddings, *Caring: A Feminine Approach to Ethics and Moral Education* (Berkeley: University of California Press, 1984); Philippa Foot, *Virtues and Vices and Other Essays in Moral Philosophy* (Berkeley: University of California Press, 1979).

whether they were neutral, impartial, and rule bound.[91] To carefully follow a set of rules to the ultimate outcome of an avoidable nuclear war would be an ethical failure of the highest degree. Ultimately, to call legislative judgment on the United Nations Charter, or on Nixon's decision to bomb Cambodia, "political" instead of "principled" is to say little about the ethics of these behaviors.

THE RELATIONAL CONCEPTION AND THE COURT: CONSIDERING YOUNGSTOWN

The Supreme Court hasn't been completely silent in the realm of war powers, and the relational conception, I believe, suggests new ways to understand its contributions. One of the most important legal expressions of a war powers theory was that offered by the US Supreme Court in its decision in *Youngstown Sheet & Tube Co. v. Sawyer* (1952).[92] Justice Robert Jackson's concurrence in this case is especially applauded. Harold Koh endorses the "unusual clarity with which it articulates the concept of balanced institutional participation."[93] Sanford Levinson calls it "the greatest single opinion ever written by a Supreme Court justice."[94] Martin Lederman and David Barron's intensive scrutiny of the history of presidentialism is set squarely within the framework of Jackson's concurrence.[95] It is also routinely cited at judicial confirmation hearings and is relevant to ongoing war powers controversies on the Court.[96] Our

91   See, e.g., Mark A. Graber, "Constitutional Politics and Constitutional Theory: A Misunderstood and Neglected Relationship," (review of *The Warren Court and American Politics* by Lucas A. Powe) *Law & Social Inquiry* 27: 2 (2002): 309–38.

92   343 U.S. 579 (1952). Henceforth *Youngstown*.

93   Harold Koh, *The National Security Constitution: Sharing Power after the Iran-Contra Affair* (New Haven: Yale University Press, 1990), 105.

94   Sanford Levinson, "Why the Canon Should Be Expanded to Include the Insular Cases and the Saga of American Expansionism," *Constitutional Commentary* 17:2 (2000), 241–66, 241.

95   David J. Barron and Martin S. Lederman, "The Commander in Chief at the Lowest Ebb—Framing the Problem, Doctrine, and Original Understanding," *Harvard Law Review* 121:3 (2008): 689–804, and "The Commander in Chief at the Lowest Ebb—a Constitutional History," *Harvard Law Review* 121:4 (2008): 941–1111.

96   U.S. Senate, Committee on the Judiciary, *Confirmation Hearing on the Nomination of John G. Roberts, Jr. to be Chief Justice of the United States: Hearing before the S. Comm. on the Judiciary*, 109th Cong. 1st Sess. (2005) (testimony of John G. Roberts, Jr.); U.S. Senate. Committee on the Judiciary, *Confirmation Hearing on the Nomination of Samuel A. Alito, Jr. to be an Associate Justice of the Supreme Court of the United States before the S. Comm. on the Judiciary*, 109th Cong. 2nd Sess. (2006), 318; U.S. Senate, Committee on the Judiciary, *Confirmation Hearing on the Nomination of Sonia Sotomayor to be Associate

perception of the links between the relational conception of war powers and "political" modes of constitutional judgment can be enriched by
considering what light the relational conception sheds on this premier
juridical expression of constitutional war powers.

This was the Court's moment to respond to the challenge that Truman
was posing to both Congress and the Court when he advanced, to both
branches, a highly insular theory of inherent executive war powers. President Truman was amplifying the policy challenge Roosevelt had made to
an old order (i.e., that US security required global security). To that claim
Truman added an institutional challenge: inherent presidential war powers as a co-attendant institutional response to new policy needs. Chapter 3 described how this construction was contested by the Taft, and later
Bricker wing of the Republican Party. When Truman advanced this claim
on the legal front, it was no less contested. In a 6–3 decision a Democratic Supreme Court told a Democratic president in the midst of a war
that he had to return the property of steel mill owners. President Truman
was told that, despite the risk of steel shortages in the Korean War, his
seizure of steel mills had been unconstitutional. The president respected
the decision and returned control of the mills to their owners. How might
we understand the *Youngstown* decision in light of the relational conception? If we use the relational conception to think about the Court in
this case, what features of its deliberative contribution come into focus?
And especially, what kinds of distinctive capacities of the Court does the
Youngstown decision reveal? Using the relational conception to theorize
Youngstown can help provide materials for considering how the underlying methodology of the relational conception might be useful for theorizing the constitutional work of juridical institutions.

While *Youngstown* is core to legal theorizing about war powers in
the United States, it is worth noting at the outset that the constitutional
politics of the Supreme Court and of Justice Jackson in this case were
inflected with partisanship several times over. All the justices had been
appointed by Democratic presidents, and Truman had appointed four of
the nine. As attorney general, Justice Jackson had overseen Roosevelt's
executive branch's seizure of the North American Aviation Company in
1941; authored the opinion supporting Roosevelt's destroyers-for-bases

---

Justice of the United States: Hearing before the S. Comm. on the Judiciary, 111th Cong.
1st Sess. (2009); *Dames & Moore v. Regan*, 453 U.S. 654 (1981); O'Connor and Thomas
opinions in *Hamdi v. Rumsfeld*, 542 U.S. 507 (2004); *Hamdan v. Rumsfeld*, 548 U.S. 557
(2006); *Medellin v. Texas*, 128 S. Ct. 1346 (2008). See also Harold Hongju Koh, "Setting
the World Right," *Yale Law Journal* 115: 9 (2006): 2350–79, 2364; John Yoo, "The High
Court's Hamdan Power Grab," *L.A. Times* (July 7, 2006); Seth Weinberger, "Restoring
the Balance: The *Hamdan* Decision and Executive War Powers," *Tulsa Law Review* 42:3
(2007): 101–18.

deal; and delivered the pro-executive *Chicago & Southern Airlines v. Waterman Steamship Corp.* decision only four years prior (1948).[97] The politics of the moment gave Truman reasons for optimism.

The security context also looked favorable for judicial deference to presidentialism. The broader Cold War was intensifying and there was active combat in Korea. Czechoslovakia had fallen. Truman was implementing containment in Greece and Turkey. Truman's claims even had a fertile intellectual field. In 1948 Clinton Rossiter published the magisterial *Constitutional Dictatorship* directly advocating the transformation of constitutional limitations as a response to security threats.[98] As one new element in his challenge to the received regime of war authority, Truman claimed not statutory but direct constitutional authority for his seizure of the mills by citing "all powers vested in the President by the Constitution as President of the United States and Commander in Chief of the Armed Forces."[99]

Justice Black's majority opinion was direct and straightforward. The president, he said, received authority only through the Constitution or statutory law; neither the Constitution nor statutory law vested the president with the power to seize private property; Truman's claim could not stand. In his call for a clear textual basis for executive power Black has been called "strangely formalistic."[100]

Jackson's concurrence emphasized the "imponderables" of politics in a separated powers system, stating that, "the Constitution . . . enjoins upon its branches separateness but interdependence, autonomy but reciprocity." Jackson then offered a test for assessing war powers. He said,

97   333 U.S. 123 (1948).

98   Clinton Rossiter, *Constitutional Dictatorship: Crisis Government in the Modern Democracies* (Princeton: Princeton University Press, 1948), see especially pp. 5, 314.

99   See Justice Jackson's concurrence, *Youngstown.* Truman's reliance on direct presidential authority was in part a function of Congress's twice-over refusal of statutory authority to seize, first in its 1947 refusal to amend the Taft-Hartley Act to authorize presidential seizure of property in emergency; and second, in its failure to ratify the seizure after he reported it to Congress. See Sen. Robert Taft's statement in deliberations over the Taft-Hartley Act: "We did not feel that we should put into the law, as part of the collective-bargaining machinery, an ultimate resort to compulsory arbitration, or to seizure, or to any other action" 93 Cong. Rec. (pt. 3) 3835 (Apr. 23, 1947). An effort to add seizure authority to the Act was defeated. Id. at 3637-45; *Congressional Record*, 82nd Cong., 2nd Sess. (April 9, 1952), 3962; the second message to Congress is at *Congressional Record*, 82nd Cong., 2nd Sess. (April 21, 1952), 4192.

100   Koh, *National Security*, 107; Tinsely E. Yarborough, "Mr. Justice Black and Legal Positivism," *Virginia Law Review* 57:3 (1971): 375-407, 390, accused Black of "rigid adherence to a rather dogmatic approach to the separation of powers concept," even as Black's "overly stringent rule" has also been defended as a form of "alarm-clock formalism." Edward T. Swaine, "The Political Economy of *Youngstown*," *Southern California Law Review* 83:2 (2010): 263–339, 296.

"Presidential powers are not fixed but fluctuate, depending upon their disjunction or conjunction with those of Congress." Presidential authority reaches it "maximum" at the point "[w]hen the President acts pursuant to an express or implied authorization of Congress." If the president is acting without a legislative expression of intent, "there is a zone of twilight" in which "any actual test of power is likely to depend on the imperatives of events and contemporary imponderables rather than on abstract theories of law." And when the president and Congress are at odds, the president's authority "is at its lowest ebb, for then he can rely only upon his own constitutional powers minus any constitutional powers of Congress over the matter," and the judiciary must "scrutinize" presidential claims "with caution."[101]

The opinion that most directly engages the security context of the moment is Chief Justice Vinson's dissent. Vinson began by describing the "extraordinary times" : "A world not yet recovered from the devastation of World War II has been forced to face the threat of another and more terrifying global conflict."[102] Describing the significance of the construction of the United Nations, the Marshall Plan, and NATO in language strikingly resonant of chapter 3's defense of cold war presidentialism, Vinson argued that "Our treaties represent not merely legal obligations, but show congressional recognition that mutual security for the free world is the best security."[103] He noted that many programs Congress has authorized "depend . . . upon continued production of steel."[104] After cataloging the global challenges of the moment and the distinctive capacities of executive branch governance, Vinson anchors his conclusion not only on past political precedents but also on the implied presidential powers spelled out in the legal precedents of *In Re Neagle* (1890) and *In Re Debs* (1895).[105]

One could argue that the dissenting Justice Vinson's opinion, with its awareness of the broader security context, advances the aims of the relational conception. However, there is no reason to believe that the judiciary has any special strengths in apprehending the meaning, significance, or proper responses of institutional design to the security problems of the Cold War. Given its comparative lack of resources, the Court is not

101   *Youngstown*, Justice Jackson concurrence, 635–39.
102   *Youngstown*, Justice Vinson dissent, 668.
103   Ibid., 669.
104   Ibid., 672.
105   *In re Neagle*, 135 U.S. 1 (1890) legally established that the president may protect the peace of the United States even without specific statutory authorization by appointing a marshal to protect officials such as Supreme Court justices. In *In re Debs*, 158 U.S. 564 (1895), the Court upheld the president's power to protect public peace by enjoining a railroad strike.

prepared to seriously engage the policy claims of another branch, but merely to replicate another branch's reasoning. I argued in chapter 5's discussion of the Iran-Contra Investigation that for a branch to advance reasoning that simply replicates the reasoning of another branch is a failure of independence, as well as a failure to insist upon and develop its own distinctive capacities. Excellent forms of constitutional argumentation in the presidency and legislature are not necessarily excellent forms of reasoning for the judicial branch.

A more appropriate use of distinctive judicial capacities was that of Black's formalism. Black's willingness to apply bright-line rules made his opinion rhetorically striking. If the case comes down in history as a sharp rebuke to overbearing presidentialism, Black's clear expression of presidential malfeasance is part of the reason. Recently, some legal scholars have begun urging a formalization of the Court's war powers regime in ways that signal appreciation for Black's expression. Stephen Vladeck, for example, endorses the reasoning of *Little v. Barreme* (1804), which "largely follows Black's 'formal' division," rather than Jackson's concurrence.[106] Black's opinion manifests one of the distinctive capacities of juridical governance: the ability to express principled lines of division and clear boundary lines in a way that clearly resolves an issue for the future and neatly communicates to the other branches the forms and procedures that are required according to the judiciary's construction of constitutional meaning.

Jackson's opinion also demonstrates some of the unique formal contributions the judiciary can make to war powers disputes. This is a counterintuitive argument: Arthur Schlesinger says that Jackson's invocation of "fluctuating intangibles of circumstance, judgment, opinion and prophecy" barred the use of a "mechanical standard"[107] in favor of a "flexible matrix."[108] Others applaud Jackson's "affirmation of the centrality of 'the *equilibrium*,'" a form of "balanced institutional participation,"[109] offering a "reciprocity model" of interbranch relations that "contemplates interbranch conflict . . . because it rejects the idea that there are clear lines

106   Stephen I. Vladeck, "Congress, the Commander-in-Chief, and the Separation of Powers after Hamdan," *Transnational Law & Contemporary Problems* 16 (2007): 933–64; Stephen I. Vladeck, "Foreign Affairs Originalism in *Youngstown*'s Shadow," *St. Louis University Law Journal* 53:29 (2008): 29–38, 37. Sarah Cleveland urges the Court to seek "explicit," not inferred, signals of congressional participation. See Sarah H. Cleveland, "*Hamdi* meets *Youngstown*: Justice Jackson's wartime security jurisprudence and the detention of 'enemy combatants,'" *Albany Law Review* 68 (2004): 1127–44, 1128.

107   Schlesinger, *Imperial*, 295.

108   Michael J. Turner, "Fade to Black: The Formalization of Jackson's *Youngstown* Taxonomy by *Hamdan* and *Medellin*," *American University Law Review* 58:665 (2008–2009): 665–98, 676.

109   Koh, *National Security*, 112.

of demarcation establishing the proper domain of each branch."[110] In the opinion itself, Jackson said that deciding the case required turning to "practical situations."[111] Stephen Vladeck notes that Jackson's opinion "solves practically nothing. . . . [T]he President can lose in category one, he can win in category three, and one is left to wonder just what category two means by 'contemporary imponderables.'"[112] In Gordon Young's words, the tests "resemble the partially completed structure of a bridge, narrowing the possible ending points, while leaving open a wide variety of possibilities."[113] Many of these echo the very challenges that the relational conception is subject to.

And yet the categories of Jackson's test pivot around the agreement or disagreement that exists between the branches. The test focuses attention on the question of reading legislative intent, especially implied intent, because central to the test is a reading of whether or not the branches are in conflict.[114] The formalism of this choice to theoretically prioritize interbranch agreement is apparent when it is contrasted to the approach of the relational conception. The relational conception cannot adopt Jackson's emphasis on interbranch agreement or disagreement as a generalized pivot for constitutional authority because it explicitly contemplates the possibility that both conflict and settlement may be *linked* to the branches' exercise of their institutional strengths. Congress and Roosevelt were at odds in the lead-up to World War II, but I have argued that both were making excellent use of their institutional capacities. Congress and Truman found some common ground in their construction of an early Cold War pro-presidency security order, and this construction was arguably constitutionally authoritative as well.

While the relational conception resists using interbranch agreement or disagreement as a *constitutional* test writ large, interbranch conflict

110   Barron and Lederman, "Lowest Ebb," 726.

111   *Youngstown*, Jackson concurrence, 635.

112   Vladeck, "*Youngstown*'s Shadow," 34.

113   Gordon G. Young, "*Youngstown, Hamdan,* and 'Inherent' Emergency Presidential Policymaking Powers," *Maryland Law Review* 66:3 (2006): 787–804, 787.

114   Koh, *National Security*, 142; Charles Tiefer, "War Decisions in the Late 1990s by Partial Congressional Declaration," *San Diego Law Review* 36 (1999): 1–39; Gordan Silverstein, *Imbalance of Powers: Constitutional Interpretation and the Making of American Foreign Policy* (New York: Oxford University Press, 1997), especially introduction; Sarah H. Cleveland, "*Hamdi* meets *Youngstown*." For examples of the dilemmas associated with reading legislative intent spurred by Jackson's framework, see Bradley and Morrison, "Historical Gloss"; Silverstein, *Imbalance of Powers*, 12; Mark D. Rosen, "Revisiting *Youngstown*: Against the View that Jackson's Concurrence Resolves the Relation Between Congress and the Commander-in-Chief," *UCLA Law Review* 54:1 (2007), 39; Michael Stokes Paulsen, "*Youngstown* Goes to War," *Constitutional Commentary* 19:1 (2002): 215–69, 234.

may nonetheless be appropriate for the *judiciary* to use as a hinge for judging when to apply its distinctive constitutional strengths such as the capacity to scrutinize formal procedures. Note that in Jackson's test, the level of judicial scrutiny moves from deference if the branches agree, to great heights, where the judiciary must "scrutinize" presidential claims "with caution," when the elected branches conflict. Jackson's test explicitly locates the Court as a participant rather than outside observer, and the extent of this participant's powers, like that of the executive and legislature, is conditioned by the terms on which it encounters the other two branches.

The decidedly legalist orientation of Jackson's approach to a war powers controversy is revealed when we see the different lines of inquiry the test suggests compared to those of the relational conception. Consider Michael Paulsen's application of the *Youngstown* framework to the War Powers Resolution and 2001 Authorization of Use for Military Force (AUMF). As discussed in the introduction, Congress's 2001 Authorization for Use of Military Force not only authorized open-ended war against "nations," "organizations," and "persons," even reaching to those who may have "harbored" those who "aided" the attacks, but also stated that "the President has authority under the Constitution to take action to deter and prevent acts of international terrorism against the United States."[115] Paulsen argues that this broad authorization is "constitutionally appropriate" because "Congress may delegate its war power so long as it supplies an intelligible standard to guide the President's exercise of his discretion." For Paulsen, because the two branches agreed, the legislature's effort to interpret the Constitution "should be treated as dispositive of any separation-of-powers legal challenge . . . unless it can be said that Congress and the President are both *wrong* as a matter of constitutional law."[116] He distinguished this position sharply from his "normative judgment of the wisdom" of this broad delegation.[117]

The relational conception would interrogate the quality of legislative process in light of the security considerations of the moment to develop an assessment of the WPR and AUMF's constitutionality. This requires reference to at least some minimal normative conclusions as part of the effort to identify whether or not legislative deliberation was appropriately far-ranging. While the case must be argued in its details, it is likely that some would see Congress's willingness to enact a massively broad delegation without considering broader Middle East foreign policy or antiterrorism policy as undermining the legislature's claim to deliberative

115   Authorization for Use of Military Force (September 18, 2001).
116   Michael Stokes Paulsen, "Youngstown," 254.
117   Ibid., 257.

responsibility. It is also likely that others would view Congress's willingness to support the president as demonstrating a responsible sensitivity to the unique dilemmas of fighting nonstate actors. Our own assessments of what was at stake partially conditions our judgment about whether Congress did a good job.

Asking only whether the branches agree or disagree elides the question—central to the relational conception—about the extent to which the branches' agreement or disagreement with one another is predicated on the application of their constitutional strengths to the matter at hand. Jackson's test should be read as a claim that judicial authority to intervene in a war powers dispute should be triggered by the presence of disagreement between the branches, a relatively formal standard. There are good reasons for courts not to get involved when the two branches are united on foreign policy, even if they are united on terms that do not ultimately pass constitutional muster.[118]

While the relational conception is not a legal theory of constitutional war powers, neither is it an antilegal theory. Courts are "political" actors in the largest sense. While this book stops short of theorizing the judicial role in war powers, there is nothing about the techniques of reasoning under the relational conception that bars judicial participation. The judiciary is one location for constitutional argumentation. Those interested in developing the significance of the methodology behind the relational conception for the judicial branch could start by considering the variety of distinctively judicial governance capacities. For example, the judiciary is well equipped to scrutinize public policy from the point of view of individual claims; to apply, and harness the benefits of, rule-based decision-making; to ensure the supremacy of law; to enforce the settlement features of constitutional governance; to enact stable precedent; to entrench policy continuity; and to enforce structural and other formal guarantees. The important governance capacities of the Court may well vary from one policy domain to another.[119] A rich and diverse contemporary literature addresses the value of judicial engagement, and on what terms, in relationship to these capacities.[120]

---

118   See *Baker v. Carr*, 369 U.S. 186 (1962)'s elaboration of political questions doctrine, emphasizing the practical importance of judicial non-interference when the branches manage to achieve a unified voice in foreign affairs.

119   Martin Shapiro, *Law and Politics*, 2, 328.

120   See, e.g., Adrian Vermeule, *Judging under Uncertainty: An Institutional Theory of Legal Interpretation* (Cambridge: Harvard University Press, 2006). In the field of war powers, for a range from emphatic resistance to court involvement to various principles of enforcing structuralism, minimalism, and perhaps even a form of "new deference," see Jonathan L. Entin, "The Dog that Rarely Barks: Why the Courts Won't Resolve the War Powers Debate," *Case Western Reserve Review* 47:4 (1997): 1305–15; Ingrid Wuerth, "An

At the same time, to adapt the methodology of the relational conception for use in analyzing courts, the terms of encounter between the judiciary and the other two branches must be freshly theorized. For, while the Constitution is indeterminate as to the relative supremacy of executive versus legislative constructions of the meaning of "defensive," it announces that the Constitution is "Supreme Law," and makes the judiciary the privileged expositor of law. This means the third condition of conflict—shared powers—can't be directly translated into a principle mediating reciprocal relationships between the courts and other branches. Different constitutional language in different areas of constitutional policy also complicates the translation of the relational conception into policy domains outside of war. While the branches, or the national government and states, share powers in a variety of areas, the text sets a variety of different terms on which those powers are shared.[121] The basic methodology behind the relational conception can be extended to other domains of constitutional policy, but its exact premises and conclusions cannot.

The image of a constitution as settlement, framework, or law elides the many other ways that constitutions function to order politics. Constitutions are law, but they are also resources with which political actors imagine themselves; ideological templates by which we imagine how to achieve in practice the goals we bring to and find in politics. From the point of view of the relational conception, it is the practical strategizing of officeholders seeking an outcome—security—in a specific institutional context that constitutionally disciplines the government's security powers. It is in the practical pursuit of goals textured by the contingencies of the moment that the Constitution is made authoritative by those it empowers.

Originalism for Foreign Affairs?" *St. Louis University Law Journal* 53:1 (2008): 5–27; Rebecca L. Brown, "Separated Powers and Ordered Liberty," *University of Pennsylvania Law Review* 139:6 (1991): 1513–66, 1515–16, 1533–38; Cass R. Sunstein, "National Security, Liberty, and the D.C. Circuit," *George Washington Law Review* 73:4 (2004–2005): 693–708; David Cole, "*Youngstown v. Crutiss-Wright*," *Yale Law Journal* 99:8 (1990): 2063–105, 2081; Kim Lane Scheppele, "The New Judicial Deference," *Boston University Law Review* 92:1 (2012): 89–170.

121   For a discussion of the many "sorting principles" that the Constitution textually advances, see Rosen, "Revisiting *Youngstown*," 1717–31.

Acknowledgments

When I consider my intellectual communities, I know what good fortune really means. In graduate school at Princeton, my dissertation committee— Christopher Eisgruber, Amy Gutmann, and Keith Whittington—deeply shaped my perspectives on politics and constitutional studies. They also gave me the experience of benefiting from the intellectual supportive- ness and critical feedback of several highly creative people over a lengthy stretch of time. It was wonderful. At Brown University's Political Theory Project, I especially benefited from the warmth, challenge, and discern- ment of Corey Brettschneider and David Estlund. Although its intellec- tual origins rest in my undergraduate and graduate studies, this book was written at Michigan, where my colleagues inspire and challenge me. A departmental book workshop generated important comments about half- way through the book's completion. I cannot thank Robert Axelrod, Pamela Brandwein, Lisa Disch, James Morrow, and Rogers Smith enough for their patience and insight at that event. Elizabeth Wingrove, Don Herzog, Anne Manuel, and Rocío Titiunik have also made academic life more precious with their friendship.

I am grateful for the sharp eyes and ears of audiences at the Univer- sity of Virginia, Columbia Law School, Harvard Law School, Princeton University, the University of Illinois College of Law, Washington Univer- sity, Cornell Law School, the James Madison College at Michigan State University, Notre Dame University, the University of Wisconsin, and the University of Maryland. A few of these audiences were assembled for Constitutional Law "schmoozes," and may these gatherings continue to flourish. A generous leave from the University of Michigan, and a Stephen L. Tatum fellowship from the University of Texas at Austin School of Law, allowed this book to benefit from the intellectual resources of Mitch Berman, Lawrence Sager, and UT's legal theory workshop. An incomplete list of people I am indebted to for their responses includes Jack Balkin, Sot Barber, Colin Bird, Randall Calvert, Josh Chafetz, Benjamin Kleiner- man, Marty Lederman, Sanford Levinson, Matthew Mancini, Trevor

Morrison, Kirsten Nussbaumer, Kim Scheppele, and Claire Timperley. Most especially and always I must thank Rogers Smith and Mark Graber, not only for their faith in this project, but for the many ways they support young(er) scholars in the discipline. Lawrence Solum, Don Herzog, Stephen Griffin, Pam Brandwein, and several anonymous reviewers also improved the full manuscript immeasurably with their comments. I apologize to the many others I have not acknowledged here. Citing these tremendous resources makes me very aware of the limitations of this work. Of course its mistakes are all my own.

Several research assistants—Shane Redman, Naomi Scheinerman, Erin Baribeau, and especially Boris Litvin—dedicated their serious, ongoing editorial effort, and for their work I am very grateful. It is a pleasure to thank Chuck Myers and Karen Carter at Princeton University Press for their editorial feedback, professionalism, and generosity. An early version of chapter 4 was published in *The Limits of Constitutional Democracy*, edited by Stephen Macedo and Jeffrey Tulis (Princeton University Press, 2009). I also acknowledge the wonderful undergraduates I have encountered at Brown and at the University of Michigan who make academic life so lively.

There are some I must thank for their personal gifts. I thank my mother, Madeline Bailey, for her many gifts of life and for her supportiveness of my academic career. My brother Alexander Zeisberg inspires me, provokes me, tolerates me, makes me proud, and makes me laugh—a lot. I am so proud of his service to our country and I hold dear his adventurous spirit. Love you bro. Stephen Coyle, Rose Coyle, Becca Bradburd, Natalie Ford, Kelly Karsnia, Remo Strotkamp, Lawrence Solum, and Mikaela Luttrell-Rowland have all offered me gifts that continue to bear precious fruit. Sara Gharacheh and her basement office offered important support in the final intense months of editing the book. And my sweet friend Preacher was such a good buddy through so many years of writing. I also thank my delightful wildflower sangha for community and friendship along the way.

I will never forget the moment in my second year of college when my esteemed professor Jeffrey Tulis told me there was a place called graduate school where I could be paid a stipend to read books. Nor will I forget the fragrant and warm Texas air the night I found out I would attend. I don't know if I could have even started the work I wanted to do without Christopher Eisgruber, who is insightful and kind and imaginative and rigorous all at the same time. Of course, my very best teacher is also my very best friend, Maryrose Hightower-Coyle. It is hard to find words for her brilliance, but anyone who knows her knows how lucky I am. These three teachers have shaped me intellectually but more importantly as a human being, and the book is dedicated to them.

Index

Abrams, Creighton, 177
Acheson, Dean, 100n18, 133, 138
Ackerman, Bruce, 41–42, 238n48
Adams, John Quincy, 59
agendas, 33, 38, 83, 158, 183, 186, 219–20
Agnew, Spiro, 176
agrarianism, 107, 217–18, 233
Aiken, George, 166
Alexander, Larry, 226–27, 230, 232–35,
  240n57
Allison, Graham, 35–36, 149, 171,
  216n122
ambiguous text, 5
Ampudia, Pedro de, 58
Anderson, Elizabeth, 33n94, 44
Austin, Warren, 129–30
Authorization for Use of Military Force
  (AUMF) of 2001, 49, 258–59

Balkin, Jack, 24
Ball, Joseph H., 125–26, 127
Bancroft, George, 71
Barron, David, 18n63, 253
Baruch, Bernard, 195
Bayard, James, 136n172
Benton, Thomas Hart, 59, 78
Berlin, 110, 148–49, 161, 169
Biden, Joe, 3
Bidlack Treaty, 116–17
bimodal compliance, 46–47
bipartisan consensus, 12–13, 90–91, 101,
  135–38, 143, 159, 179; Cuban Missile
  Crisis and, 161–63, 169; Vietnam War
  and, 163–68, 182, 250n80
Black, Hugo, 255, 257
Bloom, Sol, 127

Boehner Resolution (H. Res 292), 2nn7–8
Bohlen, Charles, 100n18
Boland Amendment, 190, 199, 212–13
Borah, William, 61n26, 250
Bork, Robert, 15n49, 16n56, 155n42
Bosnia, 251
Boumediene v. Bush, 243
Bradley, Curtis A., 18n62, 225n8, 251
Bricker, John W., 140, 250
Bricker Amendment, 141–42
Bridges, Styles, 138n176
brinksmanship diplomacy, 112, 165n80
Britain, 249; War of 1812 with, 47; West-
  ern hemisphere imperialism of, 66–67,
  79, 102, 106, 117–18; during World War
  I, 204, 207, 210; during World War II,
  61–63, 76, 79, 84–85, 87
Brown v. Board of Education, 233, 239–40
Buchanan, James, 71–72
Bundy, McGeorge, 150–51
Burton, Theodore E., 125–26, 130
Bush, George H. W., 7, 14, 191
Bush, George W., 7; Authorization for Use
  of Military Force of 2001 of, 49, 259;
  Iraq War of, 47
Bushfield, Harlan, 130
Bush v. Gore, 231
Butterworth, Walton, 137
Byrd, Robert, 191–92

Calhoun, John C., 59, 67, 79n108, 80
Cambodia: Chinese and North Vietnamese bases in, 151–52, 154, 177; Khmer
  Rouge in, 154; lack of bipartisan consensus on, 163–68, 182; Lon Nol's coup in,
  152, 154, 177, 180; official neutrality of,